I0809306

THE GHETTO MEN

by French MacLean

The Cruel Hunters: SS-Sonderkommando Dirlewanger

The Camp Men: The SS Officers Who Ran the Nazi Concentration Camp System

The Field Men: The SS Officers Who Led the Einsatzkommandos - the Nazi Mobile Killing Units

The Ghetto Men: The SS Destruction of the Jewish Warsaw Ghetto - April-May 1943

THE GHETTO MEN

The SS Destruction of the Jewish Warsaw Ghetto - April-May 1943

French L. MacLean

Schiffer Military History
Atglen, PA

Book Design by Robert Biondi.

Copyright © 2001 by French L. MacLean.
Library of Congress Catalog Number: 00-108341.

All rights reserved. No part of this work may be reproduced or used in any forms or by any means – graphic, electronic or mechanical, including photocopying or information storage and retrieval systems – without written permission from the copyright holder.

"Schiffer," "Schiffer Publishing Ltd. & Design," and the "Design of pen and ink well" are registered trademarks of Schiffer Publishing, Ltd.

Printed in China.
ISBN: 0-7643-1285-5

We are interested in hearing from authors with book ideas on military topics.

Published by Schiffer Publishing Ltd.
4880 Lower Valley Road
Atglen, PA 19310
Phone: (610) 593-1777
FAX: (610) 593-2002
E-mail: Schifferbk@aol.com.
Visit our web site at: www.schifferbooks.com
Please write for a free catalog.
This book may be purchased from the publisher.
Please include $3.95 postage.
Try your bookstore first.

In Europe, Schiffer books are distributed by:
Bushwood Books
6 Marksbury Ave.
Kew Gardens
Surrey TW9 4JF
England
Phone: 44 (0)208 392-8585
FAX: 44 (0)208 392-9876
E-mail: Bushwd@aol.com.
Free postage in the UK. Europe: air mail at cost.
Try your bookstore first.

CONTENTS

"I have cleared out great Jewish ghettos in the base areas. In Warsaw we had four weeks' street-fighting in a Jewish ghetto. Four weeks! We cleared out approximately 700 bunkers there. The whole ghetto made fur coats, clothes and suchlike. Earlier if one wanted to reach in there, it was: Stop! You are disrupting the war economy! Stop! Armaments concern . . . It is the part of the alleged armaments concerns, which Parteigenossen Speer and I want to cleanse together in the next weeks and months . . . With that I should like to conclude the Jewish question."[1]

- Heinrich Himmler, October 1943

• • •

"Considering that the greater part of the men of the Waffen-SS had only been trained for three to four weeks before being put on this action, high credit should be given for the pluck, courage and devotion to duty they showed. It has to be stated that the Army Engineers, too, executed their demolition of bunkers, sewers and concrete buildings with indefatigableness and great devotion to duty. Officers and men of the Police, some of whom had already served at the front, again excelled through their dashing spirit."[2]

SS Brigadeführer Jürgen Stroop, from his report to Heinrich Himmler

• • •

"The dirty arrogant SS swine! Imagine writing a 75-page boastful report on a little murder expedition, when a major campaign fought by soldiers against a well-armed enemy takes only a few pages!"[3]

- Colonel General Alfred Jodl, German Armed Forces High Command

Notes:

[1] Peter Padfield, *Himmler* (New York: Henry Holt and Company, 1990), p. 470.

[2] International Military Tribunal, *Trial of the Major War Criminals Before the International Military Tribunal, Nürnberg, 14 November 1945 - 1 October 1946. Volume XXVI, Documents and Other Material in Evidence, Numbers 405-PS to 1063 (d)-PS.* (Buffalo, NY: William S. Hein & Co. Inc., 1995), Document 1061-PS, Report: "The Warsaw Ghetto Is No More" by the Chief of the SS and Police in the Warsaw District, 16 May 1943, Report for 19 April 1943.

[3] Raul Hilberg, *The Destruction of the European Jews.* (Revised and Definitive Edition). New York: Holmes & Meier, 1985), p. 514.

INTRODUCTION

"In any case the former living quarter of the 500,000 sub-humans must disappear, and the city of Warsaw, always a dangerous seat of decay and subversion, be reduced in size."[1]

- Heinrich Himmler, February 1943

Warsaw was a cesspool in the mind of *Reichsführer-SS* Heinrich Himmler, the head of the dreaded SS, and second only to the *Führer*, Adolf Hitler, as a holder of power in Nazi Germany. The Jews were the worst. Despite the efforts of dozens of euthanasia experts assigned to *Operation Reinhard*, Himmler's project to kill the Jews in the General Government of former Poland, tens of thousands of Jews scurried about the former Polish capital like so many vermin in one of Julius Streicher's notorious pre-war anti-Semitic films.[2] Three hundred thousand Jews had been "resettled" from the Jewish Ghetto in Warsaw over the last six months, "resettled" to the gas chambers of the extermination camp at Treblinka. Still the Jews remained like an invidious virus. Perhaps 60,000 of them were left in the Ghetto.[3] No one really knew for sure. Counting Jews in a Ghetto was like counting rats on a garbage heap. You would see a shadow here and a twinkling of movement there. Sometimes one would even see a flash of teeth. There were reports that some of the Jews had turned on their pursuers; orders had been ignored, shots had been fired. The ethnic enemy had not been eradicated. It was racial anarchy.

The Polish resistance was almost as bad. Non-Jews – but still considered loathsome creatures – they operated in the Home Army, directed from the exiled Polish government in London, and in the various communist cells controlled by Moscow. Unrest was on the upswing. Assassination attempts were on the rise. The streets of Warsaw were unsafe for German soldiers traveling singly at night. Polish black marketeers were buying small arms and other items of equipment from disgruntled Axis soldiers returning from the hell of the eastern front – or so Josef Goebbels, Germany's propaganda minister, proclaimed as he bad-mouthed Himmler's security apparatus to the *Führer*. A pistol would fetch 15,000 zloty, a rifle 25,000; the swine were not even dealing in German marks.[4]

The bad actors were not confined to the *Untermenschen*, the sub-humans. German entrepreneurs in the city were growing richer by the day on the backs of Jewish labor employed in their factories and shops. German workshop managers were seeking to preserve their war-essential status by ordering and storing materials more than that needed to produce their finished products. Against the wishes and instructions of the *Reichsführer-SS*, the *Wehrmacht* Armaments Inspectorate was employing tens of thousands of Jews in machine shops. Didn't the vaunted German *Wehrmacht* know how to follow orders?

An even more treacherous situation was rumored to exist within Himmler's empire. Senior SS and police officials, Himmler's *Herrenmenschen* – the ruling class – were amassing caches of stolen money, furs, paintings and other valuables confiscated from the Jews already "sent east."[5] The Higher SS and Police Leader for Warsaw himself, *SS-Oberführer* Dr. Ferdinand von Sammern-Frankenegg – a man personally appointed by Himmler to this trusted position – was reported to be indulging in wine and women. No doubt he was indulging himself at the expense of the *Reich*.[6]

Heinrich Himmler would fix this situation; he would correct these deficiencies even if it took a personal visit to this miserable cesspool during the depths of a wretched Polish winter. He just might have to bring in *SS-Brigadeführer* Jürgen Stroop to Warsaw as well. General Stroop had a backbone. Yes, heads would roll. Heads would roll in Warsaw.

• • •

On the other end of the ax the *Reichsführer* was swinging was *SS-Obersturmbannführer* Walter Bellwidt, the battalion commander of the 3rd SS Panzergrenadier Training and Replacement Battalion. Lieutenant Colonel Bellwidt could care less about the war profiteers, the Nazi bigwigs, the Jews or the Ghetto. He had a job to do, and that job was to provide trained replacements to the 3rd SS Division "*Totenkopf*" that, at the moment, was fighting for its life deep in Russia.[7] Unfortunately for Bellwidt, demand for his product was high. In just the first nine months of the war in the East, the *Totenkopf* had sustained 12,625 casualties and since then the fighting had only intensified.[8] To make matters worse, *SS-Obersturmbannführer* Walter Bellwidt was running out of raw material. He was starting to see recruits from year group 1925, young boys only now turning eighteen. He would have to whip them into shape or the T-34 tanks of the Red Army would drive them into the ground like so much crimson slush. Bellwidt did have some combat veterans returning from convalescent hospitals – some had been wounded three and four times – and he did have a core of experienced officers and non-commissioned officers. He thanked God that he had *SS-Hauptscharführer* Derichs. The sergeant major was a rock. Derichs had been busting heads for a long time; he had even been at the concentration camp at Dachau before the war making sure that rabble did not get out of control. Derichs had won an Infantry Assault Badge, an Iron Cross 2nd Class and even an Iron Cross 1st Class, so he knew his way around a battlefield – unlike these kids he was trying to train. The fighting in the Ghetto would be a nasty business of close quarter gunfights, a type of warfare different from the battalion's normal training routine, but it should be over in a few days and then Bellwidt could get back to his real mission.

• • •

Mordechai Anielewicz, the twenty-four year old commander of the Jewish War Organization, had seen hundreds of thousands of his fellow Warsaw Jews report to the *Umschlagplatz* for rail transportation to the East.[9] He had heard the story that belied the German claims of resettlement; he had witnessed what compliance and non-violence had earned for the Jewish elders. Ironically, the German process of deportations had been a form of natural selection and those people remaining in the Ghetto were generally younger and fitter to fight. The weak, the helpless and the sick, as well as most children and older citizens, had largely already been sent to Treblinka before the outbreak of the Warsaw Ghetto Uprising. What remained were capable, tough, determined fighters. Anielewicz had twenty-two platoon-size fighting groups located around the Ghetto with only knowledge of the terrain and a few homemade bunkers as tactical advantages over the enemy. They had relatively few weapons, no communications equipment and no idea of the size of the German attacking formations. And they had nowhere to run.

• • •

Of course, we will never really know if these thoughts actually ran through the minds of Heinrich Himmler and Walter Bellwidt. Himmler would never tell; he committed suicide after Germany's defeat in May 1945. After the war, Walter Bellwidt apparently suffered from selective memory loss, as did many of his comrades, as we shall later see. *The Ghetto Men* is the story of the German effort to crush the Warsaw Ghetto Uprising in April-May 1943. The simple story of the Warsaw Ghetto Uprising is this; for over two years after the invasion of Poland in 1939 the Germans concentrated several hundred thousand Jews into what became known as the Warsaw Ghetto, an area of only four square kilometers. The Germans believed that this concentration would serve to identify, weaken and alienate the Jewish population so that later efforts at direct extermination would be successful. In July 1942 Nazi authorities began a two-month operation to transport about 300,000 Jews from the Ghetto to the Treblinka extermination camp where all but a handful were murdered in the gas chambers there. For the most part the Jews did not resist, even though there is strong evidence that many knew what their fate would be. Then, in September 1942 the Germans stopped the deportations. Many of the remaining 50,000 to 70,000 Jews in the Ghetto, who had temporarily escaped death due to their participation in German war-essential industries, began to organize a resistance movement to prepare for the day the Nazis would come back to finish the job. That day arrived in January 1943, but Jewish resistance and German war industry non-cooperation caused Dr. Ferdinand von Sammern-Frankenegg, the SS commander of Warsaw, to subsequently delay the operation until April. Heinrich Himmler was outraged at the entire situation in Warsaw and replaced von Sammern with a more brutal individual, Jürgen Stroop, who launched a twenty-eight day campaign against the Jews of the Ghetto. The Nazis burned and blasted their way through the Warsaw Ghetto in April and May 1943, killing or deporting at least 56,000 victims to extermination and slave labor camps. Considering the raw numbers of casualties, the Nazis won and the Jews lost. It wasn't even close.

However, the impact of this event was not so simple. The twenty-eight day siege of the Warsaw Ghetto was one of the most protracted large-scale urban battles in World War II. Only the fighting at Leningrad from 1941-1943, Stalingrad in 1942-1943, the Warsaw Rebellion of 1944 and Budapest in 1944-1945 lasted longer. The Jews had resisted *en masse* and had created a legend that would transcend the war and continue even to this day. Much has been written on this heroic – perhaps the word epic is a better description – struggle from the standpoint of the young men and women of the Jewish War Organization. Israel Gutman's *Resistance: The Warsaw Ghetto Uprising* and his earlier *The Jews of Warsaw 1939-1943, Ghetto, Underground and Revolt* are classic accounts of the action as is *A Surplus of Memory: Chronicle of the Warsaw Ghetto Uprising* by Yitzhak Zuckerman. The number of excellent sources from this perspective is extensive and I have attempted to list most of them in the bibliography.

Nevertheless, until now a book from the German perspective has yet to be written that captures all aspects of the fight from the standpoint of the attackers other than the Stroop Report, one of the most interesting documents to survive the war.[10] At the conclusion of the Warsaw Ghetto operation, Jürgen Stroop gathered copies of his daily reports, added a foreword and conclusion, and supplied numerous photographs – many of which appear in this work. Stroop made three copies of this report; he gave one to Heinrich Himmler, a second copy to Friedrich-Wilhelm Krüger, his immediate superior officer, and kept a third copy for himself as a memento. Many works give the German standpoint of the Warsaw Ghetto Uprising scant shrift. Heinz Höhne, author of an acknowledged masterpiece, *The Order of the Death's Head: The Story of Hitler's SS*, mentions not a word about the action. George H. Stein wrote only a few paragraphs on the subject in his equally respected *The Waffen-SS: Hitler's Elite Guard at War, 1939-1945*. Hanns Bayer did not discuss the operation in his *Kavallerie-Divisionen der Waffen-SS im Bild*, although the SS Cavalry Replacement Detachment of the 8th SS Cavalry Division was present at the fight. Even my good friend Dr. Charles Sydnor, author of the single best book on the 3rd SS Division, *Soldiers of Destruction: The SS Death's Head Division, 1933-1945*, did not have space to discuss the action, even though the division's replacement battalion played a significant role in the operation.

We do have, however, the previously mentioned Stroop Report, which will be discussed in great detail later in the book. Justice Robert H. Jackson, chief American prosecutor at the International Military Tribunal, stated the significance of this document during the 1946 Trials of Major War Criminals in Nürnberg. Justice Jackson opined:[11]

> I hold a report written with Teutonic devotion to detail, illustrated with photographs to authenticate its almost incredible text, and beautifully bound in leather with the loving care bestowed on a proud work. It is the original report of SS-Brigadier General Stroop, in charge of the destruction of the Warsaw Ghetto and its title page carries the inscription "the Jewish Ghetto in Warsaw No Longer Exists." It is characteristic that one of the captions concerned shows the driving out of Jewish "bandits;" those whom the photograph shows being driven out are almost entirely women and little children . . . It contains a day-by-day account of the killings mainly carried out by the SS . . .

Many post-war works have covered the German point of view in an incomplete manner. In 1979 Sybil Milton and Andrzej Worth edited the Stroop Report (referred to by Colonel General Alfred Jodl at the beginning of this book). In their work *The Stroop Report: The Warsaw Ghetto is No More!* the authors did not, however, attempt to analyze this primary source from a military perspective, nor did they examine archival SS records to see how the German effort developed and who participated. Another significant German primary source chronicle is a series of reports from Wilhelm Ohlenbusch of the Propaganda Department of the General Government. Ohlenbusch sent these reports, during the Ghetto Uprising, to the German Ministry of Propaganda in Berlin. These reports gained interest in an article by Joseph Kermish entitled, "The Warsaw Ghetto Uprising in the Light of a Hitherto Unpublished Official German Report," found in Volume IX (1973) of the *Yad Vashem Studies on the European Jewish Catastrophe and Resistance*. Kazimierz Moczarski wrote a fascinating account of jail cell discussions with Stroop, as the SS commander awaited trial in Poland, in his work *Conversations with an Executioner*.[12] Moczarski also did not have access to many archival records that could help to separate fact from bravado in Stroop's recollections. Wolfgang Scheffler and Helge Grabnitz produced an excellent work, *Der Ghetto-Aufstand Warschau 1943*.

This book will hopefully go further. A military intelligence colleague of mine once told me, when we were at the United States Army School of Advanced Military Studies at Fort Leavenworth, that there were only two important intelligence questions in assessing a military situation. The first is "What do we know?" The second key question is "What do we not know?" The first question may seem obvious. Just as important though, if we can answer the second question it will lead us to search for the correct answers that increase what we do know. In the case of the Germans at the Warsaw Ghetto Uprising, historically we know the following:

- the names of about five or six officers involved,
- the names of about seventy enlisted men in the action, who were reported by Stroop as wounded or killed in the fighting,
- the unit designations of the organizations involved,
- and the events of the action described in the Stroop Report (which may or may not be completely accurate.)

What do we not understand some fifty-six years after the event? At this point, we do not have in the public domain the names of the many more officers who must have taken part in the action based on the scope of the German effort. Six officers simply do not command two thousand troops. Nor have we identified the bulk of the enlisted troops who fought there. We do not really know how Stroop fought, such as how he emplaced his support weapons with any great detail, nor do we know how he really employed his troops. We have not analyzed Jewish survivor reports against the German battle reports. This is what we do not know. It indicates we have much to do, but it is a start.

It may be helpful at this point to recall that there were two uprisings in Warsaw during World War II. The Warsaw Ghetto Uprising transpired from 19 April to 16 May 1943 and was generally confined to the area of the Jewish Ghetto. On 1 August 1944 the entire city rose in revolt against the Germans as the Soviet Army approached the city from the east. This second revolt is historically known as the Warsaw Uprising. Since many of the Germans in this book took part in both uprisings, the distinctions between the two might sometimes blur. This book is about the Warsaw Ghetto Uprising.

My analysis began with the Stroop Report to obtain leads on what units participated in the fighting and what individuals were in these units. I then went to the National Archives to determine if the units involved had other records on file. They did; the National Archives had daily reports for the 3rd SS Panzergrenadier Training and Replacement Battalion, the largest unit to participate in the fighting. From these records I found the names of more soldiers and officers involved and found organizational information on the various *Waffen-SS* units. From there I went to Main Commission for the Investigation of Nazi War Crimes in Poland to examine the trial records of General Stroop from 1951 and to review their extensive photograph collection. Finally, in Poland, I had to walk the ground in the area of the former Ghetto to get a feel for the size of the area.[13]

After returning from Poland, I reviewed a set of records at the National Archives known as Microfilm Publication A3343, *Records of SS Personnel from the Berlin Document Center, Series SSO – SS Officers*. These reels of microfilmed SS officers' service records consist of the personnel dossiers (known as a *personalakt* in German, and referred to as such in the footnotes) for more than 61,000 SS officers (with the rank of second lieutenant and above) in this large and complex organization. The date span of the records contained in the dossiers extends from 1932 to March 1945 in some cases. These records are truly an open book into the careers of these men; the folders include marital status, religion, court-martial proceedings, promotions, recommendations for awards, transfers, assignment instructions, letters of reprimand, medical histories and family background. This covered the officers and those enlisted personnel who were later promoted to the officer ranks. A parallel set of records, Microfilm Publication A3343, *Records of SS Personnel from the Berlin Document Center, Series SSM – Enlisted Personnel,* provided similar information for about one third of the enlisted personnel at the action. This information was supplemented by Microfilm Publication A3343, *Records of SS Personnel from the Berlin Document Center, Series RS – SS Race and Settlement Office* (*RuSHA, Rasse-und Siedlungshauptamt*). This office had the responsibility of safeguarding the racial purity of the SS – by serving as an oversight board for prospective marriages. The collection has 240,000 dossiers for individual SS personnel and their prospective spouses, who submitted detailed personal and family background information to receive permission to marry. I then found an extremely valuable tool known as the Microfilm Publication A3343, *Records of SS Personnel from the Berlin Document Center, Series SS – SS Lists*. These reels of microfilm detailed, among many other items, the day-to-day battalion orders for the 3rd SS Panzergrenadier Training and Replacement Battalion, one of the major units in the fight. By examining who arrived and who departed the unit I was able to ascertain those soldiers present in the unit during the Warsaw Ghetto Uprising.

Then I searched for post-war testimony. Such testimony, however, requires a fine-tooth comb. First, post-war German legal documents, in the interest of German privacy laws, often indicate witnesses – and those ultimately acquitted of crimes – only by the person's initials. While this may serve to shield the witnesses from undesired public attention, it makes it more difficult for historians to identify who could have seen what. Additionally, many Nazis involved in suppressing the Warsaw Ghetto Uprising, including one Georg Michalsen, a former SS officer, seem to have suffered massive cases of amnesia after the war, as shown below (emphasis added by the author.):[14]

> [*Question*] Which members of the Lublin office were present during the Stroop Action in Warsaw?
>
> [*Michalsen*] As I already stated [*SS-Oberscharführer*] Slany and I went together by car from Lublin to Warsaw. In all probability, I arrived in Warsaw about two days before the beginning of the action. I was still in negotiation

with Schultz concerning transfer matters, and then there was the large conference at the SS and Police Chief's office in Warsaw. At that time there was still much pending work accompanying the transfer of the firms. As far as I remember – **but my recollection is not dependable** – after me, there were two commandos who went from Lublin to Warsaw. The leader of one of the commandos could have been Mohwinkel. Most probably [*SS-Untersturmführer* Otto] Hantke and [*SS-Unterscharführer*] Lehnert accompanied him. I have already made statements about the tasks of this commando. But I must stress that **I cannot state with certainty** whether Lehnert took really part in it. The third commando consisted either of [*SS-Oberscharführer*] Bartetzko alone or of Bartetzko and this or that other person. **I do not have exact knowledge about that**. Bartetzko was responsible for the transfer of the Schultz people. **I do not know** if [*SS-Scharführer*] Napieralla was in Warsaw. **I also cannot make a statement** whether Gross was in Warsaw during the Stroop Action. In any case, some SS members from the Camp of Trawniki were in Warsaw together with the Ukrainians. **I do not remember** who was the leader of the commando of the Trawniki people. Most probably, it could have been [*SS-Untersturmführer* Herbert] Schwarzenbacher. **I knew none** of the subordinate commanders.

All was not lost in deciphering these sources, as can be seen by the author's additions in brackets above. By entering the names of all personnel I found in the above sources, I was able to create a computer database that could sort on initials and put names to "faded" memories.

It would have been ideal to locate former German participants in the action and to speak with them face to face. Unfortunately, I was unable to do so. Most of the men depicted here are, I believe, long dead. The survivors probably fear potential prosecution. I located the son of one of the *Gestapo* officers at Warsaw and wrote him for information but received no reply. Thus, we are forced to rely on records and reports, as well as previous testimony by some participants.

While this book is organized along the lines of two of my previous works on the Holocaust, *The Camp Men* and *The Field Men*, it does differ in one significant point.[15] The previous works dealt with true, and in many cases legally proven, perpetrators who operated the concentration camp system and the *Einsatzkommandos*, the Nazi mobile killing formations, respectively. The personnel listed in those two books were all commissioned officers. While they may not have been volunteers for the particular assignment in which they found themselves, they went into their obligation with their eyes open. This is not totally the case in *The Ghetto Men*. The officers described herein of the security service (SD and *Sipo*; both described later) undoubtedly were an integral part of the Final Solution. However, many of the young enlisted soldiers in the fight, listed later in this book, were simply in the wrong place at the wrong time.[16] We should, therefore, look at them in a somewhat different light. Clearly some – perhaps quite a few – of these troops executed captured resistance fighters and shot unarmed civilians, both actions certainly war crimes. Some photographs clearly show SS troopers enjoying their work. Just as surely, many other German soldiers in the action were simply fighting for their lives in dark rooms, underground sewers and flame-drenched alleyways. They did not think the action was some type of game. For those soldiers there was no time to contemplate racial theories or their place in history. For them and for all of the gallant Jewish defenders it was quite simply "kill or be killed."

In short, the hundreds of biographies in *The Camp Men* and *The Field Men* can be considered a compilation of the most likely perpetrators in the concentration camps and the *Einsatzkommandos*, respectively. However, information of the 900-plus enlisted personnel in this work should be viewed instead as the most likely witnesses to the 1943 Warsaw Ghetto Uprising.

I suspect that not everyone will appreciate a book of this nature. The Holocaust is an emotional subject. One simply has to read works such as Reuben Ainsztein's *The Warsaw Ghetto Revolt* to feel the almost venomous condemnation of other historians who disagree with him concerning German losses during the fight. Writing about the Germans at the Warsaw Ghetto Uprising is a little like writing about General Santa Anna and the Mexican Army at the Alamo. Everyone "knows" that Davey Crockett died swinging his musket in the final stand; we accept as "truth" that Jim Bowie killed five or six attackers with his famous fighting knife before he was slain as he lay on his sick bed. To state anything else is viewed by some as heresy. As for the Warsaw Ghetto Uprising, providing information about the German effort may intrude on previously accepted "facts" concerning the epic fight by the Jewish defenders. However, my view is that we must discover as many pieces of information as possible to record what really happened, rather than to use history to report what we wish had happened.

Samuel Rajzman, a survivor of Treblinka, presents an unusual conclusion in *The Death Camp Treblinka: A Documentary* that seems to me to be applicable to my efforts in this book. Rajzman concludes that:[17]

> In writing about the Holocaust, we don't need authors with great imaginations. We need people who can depict the reality as it was. It was so overpowering that the facts speak for themselves.

Within this work you may well find grammatical errors, syntax blunders and even the occasional misspelled word. My chosen profession is that of an army officer, not a full-time author. It is that perspective which may be of value to a work of this kind – a perspective from almost thirty years of military service as an infantry officer in both peacetime and war. Having carried out, and moreover given thousands of military orders, I understand what goes into an order's process and how command and control of battalions works, just like the *Waffen-SS* battalions that assaulted the Warsaw Ghetto. I understand their reasons for employing heavy machine-guns and twenty-millimeter cannon because I have emplaced hundreds of heavy infantry support weapons for almost three decades myself. I can tell when an after- action report, such as the Stroop Report presented herein, is truthful or when it is exaggerated because I have read hundreds of reports of both varieties. I understand what an effective span of command is for a lieutenant, a captain, and a lieutenant colonel and why the German officers of the 3rd SS Replacement Battalion would not have sent their men into the fight unless these same officers accompanied them. When I read an account of wounds in combat, I can often discern those injuries likely caused by enemy action and which wounds may have been from "friendly fire." The relationship between officers, senior non-commissioned officers and junior enlisted men may appear complex to some civilian historians but it is second nature to any infantry officer. Hopefully that experience will assist in this effort; perhaps my non-traditional background can help to provide information about the subject that others might miss. My objective in this book is to present every fact possible concerning who, when, with what and how SS troops razed the Warsaw Ghetto. The men and officers are here as well as the units, weapons and tactics. I have even taken the liberty to portray how I believe Heinrich Himmler felt about much of the operation, which forms the lead-in to several chapters. It is not a pretty story, but it is, I believe, an accurate one.

Notes:

[1] Peter Padfield, *Himmler*, p. 445.

[2] Julius Streicher was a National Socialist politician whose hatred of the Jews amounted to a fixation. Even other Nazis called him the *Judenfresser*, or "Jew Eater" due to his virulent anti-Semitism. He was the founder of the publication *Der Stürmer*, Germany's most violent anti-Semitic journal. On 16 October 1946 Streicher was hanged at Nürnberg. His final words were "*Heil Hitler*!"

[3] Dr. Richard Korherr, the chief statistician of the SS, submitted a report dated 23 March 1943 that stated that there were 50,000 Jews, as of 31 December 1942, in the Warsaw Ghetto.

[4] One US dollar was worth 100 zloty in 1942-1943.

[5] A German euphanism for Jews sent to an extermination camp. SS officials maintained that the victims were merely traveling east to occupied areas of Russia.

[6] Grade and rank equivalents are found at Appendix 1. German grades and ranks are used in their original throughout.

[7] And the fight was not going well for the division; even the division commander had fallen recently. During February 1943, the SS Division "*Totenkopf*" participated in the German counteroffensive that retook Khar'kov. On the afternoon of 26 February 1943 the division was involved in a lengthy pursuit of Soviet forces. A long radio silence from the division armored regiment caused Theodor Eicke, the division commander, to take to the air in his Fieseler *Storch* light observation plane to attempt to gain contact with the unit. At approximately 1630 hours, Eicke and his pilot spotted a company of the regiment in the village of Michailovka, and the aircraft approached to land. Dropping to 300 feet Eicke passed over some unseen Russian positions in an adjoining village of Artelnoye. The enemy immediately opened fire with intense small arms and anti-aircraft fire. The *Storch* was ripped apart in midair, crashed between the two villages and burned fiercely leaving no survivors. That night SS troops attempted to reach the wreckage with no success. The following morning, a reinforced company succeeded, and recovered the charred bodies of Eicke, his division adjutant and his pilot. Source: French MacLean, *Quiet Flows the Rhine: German General Officer Casualties in World War II*. (Winnipeg, Canada: J. J. Fedorowicz Publishing, 1996), p. 120.

[8] Charles W. Sydnor Jr., *Soldiers of Destruction: The SS Death's Head Division, 1933-1945*. (Princeton, NJ: Princeton University Press, 1977), p. 222.

[9] *Umschlagplatz* (transfer place): term applying to the area near the railway spur in Warsaw, only a few hundred meters from the Ghetto, from which the Jews were sent to Treblinka.

[10] Wladyslaw Bartoszewski's *Warsaw Death Ring, 1939-1944* is an excellent source on the Security Police in the city

[11] Rupert Butler, *The Black Angels: A History of the Waffen-SS*. (New York: St. Martin's Press, 1979), p. 179. I have personally seen two of the three copies; one is at the National Archives, another is in Warsaw.

[12] *Conversations with an Executioner* is a dangerous source in my opinion. If the author's recollections are complete – he was a cellmate of Stroop in Warsaw in 1950 – and if Stroop was accurate in his recollections, then the book is quite a valuable reference. If either of the above conditions is not correct, then the work could be a misleading one. The portion of the book dealing with the Warsaw Ghetto Uprising has a ring of truth to it, but Stroop's musings concerning several events in 1944 seem completely exagerated, in my opinion.

[13] The area was totally destroyed but one can still get a good impression of the small confines of the Ghetto.

[14] Wolfgang Scheffler and Helge Grabnitz, *Der Ghetto-Aufstand Warschau 1943*. (Munich, Germany: Goldmann Verlag, 1993), pp. 199-200.

The testimony concerns *Operation Reinhard* (*Aktion Reinhard*), which will be described in much greater detail later. It was the code name for the Nazi plan to kill the Jews of the General Government. The operation was named for *SS-Obergruppenführer* Reinhard Heydrich, director of the Central Office for Reich Security (RSHA), who died in June 1942 as a result of injuries sustained during an assassination attempt by Czech partisans on 29 May 1942. The RSHA was the office responsible for coordinating deportations to the killing centers. SS officials directed *Operation Reinhard* from headquarters in Lublin.

[15] *The Camp Men: The SS Officers Who Ran The Nazi Concentration Camp System* and *The Field Men: The SS Officers Of The Einsatzkommandos*.

[16] The "Final Solution" has gained historical acceptance as a shortened version of "The Final Solution of the Jewish Question" (*die Endlösung der Judenfrage*), a German description of the total destruction of European Jewry.

[17] Alexander Donat, editor, *The Death Camp Treblinka: A Documentary*. (New York: Holocaust Library, 1979), p. 16.

ACKNOWLEDGMENTS

Once again I must acknowledge that this book was a team effort. I would first like to thank Dr. Thomas Veve of Dalton State College in Georgia. Tom, one of my oldest friends from my early Army days as a second lieutenant, is my truest source for telling me what is right with a book draft – and more importantly, what needs to be changed. As young officers together, we searched for history in Germany a quarter century ago. It is one of my greatest hopes to co-author a book in the near future with "the Swami."

The rest of my heartfelt acknowledgments will go out in alphabetical order, as I cannot say that any of you were less than top-notch in helping me complete this work. Dr. Peter Black of the United States Holocaust Memorial Museum (USHMM) is an acknowledged expert on the events in Warsaw and served as an excellent source for my efforts. Ms. Judy Cohen of the photography archives of the USHMM greatly aided me in finding many extraordinary photographs used in this work. In addition, she showed genuine interest in my work. Thanks again, Judy. And Aaron Kornblum provided his usual expert archival advice. Niels Cordes of the National Archives in College Park, Maryland was instrumental in helping me find document after key document among the cavernous holdings of microfilm. I looked forward to my Saturday morning visits when Niels would invariably greet me with the welcome phrase, "Have you seen this?" Niels, you will be sorely missed.

My "critical eyes" played key roles in this book. I am the world's worst proofreader. Marianne Driscoll is one of the best and I thank her for her diligence in proofing this work. Any errors left within are those resulting from not listening to her sage advice. I must also thank Mary and Georgia Garrett, two of the best neighbors one could ever have. They were always ready to look after my wife Olga and "son" Max whenever I was gone on research and also appeared to always be interested in my endless discussions on the subject – even when they probably weren't!

From across the "pond," Professor Witold Kulesza of the *Instytut Pamieci Narodowej* provided access to the extensive Polish archives on the subject in Warsaw. During this visit he even let me extensively review one of only three copies of the Stroop Report in existence – a dream of many researchers. From the Netherlands, Dick de Mildt, co-author (with C.F. Rüter) of *Die Westdeutschen Strafverfahren wegen Nationalsozialistischer Tötungsverbrechen 1945-1997*, graciously sent me a copy of this valuable new book on post-war judicial proceedings in West Germany and answered many questions concerning post-war judicial processes. I look forward to this splendid team's future works, which include a similar treatment of proceedings in the former East Germany.

Two persons, whom I have never met, nevertheless played a much-appreciated role in securing additional photographs and images. Andrew Mollo from France provided suburb photographic assistance (as he has done so well in the past) in addition to furnishing a rare Police identity book for a participant in the operation. Mrs. E. Stielow, of the *Bildarchiv Preussischer Kulturbesitz*, provided important explanations concerning several of the photographs found in this book.

I would like to thank two of the world's greatest booksellers. Bob Ruman, owner of *Articles of War*, has – for my money – the finest military bookstore in the United States. Bob invariably lets me know whenever books are published that I may find useful. He simply knows what I want and need without asking. Mr. Christian Schmidt and his family in Munich did yeoman's work as well through their excellent military history bookstore in that city, *Christian Schmidt Buchhandlung*. Whenever I needed to find and purchase a German language source book, they tracked it down with little information. If Bob Ruman is the best mlitary book dealer in the United States, then Christian Schmidt must hold that title in Germany.

I would also like to thank the many people who have written Schiffer Publishing with responses to my previous works. When I receive your letters stating your interest or providing critical observation, I know that my efforts in writing about these subjects have not fallen on deaf ears. I would especially like to thank the following: Tom Albright, Andrew Alton, Bart Baeyens, John Day, Mike Miller, Tony Munoz (whose own works on German forces in World War II are indeed impressive and whose publication on the German Police was especially invaluable to this book,) David Richardson, Jamie Selko and Pierre Verheye (a former inmate at the Buchenwald concentration camp.) Pierre provided absolutely superb advice on the complicated German rank and grade structure.

Dr. Charles Sydnor – currently at Virginia Public Television – whose work, *Soldiers of Destruction; The SS Death's Head Division, 1939-1945*, is – I am convinced – a model for every author in the field of the *Waffen-SS* in the last two decades, was in my corner as well. His encouragement helped me stay the course and complete this work in a timely manner. I look forward to his upcoming works on Reinhard Heydrich, the mastermind of the Holocaust.

Henryk Tacik, an old friend from my War College days, smoothed over all obstacles during my visit to Warsaw early in the research for this book. Without his help, I would not have been able to spend so much needed time visiting the site of the former Ghetto and also touring Treblinka. In the nine degree above zero weather, I did not need to be blundering about a city or countryside with which I was unfamiliar. Henryk ensured that I did not blunder!

Mr. Simon Wiesenthal, a man who needs no introduction, provided excellent comments on this project. His challenge to not let history fade provided a motivating factor that was much appreciated.

Finally, I would like to thank my wife Olga. Through thick and thin she has always been my best friend. Army separations never caused her to waver in the slightest. My interest in old, sometimes forgotten, history never prompted her to tire of me. She encourages me to write because it interests me to do so; that it brings in meager financial profit disturbs her not in the slightest. She is a saint.

1

INFERNAL WARSAW

"The death figure in the Ghetto still hovers around 5,000 per month. A few days ago, the first case of hunger cannibalism was recorded."

- General Government Warsaw Propaganda Division Report, 1942

Warsaw in the 1930s was the capital of Polish Jewry and a significant world Jewish center. The main offices of Jewish political parties were located in the city as were a large number of Jewish welfare and educational institutions. Warsaw was the center of many Jewish trade unions, sports organizations and youth movements. Jewish magazines and newspapers, published in many languages and distributed worldwide, originated on the printing presses of the city.[1] Because Warsaw was the largest Jewish community in Europe and second grandest in the world next to New York City, it served as a magnet for Nazi interest in solving the "Jewish question." Peter-Heinz Seraphim, a Nazi expert on the East and Jews, described eastern Jewry as:[2]

> The greatest concentration of Jews anywhere, the spiritual center of Orthodox Jewry and, above all, the inexhaustible reservoir from which the Jewish migrations were fed and which, again and again, had released smaller and larger groups of Jews to be soaked into other countries.

Raul Hilberg, noted Holocaust historian and author of *The Destruction of the European Jews*, described Poland's Jews as the center of gravity for eastern Jewry. Such a Clauswitzian idea was probably not lost on the Nazi leadership. They would have to destroy the Jews of Poland – and hence Warsaw – or, by their logic, they would be destroyed themselves. That effort in the city culminated in the destruction of the Warsaw Ghetto in April and May of 1943.

The seeds for the Warsaw Ghetto Uprising in 1943 were planted some forty-two months previously in October 1939 at the conclusion of Germany's highly successful invasion of Poland. To begin, one must first understand the National Socialist concept of the Pole and of the Polish Jew. In the Nazi mind a Pole was lower, without a doubt, than a German. Teutonic reasoning then deduced that a Polish Jew was lower than a German Jew and thus was on the bottom of the German ethnic scale. The Nazis referred to Eastern Jewry, and this included Polish Jewry, as "subhumanity" (*Untermenschtum*). Within Germany proper, the bureaucracy that dealt with the Jewish question was concerned with the privileges and rights of Germans and therefore was always careful to deflect destructive measures of the German Jews from the German population.[3] This forethought did not apply to Poland, where it did not matter to the Germans if a non-Jewish Pole was hurt as a consequence of a measure directed at Polish Jews.[4]

Furthermore, it is important to understand what the Germans had in mind for Poland. The Nazi civil administration and the SS followed closely on the heels of advancing German units into Poland. The German plan was to divide Poland into several areas for administration. Portions of Poland in the north, south and west were incorporated into the *Reich* to enlarge East Prussia and both Upper and Lower Silesia. The official term for this nearly 35,000 square mile landmass (a quarter of prewar Poland) was "Incorporated Eastern Territories" (*Eingegliederte Ostgebiete*). The largest area not incorporated into the *Reich* was designated the "General Government for the Occupied Areas of Poland" (*Generalgouvernement für die Besetzten Polnischen Gebiete*). Adolf Hitler appointed *Reichs* Minister Dr. Hans Frank as Governor of the General Government.[5] As the chief of the civil administration, he theoretically held the most power in the quasi-state.[6] The Germans initially subdivided the General Government into four districts: Warsaw, Kraków, Radom and Lublin. In the summer of 1941 the Germans added a fifth district of Galicia. In October 1939 the General Government contained 11,835,510 people of whom some 1,457,378 were Jews.[7]

The Germans planned for the Poles to serve as low-paid workers for the new Germanic empire in the East. The Germans would teach them rudimentary skills, but it would be clear to all that the Poles were only there to serve their German masters. For the Polish Jews, the idea was even simpler. They would ultimately be killed.

SS-Obergruppenführer Reinhard Heydrich, Himmler's chief deputy and mastermind of the Final Solution, had a two-phase plan for the concentration and ultimately the destruction of Polish Jews. First, the Germans would move approximately 600,000 Jews from the incorporated territories to the General Government; that would raise the overall Jewish population there to about 2,000,000. Second, the Germans would concentrate all 2,000,000 into closed quarters (later called Ghettos). One of the largest of these Ghettos would be at Warsaw.[8]

Heydrich met on 21 September 1939 with key *Reich* Security Service personnel engaged in the invasion of Poland. His plan for the Jews of Poland had the following key provisions:[9]

- Concentrate the Jews in cities as soon as possible.
- Transfer Jews from the *Reich* to Poland.
- Transfer the 30,000 remaining Gypsies in the *Reich* to Poland.
- Establish Jewish Councils (*Judenräte*) in the Jewish communities. These councils would be fully responsible for the exact and punctual execution of all directives issued or that would be issued in the future.
- Carry out the actions in coordination with the military and the civil administration, and should there be a clash of interests between the Security Police [a component of Heydrich's forces] and the civil administration elevate the problem to Heydrich immediately for resolution.
- Submit detailed reports on actions carried out.

On 28 September 1939 Warsaw capitulated and German troops quickly occupied the city. On 5 October the German *Führer* Adolf Hitler reviewed a victory parade along Ujazdowskie Avenue. Freshly decorated German Army troops paraded before their *Führer* while wave after wave of *Luftwaffe* aircraft passed in review.[10] While this was a notable day for the infantry and tank men, conditions in Warsaw for the Jews began to deteriorate that very day. To ensure security during the event, the Germans seized numerous hostages including several prominent leaders of the Warsaw Jewish community.[11] On 12 October 1939 the Germans issued the "*Führer's* decree regarding the administration of the occupied Polish territory."[12] This decree imposed German law on the General Government, including the Nürnberg Laws that pertained to limiting Jewish freedoms.[13] This decree was the first of many that would result in backing the Jews into a corner and causing the conditions that would lead to the Ghetto Uprising.

On 22 October, the Germans ordered the Jewish Council to deliver 360 persons for forced labor. This first demand for labor would be followed by similar requirements for workers in the months and years to come. The next day, the Nazis established a formal *Judenrat* (Jewish Council). The organization quickly announced that Adam Czerniaków, a Warsaw Jewish elder, would serve as the chairman. October events ended on the 26th when General Governor Hans Frank issued a decree that made it obligatory for Jews to perform forced labor with no compensation.[14] The same day, Frank delivered his first address to the "Polish men and women." In the speech was an ill omen for the Jews of Warsaw and the other areas of the occupied region. Frank stated:[15]

> But there is no place for agitators, profiteers or Jewish parasites in the area that has been placed under German sovereignty.

As part of Heydrich's aforementioned plan, in almost every Jewish community overrun by the Germans, the Nazis set up and selected members for a Jewish council, a *Judenrat*. The function of such a body was to help implement and facilitate Germany's Jewish policy on the local level. The *Judenrat* had three functions from a Nazi point of view. The *Judenrat* would provide Nazi authorities with updated lists of Jews and their possessions. Second, the council would pay levies when required. Finally, the *Judenrat* would provide Jewish laborers for German-sponsored work projects. The senior Jewish official in a *Judenrat* was known as the *Judenälteste*, Jewish elder. Additionally, the Nazis also established a Jewish auxiliary police force (*Jüdischer Ordnungsdienst*). Their role was to ensure Jewish compliance with Nazi regulations and to help round up Jews for "resettlement" actions.[16]

Anti-Jewish measures assumed an even more draconian nature in November. On 13 November the Germans seized 53 Jews as hostages, in retaliation for the shooting of a patrolman of the so-called "Navy Blue Police" (the Polish police [Granatowa Policja]). The *Judenrat* promptly raised and paid a "contribution" of 300,000 zloty, but the Nazis shot the 53 hostages anyway. On 18 November the Germans marked the boundaries of the Jewish quarter of Warsaw with special signs in both Polish and German. These signs read:[17]

> Area infected with typhus. Only transit permitted.[18]

On 23 November 1939, German authorities in Warsaw, under the leadership of SS and Police Leader (*SS und Polizeiführer* [SSPF]) "Warsaw" *SS-Gruppenführer* Paul Moder, announced that all Jewish stores and shops would be required to prominently display a yellow Star of David.[19] Beginning in November as well, was an influx of Jews from previously western Poland as German *Gauleitern* Arthur Greiser and Albert Förster[20] began to expel the Jews from their territory.[21]

The first of December was marked by the Nazi command decree mandating that all Jews above the age of twelve would wear a white armband with a blue Star of David on their right sleeves. (Decree regarding the identification badges of Jews in the General Government.)[22]

Ludwig Fischer, German governor of the Warsaw district, announced yet another decree on 11 December 1939.[23] The "First implementation provision to the decree regarding the initiation of forced labor for the Jewish population in the General Government" had four major provisions.[24] All Jewish males from age twelve to sixty would register for forced labor requirements. All Jews were barred from leaving their homes between 2100 hours and 0500 hours without obtaining special permission. All Jews entering the General Government were required to immediately report to the Police. All Jews living in the General Government were forbidden to change their residences without first obtaining permission.[25]

Thus 1939 marked initial German attempts to identify and concentrate Jews into semi-restrictive areas. These were the first steps in what would become a program of indirect genocide. However, there was really no consistent policy at this stage of the war toward the Jews. To be sure, Heydrich and many other Nazis wanted to remove the Jews; but other German officials felt that a continuing presence of Jews would be essential to *Reich* economic stability.[26] The argument would manifest itself again and again in the General Government. The clash between these two schools of thought meant that the Jews as a whole would die a slow death.

• • •

In 1939 Jewish resistance was non-existent; the population, at this time, believed that cooperation with the Germans offered the best chance of improved living conditions. One vehicle of cooperation was the *Judenrat* system. The Warsaw *Judenrat* was composed of numerous departments that oversaw various functions of day-to-day life. These departments included: Birth Certificates, Commerce, Complaints, Economics, Emergency Affairs, Finance & Budget, General Operations, Health & Hospitals, Housing, Insurance, Labor, Legal Affairs, Police, Population Registration, Post Office, Production, Real Estate, Social Welfare, Statistics, Taxation and Vocational Training.[27] It all seemed so orderly and efficient – that efficiency would ultimately mean death.

• • •

In 1940, the Nazis continued the crackdown on the Jews. At the beginning of January the Nazis closed all Jewish synagogues and houses of prayer. The system of food rationing began this month as well. Jews received a different color ration card, also marked by a Star of David, than other Poles. Initially the authorized amounts of food that could be bought were the same for both groups, but future months would bring a reduction in Jewish foodstuff allotments.[28] Records show the daily caloric intake of food was determined in part by social strata:[29]

- *Judenrat* and Supply Authority personnel – 1,665 calories
- wholesale merchants – 1,429 calories
- independent craftsmen – 1,407 calories
- unemployed intelligentsia – 1,396 calories
- street merchants – 1,277 calories
- doormen – 1,300 calories
- workshop employees – 1,229 calories
- refugees in hostels – 807 calories
- street beggars – 784 calories

A diarist in the Ghetto put this rationing system in more human terms when he wrote:[30]

> The Ghetto contains 20,000, maybe 30,000 persons who have enough to eat, and these are the social elite. At the other end of the ladder are about a quarter of a million people who are all beggars completely bereft of everything, and who wage a daily struggle to postpone their death by starvation. In between these two extremes are about 200,000 people, the 'average,' who somehow manage, are still able to take care of themselves, look clean and dressed, and their bellies not swollen from hunger.

Little by little, the Jews of Warsaw sold or bartered more and more of their resources, as one by one, the Jews became penniless and thus faced this slow death by starvation.

Governor Frank issued another decree on 24 January. The "Decree regarding the duty of registration of Jewish property in the General Government" canceled all debts owed to Jews. It also restricted Jewish real estate ownership.[31] On 26 January 1940 the Germans prohibited Jews from traveling by railroad.[32] Violators would be punished with either a fine or imprisonment.[33]

The Nazis issued an additional decree on 1 March 1940 that regulated Jewish finances and forbade Jews to buy or sell gold or silver without a special license.[34] Six days later, on 7 March, the General Governor issued yet another decree barring Jewish doctors from treating Aryan patients.[35] In April 1940 the Nazi administration began construction of the walls that would enclose the future Ghetto. The area in the northwestern part of Warsaw was defined as a "plague-imminent area" (*Seuchensperrgebiet*).[36] Ludwig Fischer later explained the intent of this action:[37]

> The main purpose of the campaign to explain and demonstrate the dangers of typhus, executed in collaboration with the department of health, was to point out that the Jews are the disseminators of typhus. The principal slogan of the campaign is "The Jews – Lice – Typhus." The matter has been demonstrated and clarified to the [Polish] community with the help of 3,000 large posters, 7,000 smaller posters and 500,000 pamphlets. The Polish press and the radio have shared in the distribution of this information. In addition, the children in Polish schools have been warned of the danger every single day.

In mid-May the Nazis directed that the *Judenrat* deliver 7,000 people daily for several weeks of forced labor. Much of this work was directed at construction of the aforementioned Ghetto walls.[38]

On 18 July 1940 the Nazis issued a decree prohibiting Jews from entering public parks. They were also prohibited from using public benches outside these parks. This measure was designed to further alienate Jews from the rest of society. The German administration issued an edict on 24 July that expanded the Nürnberg racial laws in occupied Poland in the "Decree regarding the determination of the concept 'Jew' in the General Government."[39] On 7 August 1940 the Germans issued yet another decree, and this order had significant ramifications for further disastrous overcrowding conditions. All Jews arriving in Warsaw would be required to settle within the planned Jewish district. This area was partially surrounded by walls begun five months earlier.[40]

September was a light month for decrees by Nazi standards. Authorities issued only one major decree during the month; it stated that Jews could only travel in streetcars that were marked "For Jews Only." On 2 October 1940 the Germans defined the boundaries of the Jewish district and officially titled the area as the "Jewish quarter" (*Jüdische Wohnbezirk*).[41] All non-Jewish Poles living inside the area were ordered to vacate the location by 31 October. All Jews living outside the Ghetto were ordered to move inside. The Jews were allowed to bring only their personal belongings and bed linen into the Ghetto. All other possessions (such as furniture) would be left behind. As a result of the order, 115,000 Poles moved out of the Ghetto area and 140,000 Jews moved into it. It was a pitiful sight, with many Jews bent over double, attempting to carry in as many foodstuffs and other necessities as they could manage.[42] Even though this was a net increase in Ghetto population, on 19 October the Germans reduced the size of the Ghetto by moving its western border from Okopowa Street and Towarowa Street to Zelazna and Wolnosc Streets.[43]

On 15 November 1940 the Germans finally sealed off the Ghetto with inhabitants permitted to leave the district only with a special pass.[44] The Germans issued 53,000 such passes; there were twenty-eight points of entry and exit for these pass holders. However, a senior German health official campaigned successfully to reduce the number of gates to fifteen.[45] City streetcars were permitted to cross the Ghetto but could not stop to pick up or discharge passengers and were under constant police surveillance.[46]

The Germans monitored the some 350,000 Warsaw Ghetto inhabitants with three police forces. Thirty-seven German police officers stood at the top of the pecking order. The German Police came from "Police Regiment Warsaw," a unit formed in the former Polish capital on 4 November 1939.[47] The regiment was composed of three units – the 301st, 304th and 307th Police Battalions.[48] The Polish "Navy Blue Police" (so described because of their uniforms) stood next in the Warsaw Ghetto law enforcement hierarchy. The newly established Jewish Order Service, subordinated to both the *Judenrat* and the German administration, occupied the bottom rung. The Jewish Order Service wore white armbands with the words "Sluzba Porzodkowa," Polish for Order Service.[49] Some Jewish collaborators assisted the Germans in their tasks. A special Jewish economic unit, the Trzynastka, Polish for "The Thirteen," operating under the *Gestapo*, had a mission of spying on fellow Jews, confiscating needed smuggled goods and seeking out Jews with counterfeit Aryan papers. Abraham Ganzeweich headed the unit, which was located at 13 Leszno Street inside the Ghetto. The group was not accountable to either the *Judenrat* or the Jewish Order Police.[50] Both the German Police and the Polish "Navy Blue Police" carried firearms; the Jewish Order Service carried clubs.[51]

On 20 December 1940 the German administration published the "Decree regarding the introduction of work cards to the General Government." Thus Jews were to receive special work certificates different from that issued to Poles.[52]

The year ended on a slightly more positive note for the Ghetto inhabitants. Perhaps sensing an imminent medical catastrophe, German authorities transferred the Orthodox Jewish Hospital, which lay outside the Ghetto boundaries, to three locations inside the Ghetto. However, perhaps the move had different motivations and was designed to reduce the number of Jews leaving the Ghetto for medical treatment.[53]

Part of the problem stemmed from overcrowding. The Ghetto covered a mere 2.4 percent of the area of Warsaw but contained 30 percent of the population. At times, some 30 percent of the Ghetto's population were refugees.

• • •

The year 1940 saw only a slight increase concerning Jewish resistance. The Dror He-Halutz "Freedom" underground group was created in the Warsaw Ghetto from members of Ha-Shomer ha-Za'ir in 1940, but remained at this point in the organizational stage. In 1942 it would become one of the founding parties of the Zydowska Organizacja Bojowa (ZOB) which will be explained later.[54] The date of 29 May 1940 marked the establishment of the Jewish Mutual Aid Organization (Zydowskiej Samopomocy Spolecznej [ZSS]). This organization would oversee all Jewish welfare organizations and charities.[55] This was because charity was not in the Nazi vocabulary.

• • •

The year 1941 began with harsh measures. Nazi authorities decreed on 14 January that more severe punishments would be given to those who attempted to cross the borders of the Ghetto without a pass. Crossing the Ghetto perimeter was a daunting task by itself. The encircling Ghetto walls were made of brick and were three meters tall (nine feet, nine inches) and were further topped with one meter of barbed wire (three feet, three inches). Beginning in January, and lasting three months, the Germans continued to resettle some 50,000 Jews from the western portions of the Warsaw district to the Ghetto. During February, the Nazi administration prohibited all non-Jews from outside the Ghetto from giving or selling any objects or goods to Jews. Those caught doing so were subject to fines, prison or forced labor.[56]

On 20 February 1941 German administrators issued a decree prohibiting Jews from using any taxis, streetcars or railways.[57] On 19 March the Germans closed the transit gates on Leszno Street that barred the way for Polish streetcars to enter the Ghetto. During April the Germans established several so-called "workshops" that employed Jews in the Ghetto in German-owned manufacturing plants.[58]

On 14 April 1941 the Germans officially established an agency of the German Ghetto administration known as the Transfer Department (*Transferstelle*). Located on the Aryan side of the Ghetto border, next to a side spur of the railroad, this department was charged with overseeing the economic life in the Ghetto and played a key role later in preventing food imports into the Ghetto.[59] The first chief of this office was Alexander Palfinger, who had previously worked in the Lodz Ghetto; Max Fischer, a German economist, later replaced him. An economic structure gradually arose in the Ghetto that sustained a small upper stratum composed of people who smuggled food into the Ghetto and smuggled valuables out to the "Aryan" side of Warsaw, and of skilled craftsmen who made deals, some legal and some illegal, with German enterprises. However, this structure could not support the vast bulk of the Ghetto population, who kept sinking closer to the starvation abyss. According to one calculation of the period, 65,000 persons in the Ghetto had jobs, but over 200,000 had no means of support.[60]

On 13 May the Germans restricted the importation of goods into the Ghetto to just two gates, one at the intersection of Chlodna and Zelazna Streets and the other next to the Krasinski Park on Nalewki Street.[61] In practice only some goods, notably food shipments into and official manufactured products out of, passed through the *Transferstelle*. The majority of economic activities in the Ghetto were illegal by German standards – namely the smuggling of food into the Ghetto and the illegal export of products manufactured inside the Ghetto.[62]

During June the Germans relaxed some of the restrictions. We do not know exactly why they took these actions, but it may have been linked to the imminent invasion of Russia. It is possible that the Germans, unsure about a potential flash point in a Ghetto of 300,000-plus people, were concerned that an outbreak of trouble in a key transportation center could disrupt rail traffic to the front. At any rate, the Nazis partially lifted the bans on education, culture and religious life. They introduced a day off on the Sabbath and permitted some theaters in the Ghetto to open and give performances in both Yiddish and Polish. The Germans permitted the Great Synagogue at Tlomackie Street to open on 16 June.[63]

The relaxation was soon over. On 18 September 1941, the SS in Warsaw – now under the leadership of SS and Police Leader "Warsaw," *SS-Oberführer* Arpad Wigand – shrank the Ghetto's size even further by excluding areas west of Zelazna Street and east of Bonifraterska Street from the Ghetto proper.[64] On 15 October the Nazis introduced the death penalty as the punishment for any Jew who left his district without authorization or for non-Jews who were found to be deliberately hiding Jews.[65]

For those Nazi bureaucrats in Berlin, who may not have been aware of the true magnitude of what was transpiring in Warsaw, Ludwig Fischer described the overall situation that September in a biannual report entitled "The Jewish Quarter in Warsaw:"[66]

> In view of the large number of Jews to be found in Warsaw, at the very beginning of German rule, thought was being given to concentrating the Jews in the Jewish quarter. The intention was, first and foremost, to separate the Jews from the Aryan surroundings and from general political considerations of our world-view. There were in addition other important reasons, health-wise and economic . . . in general, 700 ethnic Germans, 113,000 Poles and 138,000 Jews were evacuated, making 251,000 in all. In this fashion, 11,567 Jewish apartments in the quarter and some 13,800 Jewish apartments in other parts of the city were made available. The transfer was made in the course of some six weeks in a tremendous organizational undertaking. The quarter was an area of 403 hectares, with a population of 450,000 to 500,000 Jews living in an unusually crowded state. A calculation has been made that 108,000 Jews live in one square kilometer of the quarter, as compared with 38,000 [people] per square kilometer in the residential area of Warsaw, which is also above average.

On 17 November, the Germans executed eight Jews for illegally leaving the Ghetto area.[67] Four days later the Germans issued a regulation concerning the banning of shipment of parcels and packages from Jewish senders.[68] Despite these measures, however, the clash continued between those Nazi officials who wanted the Jews gone and those who saw a certain utility in continued Jewish presence in the *Reich*. In November 1941, General Governor Hans Frank told an audience at the University of Berlin:[69]

> Not all these Jews are parasites from our point of view. Surprisingly there are Jews of a different category – I have seen this for myself. It is hard to believe but there are really Jews who work and are employed in factories as transport workers or building workers or skilled tailors, shoemakers and others. With the help of the Jewish artisans, Jewish workshops were set up in which, in exchange for food and other basic necessities, their production went far towards lightening the load of German industry.

While that may have been Frank's view in an academic setting, the harsh realities for all Jews in his kingdom – Frank was frequently called "King Frank" behind his back – remained. The year ended with a 25 December decision ordering all Jews to submit furs and fur-lined clothing to German authorities by the 28th.[70]

• • •

Ghetto population increased during the year to peak in May at over 442,000 inhabitants. This compares to 360,000 Jews in Warsaw in October 1939 and 392,000 present in the city in December 1940.[71] The following table shows the monthly figures for both overall Ghetto population statistics and mortality rates in the Ghetto:[72]

TABLE 1
WARSAW GHETTO
POPULATION AND MORTALITY
JANUARY 1941 – JULY 1942

1941	**Population**	**Deaths**
January	380,740	898
February		1,023
March	445,000	1,608
April		2,061
May	442,337	3,821
June	439,309	4,290
July	431,874	5,550
August	420,116	5,560
September	404,300	4,545
October		4,716
November		4,801
December	416,700	4,366
1942		
January		5,123
February	368,902	4,618
March		4,951
April	400,000	4,432
May	400,000	3,636
June		3,356
July	335,514	3,672

Another source, Charles G. Roland, in his *Courage Under Siege: Starvation, Disease, and Death in the Warsaw Ghetto*, did a more detailed analysis of Jewish mortality in the Ghetto. Roland found that from September 1939 to July 1942 some 2,724 inhabitants perished from typhus, 18,320 persons died from hunger and exhaustion, 30,175 people succumbed to tuberculosis and 46,946 victims died from undetermined maladies.[73] Cold, frostbite and hopelessness added to the lethal mix.[74] To a large degree, these 98,165 people, according to

Roland, expired because of the conditions imposed by the Nazi authorities in the Ghetto.

Casualty figures can only begin to describe the conditions in Warsaw. Israel Gutman, in *Resistance: The Warsaw Ghetto Uprising*, presents a vivid, graphic account of the situation:[75]

> Crowded in the narrow streets of the ghetto lived a population equal to that of a city in other parts of the world: 26,000 people lived in Pawia Street, 20,000 in Mila Street, and 20,000 in Gesia Street. The sidewalks were filled with masses of people whose threadbare clothing reeked with the smell of rotting foodstuffs and human sweat. The odor of waste and refuse filled the air.

• • •

The year 1942 would mark the change from Nazi indirect genocide to direct genocide of the inhabitants of the Warsaw Ghetto, although the year began with no indicators of the horrific events that would come. By 16 February 1942 the Germans had finished constructing all walls around the new and reduced-size Ghetto. By now, the Ghetto was two parts, known as the Small Ghetto and the Large Ghetto. To connect the two without allowing the Jews to encounter the non-Jewish population, the Germans constructed an elevated wooden bridge over Chlodna Street (see picture in photograph section).[76]

Beginning in March 1942, the Nazis began to resettle the Jews from the eastern parts of Warsaw, to include the city section of Praga, to the Ghetto. They also began to resettle approximately 4,000 Jews from German cities, including Magdeburg, Berlin and Hannover, to the Ghetto.[77]

Violence returned to the Ghetto on 17 April 1942. Late that night the *Gestapo* swooped in on several apartments within the Ghetto and dragged 52 men into the streets. There, the Germans proceeded to shoot the men in front of their families and neighbors. During the night of 10/11 June, the Nazis murdered several dozen more men suspected of being involved in smuggling. On 2 July 1942, the Germans killed one hundred ten Jews, including ten officers of the Jewish Police. The punishment was in retaliation to Jewish tardiness at obeying decrees by the German Police. On 21 July 1942, the Germans took several dozen people hostage at the Community building. The same day, the Nazis executed a group of Jews on Chlodna Street.[78]

But the worst was yet to come. For the first three years the Germans had been bent on indirect genocide of the Jews in Warsaw. That was about to change. On 18 June 1942, top German administrative and security officials met in Kraków to discuss their future plans. Dr. Herbert Hummel,[79] Ludwig Fischer's representative from Warsaw to the meeting, relayed his boss's hope:[80]

> . . . That before long the city of Warsaw will be disburdened of its dead weight of unemployable Jews.

In an ominous move, Governor General Frank issued an order on 3 July 1942 that placed Jewish affairs under the jurisdiction of the Security Police of the SS.[81] Eighteen days later, the Nazis would subject the Jews of Warsaw to more direct extermination procedures, *Operation Reinhard*.

Notes:

[1] Israel Gutman, editor in chief, *Encyclopedia of the Holocaust.* (New York: MacMillan Publishing Company, 1990), Volume 4, p. 1601.

[2] Raul Hilberg, *The Destruction of the European Jews.* (Revised and Definitive Edition). (New York: Holmes & Meier, 1985.), p. 542.

[3] The German legal system and other governmental bureaucracies gave much thought to such problems as couples in mixed Jewish-Aryan marriages, disruption of German-Jewish business relationships, children of mixed marriages and Jews who had served in World War I or given significant civil service to Germany.

[4] Raul Hilberg, *The Destruction of the European Jews*, pp. 188-189.

[5] Frank had little direct control over events at the Uprising although he was heavily involved in the anti-Jewish actions throughout the General Government. He was born 23 May 1900 in Karlsruhe; he served one year in World War I and then joined a *Freikorps* to fight Communists in Munich in 1919. He attended the Universities of Kiel and Munich and obtained a law degree. During the 1920s he played a prominent role in defending various party members. Frank served as the Minister of Justice for Bavaria in 1933 but generally held positions of lesser stature before World War II. In October 1939 Hitler appointed him to head the General Government, a position he would occupy for the entire war. However, his relations with Hitler soured. Frank saw himself as the head of a new "crusader kingdom" of Germany's campaign in the East, but Hitler and Himmler saw the General Government more as a racial dumping ground and slave labor reservoir. Frank, at times, tended toward less arbitrary oppressive treatment of the Poles – although he definitely saw the Poles as slaves of a Greater German Empire – than the *Führer* desired, and matters quickly came to a head. On 5 March 1942 a tribunal consisting of Himmler, Hans Lammers and Martin Bormann stripped Frank of all jurisdiction over police and racial matters. Hitler additionally stripped Frank of all party positions and forbade him to publicly speak in Germany. However, Hitler would not accept Frank's numerous letters of resignation. The Allies tried Frank after the war among the major war criminals in the Nürnberg Trials. The court convicted him of war crimes and crimes against humanity and hanged him on 16 October 1946.

[6] Mark C. Yerger, *Riding East: The SS Cavalry Brigade in Poland and Russia 1939-1942.* (Atglen, PA: Schiffer Publishing, 1996), p. 30.

[7] Charles G. Roland, *Courage Under Siege: Starvation, Disease, and Death in the Warsaw Ghetto.* (New York: Oxford University Press, 1992), p. 15.

[8] Raul Hilberg, *The Destruction of the European Jews*, p. 205.

[9] Israel Gutman, *The Jews of Warsaw, 1939-1943: Ghetto, Underground, Revolt.* (Bloomington, IN: Indiana University Press, 1982), pp. 14-15.

[10] German war film footage in the British Broadcasting Corporation Television program *The Warsaw Ghetto*, (London: 1969. Re-released by Hollywood Home Theater), shows German troops marching with Iron Cross 2nd Classes pinned to their uniforms. Standard procedure was to separate the medal from the ribbon after the ceremony and just wear the ribbon on the service uniform. Therefore, any photograph showing a German soldier wearing both medal and ribbon on his service uniform can be assumed to be taken the day of the award.

[11] Jan Jagielski and Tomasc Lec, *Nie Zatarte Slady Getta Warszawskiego (The Remnants of the Warsaw Ghetto)*. (Warsaw: Zydowski Instytut Historyczny INB, 1997)

[12] *Erlass des Führers über die Verwaltung der Besetzten Polnischen Gebiete.*

[13] Abraham J. Edelheit and Hershel Edelheit, *History of the Holocaust: A Handbook and Dictionary*. (Boulder, CO: Westview Press, 1994), p. 327.

[14] *Verordnung über die Einführung des Arbeitszwangs für die jüdische Bevölkerung des Generalgouvernements.* Jan Jagielski and Tomasc Lec, *Nie Zatarte Slady Getta Warszawskiego (The Remnants of the Warsaw Ghetto).*

[15] Israel Gutman, *The Jews of Warsaw, 1939-1943: Ghetto, Underground, Revolt*, p. 15.

[16] The assistant commandant of the Jewish police in the Warsaw Ghetto was Jakob Lejkin whom the Germans nicknamed "The Jewish Napoleon" (*Der Jüdischer Napoleon*). Many Jews termed the Jewish police "The disgrace of mankind."

[17] Jan Jagielski and Tomasc Lec, *Nie Zatarte Slady Getta Warszawskiego (The Remnants of the Warsaw Ghetto).*

[18] The Nazis frequently used various signs indicating some sort of contagious zone (*Ansteckungsgebiet*); by this act the Nazis could claim they were protecting non-Jewish inhabitants from highly contagious diseases. The effect was to alienate the Jews from the rest of society. Body lice and fleas transmitted epidemic typhus, an often-fatal disease.

[19] *Verordnung über die Bezeichnung der Geschäfte im Generalgouvernement.* Paul Moder was born in Neheim on 1 October 1896. He served in an artillery battalion in World War I and won the Iron Cross 2nd and 1st Class. He was wounded in action during the conflict. Moder joined the Nazi Party 6 July 1925 that qualified him for award of the Golden Party Badge (Party number 9425). He entered the SS on 1 September 1931 with SS number 11716. After holding several significant SS positions in the 1930s, he became SS and Police Leader for Warsaw on 14 November 1939. He held this position until 4 August 1941. Then he went to the front in Russia with the artillery regiment of the SS *Totenkopf* Division. Moder was killed in action on 8 February 1942 while leading a battle group near the village of Kalinitz south of Lake Ilmen. He had received the Clasp to the Iron Cross 2nd Class on 26 June 1940 and the Iron Cross 1st Class on 9 November 1941.

[20] The *Gauleitern* were the senior Nazi Party officials of Germany's various geographic regions. Arthur Greiser served as the *Gauleiter* of the *Wartheland* from 1939 until the end of the war. He was extradited to Poland where he was tried, found guilty of war crimes and hanged at Poznan on 21 July 1946. Albert Förster served as *Gauleiter* of Danzig-West Prussia. On 29 April 1948 a Polish court sentenced him to death. The Poles hanged him in Warsaw on 28 February 1952.

[21] Jan Jagielski and Tomasc Lec, *Nie Zatarte Slady Getta Warszawskiego (The Remnants of the Warsaw Ghetto).*

[22] *Verordnung über die Kennzeichnung von Jüden und Jüdinnen im Generalgouvernement.* Ibid.

[23] Ludwig Fischer served as the governor of the Warsaw district from October 1939 to January 1945. Born 16 April 1905 in Kaiserslautern, he joined the Nazi Party on his twenty-first birthday, 16 April 1926 (Party number 36499) and was elected to the *Reichstag*, the German parliament, in 1937. During the pre-war period, he served in the SA and achieved a rank of *SA-Gruppenführer*. Besides serving in Warsaw, Fischer was the acting governor of the Lublin district in April and May 1943. He was arrested in West Germany after the war and extradited to Poland. The Polish Supreme National Court placed him on trial for war crimes beginning 17 December 1947. The court found him guilty of crimes against the population of Warsaw, as an accomplice in establishing the Warsaw Ghetto and for complicity in the Treblinka extermination camp. The Poles hanged him shortly thereafter.

[24] *Erste Durchführungsvorschrift zur Verordnung über die Einführung des Arbeitszwanges für die jüdische Bevölkerung des Generalgouvernement.*

[25] Abraham J. Edelheit and Hershel Edelheit, *History of the Holocaust: A Handbook and Dictionary*, p. 328.

[26] Israel Gutman, *Resistance: The Warsaw Ghetto Uprising*. (Boston: Houghton Mifflin Company, 1994), p. 73.

[27] Ibid., p. 264.

[28] Jan Jagielski and Tomasc Lec, *Nie Zatarte Slady Getta Warszawskiego (The Remnants of the Warsaw Ghetto).*

[29] Israel Gutman, *The Jews of Warsaw, 1939-1943: Ghetto, Underground, Revolt*, p. 436.

[30] Israel Gutman, editor in chief, *Encyclopedia of the Holocaust*, Volume 4, p. 1610.

[31] *Verordnung über die Pflicht zur Anmeldung jüdischen Vermögens im Generalgouvernement.* Abraham J. Edelheit and Hershel Edelheit, *History of the Holocaust: A Handbook and Dictionary*, p. 329.

[32] *Verordnung über die Benutzung der Eisenbahn durch Juden im Generalgouvernement.* Ibid., p. 329.

[33] Many other "crimes" in Warsaw were punishable by death. These included: arson against German property, incitement of disobedience, knowledge of a conspiracy, contamination of a German with a venereal disease and any violation against the German Reich. Source: Tadeusz Bielecki, and Leszek Szymanski, *Warsaw Aflame: The 1933-1945 Years*. (Los Angeles: Polamerica Press, 1973), p. 30.

[34] *Anordnung #7 des Leiters der Abteilung Devisen im Amt des Generalgouverneurs.* Abraham J. Edelheit and Hershel Edelheit, *History of the Holocaust: A Handbook and Dictionary*, p. 329.

[35] *Zweite Verordnung über die Sozialversicherung im Generalgouvernment (Unterstützungen und Verfahren).* Ibid., p. 329.

[36] Jan Jagielski and Tomasc Lec, *Nie Zatarte Slady Getta Warszawskiego (The Remnants of the Warsaw Ghetto).*

[37] Israel Gutman, *Resistance: The Warsaw Ghetto Uprising*, p. 89.

[38] Ibid.

[39] *Verordnung über die Bestimmung des Begriffs "Jude" im Generalgouvernment.* Abraham J. Edelheit and Hershel Edelheit, *History of the Holocaust: A Handbook and Dictionary*, p. 330.

[40] Jan Jagielski and Tomasc Lec, *Nie Zatarte Slady Getta Warszawskiego (The Remnants of the Warsaw Ghetto).*

[41] The Germans seemed to be careful in the use of the term "ghetto" preferring to speak in general terms of a Jewish Residential Quarter of Warsaw instead. They demanded that the Jews use the same terminology but this appears to have never happened.

[42] British Broadcasting Corporation Television, *The Warsaw Ghetto*. London: 1969. Re-released by Hollywood Home Theater.

[43] Jan Jagielski and Tomasc Lec, *Nie Zatarte Slady Getta Warszawskiego (The Remnants of the Warsaw Ghetto).*

[44] Ibid.

[45] Raul Hilberg, *The Destruction of the European Jews*, Volume 1, p. 226.

[46] Jan Jagielski and Tomasc Lec, *Nie Zatarte Slady Getta Warszawskiego (The Remnants of the Warsaw Ghetto).*

[47] Hans-Joachim Neufeldt, Jürgen Huck, and Georg Tessin, *Zur Geschichte der Ordnungspolizei, 1936-1945*. (Freiburg, FRG: Bundesarchiv, 1957), p. 29.

[48] The 301st Police Battalion remained in Warsaw until July 1942 when it deployed to central Russia. The 304th Police Battalion also departed in July 1942 but went to southern Russia. The 307th Police Battalion left earlier in the summer of 1941 for central Russia.

[49] Jan Jagielski and Tomasc Lec, *Nie Zatarte Slady Getta Warszawskiego (The Remnants of the Warsaw Ghetto).*

[50] Abraham J. Edelheit and Hershel Edelheit, *History of the Holocaust: A Handbook and Dictionary*, p. 434.

[51] British Broadcasting Corporation Television, *The Warsaw Ghetto*.

[52] *Verordnung über die Einführung einer Arbeitskarte in Generalgouvernement.* Abraham J. Edelheit and Hershel Edelheit, *History of the Holocaust: A Handbook and Dictionary*, p. 330.

[53] Jan Jagielski and Tomasc Lec, *Nie Zatarte Slady Getta Warszawskiego (The Remnants of the Warsaw Ghetto).*

[54] Abraham J. Edelheit and Hershel Edelheit, *History of the Holocaust: A Handbook and Dictionary*, p. 403.

[55] Jan Jagielski and Tomasc Lec, *Nie Zatarte Slady Getta Warszawskiego (The Remnants of the Warsaw Ghetto).*

[56] Ibid.

[57] *Verordnung über die Benutzung öffentlicher Verkehrsmittel durch Juden im Generalgouvernement.* Abraham J. Edelheit and Hershel Edelheit, *History of the Holocaust: A Handbook and Dictionary*, p. 330.

[58] Jan Jagielski and Tomasc Lec, *Nie Zatarte Slady Getta Warszawskiego (The Remnants of the Warsaw Ghetto).*

[59] Abraham J. Edelheit and Hershel Edelheit, *History of the Holocaust: A Handbook and Dictionary*, p. 243.

[60] Israel Gutman, editor in chief, *Encyclopedia of the Holocaust*, Volume 4, p. 1610.

[61] Jan Jagielski and Tomasc Lec, *Nie Zatarte Slady Getta Warszawskiego (The Remnants of the Warsaw Ghetto).*

[62] Israel Gutman, editor in chief, *Encyclopedia of the Holocaust*, Volume 4, p. 1611.

[63] Jan Jagielski and Tomasc Lec, *Nie Zatarte Slady Getta Warszawskiego (The Remnants of the Warsaw Ghetto).*

[64] Arpad Wigand was born 13 January 1906 in Mannheim. He joined the SS on 1 August 1930 with membership number 2999 and the Nazi Party on 15 February 1926 (Party number 30682). Wigand assumed duties as Inspector of the Sipo and SD in Breslau in September 1937 and held this post until assum-

ing SSPF duties in Warsaw on 4 August 1941. Himmler replaced him as SSPF on 22 July 1942 with *SS-Oberführer* Dr. Ferdinand von Sammern-Frankenegg. From Warsaw, Wigand went to the 7th SS Division "*Prinz Eugen*," where he served as a regimental adjutant with a *Waffen-SS* rank of *SS-Untersturmführer*. From November 1943 to February 1945 Arpad Wigand commanded the 3rd Battalion, 13th SS Mountain Regiment "*Artur Phleps*" during fighting in Yugoslavia and the Balkans. Wigand owned the Golden Party Badge. The British captured him at the end of the war and extradited Wigand to Poland. There he was tried for war crimes and sentenced to 15 years in prison. Wigand was released in 1956 but was tried again for other war crimes in 1981 in Hamburg. He was sentenced to 12 years in prison at this time. Arpad Wigand died on 26 July 1983 in Monschau, Germany.

[65] Ibid.

[66] Israel Gutman, *Resistance: The Warsaw Ghetto Uprising*, pp. 81-82.

[67] Ibid.

[68] *Anordnung über die Einstellung der Beförderung von Päckchen und Paketen von jüdischen Auslieferern*. Abraham J. Edelheit & Hershel Edelheit, History *of the Holocaust: A Handbook and Dictionary*, p. 330.

[69] Israel Gutman, *Resistance: The Warsaw Ghetto Uprising*, p. 74.

[70] Jan Jagielski and Tomasc Lec, *Nie Zatarte Slady Getta Warszawskiego (The Remnants of the Warsaw Ghetto).*

[71] Charles G. Roland, *Courage Under Siege: Starvation, Disease, and Death in the Warsaw Ghetto*. (New York: Oxford University Press, 1992), p. 225.

[72] Israel Gutman, *The Jews of Warsaw, 1939-1943: Ghetto, Underground, Revolt*, pp. 63-64.

[73] Charles G. Roland, *Courage Under Siege: Starvation, Disease, and Death in the Warsaw Ghetto*, p. 225.

[74] My father, an American infantryman in the 9th Infantry Division, was captured in the Hürtgen Forest in January 1945. Transported to *Stalag VIG*, he was incarcerated with thousands of other allied soldiers. In recounting his experiences, he mentioned on numerous occasions how some Polish and Russian prisoners, who had been held in captivity for many years, simply sat down in the middle of the camp and died – with no outward sign of illness or injury. While the Americans in the camp would try and explain to their Polish comrades that victory was not that far away, many of these prisoners simply lost their will to live.

[75] Israel Gutman, *Resistance: The Warsaw Ghetto Uprising*, pp. 82-83.

[76] Jan Jagielski and Tomasc Lec, *Nie Zatarte Slady Getta Warszawskiego (The Remnants of the Warsaw Ghetto).*

[77] Ibid.

[78] Ibid.

[79] Dr. Herbert Hummel was born 7 May 1907 in Landshut. A lawyer, he attended the Universities of Munich, Innsbruck and Würzburg. He entered the Nazi Party on 1 March 1932 with Party number 992585. Hummel was awarded the War Service Cross 2nd Class in 1940 and the 1st Class on 30 January 1942.

[80] Arno Mayer, *Why Did The Heavens Not Darken?* (New York: Pantheon Books, 1988), p. 397.

[81] Israel Gutman, *The Jews of Warsaw, 1939-1943: Ghetto, Underground, Revolt*, p. 199.

2

OPERATION REINHARD

"I hereby order that the resettlement of the entire Jewish population of the General Government be carried out and completed by 31 December 1942."[1]

- Heinrich Himmler, 19 July 1942

By the summer of 1942 Heinrich Himmler's empire stood at its high-water mark. From the Bay of Biscay in the west, to almost the Caspian Sea in the east, the *Reichsführer-SS's* security machine seemed like an omnipotent, malevolent monster affecting the lives of several hundred million people. At this very moment, Himmler's *Einsatzgruppen* were murdering hundreds of thousands of Jews in Russia, the Ukraine and the Baltic States. Meanwhile his concentration camps at Auschwitz, Mauthausen and other places that would later be remembered in infamy were preparing to devour thousands more in technologically advanced gas chambers and crematoria. But the torrent of blood was not enough. All the Jews would have to go.

• • •

In mid-July a secret SS detachment arrived in Warsaw under the direction of *SS-Sturmbannführer* Hermann Höfle. On 21 July these men directed forces of the Polish "Navy Blue Police," and some four hundred soldiers in several Ukrainian, Lithuanian and Latvian support elements to begin seizing hostages. This round up included several members of the *Judenrat* and their families. Some two thousand Jewish Order Service would assist the support elements; the Jewish Order Service incorrectly believed that they and their families would not be included in the deportations. The following morning Höfle met with Adam Czerniakow, still chief of the *Judenrat*, and informed him that all Jews of Warsaw, with some certain exceptions, would be deported to the East over the next several weeks. The SS officer went on to say that the Germans would ship the first 6,000 Jews that very day, and that several thousand would depart each day thereafter. Höfle added that should Czerniakow hinder the deportation in any way, then his wife would be the first one to be shot as a hostage. The following day Adam Czerniakow took his life.[2]

• • •

Höfle and his small detachment of men, including SS officers *SS-Hauptsturmführer* Georg Michalsen and *SS-Hauptsturmführer* Reinhold von Mohrenschildt, belonged to a secret organization headquartered in Lublin, *Operation Reinhard.* Led by *SS-Brigadeführer* Odilo Globocnik, handpicked by Heinrich Himmler for the mission, the purpose of the operation was to exterminate the Jews of the General Government. Himmler issued no written orders or instructions to Globocnik. However, the tasks that Globocnik, the SS and Police Leader for Lublin, were to accomplish can be summarized as follows:[3]

- prepare the overall plan to deport and kill the 2,000,000 Jews of the General Government;
- build three death camps where the killing would take place;
- coordinate the deportation and transportation of Jews to the death camps;
- kill the Jews at the camps;

• seize the valuables and assets of the victims and transfer these objects to appropriate *Reich* officials;
• execute the entire operation under the conditions of greatest secrecy.

We do not know the exact date that Globocnik received his initial order to begin planning for the operation. We do know, however, that beginning in October 1941 German euthanasia specialists began to report for duty in the new undertaking. Globocnik could count on a force of 450 personnel to operate the endeavor. This included 153 SS and Police officials, who served under Globocnik's command in the Lublin district, 205 SS and Police officials in supporting units and 92 euthanasia specialists from the Chancellery of the *Führer*.[4] The operation was dedicated by name to *SS-Obergruppenführer* Reinhard Heydrich, who had been shot in May 1942 by members of the Czech underground, on the outskirts of Prague, and had died a week later.

The SS located the headquarters for *Operation Reinhard* in the former Stefan Batory College in Lublin. Other *Operation Reinhard* facilities included the SS training camp at Trawniki, the SS clothing workshops located at the old airport at Lublin and the three death camps themselves at Belzec, Sobibór and Treblinka.[5] Each camp served a general region; the Germans would send the Jews of the Warsaw Ghetto to a small hamlet known as Treblinka.

The village of Treblinka is located about fifty miles northeast of Warsaw. During the war it was located in the northern region of the General Government. In June 1941 the Germans established a labor camp known as Treblinka I near the village. At this location the Nazis forced the one to two thousand Poles and Jews imprisoned there to work in quarries to extract materials for the construction of fortifications along the 1939 German-Soviet demarcation line. The labor camp was under the authority of the SS and Police Leader Warsaw. *SS-Hauptsturmführer* Theodor van Eupen served as the commandant. The Treblinka killing center, on the other hand, was located about one mile from the labor camp in a sparsely populated area near the Polish village of Wolka Okraglik along the Malkinia-Siedlce railway line. The camp was situated two and a half miles southeast of the village and the railway station of Treblinka. The Germans extended a branch railroad track from the labor camp to the extermination camp, that became known as Treblinka II, and continued it to the nearby railway station in the village of Treblinka. One of the prime considerations for site selection was that it was heavily wooded and hidden from view.[6]

SS-Obersturmführer Richard Thomalla laid out the extermination camp, in late May or early June 1942, in a trapezoid of 1,312 by 1,968 feet.[7] *SS-Unterscharführer* Erwin Herman Lambert, a foreman of the building team, ensured that branches woven into the three to four meter-high barbed-wire fence and trees planted around the perimeter served as camouflage. This blocked any view into the camp from the outside. The Germans constructed 26 foot-high watchtowers along the fence and at each of the corners. Thomalla divided the camp into three parts: the reception area (*Auffanglager*), the living area (*Wohnlager*), and the extermination area (*Totenlager*). The living area contained housing for German and Ukrainian guards assigned to the camp, offices, a clinic, storerooms and workshops. One section of the living area contained barracks that housed Jewish prisoners forced to work in the camp.[8] Construction went smoothly. On 7 July 1942, *SS-Obersturmführer* Dr. Irmfried Eberl, the first commandant of Treblinka, notified the commissar of the Warsaw Ghetto, Dr. Heinz Auerswald, that Treblinka was ready to accept "resettlers."[9] [10]

Incoming trains from Warsaw, generally with fifty to fifty-seven cars, first stopped at the Treblinka village railway station.[11] The Directorate General of the Eastern Railroad (*Generaldirektion der Ostbahn*), called "*Gedob*" for short, administered all the trains. Dr. Adolf Gerteis headed this organization that was subordinated to the *Reichsbahn* (German Railroad) under the Ministry of Transport. *Gedob* had several missions to perform regarding *Operation Reinhard* to include:[12]

• coordinate the traffic schedule with SS authorities in charge of the deportations;
• determine at which railway stations the deportation trains would be waiting;
• determine the number of freight cars needed for each deportation;
• determine the timetable and destination for each train;
• coordinate the deportation schedule in accordance with other important military and transportation requirements;
• conduct the transportation with the greatest secrecy.

The *Gedob* classified each train with Jewish deportees as a special train (*Sonderzug*). As a rule, the freight cars were closed but on some occasions the Germans used open-top cars. Within each car the Nazis found it possible to cram up to one hundred individuals.[13] Additionally, each train normally had one or two passenger cars for the guards. The trains used in the deportation of the Warsaw Ghetto generally loaded at the *Umschlagplatz* from 1600 to 1700 hours daily. This became a problem. *Gedob* had set daily departure times at 1225 hours. It was a four-hour trip to Treblinka; *Gedob* posted the Treblinka arrival time of 1630 hours.[14] Given a two and one half-hour turn-around time at Treblinka and the trip back to Warsaw, the deportation train would be back in Warsaw at 2319 hours, ready for the next day. However, the SS men at Treblinka did not want the killing operations to continue in hours of darkness; it placed too great demands on security. As a practical matter, trains often arrived at Treblinka at 2100 hours and remained sealed until the following daybreak.[15] Delays often caused trains enroute to death camps to arrive several days late and many of the cattle car occupants, starved of food and water, would be dead.

At Treblinka, German railway workers Rudolf Emmerich and Willi Klinzman detached nineteen cars at a time from the train and brought them into the camp. They detached nineteen, because that was the capacity of the unloading ramp at Treblinka.[16] The Nazis ordered the victims to disembark in the reception area, which contained the railway siding and platform. *SS-Hauptsturmführer* Franz Stangl and *SS-Oberscharführer* Kurt Franz announced that the deportees had arrived at a transit camp and were to hand over all valuables. The reception area also contained a fenced-in "deportation square" with two barracks, in which deportees – men separated from women and children – had to undress, and two large storerooms where victims' possessions, confiscated upon arrival, were sorted for shipment back to Germany. *SS-Scharführer* Franz Suchomel was a prominent non-commissioned officer in this area.[17]

A camouflaged, fenced-in path, referred to as the "tube," led from the reception area to the extermination area. Camp officials forced the victims to run along this path and enter the gas chambers, labeled as showers. Once the SS sealed the chamber doors, they started an engine installed in a room attached to the gas chambers. Exhaust pipes funneled carbon monoxide into the gas chambers killing the victims inside. The death process usually lasted twenty-five minutes but sometimes there were mechanical malfunctions that caused major delays of over an hour. Jewish prisoners then interred the bodies of the gassing victims in huge trenches. The Germans repeated the process until the train was empty of victims.[18]

The SS told deportees, who were too weak to reach the gas chambers on their own, that they would receive medical attention. The Nazis took them instead to a camouflaged area, known as the *Lazarett* (Aid Station), which was disguised with a Red Cross flag as a hospital, and they were shot by *SS-Scharführer* August Miete.

No one really knows exactly how many people were killed at Treblinka during the seventeen months of its operation. Dr. Helmut Krausnick, a respected historian and director of the Munich Institute of Contemporary History, believed 700,000 perished. The official Polish figure, as given by Z. Lukaszkiewicz, was 800,000. Dr. Wolfgang Scheffler, an expert witness for the prosecution at the second post-war Treblinka trial in 1965, asserted that 900,000 died. Franciszek Zabecki, a transport controller at the Treblinka railroad station, kept a daily log that put the figure closer to 1,200,000. Whatever the number, Treblinka must certainly rank as one of the largest, most deadly efficient murder machines of all time.[19]

Not everything ran smoothly. *Operation Reinhard* had over-scheduled incoming transports to Treblinka. The camp was designed to process 5,000 to 6,000 victims per day. However, the total frequently exceeded that number during the period in late summer 1942 when the Warsaw Jews were being deported. Trains also arrived from the Radom district and the Lublin district. Some 30,000 Jews arrived from Radom between 5 and 17 August. Another 21,000 victims came from Kielce between 20 and 24 August and 11,000 deportees arrived from Radzyn from 25 to 26 August.[20] *SS-Obersturmführer* Dr. Irmfried Eberl could not maintain control and was relieved of command and replaced with *SS-Hauptsturmführer* Franz Stangl. Kurt Franz, the incoming deputy commandant, reported on what he found at Treblinka:[21]

> It was midsummer or early autumn 1942 when I arrived at Treblinka from Belzec. I left Malkinia station on foot and it was already dark by the time I reached Treblinka. In the camp there were bodies lying everywhere. I seem to recall that they were all swollen. Jews dragged these bodies through the camp to the upper section. The working Jews were forced to keep moving by the [Ukrainian] guards, also by the Germans. I also saw them being beaten. What they were beaten with I can no longer say. There was tremendous confusion and a horrible din . . .
>
> That evening I went walking around the camp. During my walk I had established that some of the guard squads were with girls and had put down their rifles. Then, as far as I could, I established order.
>
> The next day very early in the morning I looked around the camp. I could no longer see any bodies lying around. At about 0900 hours – it could have been somewhat later – a transport arrived. When I got there, the men were already standing naked in the so-called reception yard.

Franz Stangl, the incoming commander who would replace Eberl, remembered the scene this way:[22]

> I think it started the day I first saw the *Totenlager* in Treblinka. I remember [*SS-Hauptsturmführer* Christian] Wirth standing there, next to the pits full of blue-black corpses. It had nothing to do with humanity – it could not have; it was a mass – a mass of rotting flesh. Wirth said, 'What shall we do with this garbage?'

Order had been restored. The killing factory resumed work. The "garbage" was disposed. The deportations from Warsaw could resume.

• • •

SS-Sturmbannführer Hermann Höfle directed the Warsaw deportation from two locations in the Ghetto. He established his command post, along with a dozen SS officers and enlisted personnel at 103 Leszno Street. The SS set up a second command post at the headquarters of the Jewish Order Police on Ogrodowa Street; this location had SS and *Gestapo* officers who had been in Warsaw for some time.[23]

Assisting Höfle in his ghastly work were the 22nd Latvian, 272nd Latvian and 274th Latvian Police Battalions that had been brought in from the Baltic states.[24] Once the German *Wehrmacht* had cleared Latvia in 1941, during their attack on the Soviet Union, they established voluntary Latvian police units under German control. Initially these units, some 500 to 550 men in strength, were assigned security duties in rear areas.[25] The three units reported to Warsaw in July 1942, ostensibly linked to the beginning of the deportations.[26] Also assisting in the effort was the German 61st Police Battalion from Dortmund, which had been assigned to duties in the General Government the month before.[27]

The Germans conducted the deportations in four phases, although it is not clear that this was their plan from the start. From 22 to 30 July the Jewish Order Police began to evacuate the streets of the Ghetto. They rounded up unregistered Jews, as well as those Jewish refugees from other areas that had no permanent dwellings, in the first phase of the operation. The SS men established quotas of deportees each day, issued orders, conducted surprise inspections, increased the number of guards at the entrances of the Warsaw Ghetto and directly supervised deportees at the *Umschlagplatz* (transfer point north of the Ghetto next to a railway spur). During this phase Jews who had proper work papers listing them in an exempt category were excluded from deportation. The Germans deported 58,130 Jews from the city during this phase.[28]

The Germans deported the Jews by first marching them on foot from the Ghetto north on Zamenhof Street to the *Umschlagplatz*. This was a short distance, less than half a mile. The *Umschlagplatz* was a holding area eighty meters by thirty meters just north of the corner of Niska and Zamenhof Streets. This open area was situated next to the four-story Czyste Hospital in which Jews were sometimes held overnight before deportations. Most of the Jews sat or stood in the *Umschlagplatz* for several hours until a freight train pulled into a spur line about one hundred meters north. Then, the Germans marched the Jews on a path north to the waiting cars. It appears that the Jews moved between two lines of troops, in some sort of selection process, with German Police to the left (west) and Ukrainian and Latvian security troops on the right (east). During the short march, the Germans selected a small number of Jews to be future slave laborers and held these personnel in a separate area just south of the rail cars. These laborers would travel to Trawniki or Poniatowa as a temporary reprieve. The vast majority would entrain up wooden ramps to the awaiting fright cars that would transport them to their deaths at Treblinka.[29]

The second phase lasted from 31 July to 14 August. During this phase the Nazis assumed full control of the operation in the streets of the Ghetto. Some two hundred men, which included SS, German Police, Lithuanians, Latvians and Ukrainians, conducted dragnets and systematically combed blocks of buildings for potential deportees. The Germans honored some exemption papers, but at the end of each day it appears that if a quota had not yet been met, then persons with valid exemption papers were often rounded up and sent to the *Umschlagplatz* anyway. The Germans deported some 97,333 Jews from Warsaw during this phase.[30]

Phase three took place from 15 August to 6 September. It included two operational pauses when the *Operation Reinhard* staff left Warsaw to conduct actions elsewhere, and as we have seen, when the killing machine at Treblinka temporarily was overloaded. Exemption papers became almost meaningless and the SS started to take Jewish workers out of the war-related industries. The SS conducted even more raids and detailed searches of buildings to meet their daily quotas of deportees. During this period the Germans deported 50,549 Jews.[31]

The final phase lasted from 6 to 21 September. The Jews proved even harder to process and the Nazis ordered all people to evacuate their apartments and assemble next to the *Umschlagplatz*. So terrible were the selections that the surviving Jews referred to the period as "the cauldron." The Germans ruthlessly combed all the workshops setting individual deportation quotas for each work section. The final deportation occurred on 21 September and included more than a thousand Jewish Order Police and their families as victims to be sent to the *Umschlagplatz*. To the Jewish policemen, their cooperation with the Nazis had finally turned to be a cruel hoax. Nazi authorities sent some 44,253 Jews on the trains from Warsaw to Treblinka, and their deaths, during this period.[32]

The original German plan was apparently to leave some 35,000 Jews in the Ghetto after the *Operation Reinhard* action. During the four phases, the Nazis deported 253,741 Jews to Treblinka.[33] Besides these victims, who went directly to Treblinka, the Germans sent 11,580 persons to a transit camp (*Durchgangslager*) near Lublin. Israel Gutman in his *The Jews of Warsaw, 1939-1943: Ghetto, Underground, Revolt*, asserts that a further 10,380 died or were killed during the operation.[34] Thus, it would seem that the Jewish population in the Warsaw Ghetto dropped by at least 275,701.

Judenrat statistics from the period reveal that 6,687 Jews were shot in the Ghetto during the *Operation Reinhard* action to include 1,224 in July, 2,305 in August and 3,158 in September. This compares with 81 deaths by gunfire in April in the Ghetto, 54 in May and 90 in June. Most of the shootings during the *Operation Reinhard* months involved Jews trying to escape the deportations.[35]

Many historians have commented on the degree of passivity and submission of the Warsaw Jews during the *Operation Reinhard* deportations. While it is not the purpose of this work to examine the psychological factors at work that summer, clearly Jewish resistance was less than it would become in January, April and May of 1943. Yisrael Gutman proposes several factors that he believes significantly influenced the behavior and response of the Warsaw Jews during the summer deportations. He summarizes them as:[36]

- perpetual ignorance and uncertainty as to the true fate that awaited the deportees;
- an assumption that the Germans would only deport a portion of the Ghetto population that would primarily consist of those Jews who were refugees or lacking a stable means or support;
- belief that the action was always about to end – that it was always almost over;
- an assumption that resistance would make matters worse for all;
- a resignation that a part of the population of the Ghetto might have to be deported so that safety could be secured for the remainder;
- the total consummation of all emotional and physical strength just to cope with the stress generated by the action, which left no energy for resistance;
- a paralysis of the will to resist caused by the steadily deteriorating circumstances in the Ghetto.

Gutman goes on to say that *Operation Reinhard* revealed a tragic paradox of history. He concludes that Hitler's National Socialists regime viewed the Jews as the most powerful and deadly racial and political enemy of the *Reich*. The horrible paradox was that this enemy, the Jews, against whom a comprehensive program of total annihilation was planned and ultimately executed, was "actually the embodiment of weakness and helplessness."[37] While the Germans may have gained this impression in Warsaw during the summer deportations, they would find a much different situation there just a few short months later.

Notes:

[1] Yitzhak Arad, *Belzec, Sobibór, Treblinka: The Operation Reinhard Death Camps*. (Bloomington, IN: Indiana University Press, 1987), p. 17.

[2] Ibid., p. 203, 206.

[3] Ibid., p. 16.

[4] Ibid., p. 17.

[5] Ibid., pp. 18-19.

Belzec was the second Nazi killing center to begin operation, and the first of the *Operation Reinhard* camps. The small town of Belzec is located between the cities of Zamosc and Lvov (Lwów) in southeastern Poland. In early 1940, the Germans established a labor camp for Jews in Belzec, where Jews were forced to build fortifications and antitank ditches along the demarcation line between German- and Soviet-occupied Poland. This labor camp was liquidated in the fall of 1940. The availability of good rail connections and Belzec's location in the center of the large Jewish populations of the Lvov, Kraków, and Lublin regions led to the construction of the extermination camp there in November 1941. Located along the Lublin-Lvov railway line, the extermination camp was 1,620 feet from the Belzec railway station. A siding connected the camp and the station. Belzec was divided into a combined administration-reception area and an extermination compound. A narrow enclosed path called the "tube" connected the two. The reception area held the railway siding and a ramp. The extermination area included the gas chambers and mass graves. Each side of the camp measured 886 feet. The SS guards assigned to the camp were housed in a separate compound near the Belzec train station. Gassing operations began in mid-March 1942. Between March and December 1942 at least 600,000 people were deported to Belzec and killed. Most of the victims were Jews from the Ghettos of southern Poland. The Germans also deported Jews from Germany, Austria, and Bohemia and Moravia to Belzec. Several hundred Gypsies were deported to the camp and murdered as well. After deportations to Belzec ceased in December 1942, prisoner detachments exhumed bodies from burial pits and cremated them in an effort to obliterate all traces of mass murder. The Belzec killing center was finally dismantled in July 1943. The remaining prisoners, who had been assigned to the camp's work force, were deported to the Sobibór extermination camp and killed. After Belzec was dismantled, the Germans established a farm at the site, planting trees and crops to disguise the area. A Ukrainian, a former guard at the camp, farmed the land. Soviet forces liberated the Belzec camp area in the summer of 1944

The small village of Sobibór is in central Poland, about three miles west of the Bug River and five miles south of Wlodawa. Sobibór was the second killing center constructed as part of *Operation Reinhard*. It was built along the Chelm-Wlodawa railway rail line, in a wooded, swampy, and thinly populated region. The camp covered a rectangular area of 1,312 by 1,969 feet. A minefield 50 feet wide surrounded the entire camp. The Sobibór camp was divided into three parts: an administration area, a reception area and an extermination area. The administration area included camp offices, housing for the German and Ukrainian guards assigned to the camp, and barracks for the prisoner labor force. The reception area held the railway siding, ramp, barracks where the victims disrobed, and warehouses for the victims' possessions. The extermination area included gas chambers, mass graves, and barracks for prisoners assigned to forced labor. Deportations to Sobibór began April 1942 and lasted until the fall of 1943. Jews deported to Sobibór came mainly from the Ghettos of eastern Poland, especially from the Lublin area. Jews were also deported to Sobibór from German-occupied Soviet territory, from Bohemia and Moravia, Austria, the Netherlands, Belgium, and France. About 250,000 people were killed at Sobibór.

[6] United States Holocaust Memorial Museum, *Historical Atlas of the Holocaust*. (New York: Macmillan Publishing USA, 1996), pp. 90-91.

[7] Yitzhak Arad, *Belzec, Sobibór, Treblinka: The Operation Reinhard Death Camps*, p. 37.

[8] United States Holocaust Memorial Museum, *Historical Atlas of the Holocaust*, pp. 90-91.

[9] Heinz Auerswald served as the German commissar of the Warsaw Ghetto from May 1941 to November 1942. Born 26 July 1908 in Berlin, he was a lawyer by profession. Auerswald joined the SS on 7 June 1933 (SS number 216399) and entered the Nazi Party with membership number 4830479. Auerswald was promoted to *SS-Unterscharführer* on 20 April 1937. He served with a Police battalion in Warsaw in 1939 before being transferred to the civil administration established to govern the city. Initially he was in command of the ethnic German affairs section until his appointment as commissar. After the mass deportations of Warsaw Jews to Treblinka between July and Septem-

ber 1942, Auerswald became the district administrator for the Ostrów region. He was drafted into the army in January 1943. Auerswald survived the war. He was investigated for possible war crimes by German judicial authorities in the 1960s but was never indicted.

[10] Alexander Donat, editor, *The Death Camp Treblinka: A Documentary*. (New York: Holocaust Library, 1979), p. 13.

[11] The ramp at the extermination camp could only accommodate nineteen cars at a time. Source: Jaroslaw M. Rymkiewicz, *The Final Station: Umschlagplatz*. Translated by Nina Taylor. (New York: Farrar, Straus and Giroux, 1994), p. 150. Therefore, maximum efficiency dictated that the train pull either thirty-eight or fifty-seven cars (multiples of nineteen) to provide for an even break. A few cars less than fifty-seven would not matter to the SS personnel in the camp. However, a few cars more than fifty-seven would mean that the SS would have to conduct four cycles of the killing operation instead of three that would have added perhaps one to two additional work hours to their day. Such an occurrence would have also delayed the train's return to Warsaw by at least one hour. For these reasons, I believe that the camp commandant, through Globocnik, would have asked the *Gedob* not to send more than fifty-seven cars on any one train. Globocnik's men at Warsaw, who would have packed more people into each car to ensure that the train had a maximum of fifty-seven cars, could have accomplished this.

[12] Yitzhak Arad, *Belzec, Sobibór, Treblinka: The Operation Reinhard Death Camps*, p. 49.

[13] Rupert Butler, *The Black Angels: A History of the Waffen-SS*. (New York: St. Martin's Press, 1979), p. 167.

[14] Raul Hilberg, *Sonderzüge nach Auschwitz*. (Mainz, FRG: Dumjahn Verlag, 1981.), p. 178. The actual schedule showed the train at the Warsaw Danzig Station (Warsawa Gdanska) leaving at 1225 hours and passing through Warsaw Marki at 1242 hours, Tluszcz at 1400 hours, Malkinia at 1554 hours and arriving at Treblinka at 1630 hours.

[15] Yitzhak Arad, *Belzec, Sobibór, Treblinka: The Operation Reinhard Death Camps*, pp. 60-66.

[16] Jaroslaw M. Rymkiewicz, *The Final Station: Umschlagplatz*. Translated by Nina Taylor. (New York: Farrar, Straus and Giroux, 1994), p. 150.

[17] United States Holocaust Memorial Museum, *Historical Atlas of the Holocaust*, pp. 90-91.

[18] Ibid., pp. 90-91.

[19] Alexander Donat, editor, *The Death Camp Treblinka: A Documentary*, p. 14.

[20] Yitzhak Arad, *Belzec, Sobibór, Treblinka: The Operation Reinhard Death Camps*, Appendix A.

[21] Ernst Klee, Willi Dressen and Volker Riess, *The Good Old Days: The Holocaust as Seen by Its Perpetrators and Bystanders*. (New York: Koneck & Koneck, 1991), p. 244.

[22] Tom Segev, *Soldiers of Evil: The Commandants of the Nazi Concentration Camps*. (New York: McGraw-Hill Book Company, 1987), p. 202.

[23] Israel Gutman, *The Jews of Warsaw, 1939-1943: Ghetto, Underground, Revolt*. (Bloomington, IN: Indiana University Press, 1982), p. 207.

[24] German film footage of the *Umschlagplatz*, shown in the British Broadcasting Corporation Television program *The Warsaw Ghetto* (London: 1969. Re-released by Hollywood Home Theater), shows Latvian and/or Ukrainian personnel wearing what appear to be uniforms of dark blue tunics and black trousers.

[25] David Littlejohn, *Foreign Legions of the Third Reich. Volume 4: Poland, the Ukraine, Bulgaria, Romania, Free India, Estonia, Latvia, Lithuania, Finland and Russia*. (San Jose, CA: R. James Bender Publishing, 1987), p. 171.

[26] Hans-Joachim Neufeldt, Jürgen Huck, & Georg Tessin, *Zur Geschichte der Ordnungspolizei, 1936-1945*. Teil II, p. 102 & 107.

[27] C.F. Rüter & D.W. de Mildt, *Die Westdeutschen Strafverfahren wegen Nationalsozialistischer Tötungsverbrechen 1945-1997*. (Amsterdam: Holland University Press, 1998), p. 91. Twenty personnel from this unit were tried in Dortmund in 1954 for the murder of 110 Jews in Warsaw in June and July 1942, but all twenty defendants were acquitted.

[28] Israel Gutman, *The Jews of Warsaw, 1939-1943: Ghetto, Underground, Revolt*, pp. 209-210.

[29] Jaroslaw M. Rymkiewicz, *The Final Station: Umschlagplatz*, pp. 6 and 149.

[30] Israel Gutman, *The Jews of Warsaw, 1939-1943: Ghetto, Underground, Revolt*, p. 210.

[31] Ibid., p. 210.

[32] Ibid., pp. 211-212.

[33] Ibid., pp. 221-223.

[34] Ibid., p. 213.

[35] Ibid., p. 213.

[36] Ibid., p. 227.

[37] Ibid., p. 227.

3

THE JANUARY PROBLEM

"[In Warsaw] only those Jews have the right to live who work to supply the German Army . . . A people that hates the Germans with every fiber of its being can purchase its life only at the price of helping its foe to victory – the very victory that means the complete annihilation of Jewry from the face of Europe, if not of the whole world."[1]

- Dr. Emmanuel Ringelblum, Jewish historian, Warsaw 1942

Heinrich Himmler was restless. The Russians had stopped the German blitzkrieg and conducted a successful counterattack at Stalingrad. The German 6th Army was in its last death throes, which did not bode well for continued German occupation of *Lebensraum*, living space, in the Ukraine. Czech resistance fighters had assassinated *SS-Obergruppenführer* Reinhard Heydrich the previous summer, leaving Himmler as the main driving force behind the destruction of the subhumans in Poland and the east. But the necessities of war were blurring the sharp lines of the *Reichsführer's* racial ideas. Would Himmler win the battle to destroy the Jews or would the Army prevail with their arguments concerning armaments production? Or would the solution be a combination of the two views? Those were the questions.

If the remaining Jews of the Warsaw Ghetto thought that their nightmare was over, they were sadly mistaken. Heinrich Himmler had further designs on the area, initially economic. Throughout the war Himmler sought to make the SS economically self-sufficient. He created the SS Economic-Administrative Main Office (WVHA), which not only controlled the concentration camps, but also exploited slave labor. By September 1939, the SS controlled four giant economic enterprises. The German Excavation and Quarrying Company Limited (*Deutsche Erd-und Steinwerke GmbH*) produced building materials in fourteen stone, brick and clinker works. The German Equipment Company Limited (*Deutsche Ausrüstungwerke GmbH*) owned a variety of trades to include iron foundries, woodworking, cutlery and bread making. The German Experimental Establishment for Foodstuffs and Nutrition Limited (*Deutsche Versuchsanstalt für Ernährung und Verpflegung GmbH*) dealt with food production, forestry and fisheries. Finally, the Society for Exploitation for Textile and Leather-Work Limited (*Gesellschaft für Textil-und Ledervewertung GmbH*) produced uniforms for the *Waffen-SS*.[2]

All these SS economic enterprises needed not only cheap labor, which they often got from the inmates of the regular concentration camps, but also machinery and equipment. The Warsaw Ghetto had plenty of both. On 1 December 1942 Himmler wrote to his chief of the WVHA, *SS-Obergruppenführer* Oswald Pohl, an interesting letter. Himmler, it seems, had just had a look at the machinery and equipment in the Warsaw Ghetto; in the opinion of the *Reichsführer-SS*, the stores and tools were worth hundreds of millions of *Reichsmarks*. He instructed Pohl to remove the machines from the Ghetto as quickly as possible. Pohl immediately sent three experts to Warsaw to inventory the equipment and then quickly informed the *Reichsführer-SS* that all preparations were in place to move the equipment. Himmler gave him the go-ahead and told Pohl to let the Economic Ministry know what was happening.[3]

The *Wehrmacht* had designs on the city as well. The German Army was in urgent need of brushes, clothing, metal ware and even beds and was willing to buy these goods directly from Jewish manufactures in order to avoid the higher prices that German manufacturers and middlemen exacted in the transactions. Thus, on many occasions the army deliberately circumvented the civilian administration of the General Government and the *Transferstelle* to avoid the high duties.[4]

On 18 September 1942, General Curt Freiherr von Gienanth, the commander of all troops stationed in the General Government, voiced his concern about supplies for his forces in the days ahead.[5] The *Reich* Economic Ministry instructed von Gienanth to put more Jews to work to free Ukrainian and Polish workers for forced labor in Germany itself. The problem was a shortage of skilled laborers. There were just over one million workers in the General Government; 300,000 were Jews and of these 100,000 were skilled workers. In the firms producing goods for the *Wehrmacht*, von Gienanth pointed out that Jews held 25 percent to 100 percent of the skilled worker positions. Of 22,700 workers employed in the private manufacture of uniforms, some 22,000 were Jews. According to von Gienanth, to remove these workers, without first bringing in trained replacements, would:[6]

> . . . considerably reduce the war potential of the *Reich* and momentarily paralyze the provisioning of the troops at the front and in the General Government.

Von Gienanth concluded by asking the High Command of the Armed Forces (*Oberkommando der Wehrmacht* [OKW]) to persuade *Reichsführer-SS* Himmler not to uproot the skilled Jews too rapidly as it could possibly damage critical war production. Interestingly enough, von Gienanth went into retirement thirteen days after writing his letter. Perhaps his letter had made waves.

There were other players in the power grab. On 5 September 1942, Field Marshal Wilhelm Keitel, Chief of the OKW, had provided "impossible" orders to his unruly subordinate, von Gienanth:[7]

> The Jews employed in the general Government by the *Wehrmacht* for military auxiliary services in the armaments industry are instantly to be replaced by Poles, that is, non-Jews. The implementation is to be reported.

Albert Speer, Minister of Armaments and War Production, stated in his book *Infiltration: How Heinrich Himmler Schemed to Build an SS Industrial Empire*, that Keitel knew that this edict would cause immense difficulties for von Gienanth because it would be simply impossible to expeditiously replace Jewish manpower with Poles.[8] Speer stated that von Gienanth was actually replaced rather than retired.[9]

On 22 September 1942, Hitler held an economic meeting to resolve the dispute. At the conclusion of the conference Hitler stated:[10]

> The *Führer* agrees with *Gauleiter* Sauckel's [Plenipotentiary for Labor Allocation] proposal to have Jewish skilled workers remain in the General Government.

Himmler probably felt that several of the parties had gone over his head. Undoubtedly, in his mind it was close to anarchy in Warsaw. Just how did the Germans in Warsaw get in this predicament?

German civilian manufacturers surfaced in the Warsaw Ghetto in the summer of 1941 after first obtaining permission from the *Reich* Economic Office to operate in the Warsaw area. A carpentry company, led by Bernhard Hallmann, arrived in July, while the Fritz Schulz Company, a fur establishment from Danzig (now Gdansk), became active in September.[11] One of the largest private firms in the Ghetto, owned by Germans but staffed by Jews, was that of textile manufacturer Walther Caspar Többens. Többens was part of the *Deutsche Firmengemeinschaft Warschau m.b.H.* and by July 1942 he employed over 4,500 Jews. Többens produced articles for the German Army by exploiting Jewish property and labor. These products included tailoring, fur making, leather goods.[12]

Although the Jews hired by Többens and the other German factory owners toiled like beasts of burden in horrid labor conditions over long hours, they considered themselves fortunate. They had work permits, and these permits served as protection against being sent to a labor camp or worse. Additionally, some 3,000 to 4,000 Jews worked in shops located outside the Warsaw Ghetto. At dawn each morning the SS and Jewish Police would herd these workers together, march them through the streets and transport them to nearby shops. Each evening the dead-tired workers would stumble back into the Ghetto to their cramped apartments after a dozen, or even more, hours of backbreaking work.[13]

After the deportations of the previous summer, the survivors were herded into three main areas. The first, and largest of these locations, was the Central Ghetto in the north, which was the size of about a dozen square blocks. As only one large factory producing goods for the *Wehrmacht* was in this area, the Jews in this district were mainly "nonproductive" Jews who were the most expendable should another deportation begin. To the north of the Central Ghetto lay the *Umschlagplatz*. Within the area lay the *Judenrat* Building, the Czyste-Benson-Bauman Hospital and the headquarters for most of the Jewish resistance forces.[14] A closed off section of the Central Ghetto contained the *Werterfassung* – an organization commanded by *SS-Obersturmführer* Franz Konrad – the SS enterprise devoted to collecting, classifying, sorting and storing all transportable Jewish property left behind in the deserted apartments and buildings of the Ghetto. As the Central Ghetto contained what remained of the Ghetto's public institutions, and as it was home to over half the Jews left in Warsaw (probably at least 30,000 lived in the area), it served as the nucleus of the underground and resistance movements.[15]

Just to the east of the Central Ghetto, and separated by a wall, were several square blocks, known as the Brushmaker's District. Here, several factories churned out brushes of every size and type for military consumption.[16] The boundary of this district ran along Swietojerska, Bonifraterska, Walowa and Franciszkanska Streets. The Brushmaker's District contained about 4,000 Jews.[17]

The third major Ghetto area was the Productive Ghetto, some three isolated streets in the south that housed most of the factories. Around each factory and its workers' quarters were stone walls. The Jews of each factory had to remain within the walls or face deportation or death. The most prominent of these factories were Többens (Leszno Street), K.G. Schulz (Leszno Street), and Fritz Schultz (Nowolipie Street). Smaller "shops" included Oskar Schilling, Kurt Röhrich, Bernard Hallmann and several others. Leszno, Zelazna, Nowolipie, Smocza, Nowolipki and Karmelicka Streets bound the Productive Ghetto. Almost 20,000 Jews were crammed into this area.[18]

Between the Central Ghetto in the north and the Productive Ghetto in the south lay the Wild Ghetto, a barren wasteland uninhabited since July of 1942. Uninhabited may be too formal a term for the area. Jews, Poles, criminals and anyone hiding from the Nazi authorities made their way constantly through the territory while on the run. The Pawiak Prison – run by the *Gestapo* – was located in the section of the Wild Ghetto. Finally, at the southwestern corner of the previous Ghetto, and separated from the Productive Ghetto by several blocks of deserted buildings, lay the Small or Little Ghetto where 2,000 Jews worked in the "Little Többens" German factory, a part of the W.C. Többens enterprise, on Prosta Street.[19]

Each section of the Ghetto had rules that the Jews had to follow. On 14 September, toward the end of the deportations, *SS-Oberführer* von Sammern issued a regulation concerning the Jews concentrated in the "shops" that included the following points:[20]

> • All the certified enterprises in the Jewish quarter must ensure that the area of the factory and the housing block for the Jewish workers are adjacent and constitute a single, closed unit.
> • For this reason, walls or appropriate barriers must surrounded the factories and housing blocks.
> • The Jews are forbidden to leave the factories or housing blocks, and sentries of the *Werkschutz* [Ukrainian factory guards] should be posted on the boundaries of the area.
> • If the areas of the factory and the housing block are not adjacent, the Jewish workers are to be led [to work] in orderly formations. This is also binding on the Jews who work outside the Ghetto.
> • The owners of the firms are personally responsible for carrying out these orders.
> • Jews found outside the factory or housing-block area, without the express personal permission of the commander of the SS, will be shot.

Even with all these rules, Himmler felt irritated about the situation. On 9 October 1942 he modified his directive of 19 July that had ordered that resettlement in the General Government be complete by the end of the year. In this modification Himmler insisted that:[21]

> . . . all the so-called armaments workers who are merely working in tailor, fur and shoemaking workshops [are to be] assembled in these places, i.e., in Warsaw [or] Lublin, in concentration camps, by *SS-Obergruppenführer* Krüger and *SS-Obergruppenführer* Pohl . . . The *Wehrmacht* is to pass their merchandise orders to us, and we will guarantee the continuance of deliveries of the clothing items they desire.

Himmler was still disturbed about the turn of events. He continued in his communication with what can only be described as a not-so-veiled threat:[22]

> [I have] given orders to proceed mercilessly against all those who believe they have to oppose this [order] with alleged armaments interests, but in reality only wish to support the Jews and their businesses.

On 14 January 1943 he paid a surprise visit to Warsaw, perhaps in his initial effort to "proceed mercilessly." Himmler notified a miffed Krüger saying, "I did not know I was going and I did not inform you." At the *Wehrmacht* Armaments Office, Himmler was informed that 24,000 Jews in the Warsaw Ghetto, many employed by Többens, were camouflaged as armaments workers, but in fact were only tailors and fur-dressers. Clearly disturbed by the turn of events, he told Colonel Freter of the Armaments Office that by 15 February 16,000 of Többens' workers would be shipped to Lublin.[23] Himmler then wrote to Krüger with his decision:[24]

> I have charged Colonel Freter to communicate to the Armaments Inspector, Lieutenant-General Schindler, my astonishment that my instructions respecting the Jews have not been followed.[25] I have once again stipulated a time limit of 15 February 1943, by which the following are to be fulfilled:

- Immediate elimination of the private firms. I consider it unconditionally necessary that the owners who have made themselves indispensable here be called up so far as practicable, and sent to the front.
- I commission the RSHA to examine the books of the firm of Walter C. Többens most rigorously under a magnifying glass. If I am not mistaken here is a man formerly without means, who has developed over the course of three years into a wealthy owner, if not already a millionaire, and indeed only because we, the state, have driven the cheap Jewish work force to him.
- Immediately take-up of the whole 16,000 Jews in a concentration camp, preferably Lublin. Guarantee to deliver to the Armaments Inspectorate the same in regard to quantity and date as formerly. I believe, moreover, that it can be done more cheaply.
- The same goes for a number of smaller Ghetto-firms that make parts of machinery or aircraft, which too can be made in a camp.
- The residue is to be gathered with utmost speed in some spot in the General Government so that one has a factory with a couple of 'shops' staffed with only Jewish workers, whose guarding and isolation are to receive the sharpest attention.

SS-Hauptsturmführer Georg Michalsen, assigned to the SS and Police Leader for Lublin and *Operation Reinhard*, testified after the war about Himmler's and Globocnik's plans for the Jews of Warsaw. Michalsen stated:[26]

> It was the intention that all Jews were to be removed from Warsaw. For this purpose, the transfers to the camps were planned and prepared. The firms themselves did not want to participate at first. Also the Armament Command was against it at first. The reason was that through the intended transfer of the enterprises the Armament Command in Warsaw would have lost all firms, and then its existence would have become without purpose.
>
> I had orders from Globocnik to transfer all recognized armament firms of Warsaw to the camps in the district of Lublin. I point out that during this time theoretically only recognized armament factories were allowed to exist in the Warsaw Ghetto. In the legal sense, other Jews would no longer have had the right to live there. I was not allotted any assistant in this task; I was on my own (except for a driver). I now started to negotiate with the firms about the transfer and I have completed the necessary contracts with the firms. In this connection I must say that an SS-man was sent to Többens, it was a [*SS-Oberscharführer*] Birmes whose name was already mentioned to me before. I am not completely sure whether he went to Többens merely for this reason and that this matter was why he came, but I believe it was so.
>
> The firms wanted to take care of the actual process of the move and transfer themselves, meaning without our cooperation. They were afraid that the Jews would become scared if we had made an appearance, because then the Jews could have assumed, rightfully so, that this again concerned a shipment to Treblinka as during last year. Többens even was authorized (which was strictly forbidden in other cases) to take Jews along in his car. He drove to Poniatowa with several Jews so that they would have a chance to convince themselves about the existence of the camp. For this, Többens had received an SS-marker for his car.
>
> The transfer efforts were successful in part. However, some of the Jews did not want to transfer because they were afraid that their own resistance fighters would shoot them because they had volunteered for the transfer. That this was actually the case and that the Jews were afraid, is a fact that was confirmed by the Warsaw Security Police to von Sammern, who in turn related it to me. I do not know who at the Security Police confirmed this to von Sammern, but I assume that it was the office that had the best knowledge about Jewish affairs, namely the office of the Security Police within the Ghetto. This still existed; I was there personally two, three or four times. As the man in charge of this office I am familiar with [*SS-Obersturmführer*] Brandt, I did not see a higher military rank at this time.
>
> Since only a part of the firms was already transferred to the camps, while the larger portion still remained in Warsaw, the firms were cut up and production suffered from it. We then insisted that the firms would continue the transfer. Despite this, one week after the other went by without a complete transfer having been accomplished.
>
> I can make the following statements about the immediate prior history of the Stroop mission: I always had to report to Globocnik about the status of my transfer preparations. When he learned from me that it did not always succeed, he wrote to von Sammern and moreover called him on the telephone. When I went to see von Sammern the next time, he told me that there was no other alternative but to stage a massive action. The firms were also told about this plan and found it to be right because they also could see that the transfer could not succeed any other way. I personally notified Mr. Schultz about this. I remem-

ber that he was living in a hotel. I do not recall who informed Mr. Többens about it. After all, Többens himself had seen Globocnik in Lublin.

Himmler was ready to pounce. It only remained to be seen if the SS authorities in Warsaw shared his enthusiasm. There had been a change since the previous summer.

• • •

Although Warsaw was not the capital of the General Government, Warsaw became the capital of underground Poland. The "Anti-Fascist Bloc" (Blok kegn Fashizm) was a Jewish underground movement established by Communists in the Warsaw Ghetto beginning in March 1942. The organization attracted support of left-wing Zionist political parties. The group suffered a serious blow when the *Gestapo* arrested a large number of Communists in the Ghetto on 30 May 1942. The bloc then dissolved; however, its remnants became some of the first component groups of the Zydowska Organizacja Bojowa (ZOB), a para-military organization dedicated to physically resisting the Nazi authorities.[27]

On 28 July 1942 a coalition of three underground parties (Ha-Shomer ha-Za'ir, Dror He-Halutz and Akiva) led by Mordechai Anielewicz, founded the Zydowska Organizacja Bojowa. By October 1942 the ZOB was sufficiently confident in its strength to begin plans for an active defense of the Jews in Warsaw.[28] The command of the new organization quickly decided to accomplish three actions that would make their presence known throughout the Warsaw Ghetto. They would:[29]

- Publish a manifesto addressed to the Jewish public in Warsaw that explained that "resettlement" meant Treblinka and that Treblinka meant certain, quick death. Therefore, the Jews must begin to forcibly resist German deportation commands.
- Produce fake work permits/work documents and distribute these documents throughout the population. It was hoped that these documents would confuse and foil German efforts at deportation.
- Resist actively the orders of the Jewish Order Service and the *Judenrat*. As part of this resistance a death sentence is issued against the commander of the Jewish Order Service, Jozef Szerynski.

The ZOB struck quickly. During the latter half of August 1942, they conducted arson operations against selected housing blocks that had been requisitioned by the Nazis, as well as in warehouses in which goods were stored. On 20 August 1942 the ZOB attempted to kill Józef Szerynski, but only seriously wounded the police commander.[30]

In late 1942, members of Betar created the Jewish Military Union (Zydowski Zwiazek Wojskowy [ZZW]). The ZZW, a revisionist Zionist movement, did not officially join the ZOB although it would coordinate operations and share weaponry. The chairman of the ZZW committee was Dr. David Wdowinski; its military commander was Pawel Frenkiel.[31]

• • •

The Nazis began to carry out Himmler's order with a planned deportation of about 8,000 Jews. At 0730 hours, 18 January 1943, German units and support elements penetrated the Ghetto. The Jews believed that the SS had come for all of them – an incorrect assumption – and few responded to the German demands to descend to the courtyards and present their work permits for inspection. While we do not have detailed figures concerning German unit participation in this action, several sources indicate that two hundred German gendarmes, augmented by eight hundred Latvians and Lithuanians, participated.[32] At the beginning of this latest action Nazi authorities attempted to round up those Jews who lacked papers, the "illegals" that Himmler wanted to purge. When SS authorities realized that they could not meet their quotas in this manner, they began to conduct indiscriminate manhunts and captured 3,000 Jews on the first day.[33]

The Nazis got more than they bargained for that day as well. On several occasions police forces ran into armed Jews. The Jews fought inside the Ghetto buildings and infiltrated columns of deportees on their way to the *Umschlagplatz*, firing at the Nazi guards before escaping into nearby hideaways. Polish underground sources stated that twelve police and SS men were killed in the four-day action and ten others were wounded. "Only" about 5,000 to 6,500 Jews were deported during the action.[34] It appears that the Nazis shot an additional 1,770 Jews during these deportations.[35] While the Jews had conducted some resistance, they were unable to stop the deportations. Von Sammern called off the action on 21 January. We can surmise that this event planted the seed in Himmler's mind that another SS leader would be needed in Warsaw when the final day of reckoning came.

• • •

The events of this second deportation also planted the seed in Jewish minds for future organized resistance. On 22 January the ZOB resistance published a manifesto, which in part warned of the dangers that lay ahead:[36]

> Jewish masses, the hour is drawing near. You must be prepared to resist and not give yourselves up to slaughter like sheep. Not a single Jew should go to the railroad cars. Those who are unable to put up active resistance should resist passively, meaning go into hiding. We have just received information from Lvov that the Jewish Police there forcefully executed the deportation of 3,000 Jews. This will not be allowed to happen again in Warsaw . . . Our slogan must be: all are ready to die as human beings.

The Jews embarked on a three-pronged strategy to prepare for this conflict. They would focus to:[37]

- purge the Ghetto of collaborators and *Gestapo* informants,
- obtain money to purchase additional arms,
- plan the battle and prepare the fighters for combat.

From almost the inception of the Ghetto, some Jews turned traitor against their own people. Anticipating the impending armed struggle, Jewish resistance elements decided to eliminate the turncoats. The resistance fighters killed Ark Kajntraub, a *Gestapo* agent, on 21 February. On 22 February they shot and killed Dr. Alfred Nossig, a member of the *Judenrat*, who had informed the Germans about hideouts. Bobi Nebel and Adas Szajn, both informers, were next to fall. Resistance fighters killed both on 28 February.[38]

• • •

Fifteen February came and went without major incident. However, instead of thousands of Jews being transferred to Lublin, it seems that only some 350 Jewish workers and a portion of the Pavia Street furrier factory were actually deported to Trawniki in mid-February.[39] On 23 February, the SS deported a further 850 Jews to Poniatowa.[40] Quite simply, only a handful of Jews believed German promises of better working conditions in the Lublin area and so only a few volunteered for deportations. The rest stayed where they were. February passed. At the beginning of March, the Germans transported 280 Jews from the Többens workshops and conducted two additional small deportations in the second half of March but we do not know how many people this entailed.[41] On 10 March the Nazis caught a number of Jews outside the Ghetto. As punishment, the Germans transported them back inside the Ghetto to Pawiak Prison and shot them. On 13 March, several Jews shot some members of the *Werkschutz*. In retaliation, *SS-Obersturmführer* Karl Brandt led a reprisal mission into the Ghetto and killed over two hundred Jews. Finally, on 15 March, the Germans deported six hundred men and one hundred fifty women from Pawiak Prison to Majdanek concentration camp.[42]

Then the SS stopped. The Germans did not come into the Ghetto to begin another round-up. Von Sammern appeared to have lost his nerve or became confused as to what to do next. With this respite, the Jews tried to get by as best they could. It is likely that *SS-Obergruppenführer* Friedrich-Wilhelm Krüger, shortly after assessing that he would need to get involved, developed battle plans for the destruction of the Warsaw Ghetto and put these before Himmler in late March or early April for approval.[43] Finally, in mid-April, *Reichsführer-SS* Himmler – although we have no existing documents that attest to his decision process – decided that he would wait no more.[44]

We do have an interesting piece of testimony from Jürgen Stroop from the Nürnberg Trials. Allied prosecutors took an affidavit from Stroop in February 1946 to be used in proceedings against former *SS-Obergruppenführer* Ernst Kaltenbrunner, Reinhard Heydrich's successor. Stroop stated (bold emphasis added by author):[45]

> *SS-Oberführer* Dr. von Sammern-Frankenegg, my predecessor, planned the action against the Warsaw Ghetto. On the day when this action started I took command and Von Sammern explained to me what was to be done. **He had the order from Himmler before him**, and in addition I received a teletype from Himmler which ordered me to evacuate the Warsaw Ghetto and raze it to the ground.

I believe that Stroop's recollections accurately show that the actual decision to liquidate the Warsaw Ghetto came from the top down and not from von Sammern. Von Sammern's role was to translate Himmler's order into action, which he apparently did on 18 April.

Franz Konrad, the SS officer in charge of the *Werterfassung*, provided his own testimony after the war concerning the mood in von Sammern's headquarters in Warsaw on 18 April 1943:[46]

> A week before Easter 1943 – it was a Sunday morning – SS and Police Leader von Sammern convened a meeting with the heads of the Security Police, *SS-Obersturmbannführer* Hahn, the commanders of the SS units in Warsaw, [the commanders] of the cavalry and infantry reserve units, the commanders of the Security Police and the Order Police and the officers in his headquarters (myself among them). At this meeting we were notified that on Monday he intended to transfer out the Jews who still remained in the Warsaw Ghetto. During the discussions about the appropriate time for sending the various SS and Police units into action, *SS-Brigadeführer* Jürgen Stroop entered and announced that he had been appointed to the post of SS and Police Leader by order of the *Reichsführer-SS*.

Former *SS-Hauptsturmführer* Georg Michalsen, who temporarily served under Stroop during the Warsaw Ghetto Uprising, remembered the meeting in this fashion during post-war testimony and provides even greater resolution concerning the details of this meeting:[47]

> [*Question*] How did von Sammern envision the technical process of this massive mission?
>
> [Michalsen] He intended to capture the underground movement and to liquidate it, and then the working Jews would volunteer for the transfer.
>
> [*Question*] It is known from other sources that a large part of the Jews were not ready to voluntarily be transferred because they were afraid that they would be sent to an annihilation camp.
>
> [*Michalsen*] I can only say what then was presented to us by the firms. According to that, the Jews in general were willing to be transferred, but that mainly they did nothing because they were afraid of retaliation by the resistance movement. However, there were also some among them who hesitated and even resisted, but we expected that these would come along after the majority of the Jews willing to transfer had been moved. It must have been primarily to remove the pressure from the resistance movement on the Jews.
>
> Since it concerned a very large building complex, namely practically the total former Ghetto area, the execution of this endeavor was not easy, and large forces were needed. Therefore, the Ghetto was firmly sealed off from the outside. In the Ghetto itself, at first about 2,500 men were slated for this action. It was intended to systematically comb through the whole Ghetto in the direction from north to south and to capture all Jews, during this occasion, who lived there illegally. It was also assumed that no significant resistance would be encountered because the German military contingent was much larger. If serious resistance would have been envisioned the whole staff would not have presented itself openly in the morning of the first day of the action in front of the Jewish Council Building. About twenty SS and Police officers stood around – like the best target.
>
> [*Question*] During the preparation for the action and while in discussion between yourself and von Sammern, was the problem of those Jews who did not belong to the resistance movement, but did live illegally in the Warsaw Ghetto, broached?
>
> [*Michalsen*] Yes, this has come up in talks between von Sammern and myself. It was known that a considerable number of such illegal Jews were present. The number given to us then is something I cannot state today, but it was a number that was not to be taken lightly and was not taken lightly. As to their treatment, I can say that von Sammern intended to put them into the same category with the resistance fighters, to capture them and to relocate them – to Treblinka.
>
> I do not remember with certainty whether there was detailed talk between von Sammern and myself that the Jews were to be taken to Treblinka. I must add that this was a matter that was not in my area of concern because I was only interested in the transfer of the working Jews into our camps. I assume with certainty that this problem of the other Jews was discussed and I also believe with certainty that it came up that they would be sent to Treblinka. They would, under no circumstances, be brought to the labor camp, on one hand because there was no desire that resistance people were brought into the camps, and moreover, because the firms themselves did not want them. In conclusion, it can be said that there were two aims for this whole action. On one hand, it was the effort by Globocnik and myself to transfer the working Jews into the work camps, while on the other hand, it was the attempts of von Sammern – in fulfillment of Himmler's order – to completely cleanse Warsaw of Jews. This means that the resistance fighters and the illegal Jews would have practically been left, and due to this fact, von Sammern had the intention described by me above to look at the illegals practically as resistance fighters and to transfer them all together to Treblinka.
>
> I can make the following statements about the strategy talks with von Sammern: besides von Sammern, Stroop also took part in this conference. Several officers of the Police and *Waffen-SS* were also present. The chief of the Trawniki unit was also there. I cannot remember today who this was, but I believe that Streibel was in command of the Trawniki people in Warsaw then. Hahn also participated in this conference and I believe that he had brought along several people from his office.
>
> During this conference, a very specific and detailed apportioning of the various units was made. Each unit received their plans and the command to comb through a specific area of the Ghetto. A systematic search of house after house, cellar after cellar, hiding place after hiding

place was to be made. For this purpose, each unit was given a section that they had to comb through and the place was noted when they had reached their final destination. Also the exact times for the mission were discussed.

The security police were heavily represented in this action. I do no longer remember their numbers. If I am confronted with a number of 33 people in the Stroop Report, I find that this number was about right. The security police were not engaged as a complete unit, but they were dealt out to the various units. This was that much more necessary in this mission because the units themselves knew the geography. In addition it was the specific task for the security police to find and catch hidden persons and resistance fighters. The military was to provide the "protective corset." In connection with this matter, the security police also must have written many reports, and these must have passed through Dr. Hahn.

[*Question*] Were the units also ordered during the meeting to transfer the firms?

[*Michalsen*] No, this order was not given because this was left to the firms themselves. The units were only to ensure the transfer in such a way that the firms with Jews who were willing to be transferred would be shielded from the repercussions of the resistance movement. Besides, it was expected that the largest portion of work forces would volunteer to be transferred at the moment when the resistance movement was stopped, and that the remainder who were hesitating and resisting the move would come along.

• • •

Heinrich Himmler and his SS lieutenants would not implement half-hearted measures. They would not tread lightly among the factory owners. The time for sending in the Latvian and Lithuanian police was over. The Germans would bring in the tanks, they would bring in the artillery and they would bring in the flame-throwers. They would not play any more games with these armed Jews. They would bring in the *Waffen-SS*.

Notes:

[1] Arno Mayer, *Why Did The Heavens Not Darken?* (New York: Pantheon Books, 1988), p. 316.

[2] Heinz Höhne, *The Order of the Death's Head: The Story of Hitler's SS.* (New York: Coward-McCann, 1985), pp. 405-406.

[3] Raul Hilberg, *The Destruction of the European Jews.* (Revised and Definitive Edition). New York: Holmes & Meier, 1985), p. 533.

[4] Israel Gutman, *Resistance: The Warsaw Ghetto Uprising.* (Boston: Houghton Mifflin Company, 1994), p. 93.

[5] Curt Ludwig Freiherr von Gienanth was born on 6 December 1876 in Eisenberg/Rheinpfalz. He entered the Army in 1896 and rose to the rank of captain before World War I began. During the conflict he served in several general staff positions. He initially retired in 1933 but was recalled to service in 1939. Von Gienanth was named as the Military Commander for the General Government on 21 July 1940; he held this post until 1 October 1942. He was awarded a German Cross in Silver on 30 June 1943. Von Gienanth survived the war; he died on 3 April 1961 in Heidelberg, Germany.

[6] Arno Mayer, *Why Did The Heavens Not Darken?*, p. 399.

[7] Ibid., p. 262.

[8] Ibid., p. 262.

[9] Albert Speer, *Infiltration.* (New York: MacMillan Publishing, 1981), p. 265.

[10] Ibid., p. 264.

[11] Israel Gutman, editor in chief, *Encyclopedia of the Holocaust.* (New York: MacMillan Publishing Company, 1990), Volume 4, p. 1611.

[12] Walter Caspar Többens was born 19 May 1909 in Meppen. He was captured by American troops in Austria. While being deported for trial in Poland Többens escaped. He was tried *in abstentia* by a West German court in 1949 and initially sentenced to ten years imprisonment. This was reduced to five years. Többens surfaced in 1952 but did not serve any time in prison. He died in an automobile accident in 1954.

[13] Irving Werstein, *The Uprising of the Warsaw Ghetto, November 1940 - May 1943.* (New York: W.W. Norton & Company, 1968), pp. 81-82.

[14] Dan Kurzman, *The Bravest Battle: The Twenty-eight Days of the Warsaw Ghetto Uprising.* (New York: G. P. Putnam's Sons, 1976), p. 26.

[15] Israel Gutman, *The Jews of Warsaw, 1939-1943: Ghetto, Underground, Revolt.* (Bloomington, IN: Indiana University Press, 1982), pp. 268-269.

[16] Dan Kurzman, *The Bravest Battle: The Twenty-eight Days of the Warsaw Ghetto Uprising*, p. 26.

[17] Israel Gutman, *The Jews of Warsaw, 1939-1943: Ghetto, Underground, Revolt*, p. 269.

[18] Ibid., p. 269.

[19] Dan Kurzman, *The Bravest Battle: The Twenty-eight Days of the Warsaw Ghetto Uprising*, p. 26.

[20] Israel Gutman, *The Jews of Warsaw, 1939-1943: Ghetto, Underground, Revolt*, p. 276.

[21] Albert Speer, *Infiltration*, p. 264.

[22] Ibid., p. 264.

[23] Gerald Reitlinger, *The Final Solution: The Attempt to Exterminate the Jews of Europe, 1939-1945.* (Northvale, N.J.: Jason Aronson, Inc., 1987), pp. 272-273.

[24] Peter Padfield, *Himmler.* (New York: Henry Holt and Company, 1990), pp. 444-445.

[25] Lieutenant General Max Schindler was the Chief of the Armaments Office for the East. He was born 11 December 1880 in Munich. He entered the Army in 1900 and served in the infantry. Schindler retired in 1935 but was recalled to duty in 1939. He survived the war.

[26] Wolfgang Scheffler and Helge Grabnitz, *Der Ghetto-Aufstand Warschau 1943.* (Munich, Germany: Goldmann Verlag, 1993), pp. 191-192.

[27] Abraham J. Edelheit and Hershel Edelheit, *History of the Holocaust: A Handbook and Dictionary.* (Boulder, CO: Westview Press, 1994), p. 403.

[28] Ibid., p. 403.

[29] Israel Gutman, *The Jews of Warsaw, 1939-1943: Ghetto, Underground, Revolt*, p. 237.

[30] Ibid., p. 240.

[31] Abraham J. Edelheit and Hershel Edelheit, *History of the Holocaust: A Handbook and Dictionary*, pp. 403-404.

[32] Israel Gutman, in his *Resistance: The Warsaw Ghetto Uprising*, mentions that Ukrainians participated in the January deportations as well.

[33] Israel Gutman, *The Jews of Warsaw, 1939-1943: Ghetto, Underground, Revolt*, pp. 307-316.

[34] Israel Gutman, *Resistance: The Warsaw Ghetto Uprising*, p. 184.

[35] Tadeusz Bielecki and Leszek Szymanski, *Warsaw Aflame: The 1933-1945 Years.* (Los Angeles: Polamerica Press, 1973), p. 92.

[36] Ibid., pp. 304-316.

[37] Israel Gutman, *The Jews of Warsaw, 1939-1943: Ghetto, Underground, Revolt*, p. 340.

[38] Tadeusz Bielecki and Leszek Szymanski, *Warsaw Aflame: The 1933-1945 Years*. (Los Angeles: Polamerica Press, 1973), p. 96. The resistance had already killed Mendel Lejkin, of the Jewish Order Service, on 29 October 1942. They then killed Yisrael First, Director of the Economic Department of the *Judenrat*, on 28 November 1942.

[39] Albert Speer, *Infiltration*, p. 267.

[40] Israel Gutman, *The Jews of Warsaw, 1939-1943: Ghetto, Underground, Revolt*, p. 333.

[41] Israel Gutman, *Resistance: The Warsaw Ghetto Uprising*, p. 194.

[42] Tadeusz Bielecki and Leszek Szymanski, *Warsaw Aflame: The 1933-1945 Years*, p. 96. We do not know how many of the persons transported to Majdanek were Jews.

[43] Peter Padfield, *Himmler*, p. 446.

[44] I am convinced that Himmler made the decision to reenter the Warsaw Ghetto and also decided to start the operation on 19 April 1943. First, von Sammern seems to have been too indecisive; he had dawdled since January. Second, Himmler moved Jürgen Stroop into position before the first day of the action, a clear indicator that it was Himmler's decision and that Himmler intended for Stroop to assume command at the first sign of trouble.

[45] International Military Tribunal, *Trial of the Major War Criminals Before the International Military Tribunal, Nürnberg, 14 November 1945 - 1 October 1946. Volume XI, Proceedings, 8 April 1946 – 17 April 1946.* (Nuremberg, Germany, 1947), p. 355.

[46] Israel Gutman, *The Jews of Warsaw, 1939-1943: Ghetto, Underground, Revolt*, pp. 368-369.

[47] Wolfgang Scheffler and Helge Grabnitz, *Der Ghetto-Aufstand Warschau 1943*, pp. 192-196.

4

THE GERMAN UNITS

"I must admit that we felt a certain joy when we would seize a Jew whom one could kill. I cannot remember an instance when a policeman had to be ordered to an execution. The shootings were, to my knowledge, always carried out on a voluntary basis; one could have gained the impression that various policemen got a big kick out of it."[1]

- A German Police trooper

In a dog-eat-dog world, staying on top was a difficult proposition. Heinrich Himmler understood that Nazi control of Germany, and later most of Europe, could only be maintained through a system of terror that featured a scientific application of force stemming from a shrewd exploitation of the fear of force. To generate that fear, the *Reichsführer-SS* would create a system that not only combated legal enemies, but also, in the most ruthless sense, would prevent potential enemies from arising. The dividing line between committing an actual offense against the law and perpetrating some perceived injustice against the Nazi Party would intentionally be left vague. One misstep and a citizen in the *Reich* or in occupied territory would find himself apprehended by the *Gestapo* and whisked to a concentration camp – or worse.

• • •

Heinrich Himmler not only controlled the concentration camps and the *Gestapo*, he had his own army as well. Beginning with just a handful of black-shirted SS men in the 1920s, Himmler had expanded his forces battalion by battalion, year by year. By 1945 there would be approximately 800,000 men in *Waffen-SS*; in April 1943, there were probably some 400,000 under arms. Even more important than shear numbers, Himmler's troops knew how to follow orders no matter how gruesome. They would do whatever it took in Warsaw, as we shall see. Before we can examine the conduct of the German forces assigned to quell the Warsaw Ghetto Uprising though, we must first examine the chain of command that controlled these units, the organization and capabilities of the formations themselves and the overall Nazi security apparatus in the city.[2] We will start with the SS chain of command in the General Government and the security units they employed.

HIGHER SS AND POLICE LEADER, THE ORDER POLICE, THE SECURITY POLICE AND THE SECURITY SERVICE

On 13 November 1937, two years before the war began, Heinrich Himmler established the positions of Higher SS and Police Leaders (*Höherer SS und Polizeiführer* [HSSPF]) in Germany. The positions were highly coveted as their office holders were considered among the most influential and powerful of all SS or Police officers. The HSSPF were directly subordinate to Himmler and were charged with ensuring all Police and SS coordination within a certain geographical area.[3]

In addition to coordinating SS and Police functions, the HSSPF were tasked to carry out any special mission directed by the *Reichsführer-SS*. On 18 December 1939 Himmler specified additional guidance concerning the function of the HSSPF. The three most important directives of this guidance were:[4]

• within his area the HSSPF is the representative of the *Reichsführer-SS* and Chief of the German Police [Himmler] for all matters which are the latter's responsibility;

• the HSSPF is responsible for all preparations common to the Order Police [*Ordnungspolizei*], the Security Police [*Sicherheitspolizei*] and the Security Service [*Sicherheitsdienst*] in furtherance of the defense tasks for which his office was created;

• the HSSPF will take over command of the *Waffen-SS*, the General SS [*Allgemeine-SS*], the Order Police, the Security Police and the Security Service in all cases when these organizations are used as a combined force for some specific mission.

The scope of the missions carried out by the various HSSPF was broad. These tasks could range from establishing bordellos for *Waffen-SS* troops in France, to supervising the diet of Muslim troops employed by the *Waffen-SS*, to implementing the scorched earth plan in the Ukraine or assisting in the capture of a dissident student group in Munich.[5] And, little did Himmler realize it at the time, but these directives would be tailor-made to execute the quelling of the Warsaw Ghetto some four years later by *Waffen-SS*, Police and security forces.

SS-Obergruppenführer Friedrich-Wilhelm Krüger served as the HSSPF "East," the Higher SS and Police Leader for the General Government region. Friedrich-Wilhelm Krüger had many missions. First, Krüger was the superior for the several subordinate district SS and Police Leaders – the SS and Police Leader (SSPF) for Warsaw was one of them – established to help the HSSPF control the large entity of the General Government. Second, for operational issues or special missions, Krüger also oversaw the activities of the Senior Commander of the Order Police (*Orpo*), for the General Government (*Befehlshaber der Ordungspolizei* [BdO]) and the Senior Commander for the Security Police and Security Service for the General Government (*Befehlshaber der Sicherheitspolizei* [BdS]). While normal administrative matters for the BdO came from Berlin and the Chief of the Order Police and the same was true for the BdS with respect to his administrative superior in Berlin at the RSHA, it was clear in the field that *SS-Obergruppenführer* Krüger was supreme in operational matters. During the time of the Warsaw Ghetto Uprising, the BdO for the General Government was *SS-Gruppenführer und General der Polizei* Herbert Becker, while the BdS for the General Government at that time was *SS-Brigadeführer* Eberhard Schöngarth.[6] Neither of these two men nor their organizations was directly involved in the suppression of the Warsaw Ghetto. They forwarded administrative issues from the *Orpo* headquarters and RSHA headquarters in Berlin to their subordinates in Warsaw, but did little else that could be viewed as direct influence on the situation. This lack of involvement did not characterize the organizations in Warsaw itself, however.

Krüger's representative in Warsaw was SSPF *SS-Oberführer* Ferdinand von Sammern-Frankenegg. He had duties similar to those of Krüger but at a lower level. In the Byzantine structure of the SS and Nazi apparatus in the General Government, von Sammern was also subordinate to Governor Dr. Ludwig Fischer. Von Sammern controlled two important entities for operational matters, the KdO and KdS, although post-war testimony by Karl Kaleschke, Von Sammern's adjutant, indicates that the KdS also received operational instructions concerning Jews and the resistance movement from Berlin.[7] These two organizations, unlike the BdO and BdS at a higher level, played a direct role in both the summer deportations of *Operation Reinhard* and the later suppression of the Ghetto Uprising. During this period, the KdO, the Commander of the Order Police (*Kommandeur der Ordnungspolizei*), was *Oberst der Schutzpolizei* (Colonel of Police) Rudolf Haring. The KdS, Commander of the Security Police (*Kommandeur der Sicherheitspolizei*), for Warsaw was *SS-Obersturmbannführer* Dr. Ernst Hahn. Hahn served as the representative on the SSPF staff for Security Police and Security Service affairs, and thus could be viewed as one of two right hand men for von Sammern. The other was *SS-Sturmbannführer* Max Jesuiter, who served as the Chief of Staff to the SS and Police Leader Warsaw during the Ghetto Uprising. Von Sammern's office was located on Ujazdowska Avenue in an ornate building that had housed the Belgian and Dutch Embassies before the war.[8]

KdS and Sicherheitspolizei

For the Polish campaign in 1939, Reinhard Heydrich, the chief of the Reich Security Service, formed six major *Einsatzgruppen der Sicherheitspolizei* (Sipo) – or *Einsatzgruppen* of security police – under the code name of *Operation Tannenberg*. Five of the groups were attached to the five advancing German armies while the other was designated for service in the Posen (now Poznan) district. They were identified by Roman numerals (*Einsatzgruppe I – VI*). The groups' subordinate *Einsatzkommando* were each attached to an army corps. The missions of the *Einsatzgruppen* in Poland included the arrest of politically unreliable persons, confiscation of weapons, gathering of evidence deemed important for police intelligence activities, and actions against Jews, the Polish intelligentsia and members of the upper class. *Einsatzgruppe IV* was commanded by *SS-Brigadeführer* Lothar Beutel and was attached to the 4th Army (General of Artillery von Kluge). After November 1939, personnel from this *Einsatzgruppe* were assigned to the *Kommandeur der Sicherheitspolizei und des SD Warschau* (Commander of Security Police and the SD for Warsaw), that later became known as the KdS.[9]

The KdS for Warsaw was a large organization patterned after the RSHA in Berlin. It was located on the Street of the Police *(Strasse der Polizei)*, the former Aleja Szucha. The KdS employed upwards of 2,000 personnel; about 800 were German. Until its reorganization in October 1942, the KdS had four departments; subsequently there were five after the revision. Department I/II was concerned with Administration and Law and was under the command of *SS-Hauptsturmführer* Arthur Füssel. Department I/II had eight sub-sections:[10]

- I A – personnel
- I B – training and education
- I C – registration and files
- I D – internal discipline
- II A – police organization and regulations
- II B – passports and aliens
- II C – finance
- II D – technical matters

Sub-section II C had several subordinate entities of its own, one of which handled the administration of the Security Service prisons. Department I/II also oversaw the *Gestapo* detention centers at Pawiak Prison (officially the *Gefängnis der Sicherheitspolizei* [Prison of the Security Police]), the Security Police jail on Szucha Street (consisting of interrogation cells in the basement of the Security Police and SD Commander's Office) and the Security Police labor education camp (*Arbeitserziehungslager der Sicherheitspolizei*) on Gesia Street.[11]

Department III was the Security Service (SD) and was one of the primary antagonists of the resistance during the Warsaw Ghetto Uprising (as well as all other times). The leaders of the Third *Reich* always realized that their control could only be maintained by the scientific application of force stemming from a shrewd exploitation of the fear of force. Such a system of terror would have been incomplete without an efficient and feared intelligence agency to collect information on every sphere of life in the German empire – hence the development of the Security Service.[12] *SS-Brigadeführer* Dr. Werner Best gave perhaps the most succinct description of the importance of the Security Service, when he stated:[13]

> The SD, finally, must investigate and explore thoroughly the background and activities of the great ideological archenemies of National Socialism and of the German People, in order to make possible a determined and effective effort for the annihilation of those enemies.

Wladyslaw Bartoszewski, in *Warsaw Death Ring, 1939-1944*, states that this department was the watchdog of all the other departments and acted as a type of political super-police that not only supervised the performance of law enforcement agencies, but also of the entire General Government administration.[14] Department III amassed reports, based on a vast private network of spies, and sent these messages – known as situation reports (*Lageberichte*) – to Berlin. Department III, commanded by *SS-Sturmbannführer* Dr. Ernst Kah, had four sub-sections:[15]

- III A – administration and law
- III B – nationality and race
- III C – culture, religion and propaganda
- III D – finance

Department IV, formally known as Enemies and Counter-Intelligence (*Gegner und Abwehr*), was the *Gestapo* office. Overall, the mission of the *Gestapo* was to detect, prevent and prosecute political crimes as defined by the Nazis. These "crimes" could include, but were not limited to: High Treason, Treason, Public Libel and Slander of the Government, Public Libel and Slander of the Nazi Party, Rioting or Inciting to Riot, Contravention of the Conscription Law and failure to promptly report treasonable acts. Fighting violators of such laws was euphemistically termed "measures for the prevention of acts, which might be harmful to the *Reich*."[16] In Warsaw, this department had the mission of combating the various underground movements and in organizing reprisals against both individuals and groups. *SS-Sturmbannführer* Walter Stamm served as the department head for this organization. This department was an extremely large element, was patterned after the *Gestapo* headquarters in Berlin and included six major sub-sections:[17]

- IV A – hostile activities and sabotage,
- IV B – religious bodies, Masonic organizations and Jewish affairs,
- IV C – protective custody, files, control of publications,
- IV D – émigrés, repatriates, hostages, foreign labor, Polish officers,
- IV E – counter-intelligence,
- IV N – coordinating information.

SS-Hauptsturmführer Gottlieb Höhmann served as Stamm's deputy and also was the leader of Section IV A. This element had numerous subsections that included:[18]

- IV A 1 – Communists, prisoners of war (excluding Polish officers) and radio offenses (listening to foreign broadcasts),
- IV A 2 – sabotage, forged passports and passes, shootings and explosions and air drops,

• IV A 3 – fight with the principal military and political resistance organizations,
• IV A 4 – personal security,
• IV A 5 – ciphers.

Section IV A 3, which was administered directly by Höhmann, had several desks, as the fight against the various resistance movements was complex. These desks included:[19]

• IV A 3a – right-wing organizations
• IV A 3b – summary court, reprisals
• IV A 3c – principal resistance organizations and secret political organizations
• IV A 3d – military and unidentified organizations

Section IV B, religious bodies, Masonic organizations and Jewish affairs, led by *SS-Hauptsturmführer* Paul Werner, had four sub-sections. They were:[20]

• IV B 1 – churches
• IV B 2 – soldiers
• IV B 3 – Free Masons
• IV B 4 – Jewish affairs

SS-Obersturmführer Norbert Graf Bergh-Trips served as the leader of Section IV C, protective custody, files and control of publications. He also served as the leader of Section IV D that handled émigrés, hostages, repatriates, foreign labor and Polish officers.[21]

SS-Obersturmführer Willfried Jopke headed Section IV E, counter-intelligence. This element had three sub-sections:[22]

• IV E 1 – general counter-intelligence, desertion, monitoring of foreign correspondence
• IV E 2 – economic counter-intelligence, industrial security
• IV E 3 – frontier-crossings, passports, aliens

Finally, Department V was the Criminal Police (*Kriminalpolizei* [*Kripo*]). Like police forces around the world, the *Kripo* was called upon to combat "ordinary" crime, with one significant difference. In Nazi Germany and its empire, the interpretation of the word "crime" was adapted to suit Nazi purposes and ideas. Thus, not only did *Kripo* detectives investigate traditional crimes, such as murder, arson and theft, but they also became involved in an ever increasing measure in prevention of crimes considered to be a menace to the German People – moreover, crimes that were a menace to the Nazi regime. It was the *Kripo's* duty to protect not merely public safety in the face of crime, but also to strengthen and safeguard the German Nation. As a practical matter, not only could the *Kripo* discover and arrest *actual* criminals, it could also track down and detain "potential" criminals – and "potential" in the Nazi sense was almost unlimited.[23]

Until 1936, the German criminal police were under the administration of the various German states (i.e., Bavaria, Hesse etc.). That year, Heinrich Himmler centralized these territorial entities by incorporating all criminal police into the Prussian criminal police. One year later the Prussian criminal police became the *Reich* Criminal Police Bureau (*Reichskriminalpolizeiamt*). Shortly thereafter, Himmler combined this bureau with the *Gestapo* as the Security Police Main Office (*Hauptamt Sicherheitspolizei*). This conglomeration was transformed once more when added to the Security Service and became the *Reich* Security Main Office (*Reichssicherheitshauptamt* [RSHA]). In this configuration, *Kripo* became Department V of the RSHA.

As stated earlier, the department's powers were not limited to traditional crime prevention and detection. This authority extended to include German-occupation offenses such as breaking curfew, failing to register a change of address, leaving the Ghetto unauthorized and sheltering persons fleeing German authorities. Department V in Warsaw, under *SS-Sturmbannführer* Harry Geisler, had four sections. Geisler's principal deputy was *SS-Hauptsturmfuhrer* Alfred Strunz.[24] Within the borders of the *Reich*, *Kripo* officers wore plain clothes in the traditional style of the detective, but when *Kripo* officers served in German-occupied countries they wore SS uniforms and SS rank corresponding to their civilian rank. This was so even when the *Kripo* officer was not a member of the SS. In these cases, the officers were declared honorary SS officers.[25]

The *Kripo* department in Warsaw was large and had eight primary sub-sections. These included:[26]

• V A – Polish matters
• V B – executive service
• V C – identification and searches
• V D – crime lab
• Counterfeit Section
• Crime Prevention and Gypsies
• Criminal Matters

Two of these sections bear further examination. Section V B, executive service, dealt with the organization, registration, weapons and equipment and summary court. The Criminal Matters (*Kriminaldirektion*) was the location within which most of the *Kripo* detectives resided. *SS-Hauptsturmführer* Erich Spruch headed the Criminal Matters section. This section had seven commissioner's offices (*Kommissariat*) that were organized as to the type of crime that they investigated, with the exception of the 7th *Kommissariat* that assisted the other six. They included:[27]

- 1st *Kommissariat* – homicide
- 2nd *Kommissariat* – grand larceny
- 3rd *Kommissariat* – petty theft and black marketeering
- 4th *Kommissariat* – fraud
- 5th *Kommissariat* – vice
- 6th *Kommissariat* – hotel and travel registration
- 7th *Kommissariat* – identification and photography

The Stroop Report indicates that three officers and thirty-two men from the Warsaw SD and Security Police were directly involved in the Warsaw Ghetto Uprising.[28] These men would have been concentrated in the command and control element for Stroop, operating radios, serving as couriers and interrogating prisoners. The personnel in this element were armed with pistols and submachine guns. We must consider that the officers and men who worked in the KdS offices also played a major role in quelling the Ghetto Uprising.

The officers and men in the KdS staff positions killed with information more than with bullets. To be sure, many of them frequently supervised or actually participated in brutal interrogations and executions in the prisons and lock-ups of Warsaw. However, their main stock in trade was intelligence. They were staff officers, and to be proficient staff officers they needed to provide their commander with timely and accurate information on the organization of the resistance in the Ghetto. They needed to ferret out names and addresses, not only of potential informants, but also likely resistance leaders. They should have been attempting to pinpoint Jewish strong points and bunkers, and determining which weapons would be needed to destroy these structures. There were many questions that fell in the category "what did they not know." First, and foremost, would the Jews fight and if so, how many would fight – all, or just a percentage? Did the Jewish resistance have weapons? If they did, how many and what kind of weapons did the resistance have? How much ammunition did they have and what were the sources for these weapons? Could the Security Police interdict the flow of arms? Did the Jewish resistance have any type of uniforms? Did they wear stolen German uniforms, and if they did, what could the Security Police do to differentiate between friend and foe? How was the resistance organized and how did they communicate orders to each other? Was it by word of mouth or did they have radios? If they would fight, what kind of tactics would they use? Where would they fight – in ambush sites, attics, bunkers or sewers? These were all questions that would have to be answered if the security forces expected to make quick work of the opposition. The KdS might be able to get these answers from informants, spies or old-fashioned intelligence analysis, and if they had gaps in their information, perhaps the Order Police could help.

Kommandeur der Ordnungspolizei
1st and 3rd Battalions, 22nd SS Police Regiment

The *Hauptamt Ordnungspolizei* – the Uniformed Police Main Office – was formed on 17 June 1936. It was responsible for all common police, fire coast guard and civil defense functions.[29] The most important subset of this office, the *Ordnungspolizei* (*Orpo*), the Order Police, was a large organization, growing from 131,000 officers and men in 1939 to some 310,000 personnel throughout the German empire by 1943. Forty-two percent were reservists. The *Orpo* was composed of two entities, the Protective Police (*Schutzpolizei*) under which police battalions operated, and the Rural Police (*Gendarmerie*).[30] Several thousand personnel belonging to the Order Police were probably in or near Warsaw in 1943.

The Protective Police conducted regular patrols of the streets, routine police duties, round-ups, house arrests and public executions. In addition, the *Schutzpolizei* conducted labor round-ups and suppressed smuggling and black-marketing on the periphery of the Ghetto. The Uniformed Police established four permanent headquarters in Warsaw. They were organized as:[31]

- Sector Watch North, located at 56 Krochmalna Street,
- Sector Watch South, located at 13 Willowa Street,
- Sector Watch Center, located at 1 Krakówskie Przedmiescie Street,
- Sector Watch Praga, located at 74 Targowa Street.

Each of these sector headquarters had one or two supplementary stations (known as *Stützpunkte*) that were manned by some twenty officers. The KdO, along with his *Schutzpolizei* forces, had at his disposal the Technical Emergency Corps, the German Railway Police (*Bahnschutzpolizei*) and a regiment of garrison police – the 22nd SS Police Regiment.

The Stroop Report mentions a handful of Technical Emergency Corps (*Technische Nothilfe* [*Teno*]) personnel involved in the Ghetto operation, but these men were important specialists. The *Teno* was a corps of engineers, technicians and skilled specialists in public utilities operation, construction work, communication and related fields. These specialists were generally men over military age, but the key to their success was in the knowledge they possessed; many had been public utility personnel in civilian life. *Teno* personnel were skilled in combating the effects of allied air raids in Germany. In Warsaw they would have provided Stroop with expertise on mines and explosive devices, electrical power lines, water lines and sewers.[32]

The German Railway Police were not an integral part of the Order Police and, therefore, did not come under the jurisdiction of the *Hauptamt Ordnungspolizei*. However, it is logical to assume that personnel from this service helped to organize the activities at the *Umschlagplatz* as the deported Jews would embark to Treblinka or labor camps in the south on the German railway system. These policemen were full-time German Railway (*Deutsche Reichsbahn*) employees. They wore uniforms and generally were armed with pistols and nightsticks. There overall mission was to maintain law and order on the railway system.[33]

The 22nd SS Police Regiment was formed on 24 February 1943 from the former 22nd Police Regiment.[34] The 1st and 3rd Battalions were from the Order Police.[35] The 1st Battalion initially provided three officers and ninety-four men to help suppress the Ghetto Uprising, while the 3rd Battalion provided three officers and one hundred thirty-four men.[36] Both units were stationed at Warsaw. The table of organization and equipment (TO&E) for an SS police battalion called for an overall authorized strength of thirty-one officers and 662 enlisted men. Such a unit was normally comprised of a battalion headquarters section (four officers and twelve enlisted), a medical detachment (one officer and six enlisted), a signal platoon (one officer and eighteen enlisted) and a motorcycle platoon (one officer and thirty-four enlisted.) The unit also had an armored car platoon (two officers and fifteen enlisted), a light infantry-howitzer platoon (one officer and twenty-five enlisted), an antitank platoon (one officer and twenty-five enlisted) and a motor-transport element (five officers and ninety-two enlisted.) The heart of the battalion's combat power lay in its organic three police companies (each with five officers and one hundred forty-five enlisted.) Each police company was organized into three rifle platoons (each platoon with three light machine-guns and four machine pistols to provide massed firepower) and one heavy machine-gun platoon that featured four heavy machine-guns.[37]

The 1st Battalion fielded the 1st, 2nd and 3rd Companies of the regiment while the 3rd Battalion was composed of the 7th, 8th and 9th Companies of the regiment.[38] Photographs indicate that the personnel of these units were armed with pistols, carbines and some submachine guns. The men of the *Orpo* police battalions tended to be older individuals, some not fit for front-line regular military service. Additionally, they received less comprehensive training and equipment than the troops in other components of the German security apparatus. But in operations against a relatively lightly armed enemy, these limitations were not considered to be significant. The 22nd SS Police Regiment later deployed to Byelorussia in July 1944, where it was soon destroyed in front-line fighting. The regiment was officially disbanded on 21 December 1944 in Danzig.[39]

3rd Battalion, 23rd SS Police Regiment

The 23rd SS Police Regiment was also formed on 24 February 1943. Its predecessor was the 23rd Police Regiment.[40] The 3rd Battalion was brought in from Posen to participate in the operation as the remnant force that would remain in the ruins of Ghetto after the official conclusion of the action. However, its stay in the city would stretch to several months. The organization of the battalion was the same as that for the other police battalions involved. The 3rd Battalion was augmented by a reserve Police battalion from Cologne for this mission.[41] The 3rd Battalion, as well as many other elements of the regiment, was later destroyed in fighting in March 1945.[42]

Two units from the *Waffen-SS*, which happened to be stationed in Warsaw, were committed to *SS-Brigadeführer* Stroop for use against the Ghetto Uprising, the 3rd SS Panzergrenadier Training and Replacement Battalion and the SS Cavalry Replacement Detachment. They played a key role as together, the two units provided three quarters of the troops assigned to eliminating the Warsaw Ghetto.

3rd SS Panzergrenadier Training and Replacement Battalion

The battalion was originally formed in 1939 as the SS Death's Head Infantry Replacement Battalion 1 (*SS-Totenkopf-Infanterie-Ersatz-Batallion I*). In 1941 the unit moved to Radolfzell am Bodensee. The unit moved in 1942, this time to Warsaw.[43] The battalion appears to have received its final designation in April 1943.

In 1940 the SS established a system of replacement (*Ersatz*) units for each of the *Waffen-SS* field divisions. Recruits reported to these units for training, while those who had completed this preparation were sent forward to the front to the field divisions.[44] On 23 January 1943 the *Oberkommando des Heeres* (OKH), the Germany Army High Command, issued an order that granted the *Reichsführer-SS* complete command authority over these replacement units. The Commander-in-Chief of the Army retained only the right to inspect these units and provide advice concerning their military training.[45] The following battalion document described the functions of the unit:

> The Panzergrenadier Training and Replacement Battalion is formed under one commander by separating units in training, the headquarters unit and the general convalescent unit. The commander of the battalion can, therefore, wholly devote himself to training, while the tasks of administering the headquarters and the general convalescent companies can be taken care of by the staff officers under his supervision. In the training companies, the training of recruits has been freed from all administrative tasks. All recruits of the same recruiting date should be gathered

> in one training company. All replacement functions are directly under the staff officer who is the representative of the commander. His tasks are of an administrative and technical nature to include all service business that lies outside the planned recruit training (e.g. management of clothing, kitchen and canteen, medical support, management of equipment and vehicles). Therefore, the Headquarters Company, as well as the General Convalescent Company, is under the command of the battalion staff. The training by the headquarters and general convalescent companies is limited by the usefulness of the men. In particular, according to their talents, accountants, those with knowledge about weapon technology, office workers, cooks, etc. are to be trained, as well as non-commissioned officers and enlisted men of the Headquarters Company.

The unit provided trained personnel to the 3rd SS Division "*Totenkopf*." This unit underwent several name changes during the war. The *SS Totenkopf Division* was formed in Dachau on 16 October 1939 from various *Totenkopf* units and throughout the war maintained a close association with concentration camp personnel. On 9 November 1942, the division was renamed *SS Panzergrenadier Division "Totenkopf."* On 22 October 1943, it received its last designation of *3rd SS Panzer Division "Totenkopf."* The formation fought in France, Russia, Hungary and Austria.[46] Some of the personnel of the training battalion were assigned to other divisions, but this was not the norm.

The German system of training replacements was designed to simulate – as much as possible – the actual conditions of the battlefield by introducing the most recent combat experience into training practice. Thus, the battalion had a large number of non-commissioned officer trainers who were recovering from wounds or simply detailed from the division for a period to Warsaw. The sixteen-week training course for recruits aimed at providing the young soldiers with a thorough mastery of their weapons. The course also stressed fundamentals of tactics by making the recruits participate in numerous company and platoon exercises. The Germans taught very little theory to these new soldiers.[47]

The Germans believed that replacements should report to the front in unit strength, not as individual replacements (as the American army did). Therefore the battalion periodically assembled marching battalions, or marching columns. Many of the same sergeants that had trained the recruits went to the front with them, providing needed moral support. To execute this plan, the different companies of the 3rd SS Panzergrenadier Training and Replacement Battalion conducted staggered cycles of training. The 1st Company, for example, would receive an entire company's worth of recruits at the beginning of a month and would then continue to train them over the next several months. The recruits of the company would "graduate" together at the end of training. Those not destined for further training elsewhere, such as at the SS Vehicle Drivers School at Schröttersburg, would then be sent to the front as a group. Meanwhile the 2nd Company would fill with more recruits, perhaps in the middle of a month, and go through the same procedure. Thus, at any given time, the different training companies would be at different stages of training.[48]

The battalion initially committed four officers and four hundred enlisted troops to the operation.[49] The unit was located at Stauffer *Kaserne* in the Rakowiec section of Warsaw that was only three miles from the site of the Ghetto Uprising. The battalion was armed with numerous types of small arms (rifles, pistols, submachine guns) and light machine-guns. The battalion additionally had a handful of captured tanks that were used to train drivers and conduct other training. Post-war accounts of the Warsaw Ghetto Uprising indicate the tanks used by the Germans were captured French vehicles.[50] An analysis of photographs at the Main Commission for the Investigation of Nazi War Crimes, in Warsaw, leads to a different conclusion. The tank photographed during the Ghetto Uprising appears to be of the Czech Light Tank LT-38 (CKD/Praga TNHP) family. The vehicle served as the standard light tank of the Czech Army; its production continued through 1942 on behalf of Germany as the PzKpfw. 38(t). The vehicle was armed with a 37mm Skoda gun and had two 7.92mm machine-guns. The tank had a top speed of 26 miles per hour, but in the close confines of Warsaw, the machines would have crawled along much more slowly.[51]

There were five training, or line, companies in the battalion as well as a headquarters company and a general convalescent company. The line companies appear to have rotated into the fighting at the Ghetto Uprising based on the casualty accounts in the Stroop Report. Despite the fact that the unit played a significant role in the destruction of the Warsaw Ghetto, West German courts tried no personnel from the battalion after the war for this operation.[52]

SS Cavalry Field Replacement Detachment

This detachment, a unit equivalent in size to a battalion, was formed in September 1942.[53] It provided replacements for the SS Cavalry Division (*SS Kavallerie Division*.) The SS Cavalry Division was created in September 1942 at Debica, Poland from elements of the SS Cavalry Brigade (*SS Kavallerie Brigade*.) On 22 October 1943 the unit was renamed the *8th SS Kavallerie Division* and shortly thereafter became the *8th SS Kavallerie Division "Florian Geyer."* The division fought in Russia and Hungary in both front-line and anti-partisan operations.[54]

Stationed in Warsaw, the detachment sent five officers and three hundred and eighty-one men to Stroop on the first day of the operation.[55] The detachment would have been armed in a manner similar to the 3rd SS Panzergrenadier Training and Replacement Battalion. Kazimierz Moczarski was a cellmate of Jürgen Stroop after the war in Warsaw. In his book, *Conversations with an Executioner*, Moczarski presents information that would suggest that the SS Cavalry Field Replacement Detachment rode horses through the Ghetto during the operation.[56] While the detachment undoubtedly conducted mounted training, there is no additional evidence that the detachment took their mounts into the city. There are no photographs to support this, nor would it have been militarily prudent to use mounted cavalrymen in a large urban area.

1st Guard Battalion, Trawniki Labor Camp "Trawniki Men"

The Germans deployed one guard battalion from the Trawniki labor camp with a strength of two officers and three hundred thirty-five men.[57] Trawniki served as a training camp for *Volksdeutsche*, Ukrainians and Russians who volunteered to assist the Germans.[58] *SS-Sturmbannführer* Karl Streibel served as the camp commandant since October 1941.[59] To obtain needed personnel, Streibel toured prisoner of war camps in the Lublin district and went as far as the Kiev area. Some 2,000 to 3,000 guardsmen trained at Trawniki during the two and a half years of its existence. Streibel organized the guards into two battalions, each of four companies. These companies were between 100 and 200 men strong. The 1st Guard Battalion deployed to Warsaw on 19 April 1943 and remained there until 19 June 1943. The "Trawniki Men," as they were called, played an important role in *Operation Reinhard*. Along with deploying to towns and cities, such as Warsaw, to help with the deportations, they additionally served as guards at Treblinka, Sobibór and Belzec.[60] That several hundred were deployed to Warsaw is proof positive of the intent of the Nazis to continue the destruction of the Warsaw Jews.

SS-Untersturmführer Johann Schwarzenbacher, a German from Munich, served as the commander of the battalion at Warsaw. He took three companies with him for the mission.[61] Most of the platoon leaders and many of the squad leaders were *Volksdeutsch*, ethnic Germans who were people of German language and culture but who were not citizens of the German *Reich* in 1938.[62] Armed with rifles and pistols, the unit wore black uniforms.

GERMAN ARMY MILITARY COMMAND IN THE GENERAL GOVERNMENT

The German Army played a supporting role in the destruction of the Warsaw Ghetto, but it was an important role none-theless. The German Army Military Commander in the General Government (*Militärbefehlshaber im Generalgouvernement*), owned the German Army units stationed in the General Government; he took directions from the Chief of the Replacement Army, General Fromm, who was located in Berlin. General of Cavalry Curt Freiherr von Gienanth held the position until the fall of 1942 when he was placed on the retirement list. His replacement, General of Infantry Siegfried Haenicke, was in command of all German Army units in the General Government during the period of the Warsaw Ghetto Uprising. On 1 September 1942 the position was renamed the "Military District Commander in the General Government."[63]

The German Army Commandant of Warsaw, who was subordinated to the German Army Military Commander in the General Government, had operational ownership of the Army formations in the Warsaw area. He could commit these units to assist when requested.

Railroad Armored Train Replacement Detachment 1

This Army unit was based at Rembertow, a small town fifteen kilometers east of Warsaw.[64] It appears that the detachment provided an engineer commando of two officers and forty-two engineer troops and the flame-thrower section that supported Stroop.

The Railroad Armored Train Replacement Detachment was formed on 1 April 1942. It's mission was to serve as a training and replacement center for crewmembers of the German Army's numerous armored trains. The Germany Army used several dozen of these trains in combat on all fronts beginning in Poland in 1939. Each train fielded a steel-plated locomotive, several cars with artillery pieces (that could be fired while the train was moving), anti-aircraft weapons, infantry cars and a command railcar. An armored train was a self-contained fighting element; the crews slept and ate onboard. The replacement unit was stationed at Rembertow, a former Polish military base that possessed a large artillery range and impact area. This enabled the Germans to drive armored trains to the shooting area and conduct practice. Additionally, Rembertow had a tank driving area (some armored trains had cars with tanks onboard that could be driven off for pursuit operations) and an infantry/engineer dismounted training area. The detachment during the period of the Ghetto Uprising was commanded by Major (*Major*) Ernst Naumann, previously the commander of Armored Train 10. The detachment expanded in October 1942 by incorporating two training companies from the Armored Train Training Detachment, which had been under the command of Captain (*Hauptmann*) Werner Franke. With this amalgamation, the detachment had the First and Second Training Companies as well as the Replacement Company, a Headquarters Company and a Convalescence Company. It probably fielded two other replacement companies as well. Within the organization were infantry troops, artillerymen, engineers, panzer troops and technical troops as the armored trains were crewed by all five branches. The unit received its official designation, the Railroad Armored Train Replacement Detachment (*Eisenbahn-Panzerzug-Ersatz-Abteilung*) on 28 March 1943.[65]

The greatest capability the engineers would provide Stroop was in the area of demolition and the flame-thrower. German engineers had a wide variety of demolition charges that could force open bunkers or destroy fighting emplacements. These included the 1 Kilogram Slab (*Sprengbüchse 24*) and the 3 Kilogram Slab (*Geballte Ladung 3 Kg.*) both of which used TNT as the explosive charge. A larger 12.5 Kilogram Hollow Charge and 13.5 Kilogram Hollow Charge (*Hohlladung*) were designed to blow holes through even the thickest of concrete structures.[66]

The portable flame-thrower most likely would have been a Model 41 or 42. Both were similar machines weighing 35 to 40 pounds carried and operated by one man. The device was capable of spewing five to six blasts of fuel oil, which smelled like creosote, some 25 to 35 yards. These five to six shots consumed a total of 7-1/2 gallons of fuel. The fuel was ignited as it left the firing nozzle.[67]

After the war, a former soldier of the unit provided extremely valuable testimony concerning the role and mission of the unit during the suppression of the Warsaw Ghetto Uprising. He stated:[68]

> I am familiar with the cleaning out of the Warsaw Ghetto in the spring of 1943. I personally had to participate in a mission in Warsaw. However, I was told by Battalion Commander N [Ernst Naumann] that we were to be engaged in breaking up the resistance during a riot in the Warsaw Ghetto. I remember clearly that we received this order only two or three days before the action. If you are telling me that the sergeant was wounded on the second day of combat in Warsaw, then it is clear to me that this is the day that we were first ordered to Warsaw. I remember this fact well because I was present when Sergeant S [Siegert] was wounded and, therefore, know exactly that this happened during the first hours of our engagement.
>
> I had received the order from Major N to report to SS-General Stroop. I had done so. I can also remember Stroop quite well and know that he preferred to be addressed as "General" by us instead of being addressed by his SS service rank. Also at the very first reporting I met Stroop right at the entrance to the Ghetto at a command post. He explained that the Jews had countered with heavy resistance during the operation and that they were located in fortified bunkers. We were supposed to explode these bunkers. To phrase it more exactly, we were supposed to free the entrances and openings of the bunkers by using explosives.
>
> For this purpose, the thirty men of my commando, split up into groups of five to six men, were subordinated to the battle troops of an SS unit. During the days of fighting I did not have an overall knowledge of the particular activities of this group. However, since every evening we returned to Rembertow with our truck, I learned from my men that they, as previously mentioned, were to open up access to the various bunkers by using explosives. For the same reason, we also blew up basements or houses when they contained nests of resistance.
>
> During the first one or two days – as far as I remember – the action took place without much planning. It was found that the nests of resistance were not identical to one another. Therefore, I am of the opinion that due to the heavy losses, which the units suffered during the first and second day of fighting, we were not ordered into fighting during the following three/four days. Only later, meaning on the fifth or sixth day, did things continue more according to plan and we had a clearer picture about the location of possible bunkers and hiding places.
>
> I personally was engaged in action with my whole unit only during our first day of engagement. We had been ordered to fight several nests of resistance, which had been established on several floors of a large housing complex and in the attic. We combed through this housing complex, starting with the ground floor, and broke resistance with hand grenades and hand firearms. When we reached the attic, resistance became so heavy that due to heavy losses on our side we had to withdraw. Here in the attic, Sergeant S [Siegert] was heavily wounded by a shot in the lungs. I still remember clearly that it was very difficult to get him out to safety. During the following days, when my pioneers were given to the various battle groups of the SS, I had no longer control over the immediate engagements of my men and I therefore had no influence over their actions. SS officers or sergeants led the battle groups. During that time, I stayed mostly close to the command post and also at times completely distanced myself from the entire action.
>
> I had full freedom of movement. I still remember that in the following days I only went to places of particular happenings when a larger object needed to be detonated and could not be overcome in any other way.

I also want to mention that besides the approximately 30 pioneers from my commando in Rembertow I also had two confiscated armored cars – they were called T 10 by Skoda – and a 76.2mm cannon, which I brought along to Warsaw. However, both types of weapons did not prove useful for fighting in the Ghetto and from the second or third day on were no longer used.

It is not possible for me to say now who was on the team that worked on the cannon. On the other side, I still remember that at least one armored car was led by Sergeant H.

As described, our commando stayed in Warsaw for about three weeks. When we were relieved, the whole Ghetto had not yet been cleansed, but there was no more significant resistance. I also remember that during the course of the battle other pioneer units supported us, i.e. that these were additionally ordered in by Stroop. They came from a place somewhere along the Vistula River [Góra Kalwaria].

It is correct that we had one flame-thrower, but as far as I know it never came into use. When whole streets were burned down later on, it was found that it was much easier to set the apartments on fire by hand. From the second or third day onward we did not take the flame-thrower along to Warsaw.

I cannot remember now to which SS units my men were attached. I can only remember that the leader of one unit was an *SS-Sturmbannführer*. He may also have been an *SS-Obersturmbannführer*. I also vaguely remember that two SS units were involved. But I do not remember names any longer. The names shown to me mean nothing. I only remember that just about every day I saw Stroop in the Ghetto.

There is no reason to doubt the details of this description. Therefore, we can conclude that this engineer unit brought with them a captured Russian 76.2mm howitzer (German artillery in this class was 75mm in caliber.)[69] This weapon would have proven quite useful in engaging defenders in the buildings, where its high explosive rounds would have caused havoc – providing the German gunners could get adequate lines of fire in the cramped section of the Ghetto. It is also possible that the unit provided the Czech tanks used in the battle as many armored train tanks were of this model.

14th Reserve Engineer Battalion

This army battalion was located at Góra Kalwaria, a small town some twenty-two miles southeast of Warsaw. One officer and thirty-four troops initially supported the operation.[70] The 14th Battalion was initially formed on 16 September 1942 in Weissenfels, Germany and shortly thereafter deployed to the General Government.[71] The engineer troops had similar equipment to those deployed from Rembertow.

Light Alarm Flak Battery 3/VIII

There appear to have been six light army *flak* (anti-aircraft) batteries in Warsaw at the time of the Ghetto Uprising.[72] One, the Light Alarm *Flak* Battery 3/VIII, was actually committed by the German Army for Stroop's use.[73]

The Light Alarm *Flak* Battery 3/VIII employed 20mm rapid-firing anti-aircraft guns primarily for use against low flying attacking aircraft. Although German anti-aircraft artillery was a combat arm of the *Luftwaffe*, the Army had numerous independent *flak* units. Each battery generally had twelve guns and was divided into three platoon-size elements (*Züge*). It appears as though one *Zug* from this battery supported the SS troops at the Warsaw Ghetto Uprising.[74]

The unit was equipped with Model 30, twenty-millimeter dual-purpose anti-aircraft guns. The weapon was introduced into the German Navy in 1930 and into ground force anti-aircraft units in 1935. The gun was fed by a twenty round magazine, was recoil-operated and could be fired either automatic or single shot. While the gun had a theoretical rate of fire of 280 rounds per minute, the practical rate of fire was 120 rounds per minute. The guns used at Warsaw probably fired much slower than that in a ground support mode. The weapon could fire a high explosive tracer round weighing just over four ounces or an armor piercing projectile, which could penetrate 1.77 inches of armor at 100 yards, weighing just over five ounces. The gun had a maximum horizontal range of 5,230 yards. In an anti-aircraft mode, the weapon had an effective ceiling of 7,215 feet. The gun was drawn on a two-wheeled carriage by either a half-track, a truck or even horse limber.[75]

The preferred method of employment in a ground support role in an urban area would have been to select fields of fire to permit the 20mm cannon to achieve a clear range of 500 to 1,000 meters. That would permit the German gunners to clearly observe both the target and the strike of the rounds, while remaining out of effective range of most small arms. During the Warsaw Ghetto Uprising, the Jews had no weapon to counter this system whenever the anti-aircraft weapon was properly employed.

Now that we have a working understanding of the German units that would be involved in quelling the Warsaw Ghetto Uprising, we can review the events as they unfolded beginning 19 April 1943.

Notes:

[1] Daniel Jonah Goldhagen, *Hitler's Willing Executioners: Ordinary Germans and the Holocaust.* (New York: Vintage Books, 1997), p. 452.

[2] When examining photographs of the Ghetto Uprising, the easiest way to distinguish Army, *Waffen-SS* and German Police personnel from each other is to look for the *Hoheitsadler*, or German War Eagle. German Army troops have an eagle above their upper pocket on the right front chest of their service tunic. *Waffen-SS* personnel wear an eagle instead on their left upper sleeve of their service tunic. German Police wear the eagle on the left sleeve but it is almost completely surrounded by a wreath.

[3] Sources: Mark Yerger, *Riding East:* The *SS Cavalry Brigade in Poland and Russia 1939-1942.* (Atglen, PA: Schiffer Publishing, 1996.), p. 32; Hans Buchheim, Martin Broszat, Hans-Adolf Jacobsen and Helmut Krausnick, *Anatomy of the SS State.* (New York: Walker & Company, 1968), p. 214.

[4] Hans Buchheim, Martin Broszat, Hans-Adolf Jacobsen and Helmut Krausnick, *Anatomy of the SS State*, pp. 218-219.

[5] Ruth Bettina Birn, *Die Höheren SS- und Polizeiführer: Himmler's Vertreter im Reich und in den besetzten Gebieten.* (Düsseldorf, FRG: Droste, 1986), p. 129.

[6] Herbert Becker was born 13 March 1887 in Torgau. He served as a captain in World War I with the 72nd Field Artillery Regiment and received both the Iron Cross 1st and 2nd Class for valor as well as earning a Wound Badge in Silver for multiple wounds. He joined the Police forces in 1919 and never left. Becker entered the Nazi Party on 1 May 1933 with a membership number of 3144750. He joined the SS on 9 November 1938 (SS number 310477) with a direct promotion to the rank of *SS-Standartenführer*; he subsequently made the rank of *SS-Oberführer* on 20 April 1939, *SS-Brigadeführer* on 20 April 1940 and *SS-Gruppenführer* on 20 April 1942. Becker served as the BdO for the General Government from 25 October 1939 to 31 October 1939 and then again from May 1942 to August 1943. In the interim, he served as the *Orpo* commander for Hamburg.

Dr. Eberhard Schöngarth was born 22 April 1903 in Leipzig. Too young to serve in World War I, he did enlist in a *Freikorps* in 1919. Schöngarth joined the Nazi Party in 1922 but left shortly thereafter. He rejoined the Party on 1 August 1933 with membership number 2848857. He joined the SS with membership number 67174 and was elevated to *SS-Untersturmführer* on 9 November 1936. Schöngarth worked at the SD main office in the late 1930s advancing to *SS-Obersturmführer* on 30 January 1938, to *SS-Hauptsturmführer* on 20 April 1938, to *SS-Sturmbannführer* on 1 August 1938 and *SS-Obersturmbannführer* on 10 September 1939. During this time he was the chief of the *Gestapo* office in Münster. Schöngarth was promoted to *SS-Standartenführer* on 1 January 1940 and *SS-Oberführer* on 30 January 1941. He went to his BdS position in Kraków, Poland in March 1941 and remained there until June 1943. During this tour of duty Schöngarth also served as an *Einsatzgruppe* leader mopping up behind *Einsatzgruppe B*; he was also promoted to *SS-Brigadeführer* on 30 January 1943. In late 1943, Schöngarth served with the 4th SS Division "*Polizei*." He then was transferred to be the senior SD and Security Police Commander in Holland. After the war the British tried Schöngarth for crimes committed in Holland and executed him on 15 May 1946 in Hameln, Germany.

[7] International Military Tribunal, *Trial of the Major War Criminals Before the International Military Tribunal, Nürnberg, 14 November 1945 - 1 October 1946. Volume XI, Proceedings, 8 April 1946 – 17 April 1946.* (Nuremberg, Germany, 1947), p. 352.

[8] Kazimierz Moczarski, *Conversations with an Executioner*. Edited by Mariana Fitzpatrick. (Englewood Cliffs, New Jersey), p.142.

[9] For a more complete description of the activities of the *Einsatzkommandos,* see *The Field Men: The SS Officers Who Led the Einsatzkommandos - the Nazi Mobile Killing Units*, by the author.

[10] Wladyslaw Bartoszewski, *Warsaw Death Ring, 1939-1944.* (Warsaw: Interpress Publishers, 1968), pp. 336-337.

[11] Ibid., p. 337.

[12] Antonio J. Munoz, editor, *The German Police*. Reprint of SHAPE G-2 Report, April 1945. (New York: Axis Europa, Inc., 1997), p. 78.

[13] Ibid.

[14] Wladyslaw Bartoszewski, *Warsaw Death Ring, 1939-1944*, p. 337.

[15] Ibid., pp. 337-338.

[16] Antonio J. Munoz, editor, *The German Police*, pp. 51, 56.

[17] Wladyslaw Bartoszewski, *Warsaw Death Ring, 1939-1944*, pp. 337-339.

[18] Ibid., p. 338.

[19] Ibid., pp. 338-339.

[20] Ibid., p. 339.

[21] Ibid., p. 339.

[22] Ibid., p. 339.

[23] Antonio J. Munoz, editor, *The German Police*, p. 64.

[24] Wladyslaw Bartoszewski, *Warsaw Death Ring, 1939-1944*, p. 340.

[25] It became obvious to many members of the *Kripo* that membership in the SS was desirable for career enhancement. Many entered the SS, therefore, without objection.

[26] Discussion between the author and Dr. Peter Black, senior historian at the United States Holocaust Memorial Museum, May 1999.

[27] Ibid.

[28] Bernard Mark, *Der Aufstand im Warschauer Ghetto.* (Berlin: Dietz Verlag, 1957), p. 233.

[29] Abraham J. Edelheit and Hershel Edelheit, *History of the Holocaust.* (Boulder, CO: Westview Press, 1994), p. 420.

[30] Daniel Jonah Goldhagen, *Hitler's Willing Executioners*, pp. 181-182.

[31] Wladyslaw Bartoszewski, *Warsaw Death Ring, 1939-1944*, pp.335-336.

[32] Antonio J. Munoz, editor, *The German Police*, pp. 37, 76.

[33] Ibid., pp. 33-34.

[34] Georg Tessin, *Verbände und Truppen der deutschen Wehrmacht und Waffen-SS im Zweiten Weltkrieg 1939-1945, Band I - XVI (4).* (Osnabrück, FRG: Biblio Verlag, 1979.), Band 4, p. 189.

[35] The 1st Battalion, 22nd SS Police Regiment was formed in July 1942 from the former 41st Police Battalion. The 3rd Battalion 22nd SS Police Regiment was formed the same month from the 53rd Police Battalion.

[36] Bernard Mark, *Der Aufstand im Warschauer Ghetto*, p. 232.

[37] Antonio J. Munoz, editor, *The German Police*, p. E7/E8. The motorcycle platoon, armored car platoon, light infantry-howitzer platoon and anti-tank platoon were all elements that were usually attached to the battalion from the regiment – that is, they were not organic to the battalion per se.

[38] Norbert Kannapin, *Die deutsche Feldpostübersicht, Band I-III.* (Osnabrück, FRG: Biblio-Verlag, 1980), Band 2, p. 368.

[39] Antonio J. Munoz, editor, *The German Police*, p. M15.

[40] Georg Tessin, *Verbände und Truppen der deutschen Wehrmacht und Waffen-SS im Zweiten Weltkrieg 1939-1945, Band I - XVI (4)*, Band 4, p. 205.

[41] C.F. Rüter & D.W. de Mildt, *Die Westdeutschen Strafverfahren wegen Nationalsozialistischer Tötungsverbrechen 1945-1997.* (Amsterdam: Holland University Press, 1998), p. 182.

[42] Antonio J. Munoz, editor, *The German Police*, p. M16.

[43] Georg Tessin, *Verbände und Truppen der deutschen Wehrmacht und Waffen-SS im Zweiten Weltkrieg 1939-1945*, Band 2, pp. 78, 214.

[44] George H. Stein, *The Waffen SS: Hitler's Elite Guard at War.* (Ithaca, New York: Cornell University Press, 1966), pp. 46-47.

[45] Ibid., p. 47.

[46] Georg Tessin, *Verbände und Truppen der deutschen Wehrmacht und Waffen-SS im Zweiten Weltkrieg 1939-1945, Band I - XVI (4)*, Band XIV, pp.241-242 & Band II, pp.212-213.

[47] Martin van Creveld, *Fighting Power: German and U.S. Army Performance, 1939-1945.* (London: Arms and Armour Press, 1983), pp. 72-73.

[48] Ibid., p. 75.

[49] Bernard Mark, *Der Aufstand im Warschauer Ghetto*, p. 232.

[50] One additional note on the incorrect identification of armored vehicles at Warsaw should be mentioned. The British Broadcasting Corporation Television program, *The Warsaw Ghetto*, shows footage of two *Jagdpanzer 38(t)* "*Hetzer*" (Baiter) self-propelled anti-tank vehicles at the Ghetto Uprising. These turretless, 16-ton vehicles were armed with the 75mm Pak 39 L/48 cannon and were crewed by four. However, given that these vehicles were not introduced into the German armored force until April 1944, the *Hetzers* shown in the film could not have been at the Uprising the previous year; thus the film is in error. Source: Burkhart Müller-Hillebrand, *Das Heer 1933-1945, Band III: Der Zweifrontenkrieg*.

[51] Peter Chamberlain and Chris Ellis, *Pictorial History of Tanks of the World 1915-45.* (Harrisburg, PA: Stackpole Books, 1972), pp. 16-22.

[52] Two soldiers from the battalion were tried for activities regarding the suppression of the Warsaw Uprising in 1944. Source: C.F. Rüter & D.W. de Mildt, *Die Westdeutschen Strafverfahren wegen Nationalsozialistischer Tötungsverbrechen 1945 - 1997*, p. 202.

[53] Georg Tessin, *Verbände und Truppen der deutschen Wehrmacht und Waffen-SS im Zweiten Weltkrieg 1939-1945, Band I - XVI (4)*, Band 3, p. 119.

[54] Ibid., Band 3, pp.119-120.

[55] Bernard Mark, *Der Aufstand im Warschauer Ghetto*, p. 232.

[56] Kazimierz Moczarski, *Conversations with an Executioner*, p. 133.

[57] Bernard Mark, *Der Aufstand im Warschauer Ghetto*, p. 233.

[58] On the eve of World War II there were about 400,000 descendants of Germans who had previously emigrated to Russia, Rumania, etc., in the second half of the eighteenth century. Their knowledge of German and other languages and their identity made them very suitable to serve in *Operation Reinhard* and similar missions.

[59] *SS-Sturmbannführer* Karl Streibel was born 11 October 1903 in Neustadt. He was a member of both the SS (SS Number 60152) and the Nazi Party (Party Number 554023). He served as the commandant of the camp until 1944. He survived the war and was acquitted of war crimes by a Hamburg court on 3 June 1979.

[60] Yitzhak Arad, *Belzec, Sobibór, Treblinka: The Operation Reinhard Death Camps*. (Bloomington, IN: Indiana University Press, 1987), pp. 20-22.

[61] Personalakt Johann Schwarzenbacher, Washington, D.C: National Archives Microfilm Publication A3343, Records of SS Officers from the Berlin Document Center, Roll SSO-123B.

[62] Definition of ethnic German, source: Charles W. Sydnor, Jr., Soldiers *of Destruction: The SS Death's Head Division, 1933-1945*. (Princeton, NJ: Princeton University Press, 1977), p. 205.

[63] Georg Tessin, *Verbände und Truppen der deutschen Wehrmacht und Waffen-SS im Zweiten Weltkrieg 1939-1945, Band I - XVI (4)*, Band 16 (Part 3), p. 174.

[64] Ibid., Band 16 (Part 3), p. 164.

[65] Wolfgang Sowodny, *Die Panzerzüge des Deutschen Reiches, 1904-1945*. (Freiburg, Germany: Eisenbahn Kurier Verlag, 1996.), pp.80-83.

[66] War Department, *Handbook on German Military Forces*. (Baton Rouge, Louisiana: Reprinted by Louisiana State University Press, 1990), p. 479.

[67] Ibid., pp. 533-534.

[68] Wolfgang Scheffler and Helge Grabnitz, *Der Ghetto-Aufstand Warschau 1943*. (Munich, Germany: Goldmann Verlag, 1993.), pp. 379-381.

[69] Sources: John Kirk and Robert Young, *Great Weapons of World War II*. (New York: Bonanza Books, 1961), pp. 236-239 and Joachim Engelmann and Horst Scheibert, *Deutsche Artillerie 1934-1945*. (Limburg, FRG: C.A. Starke, 1974).

[70] Bernard Mark, *Der Aufstand im Warschauer Ghetto*, p. 232.

[71] Georg Tessin, *Verbände und Truppen der deutschen Wehrmacht und Waffen-SS im Zweiten Weltkrieg 1939-1945, Band I - XVI (4)*, Band 3, p. 303.

[72] The designation VIII denoted that the unit belonged to *Luftgau* (air district) *VIII*. Source: Horst Adalbert Koch, *Flak. Die Geschichte der Deutschen Flakartillerie und der Einsatz der Luftwaffenhelfer*. (Bad Nauheim, FRG: Podzun Verlag, 1965.), p. 434. The commander of *Luftgau VIII* during the time of the Uprising was General of Flyers Walter Sommé. Sommé was born 27 May 1888 in Rittergut Libartowo, near Posen. He served in World War I, first an infantry officer and then as a bomber pilot. In the mid 1930s, Sommé, now a colonel, served as the commander of the "Hindenburg" Bomber Squadron. He assumed command of *Luftgau VIII* on 23 October 1941 and held this position until 31 July 1944 when he went into the Führer reserve pool of officers and then retirement. From 1945 to 1947 Sommé was held in an American prisoner of war camp. Upon his release he lived in Düren until his death on 14 May 1971. Sommé cannot be considered to have had any responsibility in the events at the Uprising. Source: Karl Friedrich Hildebrand, *Die Generale der deutschen Luftwaffe, 1935-1945, Band 1: A-G, Band 2: H-N, Band 3: O-Z*. (Osnabrück, Germany: Biblio Verlag, 1990), Band 3, pp. 311-312.

[73] Georg Tessin, *Verbände und Truppen der deutschen Wehrmacht und Waffen-SS im Zweiten Weltkrieg 1939-1945, Band I - XVI (4)*, Band 16 (Part 3), pp. 191-192.

[74] War Department, Military Intelligence Service, *German Anti-aircraft Artillery*, Special Series No. 10. (Washington, DC: Government Printing Office, 1943), pp. 7-13.

[75] Ibid., p. 12.

5

THE BATTLE

"Alle Juden herunter!"
"All Jews downstairs!"

- Nazi command to vacate a building during a resettlement action – an order that brought fear and ultimately death to thousands of people.

Heinrich Himmler had an important telephone call to make on Thursday, 15 April 1943. The *Führer's* birthday was only five days away and Himmler wanted to give his boss some good news for a change concerning Warsaw. Von Sammern-Frankenegg had diddled and dawdled for months, but was now going to make a final push to clean out the Ghetto. Himmler had little confidence in von Sammern. The SS and Police Leader was one of those Austrians that Hitler liked so much. He wasn't an early member of the Party nor was he an early member of the SS, having joined in December 1932. Nor was he particularly a good military man, but he was a protégé of fellow Austrian Dr. Ernst Kaltenbrunner. Kaltenbrunner had assumed the duties of Reinhard Heydrich, so he had some influence in Himmler's court. The *Reichsführer* once described von Sammern as a pleasant cavalryman, but unsuited to his duties.[1] But Heinrich Himmler knew a man who would fit the bill. *SS-Brigadeführer* Jürgen Stroop knew how to kill Jews and other bandits. He had done all that was expected of him in the liquidation of the ghetto at Lvov (called Lemberg by the Germans), not to mention performing admirably in several large manhunts of Polish resistance fighters in the countryside around the city. Hitler would be pleased. Himmler placed the call and ordered Stroop to report to *SS-Obergruppenführer* Friedrich-Wilhelm Krüger in Kraków on 16 April. Stroop did not have much time. He would then depart Kraków and be in Warsaw on Saturday the 17th. Himmler's words added a sense of urgency to the mission:[2]

> My dear Stroop, everything, even the most important matters, pales beside the task I have assigned you in Warsaw. The time for the great action has come. Go to Krüger; on 17 April you must be in Warsaw without exciting suspicion . . .

Heinrich Himmler had a flair for the dramatic and the occult. The *Führer's* birthday and the destruction of the Warsaw Ghetto were just days away and with a little help from the stars might just be brought into alignment.

• • •

The following is a day-by-day account of the fighting during the Warsaw Ghetto Uprising. To help clarify the events, the reader should consult with the daily maps located in the map section.

Sunday, 18 April 1943
At 1400 hours on 18 April 1943 the SS and Police Leader for Warsaw placed SS and German Police on alert. At 1800 hours the Polish police surrounded the Ghetto and began heavy patrolling outside the Ghetto wall. Everything was in order.[3]

• • •

Monday, 19 April 1943

At 0200 hours, 19 April 1943, the Germans reinforced the Polish police with German Police, Latvians and Ukrainians. *SS-Oberführer* von Sammern planned to begin clearing the Central Ghetto with two groups of troops. His first detachment would enter the Ghetto through the Nalewki Gate on Nalewski Street and begin seizure and deportation actions. Von Sammern would lead the column with Jewish Police and Latvian troops, with his German and Ukrainian forces just behind. A second group would move through Gesia Street to Zamenhofa Street. Both groups would be led by motorcyclists, which were followed by trucks with infantry. Von Sammern would initially ignore the Brushmaker's District, the Productive Ghetto and the Wild Ghetto; he believed that if he could quickly and ruthlessly deal with the Central Ghetto, then the entire Jewish population would meekly submit to the deportations.[4] Von Sammern believed the entire operation would last no longer than three days.[5]

• • •

The Jewish resistance fighters had other plans. The Jewish War Organization had spent the previous months organizing for combat and could field some 750 resistance fighters under the command of Mordechai Anielewicz. Anielewicz organized his forces into twenty-two platoon-size units termed "battle groups." Each of these elements contained about 30 young men and women aged 18 to 25. The Central Ghetto forces, led by Israel Kanal, featured nine battle groups, roughly some 270 fighters. In the Productive Ghetto Eliezer Geler led eight battle groups with about 240 fighters. The final ZOB forces were in the Brushmaker's District under the command of Marek Edelman. Edelman had five battle groups in this area, some 150 personnel.[6]

Not all the resistance fighters were under the command of the ZOB. Paul Frenkel led the Irgun Zwai Leumi, which fielded three battle groups (90 fighters.) Additionally a few Poles inside the Ghetto and some Polish partisans outside carried out diversionary attacks against the Germans, particularly near the Ghetto walls.[7] Whether the resistance fielded more than 750 armed fighters will be forever open to speculation as the defenders in many bunkers perished almost to the last man and woman. There may have been as many as 1,000 additional Jews who played an active role of scouts, lookouts and ammunition runners. But in any case, those Jews conducting the defense of the Ghetto were probably not more than three to five percent of the Ghetto population as a whole.[8]

There has been much post-war discussion concerning the armament of the Jewish resistance forces inside the Ghetto. Clearly, they were out-gunned by their German adversaries at every turn. I again turn to Raul Hilberg (*The Destruction of the European Jews*) as providing a reasonable explanation. Hilberg asserts that the resistance fielded two or three light machine-guns, perhaps one hundred rifles and carbines (the count could vary as much as several dozen), a few hundred pistols and revolvers, a few thousand hand-grenades, home-made incendiary devices (Molotov cocktails) and some pressure mines and explosive contraptions (*Höllenmaschinen*).[9] I believe that the defenders may also have possessed a few MP-40 machine pistols; these would have been carried by the leaders or those considered the best fighters. The Molotov cocktails seemed to have been the primary weapon of most Jewish defenders and there may have been many of these devices. In 1964 Polish construction workers repairing a street in the former Ghetto uncovered 100,000 Jewish-produced homemade detonators for these weapons.[10]

The resistance would initially concentrate their forces in three locations to protect the Central Ghetto streets. One group of Jewish resistance set up their defenses at the corner of Nalewki and Gesia Streets near one of the main Ghetto thoroughfares. A second unit established positions at the intersection of Zamenhofa and Mila Street. A third element took up positions at the intersection of Muranowska and Nalewki Street, just opposite of Muranowski Square. All three groups had barricaded themselves on several floors of the buildings, reinforcing the already formidable building walls with additional protection of sandbags.[11]

Additional tactical assets, available to the resistance fighters, were the bunkers. After the summer and early fall deportations, Anielewicz initiated a program of construction in and under the Ghetto. The Jews built scores and scores of bunkers and dugouts – Stroop would later claim over 600 had been found. Although most of these bunkers appear to have been isolated structures without benefit of mutual support from other locations, tunnels, trenches and ditches connected many others. Resistance leaders organized a special staff of those experts who could design and construct the fortifications, including architects, engineers, carpenters and stone masons. A well-constructed bunker was linked to the city's central water supply system, which passed under the Ghetto. This ensured a fresh supply of water. Many bunkers also had electrical power and camouflaged sources of air and entrance. When asked why they were constructing such shelters, the Jews replied that it was for protection against future Russian bombing raids.[12] The Germans bought it. While non-active (at least unarmed) fighters occupied some bunkers, armed fighters defended no less than seventy of the dugouts at the following locations:[13]

- five bunkers on Szczesliwa Street,
- two bunkers on Stawki Street,

- seven bunkers on Niska Street,
- ten bunkers on Mila Street,
- four bunkers on Muranowski Square,
- eight bunkers on Nalewki Street,
- five bunkers on Swietojerska Street,
- two bunkers on Gesia Street,
- four bunkers on Franciszkanska Street,
- two bunkers on Pawia Street,
- two bunkers on Walowa Street,
- three bunkers on Nowolipki Street,
- eight bunkers on Nowolipie Street,
- six bunkers on Leszno Street,
- one bunker on Grzybowska Street,
- three bunkers on Smocza Street.

So why did the Jews decide to fight now, or at least to support those who did, when they had not done so during the deportations the previous summer? Again we turn to Yitzak Arad for a reasonable explanation. Arad asserts there were three reasons for the change in attitude. The Jews supported resistance because:[14]

- they were convinced that the real purpose of the April deportation was to send all the Jews to the gas chambers of Treblinka;
- they believed that the strength of the underground, the fighters, was much greater than it actually was;
- they hoped that resistance would force the Germans to cease the planned deportation and liquidation of the Ghetto, as they felt it had done in January 1943.

One other feature should be mentioned, the urban terrain. On average, the Warsaw Ghetto had densely packed three-to-five story buildings on both sides of the streets. The buildings were old, but photographs show that most were of extremely solid construction with thick walls, which provided not only good concealment but excellent cover as well. The buildings were topped with tile roofs that formed triangular attics. The structures were built close together and the defenders could move from building to building by laying ladders horizontally between the attics and using these as bridges.[15] To get from one floor to another required the attackers to channelize themselves moving up winding staircases or attempting to scale the buildings from the outside. The defenders could conduct resistance at every floor; many of the buildings shared common walls, and with a great degree of forethought the defenders had burrowed holes through these common walls, which enabled them to move from building to building without having to go outside. The numerous streets crisscrossing the Warsaw Ghetto were narrow or medium width; with the inevitable rubbling that went on these arteries were not good avenues on which to drive tanks. Several of the streets had dead ends; many ended at the Ghetto wall as not every street that approached the wall had a gate to lead outside to the city. Fields of fire were relatively short, one hundred meters in some places. The only real open terrain lay at Muranowski Square toward the north of the Ghetto. Under the Ghetto, as beneath the rest of Warsaw, lay an extensive network of sewers. These were good concealed avenues to move about but were nightmares for both the resistance fighters and the attacking Germans from a navigational standpoint. It was extremely easy to get lost in the dark, dank underground labyrinth.

• • •

The first day's fighting generally took place at the corner of Gesia and Nalewki Streets, the intersection of Mila and Zamenhof Streets, the Muranowski Square and on Szczesliwa, Stawki and Lubecki Streets. The German attack began at 0600 hours. Jewish survivor accounts indicate that the first shots rang out from a house at 33 Nalewki Street and that defensive fire quickly began from numerous other locations. Several of the German and Ukrainian elements fled leaving their casualties behind. Jewish defenders collected much needed weapons and equipment from the fallen German troops. It appears that at Zamenhofa and Mila Streets the defenders let the vanguard of Latvians and Jewish police pass through the ambush site and then opened up on the Germans. At some time during the initial fighting, the Germans introduced one or two small tanks and perhaps two armored cars. The defenders set one of the tanks (and possibly both) on fire by Molotov cocktails; the crew bailed out. Given that the Czech LT-38 tank had armor of 25mm thickness in the front, the Jewish defenders did not have any other weapons, other than Molotov cocktails, that could disable the vehicles.[16]

The first round of fighting probably lasted some thirty minutes, ending at about 0630 hours, at which point the Germans withdrew. Stroop claims that six SS men and six "Trawniki Men" were wounded in these initial attacks. *SS-Oberführer* von Sammern panicked at this point. He did not foresee the possibility of these events and he had no alternate or back-up plan. He went to the Hotel Bristol at 0730 hours and reported to *SS-Brigadeführer* Stroop:[17]

> All is lost in the Ghetto! We are no longer in the Ghetto! There is no way to get in there! We have got wounded and dead!

Von Sammern went on to state that the *Luftwaffe* should commence bombing the Ghetto, but Stroop disagreed. Stroop had heard enough and promptly relieved the beleaguered von Sammern. At roughly the same time, certainly before 0800 hours, *SS-Obergruppenführer* Krüger called from Kraków for a situation update. According to postwar testimony by Stroop, he told the HSSPF the bad news at which point Krüger cursed, ranted and raved.[18] Then it was the *Reichsführer-SS's* turn to call. Himmler was calmer, according to Stroop, but told the new SSPF that all Germans in Warsaw must be put on alert, but that nothing should be done to provoke the Poles.[19] Shortly after the conclusion of the call with Himmler, Stroop led a group of officers into the Ghetto and began assessing the situation. By 1200 hours Stroop thought that enough calm had returned to his troops so that they could resume combat operations. German attacks then resumed and continued until about 2030 hours. It appears that at least ten more Germans were wounded in the afternoon and evening attacks. One source stated that German ambulances came into the Ghetto to retrieve the wounded men and that the defenders fired on these vehicles as well.[20]

The major German vehicle for reporting the conduct of the fighting, at least from the German viewpoint, in the Warsaw Ghetto was the Stroop Report. The report was actually a series of daily communiqués that *SS-Brigadeführer* Stroop transmitted to his superior, *SS-Gruppenführer* Friedrich Wilhelm Krüger. On most days of the Ghetto Uprising, Stroop submitted one summary report; on a few days he submitted two. At the conclusion of the Warsaw Ghetto Uprising, Stroop had copies of the daily reports collated, added a lengthy introduction and assembled a photographic section. As previously mentioned, the Germans made three copies; Stroop gave one to Heinrich Himmler, another to Krüger, and kept a third for himself. Max Jesuiter served as the Chief of Staff to the SS and Police Leader, Warsaw during the Ghetto Uprising. He countersigned many of the daily reports and testified after the war as to the format (emphasis added by the author):[21]

> I can make the following statements about the creation of the so-called Stroop Report:
>
> On a daily basis Teletype messages were sent to the Higher SS and Police Chief in Kraków, as they are available in copies of the report. After the mission was completed, Stroop let us copy the remaining samples of these Teletype messages. As far as I remember, three, at the most four of such copies were made. These copies were then put together as what is today known as the Stroop Report. Stroop then added an introduction and added the photo report. But all this took place only after the mission. The clerk who at that time had to make the copies was a Mrs. H.L., nee G.
>
> Miss G. was the head clerk at our office. She wrote for the chief and for me. We also had an additional typist, but I do not remember her name. As I said, the Teletype messages were written. Then at least on one copy I have checked the correctness of the copy, i.e. that it was in agreement with the original, and confirmed this with my signature. Whether I have verified all copies is something I do no longer know today. In any case, the sample shown me did not get verified by me, but on the other side the verification is available in the report which was published in book form.
>
> As I have already stated in my earlier interrogation, Stroop always came to the office in the evening. He had notations of numbers, which became the basis for his Teletype messages. I cannot tell where he had gotten these numbers because I personally never was with him in the ghetto. It can be assumed that he obtained these numbers during the daily reports from the unit leaders or from the leader of the separate search troops. However, such reports by unit leaders or troop leaders never went through our office; I have never been given such reports. Therefore, Stroop must have gotten these reports at the scene, which means in the ghetto, from the unit leaders. More accurate information about the origin of these numbers could come from [Adjutant Karl] Kaleschke who was together with Stroop on a daily basis.
>
> I want to say the following about the accuracy of the numbers given by Stroop: of course, I can neither confirm nor dispute whether these numbers were correct because I was never with him when he made these observations. It must also be considered that the numbers in the report, which Stroop received from the unit leaders or the troop leaders, were not exactly correct. But from the impression I have about Stroop, I can say that, **if there was an inaccuracy in the numbers, it could not have been significant. Stroop was very correct in his dealings with superiors and I do not believe that he presented imaginary numbers to them. If there were any deviations, they could only have been minimal.**
>
> To the question whether Stroop possibly reported less shootings than actually occurred because it is possible that Himmler was not supposed to know that so many shootings did take place in Warsaw as this was not his intention (in order not to cause unnecessary upheaval in Warsaw), I would like to state the following: I am not under the impression that Stroop under-reported the numbers in his report of the num-

bers, because I know that Himmler had always been unhappy with the SS and Police Chief in Warsaw because in his [Himmler's] opinion too little happened there. Now there was an occasion that something could happen and something did happen, and **I do not believe that Stroop held back the real numbers**. But all these are merely my opinions, and I cannot make a real statement about it.

I can add the following about the way the separate daily reports were written down. As I said earlier, Stroop always came back to the office during the evening and dictated the report. Most of the time, he dictated it to me personally. After that I did not immediately write the report on the typewriter, but took his dictation down in shorthand. Then I dictated it to Miss G. into the typewriter. It did also happen that Stroop dictated directly to Miss G. Each Teletype message shows a reference at the top. In this reference it is a group of letters, which are connected by a diagonal stroke. The first two letters were always St; that is the dictation mark for Stroop. The letters behind the stroke are the dictation marks of the typist. In most cases the reports show the dictation marks St/Gr which means Stroop-G. Also in the cases when I first took down Stroop's report in shorthand and then dictated it to Miss G, the dictation marks were Stroop-G. Who the other lady with the dictation marks Wdt (compare with the sample report of 26 April 1943) is something I do not remember; as I said before, we had an additional typist.

The fact that at times another typewriter was used should find its explanation in the fact that, as I had mentioned before, the creation of the report had to be done in great haste and that possibly other typists were used to make copies. The fact that these reports were copied on different typewriters and in different methods is shown, for instance, when comparing the Teletype message of 5 May 1943 in the book with the same example in the files. As an example, the difference of the written word "Anschein" in the first line of the text can be seen.

Stroop submitted his first daily report on 19 April 1943, which summarized the day's events.[22]

Stroop Report, 19 April 1943

Shutting off of the Ghetto commenced at 0300 hours. At 0600 hours the order was given to the *Waffen-SS* (strength: 16 officers and 850 troops) to comb out the remainder of the Ghetto. Hardly had the units fallen in when they came under strong concentrated fire by the Jews and bandits. Our tank and two armored cars used in this action were pelted with Molotov cocktails. The tank was set on fire twice. Due to this enemy counter-attack, we had to withdraw the units. Our losses in the first attack were twelve men (6 SS men and 6 men from Trawniki). At 0800 hours I began a second attack with these units. Although the enemy repeated his counterattack, we succeeded this time in combing out blocks of buildings according to plan. We caused the enemy to retire from the roofs of the buildings and from elevated positions and move into the cellars, bunkers and sewers. During this operation we caught only 200 Jews. Immediately afterward, raiding parties were directed to known bunkers with the order to capture the Jews and destroy the bunkers. We then captured 380 Jews. We discovered that the Jews had taken to the sewers. The sewers were completely inundated, to make staying there impossible. About 1730 hours we encountered very strong resistance from one block of flats, which included machine-gun fire. A special raiding party invaded that block and defeated the enemy, but could not catch the resistors. The Jews and criminals resisted from base to base, and escaped at the last moment across lofts or through subterranean passages. About 2030 hours the external barricade [around the Ghetto] was reinforced. All units were removed from the Ghetto and dismissed to their barracks. The external barricade [Ghetto wall] was reinforced by 250 *Waffen-SS* men. The operation will be continued on 20 April 1943.

Units at my disposal:

SS

SS Panzergrenadier Reserve Battalion	6 officers 400 troops
SS Cavalry Reserve Squadron	10 officers 450 troops
Police	6 officers 165 troops
SD	2 officers 48 troops
Trawniki men	1 officer 150 men

One tank (captured French model)
Two heavy armored cars

Army

100mm howitzer crew (one gun)	1 officer 7 troops

Flame-thrower	1 troop
Engineer section	2 officers
	16 troops
Medical detachment	1 officer
	1 troop
Anti-aircraft section (three 20mm guns)	2 officers
	24 troops

Total: 31 officers, 1,262 troops

After the war Jürgen Stroop was apprehended and turned over to Polish authorities for trial. While he was incarcerated in Warsaw he discussed much of his career with two cellmates, one of whom, Kazimierz Moczarski, wrote of the experience in *Conversations with an Executioner*. His recollections of the Warsaw Ghetto Uprising appear to shed additional light on the situation. Stroop recounted the following about the first day of the fight:[23]

> As early as four thirty that morning . . . armored vehicles and SS troop cars had arrived at the Ghetto's gates. As they moved through the 'Aryan' streets, the noise of their passage alerted outlying Jews and their Polish supporters to the fact that something was up . . . During the early fighting I stuck close to my phones. My hastily assembled staff, including drivers, messengers and radio and telephone operators functioned like clockwork allowing me to follow von Sammern's actions minute by minute. It was clear from the first that the Austrian [von Sammern] had entered the Ghetto at six A.M. with insufficient forces – only eight hundred and fifty men, including civilian police, security forces, *Askaris* [Trawniki troops] and the *Wehrmacht* . . . There wasn't a sound for the first five minutes. The Jews let our troops keep coming. Then just as von Sammern was probably thinking that his SS men would stroll through the Ghetto like tourists, the shooting began. Our troops started to panic under the strong, well-aimed fire, but von Sammern's officers somehow managed to keep them advancing in tight formation. Suddenly all hell broke loose . . . Within thirty minutes von Sammern's troops had been routed and the tank and one armored car had been put out of commission . . . My phones were ringing like mad. I had three talks with Krüger and one with Heinrich Himmler. They were both furious..Both men ordered that von Sammern be withdrawn from the Ghetto instantly and that a new assault be made in two hours – this time under my command.

Former *SS-Hauptsturmführer* Georg Michalsen, who temporarily served under Stroop during the Ghetto Uprising, remembered that first day somewhat differently. Michalsen testified after the war that:[24]

> The start of the fighting was a little different from what is written in the report. I have witnessed this start with my own eyes. We stood on the square in front of the building of the Jewish Council. A unit of the *Waffen-SS* was also standing there, ready for action. Then the *Waffen-SS* unit started to force itself into a street of the Ghetto; the unit proceeded along the house walls to the right and left in rifleman file formation, which means, one behind each other. After the unit had gotten about fifty meters into the street, they were fired at out of the houses. Immediately there were some dead and wounded. At first the SS people continued to proceed. The firing increased, and the order for withdrawal was given. Taking their dead and wounded along, the unit retreated. Then a second assault was made with an armored troop carrier. A tank was not employed. It concerned an open armored troop carrier of the SS, which was manned by *Waffen-SS* people. A Molotov cocktail was thrown on this carrier. I think there were even more than one cocktail. The armored carrier started to burn immediately and retreated with great speed. Among the *Waffen-SS* people on the armored carrier many were heavily burned. For the time being, the whole action was stopped, and a war counsel took place. At this point Stroop was notified and brought in. After his arrival, the action was resumed and Stroop sent me off, as I have already described earlier. If there is talk in the report about numerous shootings of Jews in the Zamenhof Street, I know nothing about it. I have not witnessed anything like that. After Stroop arrived, I left the square and devoted myself to the orders, which I had received.
>
> As I said, at the beginning of the action a large number of SS and police officers were standing in front of the building of the Jewish Council when the first shots were fired.
>
> [*Question*] According to various presentations, among them that of the witness Jesuiter, Stroop was not present at this event but only joined later.
>
> [*Michalsen*] Yes, since I am now confronted with this, I do remember that it is correct. Stroop was not present at first. When the shooting started, von Sammern drove away and brought Stroop. The shooting of the Jewish council member who was working on a Red Cross matter as described by me earlier occurred by order of Stroop, which means only after Stroop had arrived in the Ghetto. Now

> Stroop took the whole matter into his hand. Stroop then ordered me, in the manner described, to now go there and convince the Jews that they let themselves be transferred.

Max Jesuiter provided more details from his vantage point concerning how the events unfolded. Jesuiter stated after the war in legal testimony:[25]

> I can only say what I had heard at that time: I was present when von Sammern arrived at the office around 0700 hours completely confused and agitated. At that moment Stroop was sitting in the bathtub. I must add: since I do remember that Stroop was sitting in the bathtub, it could not have been at the office, because we did not have a bathtub there; it must have been at our quarters in the Aleja Roz. I still remember that von Sammern was completely out of control and helpless and that Stroop said something like this to him: "Now just don't get excited over this, I will take care of it." During this conversation, von Sammern reported that a troop of the Order Police was shot at during a change-over, and this is how I remember it.

What Stroop, Jesuiter and Michalsen failed to mention about that first day was that at about 1000 hours, the Germans began shooting prisoners in the courtyard of the *Judenrat* building in order to relieve potential overcrowding at the *Umschlagplatz*. Stroop personally participated in the selections.[26] The most significant aspect of the day from the German point of view was the change in perception. Von Sammern entered the Ghetto early in the morning with the thought that the action would be merely an extension of the previous summer's deportations. After the initial German setbacks, Stroop appears to have come to the conclusion that this would be a military-style action.

There was one more significant event on 19 April. Late that night, Heinrich Himmler called Stroop from Berlin to check on the progress in the Ghetto. The *Reichsführer-SS*, whose "eyes and ears" everywhere had informed him that Stroop had gained control of the situation, was in a much better mood than earlier in the day. Himmler congratulated Stroop with typical Himmleresque melodrama:[27]

> You conducted the overture magnificently. It came out extremely well, especially against the background of the clumsy attempts of that bungler, von Sammern. Since I am fond of Wagner's operas and the contemporary National Socialist musical conductors, permit me to tell you: Maestro, continue to play thus, and our *Führer* and I shall never forget it.

• • •

Tuesday, 20 April 1943, Morning

The second day's fighting centered in the area of the Brushmaker's District, on Mila Street, on Leszno, Nowolipie, and Smocza Streets and on the Muranowski Square. There were also attacks by the Polish Home Army (Armia Krajowa) along the Nowiniarska Street. The Germans again committed one or two tanks (probably the same ones that had been damaged the previous day as the LT-38 was easy to maintain, fix and put back into action) against two bastions of defenders at 7 and 9 Muranowska Street. One tank again appears to have been damaged, probably with a thrown track.[28] But the armored vehicles began to pound both houses from their positions in the street with their 37mm guns. Many of the defenders in the buildings were killed or captured although some resistance fighters escaped through a tunnel.[29] Additionally, Stroop began to employ small assault teams, which included *Waffen-SS* and Army engineers to move through the buildings.

The resistance also set up defenses in the Brushmaker's District. There, the defenders fortified ten houses on 28-38 Swietojerska Street. Resistance fighters also setup a large command-detonated mine under a small square at 6 Walowa Street.[30] They detonated the mine. Jewish recounts claim that twenty-two Germans were killed although Stroop's account does not reflect this. Stroop brought forward three twenty millimeter anti-aircraft guns and a one-hundred millimeter howitzer. All four guns began direct firing against Jewish positions. Resistance accounts also mention that the Germans employed searchlights in the fight. The Germans claimed to have lost three men killed and eight wounded; this certainly contradicts the report of the mine explosion. These losses included *SS-Panzergrenadier* Paul Jäger, 4th Company, 3rd SS Panzergrenadier, Training and Replacement Battalion, and *Gefreiter* Joseph Strupp and *Schütze* Christian Hohbein, Light Alarm Flak Battery 3/VIII, killed in action. *SS-Panzergrenadier* Valentin Malle (gunshot wound, lower right leg) and *SS-Panzergrenadier* Alfons Hausa of the 2nd Company, 3rd SS Panzergrenadier Training and Replacement Battalion, *SS-Reiter* Anton Heit, *SS-Schütze* Ludwig Schay, *SS-Unterscharführer* Robert Hauschild and *SS-Reiter* Johann Neugebauer of the SS Cavalry Replacement Detachment, *Feldwebel* Josef Siegert (gunshot through the lung) of the Engineer Commando Rembertow and *SS-Oberscharführer* Sepp Mayowski from the Trawniki camp, were wounded in action. Stroop submitted two reports, which covered the day's actions.[31]

Stroop Report, 20 April 1943, Morning

I put Major of Police Sternagel in command of today's operations subject to my further instructions if necessary.

At 0700 hours nine raiding parties were formed, each with one officer and thirty-six troops. These consisted of mixed units [probably some police and some *Waffen-SS*] who had to comb out and intensively search the remainder of the Ghetto. This search is still underway; its first objective will be completed by 1100 hours. In the meantime it has been ascertained that there are several centers of resistance that are so strong that the tank could not go through. These are in that part of the Ghetto, which contains several armaments factories; it is not inhabited, but it also has not yet been searched. Two raiding parties defeated these centers of resistance and made a passage for the tank men. In this operation we have already had two *Waffen-SS* men wounded.

The enemy is much more cautious than yesterday, since he has, of course, heard of the heavy arms at our disposal. My intention is to completely comb out the remainder of the Ghetto and then to clean out the so-called uninhabited [Wild] Ghetto in the same manner. We have ascertained in the meantime that the latter part of the Ghetto contains at least ten to twelve bunkers, some of which are even within the armament factories. The whole of the operation is made more difficult because there are still enterprises in the Ghetto that contain machines and tools which must be protected against fire and bombardment.

Stroop Report, 20 April 1943, Evening

The resistance centers ascertained within the inhabited, but not yet cleared part of the Ghetto were crushed by a battle group of *Wehrmacht* engineers and flame-throwers. The *Wehrmacht* had one wounded in this operation who was shot through the lungs. Nine raiding parties broke through as far as the northern boundary of the Ghetto. Nine bunkers were reached. Their inhabitants were crushed when they resisted and the bunkers were blown up. What losses the enemy suffered cannot be ascertained accurately. Altogether the nine raiding parties caught 505 Jews today. Those among them who are able bodied were kept ready for transport to Poniatowa. At about 1500 hours I learned from the Army Accommodation Office that the block of buildings occupied by that office, and where 4,000 Jews are reported to be employed, is to be evacuated immediately. The German building manager was asked to call upon the Jewish workers to leave the block voluntarily. Only twenty-eight Jews obeyed this order. Thereupon I resolved to either evacuate the block by force, or to blow it up. The anti-aircraft artillery (three 20mm guns) which were used for this operation had two men killed. The 100mm howitzer, which was also used, expelled the bands from their strong fortifications and also inflicted losses on them as far as we were able to ascertain. This action had to be terminated due to the fall of darkness. On 21 April 1943, we shall attack this resistance center again.

In today's action we caught, apart from the Jews reported above, considerable stores of incendiary bottles, hand-grenades, ammunition, military tunics and equipment.

Losses:

2 dead (Wehrmacht)
7 wounded (6 *Waffen-SS*, 1 Trawniki man)

In one case the bandits had laid personnel mines. I have succeeded in causing the firms W.C. Többens, Schultz & Company and Hoffmann to be ready for evacuation with their entire personnel on 21 April 1943 at 0600 hours. In this way I hope to get the way free at last for cleaning out the Ghetto. The Trustee Többens has pledged himself to induce the Jews, numbering 4-5,000 to follow him voluntarily to the assembly point for resettlement. In case he meets with little success at the Army Accommodation Office, I am going to clean out this part of the Ghetto with force as well.

I acknowledge receiving the order, which the *SS-Obergruppenführer* [Krüger] communicated to me by telephone and of the powers granted to me. My next report will be at noon on 21 April 1943.

After the war, while he was incarcerated in Warsaw, Stroop had these recollections about the day:[32]

At 0700 hours the first assault units reentered the Ghetto. I'd broken them into groups of thirty-six men, each with its own officer. Police Major Sternagel knew his orders: carefully reoccupy the area taken the day before, clean up the Remnant Ghetto [Central Ghetto], then comb the entire walled area. I thought we could complete the bulk of our job that Tuesday, and use the third and following days for mopping up . . . we weren't able to clean out the Remnant Ghetto that day. We encountered pockets of resistance every inch of the way, including hideaways con-

> cealed within living quarters. I ordered up two assault units. The tank sent along to protect them drew heavy fire, and one of its treads was damaged . . . the rest lay low, fled through those rat holes of theirs, or offered armed resistance . . . That's what forced me to bring in the engineers and the anti-aircraft guns . . . Twenty millimeter. Fast firing. But you can imagine, gentlemen, the potency of guns like that shooting straight ahead at targets no more than two hundred or three hundred meters away. The Jews responded with grenades and automatic fire aimed at our gun crews. The snipers must have been low on ammunition because they made each shot count. They managed to kill two of our light artillerymen [anti-aircraft gunners].

• • •

Wednesday, 21 April 1943

The third day's fighting took place along the Leszno, Smocza, Nowolipie and Nowolipki Streets. Additional fighting transpired on the Swietojerska, Walowa and Franciszkanska Streets. Finally, there was heavy fighting among the bunkers on the Mila, Niska, Szczesliwa, Wolynska and Pokorna Streets. Jewish resistance accounts state that the Germans used aircraft to attack the Ghetto.[33] Stroop submitted two reports for the day. From these reports it appears that Stroop had made the discovery that burning down entire buildings, or even blocks of buildings, would be an effective technique in combating the resistance. The heavy artillery he mentions in his first report is either the 100mm gun or the 20mm anti-aircraft guns.[34] *SS-Reiter* Georg Pöpl, SS Cavalry Replacement Detachment, *Zugwachtmeister der Schutzpolizei* Erich Perschke and *Zugwachtmeister der Schutzpolizei* Otto Koglin, 1st Battalion, 22nd SS Police Regiment, *Zugwachtmeister der Schutzpolizei* Kurt Czesnik, 3rd Battalion, 22nd SS Police Regiment, and *Wachmann* Nikolai Huzulak and *Wachmann* Iwan Knyhynyzkyn, Trawniki camp, were wounded in action.

Stroop Report, 21 April 1943

> Subject to the report I made earlier today at 1400 hours by telephone, I beg to report:
>
>> The forces at my disposal remain the same as that on 20 April. The whole of the Ghetto has been cordoned off since the beginning of operations on 19 April 1943. Inasmuch as the special operation concerning the block of buildings occupied by the Army Accommodation Office had to be interrupted due to darkness, one battle group reinforced by engineers and heavy artillery was sent again into the operation at 0700 hours. When it had combed the enormous block of buildings, it found a large quantity of bunkers and subterranean passages and caught 60 Jews. Although we did our best, we were unable to catch more of the 700 to 800 Jews who used to inhabit this block. They retired from refuge to refuge through subterranean passages, sometimes firing their arms. Therefore, I resolved to blow up those passages, which we had discovered, and subsequently to set the entire block on fire. Not until the building was well aflame did screaming Jews make their appearance and they were then evacuated at once. We had no losses in this operation. Precautionary measures were taken in order to ensure that the conflagration remained localized.
>>
>> The main body of our forces was ordered to cleanse the so-called inhabited, but not yet released, part of the Ghetto [Central Ghetto] by proceeding from South to North. Before we started this action, we caught 5,200 Jews who had been employed in enterprises under the supervision of the Commissioner for Armaments and transported them under armed guard to the railway station, which had been chosen for use in the resettlement. I formed three search parties to which were attached special raiding parties, who had the duty to attack and blow up the bunkers which became known to us. This operation had to be interrupted, after one half of the area mentioned had been combed out, due to intervening darkness. It will be continued at 0700 hours on 22 April 1943.
>>
>> Apart from the Jews who had been sent away, 150 Jews and bandits were killed in battle, about 80 bandits were killed in their bunkers when they were blown up. The enemy today used the same arms as on the day before, particularly homemade explosives. Samples have been kept at the SS Police Leader's office. For the first time we noticed participation of members of the Jewish Women's Battle Association (Chaluzim Movement). We captured rifles, pistols, hand-grenades, explosives, horses and SS-equipment parts.
>>
>> **Losses:**
>>
>> 2 Police troops, 2 *Waffen-SS* men, 1 Trawniki man

Stroop Report, 21 April 1943, Amendment

> Setting the block on fire by nightfall achieved the result that those Jews, whom we had not been able to find despite all our search operations, left their hide-outs under the roofs, in the cellars, and elsewhere and appeared outside of the buildings trying their best to escape the flames. Masses of them – entire families – were already aflame and jumped from the windows or endeavored to let themselves down by means of sheets tied together or the like. Steps had to be taken so that these Jews as well as the remaining ones were liquidated at once. During the whole of the night there were shots from buildings, which were supposed to have been evacuated. We had no losses in our cordoning forces. 5,300 Jews were caught for de-camping action and transported off.

After the war Stroop elaborated on the techniques of the engineers. First, the sappers would move into a building and blow-up all enemy bunkers, strongholds and passages that they could locate. Then, realizing that some defensive locations could still remain undetected, the engineers would set the house or block of houses on fire.[35]

It is possible that the *Luftwaffe* bombed the Ghetto but it would have been more difficult than would first seem. It is unlikely that any front-line bomber unit far away in Russia would have sent its aircraft, at night, hundreds of miles west, bombed the Ghetto and then return to base. One reason is that every German *flak* unit along the route would have had to be briefed well beforehand or the anti-aircraft gunners might have mistaken the planes for the Soviet air force. Secondly, such a mission would have taken valuable planes away from preparations for the upcoming offensive at Kursk. The Germans would have probably used a training unit stationed in the General Government; this was much closer and would minimize navigational errors (there was a bomber school element at Warsaw).[36] Second, there would have been a decision as to whether to use horizontal bombers or dive-bombers. The area of the Ghetto was relatively small and horizontal bombers had a large dispersal pattern for their bombs, a pattern that could have caused great collateral damage to German installations in the city. As the Germans generally left the Ghetto at night, there would have been no air-ground liaison teams to radio the bombers in and guide them to the target. Stroop could have specified that the attacking planes drop their bombs on those areas already burning; the planes would have had little difficulty spotting the large fires. Dive-bombers would have been a more accurate choice. Of course, Stroop did have some clandestine patrols in the Ghetto and they would have been at risk. This is not to say that the *Luftwaffe* did not bomb; it is an assertion that a lot of factors could have gone wrong for the Germans had they attacked at night from the air.

• • •

Thursday, 22 April 1943

The fourth day of the Warsaw Ghetto Uprising saw fighting along the Leszno and Nowolipie Street as well as on the Nalewki, Swietojerska and Franciszkanska Streets. Stroop submitted two reports covering the day's fighting. A post-war source states that the Germans blew up the gates to the Leszno houses with grenades. It may also have been explosive charges. Once the Germans penetrated the houses, they would have cleared the buildings beginning with the bottom floor and worked their way upward, destroying bunkers and barricaded rooms as they went.[37] The source also states that the Germans attacked the higher floors with grenade launchers.[38] If this report is correct, the Germans most likely used grenade launchers that fit over the muzzle of their Mauser 98 rifles. These rifle grenade launchers could fire either high explosive rifle grenades to a range of 250 meters or a hollow-charge armor piercing rifle grenade to a distance of 100 meters. The high explosive round would have thrown fragments up to 30 meters away – devastating in a confined room. While the armor piercing round was designed for use against armored vehicles, German troops may well have attempted to fire these projectiles against the reinforced fighting positions of the resistance.[39] *SS-Untersturmführer* Hans Dehmke (hand grenade explosion), SS Cavalry Replacement Detachment and *Wachmann* Willi Stark and *Wachmann* Borys Odartschenko, Trawniki camp, were killed in action. Stroop submitted two reports to *SS-Obergruppenführer* Krüger in Kraków for the day.[40]

Stroop Report, 22 April 1943, Morning

> One raiding party was dispatched to again invade a block of buildings, which had been burned out and was aflame, in order to catch those Jews who were still inside. When shooting started again from another block against the men of the *Waffen-SS*, this block also was set on fire. The result was that a considerable number of bandits were scared from their hideouts and shot while trying to escape. Apart from those, we caught 180 Jews in the backyards of the buildings. The main body of our units continued the cleansing action from the line where we terminated this action yesterday. This operation is still in progress. As in the previous days, the local resistance was broken and the bunkers we discovered were blown up. Unfortunately there is no way of preventing the Jews and bandits from taking

> refuge in the sewers below the Ghetto where we can hardly catch them after they have dammed up the torrent of water we had tried to use to get them out. The city administration is not in a position to frustrate this nuisance. Neither did we succeed in using smoke candles or by mixing creosote into the water. Cooperation between all our forces was splendid.

Stroop Report, 22 April 1943, Evening

> When the special raiding party searched the remainder of the blocks as already reported, they met with resistance at some places and had the following success: 1,100 Jews were caught for decamping, 203 Jews and bandits shot dead, 15 bunkers blown up. We captured 80 incendiary bottles and booty of other kind. Units at my disposal are the same as on 20 April.
>
> **Losses:**
>
> *SS-Untersturmfuehrer* Dehmke killed when the enemy hit a hand grenade, which he carried. One sergeant of Police was shot through the lungs.
>
> When the engineers blew up the bunkers, a considerable number of Jews and bandits were buried under the ruins. In a number of cases we found it necessary to start fires in order to smoke the gangs out.
>
> I ought to add that since yesterday some of the units have been shot at time and time again from outside the Ghetto from the Aryan part of Warsaw. Raiding parties at once entered the area in question and in one case succeeded in capturing 35 Polish bandits and Communists who were liquidated at once. Today it happened in several instances, where we had found it necessary to execute some of the bandits, that they collapsed on being shot, shouting "Long live Poland" and "Long live Moscow." The operations will be continued at 0700 hours, 23 April 1943.

Many Jewish survivor accounts of the Ghetto Uprising mention that the Germans used poison gas to attempt to flush out the bunkers and sewers of defenders. There is no hard evidence to support this assertion. No photographs of the action show German troops in protective gas masks, which they surely would have worn had true poison gas been used. What the Germans actually employed, I believe, was termed Smoke Candle 39s (Nb.K.39). This device was a metal can, 5 3/4 inches high by 3 1/2 inches in diameter filled with zinc dust and hexachlorethane. It weighed 4 3/4 pounds. Ignited by a pull-cord type igniter, the device would burn for three to four minutes and emit dark gray smoke. This smoke, when confined to a small space such as a sewer, could well suffocate an individual, but it was not a poison gas *per se*. Another smoke munition that could have been used was the Long-Burning Smoke Generator 42 (Nb.KL 42). This was a cylindrical metal container of 19 inches high by 6 5/6 inches in diameter. It contained 36 pounds of a smoke-producing mixture of zinc chloride and hexachlorethane and would burn fifteen to thirty minutes, producing whitish-gray smoke.[41] Again, large amounts of this smoke could easily kill in a confined space, but it was not classified as a poisonous gas. All armies during World War II used smoke munitions of this type; it was not a banned substance by the Geneva Convention.

Stroop's post-war recollections highlight the difficulties that his forces experienced in this type of warfare:[42]

> The second thing that struck me that Thursday was our inability to capture Jews and Poles who had fled to the sewers beneath the Ghetto. Those 'catacombs' made excellent secret passages and ambush sites, and the Jews thwarted all our effort to flood them. The few SS men who went underground were met with pistol fire. Smoke candles and the addition of creosote to the water also proved ineffectual. We never did gain control of those sewers.

• • •

Friday, 23 April 1943

The fifth day of the Warsaw Ghetto Uprising was a pivotal day. In his summary to the Stroop Report, Jürgen Stroop relates that:[43]

> On 23 April 1943 the *Reichsführer-SS* issued through the Higher SS and Police Leader East at Kraków his order to complete the comb-out of the Warsaw Ghetto with the greatest severity and relentless tenacity.

Stroop heeded the instructions and focused the fighting on Leszno and Nowolipie Streets. A Jewish resistance squad at Nowolipie and Karmelicka Streets set out, according to a post-war source, to attack a headquarters of the *Gestapo* at 103 Zelazna Street. However, the Germans intercepted the group and killed most of the fighters.[44] Stroop reports that 150 of the "Trawniki Men" were detached from his command for special purpose duties. We do not know exactly what this duty entailed. On this day it appears that the Germans expanded their tactic of setting fires to burn out the resistance fighters. *Zugwachtmeister der Schutzpolizei* Erich Waclawik (grenade shrapnel), *Wachtmeister der Schutzpolizei* Karl Neidhard and *Wachtmeister der Schutzpolizei* Oskar Hexel (right lower leg;

later amputated below the knee) of the 3rd Battalion, 22nd SS Police Regiment and *Wachmann* Grigor Iwanyschyn, Trawniki camp, were wounded in action. Stroop submitted one report for the day.[45]

Stroop Report, 23 April 1943

> The whole of the former Ghetto has been divided for the purposes of today's operations into twenty-four districts. One reinforced search party with special orders was allotted to each district. These orders had to be carried out by 1600 hours.
>
> Result of this action: 600 Jews and bandits ferreted out and captured, about 200 Jews and bandits executed, 48 bunkers, many of a quite elaborate character, were blown up. We captured some gas masks in addition to valuables and some money.
>
> The units had been informed that we intended to terminate the operation today. In the morning the Jews had already become aware of this instruction. This is why I ordered a renewed search by the search parties after an interval of one to one and a half-hours had elapsed. The result was that they, as always, found that again Jews and bandits were within the blocks. From one block shots were fired against our cordoning units. I now ordered an attack by a special battle group, and in order to smoke the bandits out, every block was now set on fire. The Jews and bandits held their fire up to the last moment and then concentrated their fire against our units. The enemy even used carbines. A number of bandits, who fired from the balconies, were hit by our men and came crashing to the ground.
>
> Furthermore, today we discovered a place, which is reported to have been a rallying point of the so-called "PPR" [Communists], which was unoccupied, and destroyed it. It was on this fifth day of the operation that we found the worst of the terrorists and activists who so far always had found a way to dodge our every searching or resettlement action.
>
> An ethnic German reported that again some Jews escaped through the sewers into the Aryan part of the city. We learned from a traitor that some Jews stayed in a certain house. A special motorized raiding party invaded the house and was able to catch three Jews, two of them female. During this operation one of our vehicles was pelted with an incendiary bottle and one explosive which caused two policemen to become casualties.
>
> The whole of the operation is rendered more difficult by the cunning way in which the Jews and bandits act. For instance, we had to discover that the hearses which were used to collect the corpses lying around, contained living Jews as well who were being driven out of the Ghetto to the Jewish cemetery where they were able to escape. Now, through our continuous control of the hearses, this way of escape has been closed.
>
> Shortly before the termination of today's operation, we again discovered that about thirty bandits had sought refuge in a so-called armaments factory. Since our forces are storing goods of great value in this building, I requested that the factory be evacuated by noon on 24 April. This will enable us to clear this large structure by tomorrow. Today 3,500 Jews were caught who will be decamped together with the enterprises. Altogether 19,450 Jews have been caught for decamping. Of these about 2,500 must still be loaded. The next train will depart 24 April 1943.
>
> Our strength today is as on 22 April but without the 150 troops from Trawniki (Trawniki Men). These personnel have already been put at the disposal of the Eastern Command as reinforcements for a special purpose.
>
> **Losses:**
>
> 2 Police sergeants wounded
> 1 Trawniki man wounded
>
> This operation will be continued on 24 April 1943 at 1000 hours. This hour was chosen so that Jews who still may stay in the Ghetto shall continue to think that the operation was actually terminated today.

Stroop reported after the war that he again committed tanks and armored cars during the fighting on this day. He also described removing hundreds of corpses from the fighting.[46]

The Germans resorted to intentional arson due to a failure of their urban tactics. German doctrine and procedures called for concentration of all heavy weapons' fire, including artillery, against a single target. During this concentration the infantry would assemble and then attack the objective immediately upon termination of artillery fire. The immediate objective of the attacking Germans was to divide the area occupied by the enemy, isolate the enemy into smaller areas and deny the enemy freedom of movement. The assaulting troops would be divided into a number of columns that each would make coordinated parallel attacks. The columns would be further subdivided into assault and mop-up groups. When possible, German tactics called for the assault groups to blast holes through the walls of rows of buildings along the route of advance in order to provide the infantry with covered and concealed approaches. German doctrine also called for the attackers to avoid streets as much as possible. When the Germans did have to advance along a street, they would move in two files, one on each side of the street, staying close to the buildings to gain some degree of quick cover should shots ring out. The attackers would enter buildings on the ground floor and then fan up to higher floors and down to basements and cellars.[47]

There were two major problems with this approach at Warsaw. First, because of the height of the buildings, the rubble and the narrowness of the streets, the Germans could not get adequate fields of fire for their support weapons. They were, therefore, unable to mass their heavy weapons' fire to the degree they wished. Second, by entering the three, four and five-story buildings on the ground floor, the Germans had an uphill fight as they moved upward in the narrow, winding stairwells. The Jewish defenders could roll grenades down the stairs, confident that the explosive devices would proceed toward the Germans until explosion. The attackers, on the other hand, might likely meet their own grenades, as these bombs frequently bounced back down the stairs if errantly thrown by young troopers. Fire presented no such problems and Stroop settled on this tactic for the remainder of the operation.

• • •

Saturday, 24 April 1943

The sixth day of the German attack featured combat on Mila, Bonifraterska, Muranowska, Leszno, Nowolipie and Nowolipki Streets. There was also fighting on Okopowa Street and Dzika Street. A post-war account states that German air attacks continued on this day. Jewish resistance fighters appear to have borrowed the German tactic of using fire. Several rebel groups destroyed the large Pfeiffer & Weigl tannery, several Army storehouses filled with woolen goods and the German military cannery. The defenders also began to send out raiding parties of their own. The rebels formed small groups of up to ten fighters, dressed them in captured German uniforms and helmets, and sent them to attack the flanks and rear of enemy patrols. News reached the Ghetto on this day that the Nazis had executed all four members of the *Judenrat* presidium who had been taken hostage at the start of the Ghetto Uprising.[48] German attacks went on through the night, not ending until 0145 hours. *SS-Unterscharführer* Fritz Vogel and *SS-Reiter* Johann Haller, SS Cavalry Replacement Detachment and *Wachmann* Emil Schmidt, Trawniki camp, were wounded in action. Stroop submitted one report for the day.[49]

Stroop Report, 24 April 1943

> Contrary to the proceeding days, I ordered the 24 search parties not to start at one end of the Ghetto, but to proceed from all sides at the same time. Apparently the Jews still staying in the Ghetto were deceived by the fact that operations did not start until 1000 hours and believed that the action had finally been terminated yesterday. Therefore, the search action had especially satisfactory results today. Our success is furthermore due to the fact that the officers and men have become accustomed to the cunning fighting techniques and tricks used by the Jews and bandits, and that they acquired great skill in tracking down the bunkers which are found in such great numbers. After the raiding parties returned, we set about to clear a certain block of buildings situated in the northeastern part of the former Ghetto. In this labyrinth of a building there existed a so-called armaments firm in which supposedly were stored raw materials and goods worth millions. I had notified the *Wehrmacht* administration of my intentions on 23 April 1943 at about 2100 hours and had requested them to have their goods evacuated by 1200 hours today. Since they did not start this evacuation until 1000 hours today, I felt obliged to extend the term until 1800 hours. At 1815 hours a search party entered the premises, which had been cordoned off, and found a great number of Jews within the building. Since some of these Jews resisted, I ordered the building to be set on fire. Not until all the buildings along the street and the back premises were well aflame did the Jews emerge from the structures and attempt to save their lives by jumping from windows and balconies to the street. They threw down beds, blankets and the like. Over and over again we discovered that the Jews and bandits returned into the flames rather than to risk being caught by us. Over and over the Jews kept up their firing almost to the end of the action. Thus, the engineers had to be protected by a machine-gun when they had to forcibly enter a concrete building tonight, which had been strongly fortified. Termination of today's operation occurred at 0145 hours, 25 April 1943.
>
> For decamping 1,660 Jews were caught. Some 1,814 Jews were pulled out of bunkers of which 330 were shot dead. Innumerable Jews were destroyed by the flames or perished by the bunkers being blown up. Twenty-six bunkers were blown up and an amount of paper money, among it many dollars, was captured. We have not counted the amount. Our strength today was the same as yesterday minus fifty *Waffen-SS* troops.
>
> **Losses:**
>
> 2 SS men and 1 Trawniki man

Altogether we have now caught 25,500 Jews, who formerly resided in the Ghetto, in this action. Since there are only quite vague estimates available concerning the actual number of inhabitants, I believe there are only a very few number of Jews and bandits still remaining in the Ghetto. The operation will be continued at 1300 hours on 25 April. I beg to acknowledge receipt of the teleprint letters of 24 April 1995. As far as can be predicted we will continue the present large-scale action until Easter Monday.

We have fixed large posters to the walls surrounding the Ghetto which state that anyone who enters the former Ghetto without being able to prove his identity will be shot.

• • •

Sunday, 25 April 1943

The seventh day of Jewish resistance continued on this Easter Sunday. Stroop started relatively late, perhaps to give the men an opportunity to attend a religious service, at least in the case of the Army troops. Stroop formed seven search/assault parties, each with seventy men, or about two platoons worth of troops per group. Some of the bitterest fighting in the day would occur at 5 and 7 Mila Street amidst the burning houses.[50] *SS-Panzergrenadier* Siegfried Böckmann (gunshot wound, left upper ankle), 1st Company, 3rd SS Panzergrenadier Training and Replacement Battalion, *SS-Rottenführer* Fritz Krenzke (gunshot wound, left foot), SS Cavalry Replacement Detachment, *SS-Scharführer* Hugo Nieratschker, *Sicherheitspolizei* and *Wachmann* Jurko Kosatschok Trawniki camp were wounded in action. The Stroop Report designation of "T II" refers to the Treblinka extermination camp.[51]

Stroop Report, 25 April 1943

The operation started at 1300 hours on 25 April 1943. For today seven search parties were formed with one officer and seventy troops in each. Each party was allotted to a certain block of buildings. Their order was, "Every building is to be combed out once more; bunkers have to be discovered to be blown up, and the Jews are to be caught. If any resistance is encountered or if bunkers cannot otherwise be reached, the buildings are to be burned down." Apart from the operations undertaken by these seven search parties, a special operation was undertaken against a center of bandits situated outside the wall surrounding the former Ghetto, and inhabited exclusively by Poles.

Today's operations of the search parties ended almost everywhere so that enormous conflagrations were started and that the Jews were forced in this manner to leave their hide-outs and refuges. Altogether 1,960 Jews were caught alive. The Jews informed us that among them are parachutists who were dropped, and bandits who had been equipped with arms by some unknown people. 274 Jews were shot. There were uncounted Jews as in the preceding days who were buried in blown up bunkers and burned in the flames, as can be observed time and again. By catching this bag of Jews today, we have caught a very considerable part of the bandits and the lowest elements of the Ghetto. Intervening darkness prevented us to carry out the liquidation at once. I am going to try and obtain a train tomorrow for T II; if not, I shall carry out the liquidation tomorrow. Today we also encountered some armed resistance. We captured five pistols and some explosives in a bunker. Furthermore, we seized considerable amounts of paper money, foreign currency, gold coins and valuables. Even now the Jews still dispose of considerable property. While last night one could see a glare of fires above the former Ghetto, tonight it is a giant sea of flames. Since we continue to discover great numbers of Jews whenever we search and clear, the operation will be continued on 26 April 1943 at 1000 hours.

Including today, 27,464 Jews formerly of the Ghetto have been caught.

Our total losses to date:

Waffen-SS	27 wounded
Police	9 wounded
Security Police	4 wounded
Army	1 wounded
Trawniki men	9 wounded
	50 wounded

and five dead, of whom:

Waffen-SS	2 dead
Army	2 dead
Trawniki men	1 dead
	5 dead

We do not know what the Germans made of the report of parachutists. If there were indeed such agents, they were most likely dropped by single Soviet aircraft flying deep behind the German frontlines.

• • •

Monday, 26 April 1943

The eighth day saw the Germans continue the tactic of burning out the resistance. The day also saw the last communiqué of the ZOB from the Ghetto. In it, the defenders mentioned tank and air attacks.[52] While the action this day appears to have been somewhat less intense, a previously unknown ammunition dump exploded when its surrounding building burned down. Stroop was unable to obtain a train to take deportees to Treblinka; the Germans either were forced to keep these thousands of people under guard or to conduct summary executions, which they did near the Pawiak Prison and at the *Judenrat*. *SS-Rottenführer* Joseph Schuster, SS Cavalry Replacement Detachment, was wounded. Stroop submitted two reports for the day:[53]

Stroop Report, 26 April 1943, Morning

> The operation on 25 April 1943 was terminated at 2200 hours. The Poles residing in Warsaw are much impressed by the toughness of our operations in the former Ghetto. As can be seen from the daily reports, the general situation is much calmer since we began the action, apart from smaller incidents, especially within the city area of Warsaw. From this fact one might conclude that up to now the bandits and saboteurs have resided in the former Ghetto, and that now all of them have been destroyed. In this connection it may be of some interest that an illegal ammunition store was seen to explode when we burned down a certain building on which we worked.

Stroop Report, 26 April, Evening

> The whole of the former Ghetto was combed through today once more by the same search parties, each of which were allotted to the same areas as before. In this way I tried to bring about that the leaders would be familiar with the thoroughfares, blocks of buildings, and backyards and thus be able to penetrate deeper and deeper into the maze of bunkers and subterranean passages. Almost every search party reported that they encountered resistance, but have broken it by firing back or by blowing up the bunkers. It becomes clearer and clearer that we are now encountering the toughest and strongest of the Jews and bandits. Several times bunkers have been destroyed and the inmates did not come to the surface of the earth during the whole of the operation. In some cases the inmates were hardly in a condition to crawl out to the surface. Captured Jews report that many of the inmates of the bunkers had become insane owing to the heat, smoke and explosions. Several Jews were arrested who had maintained close liaison with a group of Polish terrorists. Outside the former Ghetto we arrested 29 Jews.
>
> During today's operation several blocks of buildings were burned down. This is the only method, which finally forces this trash and bundle of sub-humanity to come out into the open. We again captured arms, incendiary bottles, high explosive bombs and considerable amounts of cash and foreign currency.
>
> Today I also determined that several so-called armaments enterprises will evacuate their stores from the buildings at once, so that I can comb out these buildings in which the Jews have now taken refuge. In one case we again discovered that a building which had been said to contain a giant enterprise, in fact had almost no stores or goods. One enterprise was closed without further ado and its Jews decamped. As a result of today's operation 30 Jews were decamped, 1,330 Jews were pulled out of bunkers and immediately shot and 362 Jews were killed during the fighting. Altogether we caught 1,722 Jews today. This brings the total of Jews caught to 29,186. Moreover it is very probable that numerous Jews have perished in the thirteen bunkers blown up today and in the conflagrations. At the time of writing not one of the Jews caught still remains within Warsaw. The scheduled transport to T II had no success.
>
> Our strength is the same as yesterday. We had no friendly losses. The end of today's operation occurred at 2145 hours. It will be continued on 27 April 1943 at 0900 hours.

Stroop provided an insight after the war on the fighting on 26 April. He commented:[54]

> You may be right . . . in comparing the *Grossaktion* [great operation] to a hunt. My soldiers tracked the enemy until they caught the scent. Then they went after the nooks and crannies of the Ghetto until they'd sniffed out and killed the sub-humans hiding there . . . No Jew voluntarily left his bunker that day, so every strong point and hideaway had to be stormed. We were forced to dynamite the entrance to cellars and passageways and sometimes even the ground floors and porches . . . Fighting continued in the seven sectors under the attack by our assault units. More and more houses were set ablaze. Thick smoke billowed over the Ghetto, darkened the sky. Flames shot from windows and roofs; the air was fouled with sparks, ashes, and the stench of burning. The noise was unbearable – commands, screams, curses, exploding grenades.

Stroop had to fight *SS-Gruppenführer* Odilo Globocnik, the SS and Police Leader of Lublin, that day as well. Globocnik arrived in Warsaw about 1400 hours to attempt to persuade Stroop not to destroy the industrial shops of the Productive Ghetto. Globocnik may have brought as many as thirty of his officers and men with him to intimidate those who would interfere with his economic enterprises. Stroop seemed to acquiesce; however once Globocnik had departed, Stroop called Krüger – a long-time adversary of Globocnik – who ordered Stroop to ignore the "war profiteer" and keep to the original schedule of destroying the Ghetto. Stroop did, and the factories burned.[55]

• • •

Tuesday, 27 April 1943

The ninth day of the fighting saw combat on Leszno, Nowolipie, Nowolipki, and Niska Streets and also on Muranowski Square as the SS broke into more bunkers. A post-war account of the fighting reveals that the Germans introduced a new tactic of flooding selected bunkers to drown or drive out the inhabitants. The source states that this technique was used on a bunker at 74 Leszno Street this day.[56] While it is not mentioned in the report, it is entirely possible that the attackers used this method.

SS-Panzergrenadier Friedrich Czwielung and *SS-Sturmmann* Hans Petry, both of the 5th Company, 3rd SS Panzergrenadier Training and Replacement Battalion and *Wachmann* Wladimir Stasik, Trawniki camp, were wounded in action. Stroop submitted one report for the day:[57]

Stroop Report, 27 April 1943

For today's operation I had formed twenty-four raiding parties with the same tasking on several days of last week. They had to search the former Ghetto in smaller groups. These search parties pulled 780 Jews out of bunkers and shot 115 Jews who resisted. This operation was to terminate about 1500 hours; some of the parties had to work longer because they found some more bunkers at that time.

At 1600 hours a special battle group, 320 officers and men strong, started cleaning a large block of buildings situated on both sides of the so-called Niska Street in the northeastern part of the former Ghetto. After the search, the entire block was set on fire, having first been completely cordoned off. In this action a considerable number of Jews were caught. As before, they remained up to the last moment in the bunkers, which were either below ground or in the lofts of the buildings. They fired their arms up to the last moment and then jumped down into the street – sometimes from as far up as the fourth floor – having previously thrown down beds, mattresses, etc., but not until the flames made any escape impossible.

Altogether 2,560 Jews were caught today within the former Ghetto, of whom 547 were shot. Moreover an unknown number of Jews perished when their bunkers were destroyed or who died in the flames. The sum total of Jews who formerly resided in the Ghetto and who have been caught in this action now amounts to 31,746.

We learned from an anonymous communication that a considerable number of Jews were staying in a block of buildings which adjoins the northeastern part of the Ghetto, but is in itself outside of it. A special raiding party under the command of 1st Lieutenant of Order Police Diehl, was dispatched for an attack against these buildings. The raiding party discovered a gang of about 120 men, strongly armed with pistols, rifles, hand-grenades and one machine-gun, who resisted. They succeeded in destroying 24 bandits in battle and arrested 52 bandits. The remainder could not be caught or destroyed since darkness intervened. The buildings, however, were surrounded at once so that escape will hardly be possible. This cleansing action will be continued tomorrow. Moreover we arrested 17 Poles, including 2 Polish policemen, as they should have been aware of the existence of this gang. In this operation we captured three rifles, twelve pistols, one-hundred Polish Mills bombs, twenty-seven German steel helmets, quite a number of German uniform tunics and coats – some even with the East Front ribbon attached, reserve magazines for machine-guns and three-hundred rounds of ammunition. The leader of the raiding party had a difficult task because the bandits were disguised in German uniforms. But despite this fact, he did his duty with great efficiency. Among the dead terrorists we identified with certainty some Polish terrorists. Today we succeeded in discovering and liquidating one of the founders and leaders of the Jewish-Polish resistance movement. The external appearance of the Jews whom we are catching now shows that it is now the turn of those Jews who were the leaders of the entire resistance movement. They jumped from the burning windows and balconies cursing Germany, the *Führer* and German soldiers. The SS men who had descended into the sewers discovered that a great number of corpses of perished Jews had been washed away by the water.

Our own strength from 0700 to 1900 hours (cordoning forces):

288 German Police
200 Trawniki men
140 Polish Police

Our own strength from 1900 to 0700 hours (cordoning forces)
288 German Police
250 *Waffen-SS*
140 Polish Police

Our strength in the operation (clearing forces)

German Police	3 officers	115 troops
Waffen-SS	4 officers	400 troops
Technical Emergency Corps	1 officer	6 troops
Security Police	2 officers	30 troops
Army Engineers	2 officers	21 troops

Our own losses were 3 wounded of whom 2 were *Waffen-SS* and 1 Trawniki man. The operation terminated at 2300 hours. It will be continued on 28 April 1943 at 1000 hours.

Stroop added information after the war on the day's fight that cuts to his state of mind:[58]

We were moving in slowly now, behind the line of flame. We shot anything that budged, including 'parachutists' [Jews who jumped from burning buildings]. Some sub-humans gave up and surrendered; others fought to the last, cursing and insulting us or singing the Polish anthem or some of those psalms of theirs. As we advanced, special units staffed with engineers began to sniff out and destroy bunkers in areas, which had cooled down sufficiently. Most of the holed-up Jews resisted, necessitated the use of smoke bombs and flame-throwers. Once we'd pulled that scum out of the bunkers, we divided them into groups, liquidating those who resisted or were insolent . . .

• • •

Wednesday, 28 April 1943

The tenth day of the battle witnessed an attack by resistance forces against the Ghetto wall along Sapiezynska Street. A postwar source indicates that there was fighting at bunkers on 76 and 78 Leszno Street. The same source also indicated that the *Luftwaffe* bombed the Ghetto on the night of 28-29 April, but there is no mention of this in Stroop's accounts.[59] *SS-Panzergrenadier* Walter Schmidt, 1st Company, 3rd SS Panzergrenadier Training and Replacement Battalion, *SS-Reiter* Ludwig Török, *SS-Reiter* Alexander Wiesinger, *SS-Reiter* Johann Lebisch (shrapnel to right knee; leg later amputated), all three from the SS Cavalry Replacement Detachment were wounded in action. Stroop submitted one report to *SS-Obergruppenführer* Krüger for the day.[60]

Stroop Report, 28 April 1943

The operation began at 1000 hours. Today I formed ten raiding parties for combing-out the whole of the Ghetto. These raiding parties again discovered, proceeding step by step, a number of bunkers, which were found to have been prepared as long ago as the middle of last year for use in the resistance action of the Jews. Altogether 335 Jews were forcibly pulled out from these bunkers. Apart from these operations, we continued to cleanse the resistance center used by the Jewish military organization, situated at the borders of the Ghetto. We succeeded in shooting 10 more bandits and in arresting 9, beyond those caught yesterday, and in capturing more arms, ammunition and military equipment.

In the afternoon a battle group again was directed against a block of buildings which had already been combed out, and the block was set on fire during the operation. As on previous days, masses of Jews could be seen emerging, forced out by the flames and the enormous clouds of smoke. Somewhere else an engineer officer, attached by the *Wehrmacht* to the units, opened a bunker with great difficulty situated about three meters below ground. From this bunker, which had been prepared last October and was equipped with running water, a lavatory and electric lighting, we pulled out 274 of the richest and most influential Jews. Again today we encountered very strong resistance in many places and broke it. It becomes clearer every day that we now encounter the real terrorists and activists, because the action takes longer than expected.

Today's results: 1,655 Jews caught for de-camping, of whom 110 were shot in battle. The flames killed many more Jews, moreover there were Jews in an unascertainable number destroyed in the bunkers when they were blown up. With today's result the number of Jews caught rises to 33,401. Not included in this number are Jews who were killed by fire or destroyed in the bunkers.

Our own strength is the same as yesterday. Our own losses were three wounded (one Police and two *Waffen-SS* men.) The operation terminated at 2200 hours. It will be continued on 29 April 1943 at 1000 hours.

Stroop's post-war recollections further define the characteristics of one of the bunkers captured during the day:[61]

On April twenty-eighth, after days of effort, we opened the most superb Jewish installation I've ever seen, even finer than the hideaway we'd stormed back at Rogatin. It was a two-story building, all underground, equipped with a modern ventilation system, three sources of electricity, kitchens, toilets, showers, access to the city water supply, and its own artesian well. There were fuel and water reserves, a cold storage room, and a spacious larder. The place was amazingly well laid out, with several exits through long corridors and armored doors between each room. We stumbled on it one night with the help of police dogs and sound detectors. Our acoustical equipment was almost useless during the day because of the terrible racket, but at night, in the relative calm, we could sometimes pick up the sounds of voices and hum of electric motors inside the bunkers. Our dogs were a big help, because when the wind died down in the evening, they could smell the cooking odors.

• • •

Thursday, 29 April 1943

The eleventh day of the operation centered on clearing a large block of buildings in the Productive Ghetto and attacking sewer entrances. Stroop reported no German losses for the day, while German troops claimed to have killed 106 Jews in combat and to have captured 2,359 more. *SS-Schütze* Johann Nissner, SS Cavalry Replacement Detachment, was wounded. Stroop submitted one report for the day:[62]

Stroop Report, 29 April 1943

Progress of the large action on 29 April 1943 which started at 1000 hours: As on the previous day, I formed some search parties who at this time had the special task to search those blocks of buildings which had recently been separated. A larger raiding party was directed to clean a certain block of buildings (the former enterprise of the Hallmann firm) and to burn down this block. Altogether thirty-six more bunkers used for habitation were discovered and from them and other hideouts in the burning buildings we pulled out 2,359 Jews of whom 106 were killed in battle. We captured two rifles, ten pistols, ten kilograms of explosives and ammunition of various types. When a large bunker was blown up, the entire building collapsed and all of the bandits within perished. In the ensuing conflagration, loud detonations and darting flames were observed which proved that the building must have contained large stores of ammunition and explosives. Some sewer entrances were also blown up. Two exits were discovered outside the Ghetto and were made unusable by blowing them up or by walling them up.

The depositions of some of the inmates of the bunkers are to the effect that these Jews were unable to leave the bunkers for the last ten days and that they now began to lack food, etc., because the operation has lasted so long. Furthermore, the Jews testify that Jewish and Polish bandits appeared at night, wearing black masks, who walled the bunkers up from the outside and admonished them not to give any signs of life, so that they could continue to live in the Ghetto when the action was finished. Some of the armaments factories have been evacuated in a very slow manner. In some cases one gains the impression that this is done intentionally. Thus I had to discover with regard to the firm of Schulz & Company which I had visited on Easter Monday and then requested to start evacuation at once and to have it completed within three days, that even today they had not even started.

Our own strength is the same as yesterday. We had no losses. The operation terminated at 2100 hours. It will be continued on 30 April 1943 at 0900 hours. Through today we have caught 35,760 Jews.

• • •

Friday, 30 April 1943

The twelfth day of fighting saw Stroop once again commit his large artillery piece to the fight as the Nazis destroyed some thirty bunkers. The gun would have been used against resistance fighters above ground as they continued to occupy not only intact buildings, but also as they appeared to have moved into partially destroyed ones. Stroop submitted one report for the day:[63]

Stroop Report, 30 April 1943

The action started at 0900 hours. The combing out by search parties was continued. Although some giant blocks of buildings are now completely burned down, the Jews continue to stay in the bunkers which are two to three meters below ground. In many cases we are not able to discover those bunkers unless some Jew, whom we have already caught, gives us a hint as to its whereabouts. Repeatedly Jews testified during the last days that some armed Jews emerged at night from some hideouts or bunkers and threatened the other Jews with shooting if they give any signs of life. We were able to ascertain beyond all doubt that several bunkers had been locked from the outside by these bandits who tried in this manner to prove that they meant business. Altogether thirty bunkers were discovered today, evacuated and blown up. Again we caught a great number of bandits and sub-humans. Apart from the bombing out operations, which were executed by rather small parties, two larger battle groups were occupied with bombing and burning several interconnected blocks of buildings.

Altogether 1,599 Jews were caught today, of whom 179 were killed in battle. The sum total of Jews caught to date thereby rises to 37,359. Loaded today were 3,855 Jews. The number of Jews in possession of arms was much higher than before among the Jews who were caught during the last days. Thus we captured today German arms and military equipment from them. The operation against Fort Traugutta, which was also ordered for today, did not bring any result. Inasmuch as we were able to discover subterranean exits, we either occupied them or blew them up. In order to overwhelm one of the blocks we had to use a gun.

Forces used in the operation

Police	5 officers	133 troops
Security Police	3 officers	36 troops
Waffen-SS	6 officers	432 troops
Engineers	2 officers	40 troops
Staff	3 officers	7 troops

Forces used for cordoning off the Ghetto

Waffen-SS	3 officers	318 troops
German Police	2 officers	89 troops
Trawniki men		200 troops

Our own losses: 1 wounded in action (Police)

The operation terminated for the day at 2100 hours. It will be resumed on 1 May 1943 at 0900 hours.

• • •

Saturday, 1 May 1943

The thirteenth day of the Ghetto Uprising centered on fighting at a large bunker at 30 Franciszkanska Street, and also on Nalewki, Leszno and Nowolipie Streets. *Rottwachtmeister der Schutzpolizei* Hans Bolze, 3rd Battalion, 22nd SS Police Regiment and *SS-Rottenführer* Edmund Lotholz, *Sicherheitspolizei*, were killed in action. *SS-Brigadeführer* Stroop transmitted one report for the day:[64]

Stroop Report, 1 May 1943

The operation started at 0900 hours. Ten search parties were given their orders, moreover a larger battle group was directed to comb out a certain block of buildings with the added instruction to burn down that block. Within this block of buildings there existed a so-called armaments factory which had not yet been entirely evacuated, although it had enough time to do so. It was not exempted from the operation. During today's operation we caught 1,026 Jews of whom 245 were killed either in the battle or because they had resisted. Moreover, there were among them considerable numbers of typical bandits and ringleaders. In one case a Jew who had already been made ready for transport fired three shots against a 1st Lieutenant of Police but missed his mark. All the Jews caught today were forcibly pulled out of bunkers. Not a single one gave up voluntarily after his bunker had been opened. A considerable number were pulled out of the sewers. We continued to systematically blow up or block the sewer entrances. In one case the engineers laid a strong charge and had to proceed to an adjoining entrance for protection. In the meantime a Jew emerged from the sewer and removed the fuse from the charge. In the further course of this operation we succeeded in catching this Jew who was still in possession of the fuse.

In order to ascertain the movements of the Jews during the night, I used today for the first time five scouting parties, each of one officer and nine troops who went to work at night at irregular intervals. Altogether it has to be stated that our men need extraordinary diligence and energy to discover the Jews who are still in so-called bunkers, caves and in the sewer system. It can be expected that it is the remainder of the Jews who formerly inhabited the Ghetto whom we are now catching. The sum total of Jews caught so far has risen to 38,385. Not included in this number are those who died in the flames or in the dugouts. One raiding party discovered that in the main sewer below the Ghetto there are an unascertainable number of corpses.

Since the start of the operation, outside the Ghetto within suburban Warsaw the Country Police shot 150 Jews who had escaped from the Ghetto. Again we captured pistols and explosives.

Forces used in the operation

Police	4 officers	102 troops
Security Police	2 officers	1 troop
Waffen-SS	7 officers	350 troops
Engineers	2 officers	38 troops

Technical		
Emergency Corps	1 officer	6 troops
Security Police	2 officers	1 troop

Forces used for cordoning off the Ghetto

Waffen-SS		300 troops
German Police	1 officer	71 troops
Trawniki men		250 troops

Our own losses: 1 Policeman wounded yesterday died of wounds.
Today's action terminated at 2200 hours. It will be continued 2 May 1943 at 1000 hours.

• • •

Sunday, 2 May 1943
The fourteenth day of the battle was a busy one. The fighting at the large bunker at 30 Franciszkanska Street continued. Additionally, there was fierce fighting at the Transavia factory on Stawki Street. Combat also took place at Szczesliwa and Leszno Streets. *SS-Panzergrenadier* Werner Burchardt, 1st Company, 3rd SS Panzergrenadier Training and Replacement Battalion, and *Oberwachtmeister der Schutzpolizei* Robert Linke, 3rd Battalion, 22nd SS Police Regiment, were wounded in action. Stroop submitted one report for the day but it was redundant as *SS-Obergruppenführer* Krüger personally visited Warsaw and the Ghetto, so he could see for himself how the operation was progressing:[65]

Stroop Report, 2 May 1943

The operation started at 1000 hours. Nine raiding parties combed out the whole area of the former Ghetto; moreover a larger detachment was directed toward cleansing one block of buildings which contained the two armament enterprises Transavia and Wischniewski. The raiding parties took along with them some Jews who had been caught on the previous day and who now had to show the way to more bunkers. In these operations the raiding parties extracted 944 Jews from the bunkers. During these occasions 235 Jews were shot. When the block of buildings mentioned above was destroyed 120 Jews were caught and numerous Jews were destroyed when they jumped from the attics upon the inner courtyards, trying to escape the flames. Many more Jews perished in the flames or were destroyed when the bunkers and sewer entrances were blown up. Two armaments enterprises were deprived of their Jews and their managers were requested to evacuate within a short time. Altogether we caught 1,852 Jews today. The sum total of Jews caught thereby rises to 40,237. Twenty-seven bunkers were discovered, forcibly opened and destroyed with arms and ammunition captured. When the external barricade was attacked by shooting and by an attack made by some Jews who broke out from a sewer entrance outside the Ghetto, we suffered seven losses of whom four were German Police and three were Polish Police. The scouting parties who had been used during the night encountered armed resistance by some Jews who had, under the protection of darkness, ventured to emerge from their holes and bunkers. We did not suffer losses thereby. On the other hand, a considerable number of Jews were killed or wounded in this operation.

Forces used in the operation

German Police	3 officers	98 troops
Technical		
Emergency Corps	1 officer	6 troops
Sipo	3 officers	12 troops
Engineers	2 officers	37 troops
SS Grenadiers	11 officers	409 troops
SS Cavalry	3 officers	7 troops

Cordoning off forces

German Police	2 officers	9 troops
SS Grenadiers	1 officer	300 troops
Trawniki men		200 troops

Our own losses were 4 Policemen wounded and 3 Polish policemen wounded. Present at today's large action was the Higher SS and Police Leader East, *SS-Obergruppenführer* Krüger. The operation terminated at 2030 hours. It will be continued on 3 May 1943 at 0900 hours.

Jürgen Stroop commented after the war on the visit of *SS-Obergruppenführer* Krüger to the city:[66]

On 2 May 1943, *Höhrer SS und Polizeiführer Ost*, *SS-Obergruppenführer* and General of the Police Friedrich Wilhelm Krüger arrived in Warsaw. An expert in racial matters, he attached great importance to the liquidation of all the Jews in the General Government. That's why we were in constant contact and why he finally decided to check out the Grand Operation firsthand. Krüger was absolutely fearless. He had no qualms about walking through the Ghetto in the full regalia of an *SS-Gruppenführer* . . . He accompanied me to the very front line, observing and questioning. By the time his inspection was done, he'd given me a number of instructions and some excellent advice . . . It was obvious to me during Krüger's visit that he was concerned about the *Grossaktion* dragging on . . . The *SS-Obergruppenführer's* visit greatly improved the morale of my soldiers and staff.

• • •

Monday, 3 May 1943

The fifteenth day finally saw the end of the bunker fight at 30 Franciszkanska Street. *SS-Obergruppenführer* Krüger departed the city, apparently satisfied at what he saw. It appears as though *SS-Panzergrenadier* Heinrich Meier, 5th Company, 3rd SS Panzergrenadier Training and Replacement Battalion and *SS-Schütze* Rudolf Hörnicke and *SS-Schütze* Hermann Herbst, SS Cavalry Replacement Detachment, were wounded in action. Stroop submitted one report that evening summarizing the fighting for the day:[67]

Stroop Report, 3 May 1943

The operation started at 0900 hours. In the combing out operation of the former Jewish Ghetto we discovered 19 more bunkers today. We pulled 1,392 Jews out of the bunkers, shot 95 dead and decamped 177 from the former armaments enterprises. The sum total of Jews caught thereby rises to 41,806. In most cases the Jews offered armed resistance before they left the bunkers. We had two men wounded. Some of the Jews and bandits fired pistols from both hands. Since we discovered today that on several occasions Jewesses had concealed pistols in their bloomers, every Jew and bandit will from now on be ordered to strip completely and be searched. Captured among other things were one German rifle (Model 98), two pistols (Model 08) and also some homemade hand grenades. The Jews cannot be induced to leave their bunkers until several smoke candles have been burned. According to depositions made yesterday and today, the Jews were asked during the second half of 1942 to erect air raid shelters. They then started under the cover of erecting these shelters to build bunkers, which they now inhabit, in order to use them during an anti-Jewish action. Some of the scout parties were shot at during the night. One man was wounded. These scouting parties reported that groups of armed bandits marched through the Ghetto. Our own strength was the same as yesterday. Three SS men were wounded. The operation today terminated at 2100 hours. It will be continued on 4 May 1943 at 0900 hours. Today 3,019 Jews were loaded.

We have an additional German report for this day that was transmitted from the main Propaganda Department (*Hauptabteilung Propaganda*) of the General Government Administration. The author, Wilhelm Ohlenbusch, was in charge of all propaganda in Frank's empire and it is likely that Frank saw the series of reports as did Josef Goebbels, the Propaganda Minister for the *Reich*. Ohlenbusch assumed his position on 1 February 1941; prior to that date he had been the head of the Warsaw District Propaganda Department, so he was familiar with Warsaw and its environs. While it appears that Ohlenbusch sent several telegrams during the Ghetto Uprising to Berlin, only one survives intact to analyze – that for 3 May 1943. Ohlenbusch records his observations in that report as follows:[68]

According to the reports submitted by the SS and Police Leader in the Warsaw District, it has been established as follows:

By now it has been possible to subdue the entire Jewish quarter in Warsaw to the point where it is now a matter of undertaking separate moves and systematically putting in shock-troops to comb out the still remaining nests of resistance. The bunker fighting which characterized the earlier encounters can be considered ended. All the same, from time to time the Jews still succeed in gaining a foothold anew at separate points. It turns out, moreover, that shelters, bunkers and underground passages to the Aryan residential quarters etc. have existed since as long ago as the middle of last year and have been constantly extended.

While against house-blocks in which large masses [of people] sought to offer resistance, flame-throwers and heavy infantry weapons have so far been able to break this resistance, still the defense by the last combat groups is extraordinarily tough. It has been repeatedly confirmed that bandits breaking out of the burning houses and smoke-filled bunkers go back into the flames when they realize that a breakthrough is not possible. Others who have fled before the flames to the top stories, keeping on shooting the whole time, finally jump out of the windows or let themselves down on ropes and bed-clothes. All this is a clear expression of the fact that with these groups of remnants we are dealing with the organizers of the elite body of bandits and Jews, who have completely eluded our grasp up to now. The combats with these groups are being brought to a close by hard-fought separate engagements. Whether or not bandit groups are hiding in bunkers, sewers and underground passages cannot be ascertained. In some cases it was found that even smoke candles, flame-throwers and flooding the sewers did not make it possible to reach the hidden recesses. It may be taken as proven that with the bandits, terrorists and Jews in the Warsaw Ghetto we are dealing with a body carrying out a planned operation. It is now equally beyond question that if this operation had not been challenged at this present moment in the Ghetto, it would finally have been directed against the city of Warsaw.

As for the process of the conduct of the combats in detail, it should be said that it is very difficult to get the upper hand against fortified positions. The link-up of the house blocks with each other through the cellars and the attics makes any effective onslaught on the rebels liable to misfire from the outset. Only after about six days of fighting when the Ghetto was cleared of the main masses of the Jews was it possible to get to grips with the innumerable nests of resistance, which extended even as far as inside some of the armament factories. There ensued some twenty-five shock troop attempts daily, mostly on a largish scale. At the same time, demolition teams, placed under the direction of a sapper officer, were able to locate and blow up whole series of extremely well fortified bunkers, often with every comfort installed.

The successful progress made, especially in the last few days, is to be attributed to the circumstances that the German units have in the meantime grown accustomed to the combat methods of the Jews. In the operations against the Jewish quarter in Warsaw the following units took part: the SS Panzergrenadier Replacement Battalion, with 6 officers and 400 men, the SS Cavalry Replacement Detachment, with 10 officers and 450 men, the Order Police Force, with 6 officers and 151 men, the SD, with 2 officers and 48 men and the Trawniki men, with 1 officer and 150 men. There were additionally tanks, flame-throwers and field guns. On the Jewish side, the main weapons reported were modern small arms, petrol bottles and Molotov cocktails. On 28 April 1943, 50 of the SS troops involved and 150 of the Trawniki men could be detached for guard duties outside the Ghetto. Losses on the German side amount to 5 dead: 2 Army, 2 *Waffen-SS* and 1 Trawniki man. There are 50 wounded as well: 27 *Waffen-SS*, 9 Order Police, 4 SD, 1 Army and 9 Trawniki.

In the fighting there were captured from among the bandit groups: 158, 880, 35, 203, 30, 29 (seized outside the Ghetto), 1,330 (seized after all factories were cleared), 362, 10 and 110 – a total of 2,347 men. To this must be added numberless persons buried as well as an indeterminate number of those burnt in 13 large bunkers blown up, out of about 30 that were located. All in all, 33,500 Jews were rounded up and – if not liquidated as bandits – brought to the encampment near a transport railway station. The Jews from the armament works and factories, as well as those who were not considered bandits, were sent by railway to Poniatówa. Among the Poles the opinion being heard is, 'The fighting in the Ghetto has lasted longer than the Polish campaign.'

After the war in his jail cell, Stroop voiced his concern about concealed weapons on prisoners:[69]

> I'd been receiving disquieting reports from my intelligence officers of captured fighters who cunningly concealed arms to be used on guards or during interrogations. I therefore ordered, that Monday, that all prisoners taken were to be stripped naked next to a wall manned by armed guards. The naked figures then ran fifty meters to the left, hands over head, where other armed guards took over. After a careful search of their clothing, they'd be allowed to run back . . . or maybe they wouldn't [because they were executed]. Those who returned were packed into railway carriages.

• • •

Tuesday, 4 May 1943

The sixteenth day clearly was one of reduced activity in the Warsaw Ghetto. By this point, the Nazis appeared to have discovered most of the bunkers. Those remaining were so well camouflaged that the Germans could only find there locations by using information gleaned from interrogations. Stroop stated that this information came from Jews who had turned traitor. While this may have been the case, it is equally possible that the Nazis beat the information out of captured fighters or gleaned it by other forms of interrogation. Stroop submitted one report covering the day's fighting:[70]

Stroop Report, 4 May 1943

> The action started at 0900 hours. For mopping up the bunkers a raiding party was used, one officer and sixty troops strong and reinforced by an engineer detachment provided by the army. This raiding party pulled 550 Jews out of bunkers and shot 188 in battle. Discovering the bunkers becomes more and more difficult. Often they can only be

discovered by some outside Jews who turn traitor. If the Jews are requested to leave their bunker voluntarily, they hardly ever obey. They can only be forced out using smoke candles over and over again.

The main body of troops was directed about 1100 hours to comb out, clean and destroy two large blocks of buildings containing the former firms Többens, Schulz & Company and others. These blocks were completely cordoned off and we requested the Jews who were still within the buildings to come forward voluntarily. By this measure we caught 456 Jews for decamping. Not until the blocks of buildings were well aflame and were about to collapse did a further number of Jews emerge, forced to do so by the flames and smoke. Time and again the Jews try to escape even through burning buildings. Innumerable Jews whom we saw on the roofs during the conflagration perished in the flames. Others emerged from the upper stories at the last possible moment and were only able to escape death in the flames by jumping down. Today we caught 2,283 Jews of whom 204 were shot, innumerable Jews having been destroyed in bunkers and in the flames. The sum total of Jews caught rises to 44,089.

As can be seen from depositions made by the Jews, today we caught part of the governing body of the so-called "Party." One member of the committee, a leader of the gang, will be used tomorrow for mopping up some more fortified bunkers with armed Jews inside. When the armaments enterprises were evacuated, we again observed that the goods carted away were by no means valuable military equipment as had been pretended, but trifles like used furniture and other requisitioned chattel. We at once took appropriate measures.

The scouting parties, who patrolled during the night in the former Ghetto, again reported that Jews moved about in the burned out and destroyed streets and backyards. In order to be more able to catch the Jews by surprise, the scouting parties tie rags and other material around their boots. In skirmishes between the scouting parties and the Jews, 30 Jews were shot. We captured one carbine, three pistols and some ammunition. During the conflagration a considerable amount of stored ammunition blew up. Our own strength:

Forces used in the operation

German Police	4 officers	101 troops
Technical Emergency Corps	1 officer	6 troops
Security Police	2 officers	14 troops
Engineers	2 officers	41 troops
Waffen-SS	11 officers	401 troops

Cordoning off forces

During the Day		
German Police	2 officers	87 troops
Waffen-SS	0 officers	25 troops
Trawniki men	0 officers	200 troops
Polish Police	1 officer	180 troops
During the Night		
German Police	1 officers	11 troops
Waffen-SS	1 officers	300 troops
Polish Police	1 officer	180 troops

We had no losses. The operation terminated at 2330 hours. It will be continue on 5 May 1943 at 1000 hours.

• • •

Wednesday, 5 May 1943

The seventeenth day saw forty bunkers destroyed and 126 Jews shot. *SS-Rottenführer* Fritz Wieck, SS Cavalry Replacement Detachment, was wounded. Stroop submitted one report for the day:[71]

Stroop Report, 5 May 1943

The operation started at 1000 hours. At the beginning of today's operations the raiding parties seemed to have less results than on preceding days. When the operation terminated, however, quite a number of bunkers had again been discovered owing to the tracking ability of our men and to treachery of the Jews; 40 of these bunkers were destroyed. As far as possible, it appears that the Jews who stayed in them were caught (1,070 altogether). The raiding parties were directed to comb out some areas and shot about 126 Jews. Again today the Jews resisted in several places until they were captured. In several cases the entrances (hatches) of the bunkers were forcibly held or bolted from the inside, so that we could only force them open by using a strong explosive charge which opened the bunker but destroyed the inmates. Today again we captured arms and ammunition among them a pistol (Model 08). From one enterprise still in existence (the so-called Prosta) 2,850 Jews were evacuated for decamping. These had been included in the sum total reported earlier, so that only 1,070 have to be added: the present sum total therefore amounts to 45,159. Our own strength is the same as yesterday. We lost one SS man wounded and one Policeman wounded. The sum total of our losses to date has been eight killed and fifty-five wounded. The operation terminated at 2200 hours. It will be continued on 6 May 1943 at 0930 hours.

• • •

Thursday, 6 May 1943

The eighteenth day of the Ghetto Uprising centered on bunker fighting at Wolynska and Leszno Streets. *Oberwachtmeister der Schutzpolizei* Horst Riemer and *Wachtmeister der Schutzpolizei* Rudolf Hartmann, 1st Battalion, 22nd SS Police Regiment, were killed in action while *SS-Unterscharführer* Hans Forster (grenade shrapnel in back and arm) and *SS-Sturmmann* Heinz Haushalter, 1st Company, 3rd SS Panzergrenadier Training and Replacement Battalion, were wounded. Stroop presented one report for the day:[72]

Stroop Report, 6 May 1943

The operation started at 0930 hours. Today we combed those blocks of buildings, which we destroyed by fire on 4 May 1943. Although it could hardly be expected that any living person could still exist in these blocks of buildings, we discovered quite a number of bunkers in the midst of this burning heat. From these bunkers and from other bunkers, which we discovered in other parts of the Ghetto, we pulled out 1,553 Jews. While resisting and in an ensuing skirmish, 356 Jews were shot. In this fighting the Jews fired with Model 08 pistols and other weapons and three Polish Mills bombs. One *SS-Unterscharführer* was wounded. Altogether 47 bunkers were destroyed.

Two men from the external cordoning force were wounded as well. The Jews who had broken out of the Ghetto seem to be returning with the intention of assisting the Ghetto Jews either to help them fight or to liberate them. One Jew who had broken out from Lublin was caught just before he reached the Ghetto walls. He was armed with a Model 08 pistol, ample ammunition and two Polish Mills bombs. It could not be reliably ascertained if the so-called "Party Directorate" of the Jews (PPR) has been caught or destroyed. We are on their tracks. It is hoped that tomorrow we shall succeed in tracking down this so-called Party Directorate. In order to enable us to more effectively intercept the Jews and bandits, who approach the Ghetto, I have shifted the detachments along the external walls of the Ghetto further outside in the Aryan part of the city. The former "miniature Ghetto Prosta" was searched today by the raiding parties. We caught some Jews who had stayed behind. The firm Többens was requested to evacuate this miniature Ghetto by noon on 10 May. The so-called Library, situated outside the Ghetto, has been put at their disposal for temporary storage of raw materials, etc.

The sum total of Jews caught so far rises to 47,068. The Polish Police take pains to deliver to my office every Jew who turns up in the city, because they are eager to win such premiums as have been paid in earlier cases. The undersigned received some anonymous letters in which he was notified of the fact that some Jews are staying in the Aryan part of the city. One anonymous letter draws a parallel between Katyn and the large-scale action within the Ghetto.[73]

Forces used in the operation

German Police	4 officers	101 troops
Technical Emergency Corps	1 officer	6 troops
Security Police	2 officers	14 troops
Engineers	3 officers	72 troops
Waffen-SS	10 officers	500 troops

Cordoning off forces

During the Day

German Police	2 officers	87 troops
Waffen-SS	0 officers	25 troops
Trawniki men	0 officers	200 troops
Polish Police	1 officer	180 troops

During the Night

German Police	1 officers	11 troops
Waffen-SS	1 officers	300 troops
Polish Police	1 officer	180 troops

Our own losses were one Policeman killed, one Policeman seriously wounded and one *SS-Unterscharführer* less seriously wounded. The operation terminated at 2100 hours. It will be continued on 7 May 1943 at 0930 hours.

• • •

Friday, 7 May 1943

The nineteenth day of fighting focused on bunker fighting on Smocza Street. The Germans believed they had found the bunker that served as the headquarters of the resistance, and they made plans to attack it the next day. *SS-Unterscharführer* Hugo Mielke, SS Cavalry Replacement Detachment, was wounded in action. Stroop submitted one report for the day's actions:[74]

Stroop Report, 7 May 1943

> The action started at 1000 hours. The combing out parties today discovered 49 bunkers. We caught some of the Jews in them. A considerable but unascertainable number of Jews who refused to leave the bunkers and who offered armed resistance were destroyed when the bunkers were blown up. Altogether 1,019 Jews were caught alive today with 255 shot. The sum total of Jews caught so far rises to 48,342. We again encountered armed resistance in several cases whereby we lost one SS man wounded. We captured four pistols of various caliber and some stores of ammunition.
>
> The location of the bunker used by the so-called select "Party Directorate" is now known. It will be forced open tomorrow. The Jews testify that they emerge at night to get fresh air, since to stay permanently in the bunkers is unbearable owing to the long duration of the action. On average the raiding parties shoot some 30 to 50 Jews each night. From these statements one has to infer that a considerable number of Jews still are underground within the Ghetto. Today we blew up a concrete building, which we had been unable to destroy by fire. In this operation we noticed that to blow up houses is a very lengthy process and needs an enormous amount of explosives. The best, if not the only method for destroying the Jews, therefore is and still remains to start fires.
>
> Our strength is the same as yesterday. We lost one *Waffen-SS* man wounded. The operation terminated at 2100 hours. It will be continued on 8 May 1943 at 1000 hours.

A post-war recollection of Stroop sheds light on "bunker-busting" techniques the engineers used against surface structures:[75]

> Our engineers spent hours that day destroying a concrete building. Since it couldn't be burned, they had to blow it up. The necessary drilling of holes and insertion of explosives and detonators involved considerable material and expense. Destruction by fire was so much more practical that I ordered as much housing as possible set afire on the spot. My men were exposed to the usual unpleasant explosions and shrieks. Buildings collapsed in a shower of sparks and cinders. There were flames everywhere. As the smoke thickened, Jews again appeared on roofs and balconies. When they were eventually forced to jump, my sharpshooters got their reward.

• • •

Saturday, 8 May 1943

The twentieth day saw the last stand of Mordechai Anielewicz, the commander of the Jewish War Organization. It was probably a vicious fight based on the many German losses. *SS-Panzergrenadier* Lorenz Bichler, 2nd Company, 3rd SS Panzergrenadier Training and Replacement Battalion and *SS-Panzergrenadier* Helmut Hinz, 4th Company, 3rd SS Panzergrenadier Training and Replacement Battalion were killed in action. *SS-Unterscharführer* Erich Schulz and *SS-Panzergrenadier* Klemens Kapitza, 2nd Company, 3rd SS Panzergrenadier Training and Replacement Battalion and *Schütze* Otto Kiel, Engineer Commando Rembertow, were wounded in action. Stroop transmitted one report during the day:[76]

Stroop Report, 8 May 1943

> The operation started at 1000 hours. The whole of the area of the former Ghetto today was searched by raiding parties for remaining bunkers and Jews. As already reported some days ago, there still remain a number of sub-humans, bandits and terrorists, who continue to stay in the bunkers, although the heat inside has become intolerable due to the fires. These creatures know only too well that they have only a choice between remaining in hiding as long as possible or to ascend to the surface to try and wound or kill the men of the *Waffen-SS*, Police and Army who keep the pressure up against them.
>
> We continued the operation today against the bunker of the so-called select "Party Directorate" which we had discovered yesterday as reported in my transmittal of yesterday. We succeeded in forcing open the bunker of the Party Directorate and caught about 60 bandits some of whom were heavily armed. We succeeded in catching the Deputy Leader of the Jewish Military Organization "ZWZ" and his so-called Chief of Staff and liquidated them. About 200 Jews were housed in this bunker of who 60 were caught and 140 were destroyed partly owing to the strong effect of smoke candles and partly to the effect of heavy explosive charges that were laid in several places. The Jews whom we caught had already reported that innumerable Jews had been killed by the effect of the smoke candles. True, the fight of the first six days was hard, but now we are able to state that we are catching those Jews and Jewesses who were the ringleaders. There is no bunker forced open without Jews remaining in it to offer resistance with the arms at their disposal, one machine-gun, pistols and hand grenades. Today we caught quite a number of Jewesses who carried loaded pistols in their

bloomers, the safety device released. Some depositions speak of 3,000 to 4,000 Jews who still remain in underground holes, sewers and bunkers. The undersigned is resolved not to terminate the large action until even the last Jew has been destroyed.

Altogether 1,091 Jews were caught today in the bunkers. In battle about 280 Jews were shot and innumerable numbers of Jews were destroyed when their 45 bunkers were blown up. The total of Jews caught rises to 49,712. Those buildings, which had not yet been destroyed by fire, were set on fire today. On this occasion we discovered that some Jews were still hidden somewhere within the walls or in the staircases.

Forces used in the operation

German Police	4 officers	101 troops
Technical		
Emergency Corps	1 officer	6 troops
Security Police	2 officers	14 troops
Army Engineers	3 officers	69 troops
Waffen-SS	13 officers	527 troops

Cordoning off forces

During the Day		
German Police	1 officers	87 troops
Trawniki men	0 officers	160 troops
Polish Police	1 officer	160 troops
During the Night		
German Police	1 officers	87 troops
Waffen-SS	1 officers	300 troops
Polish Police	1 officer	160 troops

Our own losses were two *Waffen-SS* men killed, two *Waffen-SS* men wounded and one Engineer wounded. One Policeman who was wounded on 7 May died today of his wounds. We captured about fifteen to twenty pistols of various calibers, a considerable store of ammunition for the pistols and rifles and a number of hand grenades, which were homemade within the former armament factories. The action terminated at 2130 hours. It will be continued on 9 May at 1000 hours.

Many resistance survivor accounts cover this most pivotal day in the course of the Warsaw Ghetto Uprising. Stroop added his remarks after the war as well when he stated:[77]

May eighth was an important date for me. That day we opened up the Mila Street bunker. ZOB headquarters turned out to be a fairly large, well-fortified underground shelter, with several entrances, outlets to the sewers, and a network of underground passages dug by the Jews. The ZOB men defended themselves ferociously. Again my forces were hindered by lack of experience in close combat. After long, hard fighting we finally took the bunker, capturing some sixty armed insurgents. A handful of others had committed suicide.

Stroop went on in the discussion to state that the Germans could not identify any of the dead defenders.

• • •

Sunday, 9 May 1943

The twenty-first day of battle featured fighting inside and outside of the Ghetto. The Nazis destroyed forty-two bunkers and killed at least 319 resistance fighters. Stroop submitted one report for the day:[78]

Stroop Report, 9 May 1943

The operations started today at 1000 hours with the following results: the raiding parties at work today discovered 42 bunkers. From these bunkers we caught 1,037 Jews and bandits. In battle 319 bandits and Jews were shot, moreover an uncertain number of them were destroyed when the bunkers were blown up. The block of buildings which formerly contained the enterprise "Moravia" was destroyed by fire. In this operation we again caught a number of Jews, although this block had been combed through several times. Again we captured some pistols and hand grenades.

Forces used in the operation

German Police	4 officers	103 troops
Sipo	2 officers	12 troops
Army Engineers	3 officers	67 troops
Waffen-SS	13 officers	547 troops

Cordoning off forces

During the Day		
German Police	1 officers	87 troops
Trawniki men	0 officers	160 troops
Polish Police	1 officer	160 troops

During the Night		
German Police	1 officers	36 troops
Waffen-SS	1 officers	300 troops
Polish Police	1 officer	160 troops

We had no losses of our own. The total of Jews caught to date rises to 51,313. Outside the former Jewish Ghetto 254 Jews and bandits were shot. The operation terminated at 2100 hours. It will be continued on 10 May 1943 at 1000 hours.

• • •

Monday, 10 May 1943

The twenty-second day of fighting saw the final phase of the battle. *SS-Rottenführer* Willi Staab, *SS-Schütze* Gottlieb Zechmeister and *SS-Sturmmann* Wolfgang Preusse, SS Cavalry Replacement Detachment, were wounded in action. Stroop submitted one report for the day's fighting:[79]

Stroop Report, 10 May 1943

The operation commenced at 1000 hours. Today I again directed raiding parties to comb out the area of the former Ghetto. As on preceding days we again pulled from the bunkers, against all expectations, a considerable number of Jews. The resistance offered by the Jews had not weakened. On the contrary, it now seems that the members of the main body of the Jewish battle groups who are still in existence and have not been destroyed, have retired into the ruins with the intention to fight from there against our men in order to weaken our strength.

Today we caught altogether 1,183 Jews alive. 187 bandits and Jews were shot. Again an unascertainable number of Jews and bandits were destroyed in the blown up bunkers. The total of Jews caught to date has risen to 52,683. Today at 0900 hours a truck drove up to a sewer in the so-called Prosta. One passenger of the truck detonated two hand grenades, which was the signal for the bandits who were standing ready in the sewer to climb out. The bandits and Jews – among them are always some Polish bandits – armed with carbines, rifles and one machine-gun, climbed out to the truck and drove away in an unknown direction. The last man of their gang who stood sentry in the sewer, and had the duty of closing the sewer cover, was captured. It was he who gave the above information. He testified that most of the members of the gang had been divided into several battle groups and had either been killed in battle or had committed suicide because they had become aware of the futility of continuing the fight. The search for the truck, which was ordered immediately, had no result. The bandits further testified that the Prosta is now the refuge for those Jews still alive because the Ghetto has become too hot for them. This is why I have resolved to deal with the Prosta in the same manner as with the Ghetto and to destroy this miniature Ghetto.

We again captured firearms and some ammunition. The *Sipo* yesterday succeeded in tracking down a workshop outside the Ghetto, which manufactured 10,000-11,000 explosive charges and other ammunition.

Our own strength is the same as yesterday. We had three SS men wounded. Owing to the excellent understanding between us and the Army the detachment of engineers has been reinforced. Moreover they put a considerable amount of explosives at our disposal. The operation terminated at 2200 hours. It will be continued on 11 May 1943 at 0930 hours.

• • •

Tuesday, 11 May 1943

The twenty-third day of the action saw battles in the ruined buildings on Gesia Street. *SS-Brigadeführer* Stroop transmitted one report to Krüger for the day:[80] *SS-Sturmmann* Heinz Lehmann, 1st Company, 3rd SS Panzergrenadier Training and Replacement Battalion was killed in action.

Stroop Report, 11 May 1943

The operation started at 0930 hours. The scouting parties sent out last night reported that there must still be some Jews within the bunkers since some of the Jews were seen roaming through the destroyed streets. The scouting parties shot 12 Jews. Because of these reports, today I formed once again some raiding parties who in combing out operations discovered and destroyed 47 bunkers altogether. Again today some Jews were caught who had taken refuge within those ruins that were still protected by something of a roof. The Jews and bandits retired into these new refuges after remaining in the bunkers became too unbearable. One bunker was discovered that contained twelve rooms equipped with plumbing, running water and separate bathrooms for men and women. Considerable amounts of food were found and seized in order to make it more and more difficult for them to store the necessary food.

Altogether 931 Jews and bandits were caught. 53 bandits were shot. More of them perished when we blew up bunkers and when we destroyed by fire a small block of buildings. The total of Jews caught to date has risen to 53,667. We captured several pistols, hand grenades and ammunition.

We have not been able to systematically smoke out the sewer system since we are short of smoke candles. The military government area headquarters [*Oberfeldkommandantur* – OFK] is ready to provide new smoke candles.

Forces used in the operation

German Police	6 officers	126 troops
Technical Emergency		
Corps	1 officer	6 troops
Sipo	2 officers	14 troops
Army Engineers	4 officers	76 troops
Waffen-SS	12 officers	508 troops

Cordoning off forces

During the Day		
German Police	1 officers	112 troops
Trawniki men	0 officers	160 troops
Polish Police	1 officer	160 troops
During the Night		
German Police	1 officers	86 troops
Waffen-SS	1 officers	300 troops
Polish Police	1 officer	160 troops

We had one SS man wounded. Our total losses to date have been 71 wounded and 12 killed. The operation terminated today at 2145 hours. It will be continued on 12 May 1943 at 0930 hours.

• • •

Wednesday, 12 May 1943

The twenty-fourth day saw limited fighting. *SS-Schütze* Otto Kyasch, SS Cavalry Replacement Detachment, was wounded in action. Stroop submitted one report concerning the action for the day:[81]

Stroop Report, 12 May 1943

The operation began at 0930 hours. When the raiding parties had been ordered to comb out the area for remaining bunkers, they succeeded in discovering 30 bunkers. 663 Jews were pulled out from them and 133 Jews were shot. The sum total of Jews rises to 54,463.

Furthermore, today I reinforced the units cordoning off the miniature Ghetto and then destroyed it by fire. A considerable number of Jews probably perished in the flames. Accurate numbers could not be ascertained because the buildings were still aflame when darkness intervened. One concrete building in the Prosta, from which we had extracted Jews, was heavily damaged by demolition. It is remarkable that the Poles, without having been warned, took appropriate measures for protecting their window-panes, etc., before the explosions started.

The transports of Jews starting from here will be directed to T. II, beginning today.

Forces used in the operation

German Police	5 officers	126 troops
Technical emergency		
Corps	1 officer	6 troops
Sipo	2 officers	14 troops
Army Engineers	4 officers	74 troops
Waffen-SS	12 officers	508 troops

Cordoning off forces

During the Day		
German Police	1 officers	112 troops
Trawniki men	0 officers	160 troops
Polish Police	1 officer	160 troops
During the Night		
German Police	1 officers	86 troops
Waffen-SS	1 officers	300 troops
Polish Police	1 officer	160 troops

We lost one *Waffen-SS* man wounded. Today's operation terminated at 2100 hours. The operation will be continued on 13 May 1943 at 1000 hours.

• • •

Thursday, 13 May 43

The twenty-fifth day of combat centered on bunker combat on Bonifraterska Street as well as on Swietojerska and Walowa Streets. Resistance fighters attacked German forces along the Ghetto wall at Bonifraterska, Mylna and Okopowa Streets. Soviet air force long-range bombers raided Warsaw during the night. *SS-Panzergrenadier* Heinz Stuwe and *SS-Panzer-grenadier* Gerhard Fritz, 3rd Company, 3rd SS Panzergrenadier Training and Replacement Battalion, were killed during the raid. *SS-Panzergrenadier* Alfred Baldt, 5th Company, 3rd SS Panzergrenadier Training and Replacement Battalion, *SS-Panzergrenadier* Otto Döppe, 3rd Company, 3rd SS Panzergrenadier Training and Replacement Battalion and *Wachtmeister der Schutzpolizei* Otto Luenen, 3rd Company, 23rd SS Police Regiment, were wounded during the fighting in the Ghetto. Stroop forwarded one report for the day:[82]

Stroop Report, 13 May 1943

The operation started at 1000 hours. When we combed out the Ghetto proper today and the miniature Ghetto (Prosta) we caught 234 Jews. In battle we shot 155 Jews. Today it became clear that the Jews and bandits, whom we are catching now, belong to the so-called battle groups. All of them are young lads and females of an age between 18 and 25 years old. When we disposed of a certain bunker, a real skirmish took place in which the Jews not only fired with Model 08 pistols and Polish Model VI pistols, but also threw Polish Mills bombs against the *Waffen-SS* men. After some of the inmates in the bunker had been caught and were about to be searched, one of the females – as quick as lightning – put her hand under her skirt and pulled a Mills bomb from her bloomers – as many others had done – undid the safety catch, threw it among the men who were searching her, and quickly jumped under cover. It is only due to the quick presence of mind of the troops that no losses occurred.

The few Jews and criminals still staying in the Ghetto are using hide outs they can still find among the ruins and then retire to bunkers at night to eat and take provisions for the next day. Now we are unable to extract information from captured Jews on the whereabouts of further bunkers. The remainder of the inmates of the bunker where a heavy skirmish took place were destroyed by using a heavier explosive charge. From one of the Wehrmacht enterprises we evacuated 327 Jews today. All Jews we catch now are sent exclusively to T. II. The total of Jews caught has risen to 55,179.

Forces used in the operation

German Police	4 officers	182 troops
Technical emergency Corps	1 officer	6 troops
Sipo	2 officers	14 troops
Army Engineers	4 officers	74 troops
Waffen-SS	12 officers	517 troops

Cordoning off forces

During the Day		
German Police	1 officers	137 troops
Trawniki men	0 officers	270 troops
Polish Police	1 officer	160 troops
During the Night		
German Police	1 officers	87 troops
Waffen-SS	1 officers	300 troops
Polish Police	1 officer	160 troops

Our own losses were two *Waffen-SS* men killed, three *Waffen-SS* men wounded and one Policeman wounded. The two *Waffen-SS* men killed lost their lives in an air attack against the Ghetto. Thirty-three bunkers were discovered and destroyed. We captured six pistols, two hand grenades and some explosive charges.

Today's operation terminated at 2100 hours. It will be continued on 14 May 1943 at 1000 hours. My intention is to terminate the entire large-scale action on 16 May 1943 and hand over the mission to the 3rd Battalion, 23rd SS Police Regiment for further action. Unless otherwise ordered, I will submit a detailed report of the action, including an appendix containing photographs to the conference of the SS and Police Leader.

After the war, while incarcerated in Warsaw, Stroop commented on the Soviet air raid and other events of the day:[83]

May thirteenth was marked by furious resistance from the insurgents, mainly young boys and girls, and by Krüger's and my decision that from then on all apprehended Jews would be sent to Treblinka. We captured and destroyed thirty-three bunkers that day, but during the evening experienced Warsaw's heaviest Russian air raid of the war. I was afraid that exploding bombs might hurt my troops, who were barricading the Ghetto. Fortunately the Russians concentrated on military targets some distance away. I did lose two *Waffen-SS* men who happened to be doing special liaison duty in the target area.

Ludwig Fischer, the governor of the Warsaw district, commented on 13 May 1943 on the situation as well. Fischer declared in an address to the Polish population of Warsaw:[84]

Lately there have been a series of murderous attacks in the city of Warsaw. The same force stands behind those attacks as those who hope one day to bring this country to the bloody rule of the Bolsheviks. Everyone's task now is to frustrate the provocation of the Communist and Jewish agents. Every Jew and Bolshevik who is still alive and free is the most dangerous enemy of the population . . . Whoever informs the authorities where such a Jewish or Communist agent moves about freely, is thereby fulfilling his obvious duty to himself and to his neighbor.

• • •

Friday, 14 May 1943

The twenty-sixth day was generally a mop-up action if one merely reads the Stroop Report. However, the fighting must have been severe based on the German casualties reported. *SS-Panzergrenadier* Franz Kosarz, 3rd Company, 3rd SS Panzergrenadier Training and Replacement Battalion, *SS-Oberscharführer* Thomas Wachter (grenade shrapnel), *SS-Unterscharführer* Martin Enzbrunner (grenade shrapnel; lost right eye), *SS-Panzergrenadier* Hans Raeder, and *SS-Rottenführer* Joseph Posch, 4th Company, 3rd SS Panzergrenadier Training and Replacement Battalion and *SS-Schütze* Johann Balogh, *SS-Schütze* Andreas Kuding and *SS-Schütze* Franz Bordican, SS Cavalry Replacement Detachment were wounded in action. Stroop submitted one report for the day:[85]

Stroop Report, 14 May 1943

> Today's operation started at 1000 hours. The raiding parties formed today went to work in their allotted areas with orders to force open additional bunkers and to catch the Jews inside. In this way a considerable number of bandits and Jews were again caught, due in part as some traces of them had been discovered last night. The night patrols collided several times with armed bandits who fired back with a machine-gun and some other firearms. In this operation we suffered four casualties: three *Waffen-SS* and one Police. Shots were repeatedly fired from the Aryan part of Warsaw against the external barricades of the Ghetto. We shot about 30 bandits and captured 9 Jews and bandits during the skirmishes. In one bunker, inhabited by 100 persons, we were able to capture two rifles, sixteen pistols, some hand grenades and some incendiary devices. Among those bandits who resisted, some wore German military uniforms, steel helmets and jackboots. Apart from the carbines, we captured 60 rounds of German rifle ammunition. One raiding party had a skirmish, on the roofs of a block of buildings along the border of the Ghetto, with a gang of between ten and fourteen men. The bandits were destroyed and we suffered no losses.
>
> The captured bandits repeatedly testified that not all the persons who remain in the Ghetto have been caught. They confidently expect that the action will be over soon, and that then they will be able to remain in the Ghetto. Several bandits stated that they had been in a position to kill the leader of the action, the "General" as they call him, but that they would not do so as they had orders to avoid risking a further intensification of the anti-Jewish measures.
>
> Today the engineers blew up some concrete buildings that served as refuge for the bandits. In order to force the bandits in the sewers to come into the open, 183 sewer entrances were all opened at 1500 hours and smoke candles were lowered into them. At that point the bandits, seeking to escape what they believed to be poison gas, crowded together in the center of the former Ghetto where we were able to pull them out of the sewer entrances there. Regarding termination of the overall action I will make a decision tomorrow. Today *SS-Gruppenführer* von Herff was present during the operations.

Forces used in the operation

German Police	4 officers	184 troops
Technical emergency Corps	1 officer	6 troops
Sipo	2 officers	16 troops
Army Engineers	4 officers	73 troops
Waffen-SS	12 officers	510 troops

Cordoning off forces

During the Day		
German Police	1 officers	138 troops
Trawniki men	1 officers	160 troops
Polish Police	1 officer	160 troops
During the Night		
German Police	1 officers	87 troops
Waffen-SS	1 officers	300 troops
Polish Police	1 officer	160 troops

Our own losses were five wounded of whom four were *Waffen-SS* and one Police. Altogether 398 Jews were caught today and an additional 154 Jews and bandits were shot in battle. The total of Jews caught for the entire operation has risen to 55,731. We captured some rifles, pistols and

> ammunition, as well as a number of incendiary bottles. The action terminated at 2115 hours and will continue on 15 May 1943 at 0900 hours.

SS-Obergruppenführer Maximilian von Herff can be considered a directed observer from Berlin who was probably ordered to visit the insurrection area by Heinrich Himmler. Von Herff could be relied upon to make an accurate assessment of the situation. From October 1942 he had been the head of the SS Personnel Office in Berlin. More importantly, von Herff was truly a highly-decorated combat commander. Prior to transferring to the *Waffen-SS*, von Herff had been a career Army officer and had served in the vaunted German Africa Corps under Erwin Rommel. While there, as the commander of the 115th Armored Infantry Regiment, 15th Panzer Division, he was awarded the Knight's Cross of the Iron Cross on 13 June 1941 for heroic action.[86] In Himmler's eyes, von Herff, with his combat experience, could be relied on to record an accurate picture of events – and transmit that information quickly to the *Reichsführer-SS*.[87]

• • •

Saturday, 15 May 1943

The twenty-seventh day saw fighting in the ruins at Mila and Gesia Streets. *Zugwachtmeister der Schutzpolizei* Alfons Czapp, 1st Battalion, 22nd SS Police Regiment, was wounded in action. Stroop submitted one report to Krüger:[88]

Stroop Report, 15 May 1943

> Today's operation began at 0900 hours. The scouting parties who patrolled the Ghetto last night report that there are only a sporadic number of Jews existing in the Ghetto. In contrast to the preceding night, the patrols were unable to shoot more than 6 or 7 Jews. The combing out actions today met with little results as well. Twenty-nine additional bunkers were discovered but many of them were no longer inhabited. Altogether we caught 87 Jews today; moreover 67 bandits and Jews were shot in battle. In a skirmish, which developed around noon, a gang of bandits using Molotov Cocktails, pistols and homemade grenades was destroyed. However, a Policeman was wounded by a shot through the right thigh.
>
> A special task force searched once more and subsequently destroyed the last block of buildings, which were still intact within the Ghetto. In the evening the chapel, mortuary and all adjoining buildings in the Jewish cemetery were blown up and destroyed by fire. The sum total of Jews caught has risen to 55,885.
>
> ***Forces used in the operation***
>
> | | | |
> |---|---|---|
> | German Police | 4 officers | 184 troops |
> | Technical emergency Corps | 1 officer | 6 troops |
> | Sipo | 2 officers | 16 troops |
> | Army Engineers | 4 officers | 74 troops |
> | *Waffen-SS* | 12 officers | 510 troops |
>
> ***Cordoning off forces***
>
> | | | |
> |---|---|---|
> | *During the Day* | | |
> | German Police | 2 officers | 138 troops |
> | Trawniki men | 0 officers | 270 troops |
> | Polish Police | 1 officer | 160 troops |
> | *During the Night* | | |
> | German Police | 1 officers | 87 troops |
> | *Waffen-SS* | 1 officers | 300 troops |
> | Polish Police | 1 officer | 160 troops |
>
> Our own losses were one Policeman wounded. We captured four large-caliber pistols, one infernal machine with a fuse, ten kilograms of explosives and a considerable amount of ammunition. The operation terminated at 2130 hours. It will be continued on 16 May 1943 at 1000 hours.
>
> I will terminate the entire large action on 16 May 1943 at dusk by blowing up the Synagogue which we did not succeed in accomplishing today, and will subsequently charge the 3rd Battalion, 23rd SS Police Regiment with continuing and completing the measures which still might be necessary.

• • •

Sunday, 16 May 1943

The twenty-eighth day of the action was its last. There appear to have been no German casualties. Stroop submitted one report for the day:[89]

Stroop Report, 16 May 1943

> The operation began at 1000 hours. Altogether 180 Jews, bandits and sub-humans were destroyed. The former Jewish Warsaw Ghetto is no longer standing. The action was

terminated at 2015 hours by blowing up the Warsaw Synagogue.

All measures to be taken with respect to the established banned areas were handed over to the commanding officer of the 3rd Battalion, 23rd SS Police Regiment. I instructed him carefully. The total number of Jews dealt with was 56,065; this includes both those Jews we caught and those, whose extermination can be proven. We had no friendly losses today. I will submit a final report to the Conference of SS and Police Leaders on 18 May 1943.

Stroop provided more colorful language concerning the final official day of the action, during which the Nazis blew-up the Great Synagogue of Warsaw, in 1950 as he awaited trial. He is quoted as saying:[90]

What a marvelous sight it was – a fantastic piece of theater. My staff and I stood at a distance. I held the electrical device, which would detonate all the charges simultaneously. Jesuiter called for silence. I glanced over at my brave officers and men, tired and dirty, silhouetted against the glow of the burning buildings. After prolonging the suspense for a moment, I shouted, '*Heil Hitler*' and pressed the button. With a thunderous, deafening bang and a rainbow burst of colors, the fiery explosion soared toward the clouds, an unforgettable tribute to our triumph over the Jews. The Warsaw Ghetto was no more. The will of Adolf Hitler and Heinrich Himmler had been done.

• • •

But the fighting was not yet over. In the summary of the operation in the Stroop Report, Jürgen Stroop details what happened next:[91]

Although the large-scale action is completed, we have to reckon with the possibility of a few Jews still living in the ruins of the former Ghetto; therefore, this area must be firmly shut off from the Aryan residential area and be guarded. The Police 3rd Battalion, 23rd SS Police Regiment has been charged with this duty. This battalion has instructions to watch the former Ghetto, and to shoot immediately anybody found inside the Ghetto without authority. The commander of the Police battalion will continue to receive further direct orders from the SS and Police Leader. In this way, it should be possible to keep the small remainder of Jews there, if any, under constant pressure and to exterminate them eventually. The remaining Jews and bandits must be deprived of any chance of survival by destroying all remaining buildings and refuges and by cutting off the water supply. It is proposed to change the Dzielna [Pawiak] Prison into a concentration camp and to use the inmates to remove, collect and hand over for re-use the millions of bricks, scrap-iron and other materials.

Bernard Mark, in his *Der Aufstand im Warschauer Ghetto*, presents great details on the post-16 May actions. On 18 May, fighting continued in the ruins along Gesia, Mila and Nalewki Streets. There was more fighting two days later along Nowolipie and Nowolipki Streets. On 28 May some resistance fighters fired at the Germans on Zamenhof Street. All during June there were sporadic actions along Bonifraterska, Kurza-Pawia and Zamenhof Streets. On 19 June the Germans attacked a bunker at Grzybowska and Prozna Streets. And on 30 June there was a night fight in some bunkers on Nowolipki Street. The first half of July saw continued strife. Fighting occurred in the ruins at Swietojerska, Walowa, Franciszkanska, Nalewki and Pawia Streets as well as in the area around the Jewish cemetery. Mark reports that the last of the resistance fighters left the Ghetto in September 1943 and crossed to the "Aryan" side of Warsaw.[92] Reuben Ainsztein details even more remarkable escapes. Ainsztein states that two Jews remained in the Ghetto until 11 January 1944, while other Jews held out in the surrounding city area until 17 January 1945 when the Russians finally liberated the city.[93]

For the first time in months there was silence in the ruin and rubble of the Ghetto. As Stroop described, apart from eight buildings, the former Ghetto was completely destroyed. Only the dividing walls remained standing. The Jews lay dead and the SS officers and men departed into historical anonymity . . . until now.

Notes:

[1] Gerald Reitlinger, *The Final Solution: The Attempt to Exterminate the Jews of Europe, 1939-1945.* (Northvale, N.J.: Jason Aronson, Inc., 1987), p. 271.

[2] Peter Padfield, *Himmler.* (New York: Henry Holt and Company, 1990), p. 446.

[3] Bernard Mark, *The Extermination and the Resistance of the Polish Jews during 1939 - 1944.* (Warsaw: Jewish Historical Institute, 1955), pp. 18-19.

[4] Ibid., pp. 18-19.

[5] Tadeusz Bielecki and Leszek Szymanski, *Warsaw Aflame: The 1933-1945 Years.* (Los Angeles: Polamerica Press, 1973), p. 100.

[6] Raul Hilberg, *The Destruction of the European Jews* (Revised and Definitive Edition). New York: Holmes & Meier, 1985), p. 512.

[7] Ibid., p. 512.

[8] Richard C. Lukas, *The Forgotten Holocaust: The Poles Under German Occupation, 1939-1944.* (Lexington, KY: The University Press of Kentucky, 1986), p. 172.

[9] Ibid., p. 512.

[10] Ibid., p. 175.

[11] Bernard Mark, *The Extermination and the Resistance of the Polish Jews during 1939 - 1944*, pp. 18-20.

[12] Irving Werstein, *The Uprising of the Warsaw Ghetto, November 1940 - May 1943.* (New York: W.W. Norton & Company, 1968), p. 120.

[13] Sources: Bernard Mark, *Der Aufstand im Warschauer Ghetto.* (Berlin: Dietz Verlag, 1957.), fold out map. Ruta Sakowska, *The Warsaw Ghetto, 1940-1943.* (Warsaw: Privately published), map; and Israel Gutman, *The Jews of Warsaw, 1939-1943: Ghetto, Underground, Revolt.* (Bloomington: Indiana University Press, 1982), map.

[14] Yitzak Arad contribution, "The Armed Jewish Resistance in Eastern Europe," in the anthology by Michael Berenbaum and Abraham J. Peck, *The Holocaust and History: The Known, The Unknown, The Disputed and The Reexamined.* (Bloomington, Indiana: Indiana University Press, 1998), p. 599.

[15] Israel Gutman, *Resistance: The Warsaw Ghetto Uprising.* (Boston: Houghton Mifflin Company, 1994), p. 198.

[16] Peter Chamberlain and Chris Ellis, *Pictorial History of Tanks of the World 1915-45.* (Harrisburg, PA: Stackpole Books, 1972), p. 22.

[17] Bernard Mark, *The Extermination and the Resistance of the Polish Jews during 1939 - 1944*, p. 24.

[18] Dan Kurzman, *The Bravest Battle: The Twenty-eight Days of the Warsaw Ghetto Uprising.* (New York: G.P. Putnam's Sons, 1976), p. 104.

[19] Ibid., p. 105.

[20] Ibid.,p. 99.

[21] Wolfgang Scheffler and Helge Grabnitz, *Der Ghetto-Aufstand Warschau 1943.* (Munich, Germany: Goldmann Verlag, 1993), pp. 181-186.

[22] International Military Tribunal, *Trial of the Major War Criminals Before the International Military Tribunal, Nürnberg, 14 November 1945 - 1 October 1946. Volume XXVI, Documents and Other Material in Evidence, Numbers 405-PS to 1063 (d)-PS.* (Buffalo, NY: William S. Hein & Co. Inc., 1995), Document 1061-PS, Report: "The Warsaw Ghetto Is No More" by the Chief of the SS and Police in the Warsaw District, 16 May 1943, Report for 19 April 1943. Hereafter cited as 1061-PS.

There are several factual differences between versions of the Stroop Report. I used the Stroop Report that is on file in the National Archives at College Park, Maryland – and that was used at Nürnberg. The English translation of this document was done in 1945. I used this translation, changing only some stilted language and also changing some of the passive tense to active.

[23] Kazimierz Moczarski, *Conversations with an Executioner.* Edited by Mariana Fitzpatrick. (Englewood Cliffs, New Jersey), pp.118 - 120.

[24] Wolfgang Scheffler and Helge Grabnitz, *Der Ghetto-Aufstand Warschau 1943*, pp. 196-199.

[25] Ibid., pp. 183-184.

[26] Dan Kurzman, *The Bravest Battle: The Twenty-eight Days of the Warsaw Ghetto Uprising*, p. 119.

[27] Ibid.,p. 132.

[28] A thrown track occurs when one (or sometimes both) of the vehicle's caterpillar tracks comes off the road wheels, the return rollers, or the drive or idler wheels. It can occur in a wide variety of circumstances; in this case the driver probably tried to abruptly change directions while crossing over rubble which caused the track to pop off. Putting a tank with a thrown track back into operation is a labor-intensive task – often lasting hours – and one best done while not under enemy fire.

[29] Bernard Mark, *The Extermination and the Resistance of the Polish Jews during 1939 -1944*, pp. 18-20.

[30] A command-detonated mine is one that is exploded by an observer, normally by electrical blasting cap. The observer waits until a large number of enemy troops are near the mine and then explodes the device.

[31] 1061-PS, Report for 20 April 1943.

[32] Kazimierz Moczarski, *Conversations with an Executioner*, pp.126 - 130.

[33] Bernard Mark, *The Extermination and the Resistance of the Polish Jews during 1939 -1944*, p. 45.

[34] 1061-PS, Report for 21 April 1943.

[35] Kazimierz Moczarski, *Conversations with an Executioner*, p.130.

[36] Georg Tessin, *Verbände und Truppen der deutschen Wehrmacht und Waffen-SS im Zweiten Weltkrieg 1939-1945, Band I - XVI (4).* (Osnabrück, FRG: Biblio Verlag, 1979), Band 16 (Part 3), p. 189.

[37] Each nation uses its own doctrine for tactical operations. Some profess that clearing buildings from the bottom up is most efficient. Others believe starting on the top floor and working downward is best.

[38] Bernard Mark, *The Extermination and the Resistance of the Polish Jews during 1939 -1944*, p. 42.

[39] War Department, Military Intelligence Service, *German Infantry Weapons*, Special Series No. 14. (Washington, DC: Government Printing Office, 1943), pp. 27-33.

[40] 1061-PS, Report for 22 April 1943.

[41] War Department, *Handbook on German Military Forces.* (Baton Rouge, Louisiana: Reprinted by Louisiana State University Press, 1990), pp. 530-531.

[42] Kazimierz Moczarski, *Conversations with an Executioner*, p.131.

[43] 1061-PS, Summary, p. 8.

[44] Bernard Mark, *The Extermination and the Resistance of the Polish Jews during 1939 -1944*, p. 50.

[45] 1061-PS, Report for 23 April 1943.

[46] Kazimierz Moczarski, *Conversations with an Executioner*, p.135.

[47] War Department, *Handbook on German Military Forces, 15 March 1945.* (Gaithersburg, Maryland: Reprinted by The Military Press, 1970), p. IV-45.

[48] Bernard Mark, *The Extermination and the Resistance of the Polish Jews during 1939 - 1944*, pp. 50-52.

[49] 1061-PS, Report for 24 April 1943.

[50] Bernard Mark, *Der Aufstand im Warschauer Ghetto*, p. 313.

[51] 1061-PS, Report for 25 April 1943.

[52] Bernard Mark, *Der Aufstand im Warschauer Ghetto*, p. 314.

[53] 1061-PS, Report for 26 April 1943.

[54] Kazimierz Moczarski, *Conversations with an Executioner*, p.143.

[55] Dan Kurzman, *The Bravest Battle: The Twenty-eight Days of the Warsaw Ghetto Uprising*, pp. 234-235.

[56] Bernard Mark, *Der Aufstand im Warschauer Ghetto*, p. 316.

[57] 1061-PS, Report for 27 April 1943.

[58] Kazimierz Moczarski, *Conversations with an Executioner*, p.145.

[59] Bernard Mark, *Der Aufstand im Warschauer Ghetto*, p. 321.

[60] 1061-PS, Report for 28 April 1943.

[61] Kazimierz Moczarski, *Conversations with an Executioner*, p.147.

[62] 1061-PS, Report for 29 April 1943.

[63] 1061-PS, Report for 30 April 1943.

[64] 1061-PS, Report for 1 May 1943.

[65] 1061-PS, Report for 2 May 1943.

[66] Kazimierz Moczarski, *Conversations with an Executioner*, p.150.

[67] 1061-PS, Report for 3 May 1943.

[68] Joseph Kermish, "The Warsaw Ghetto Uprising in the Light of a Hitherto Unpublished Official German Report" in *Yad Vashem Studies on the European Jewish Catastrophe and Resistance*, Volume IX. (Jerusalem: Yad Vashem, 1973), pp. 19-22.

[69] Kazimierz Moczarski, *Conversations with an Executioner*, p.151.

[70] 1061-PS, Report for 4 May 1943.

[71] 1061-PS, Report for 5 May 1943.

[72] 1061-PS, Report for 6 May 1943.

[73] The Katyn Forest Massacre was the mass execution of several thousand captured Polish officers in a forest near Smolensk by Soviet security troops, probably in 1940. The Germans uncovered the graves in April 1943 and publicized the findings. The Soviets denied complicity. The western allies did not press the matter, fearing a rift with their Soviet partner.

[74] 1061-PS, Report for 7 May 1943.

[75] Kazimierz Moczarski, *Conversations with an Executioner*, p.160.

[76] 1061-PS, Report for 8 May 1943.

[77] Kazimierz Moczarski, *Conversations with an Executioner*, pp.161-162.

[78] 1061-PS, Report for 9 May 1943.

[79] 1061-PS, Report for 10 May 1943.

[80] 1061-PS, Report for 11 May 1943.
[81] 1061-PS, Report for 12 May 1943.
[82] 1061-PS, Report for 13 May 1943.
[83] Kazimierz Moczarski, *Conversations with an Executioner*, p.163.
[84] Israel Gutman, *Resistance: The Warsaw Ghetto Uprising*, p. 253.
[85] 1061-PS, Report for 14 May 1943.
[86] Walther-Peer Fellgiebel, *Die Träger des Ritterkreuzes des Eisernen Kreuzes 1939-1945*. (Friedberg, FRG: Podzun-Pallas-Verlag, 1986), p. 223.
[87] Von Herff was born 17 April 1893 in Hannover. He died in a British prisoner of war camp at Ulverstone, England on 6 September 1945 of natural causes.
[88] 1061-PS, Report for 15 May 1943.
[89] 1061-PS, Report for 16 May 1943.
[90] Kazimierz Moczarski, *Conversations with an Executioner*, p.164.
[91] 1061-PS, Summary, p. 11.
[92] Bernard Mark, *Der Aufstand im Warschauer Ghetto*, pp. 405-406.
[93] Reuben Ainsztein, *The Warsaw Ghetto Revolt*. (New York: Holocaust Library, 1979), pp. 166-167.

6

THE OFFICERS

"For an SS officer, there are no problems – his task is continually to remove problems himself immediately [when] they appear! Over the how, you blow your brains out, not I!"[1]

- Heinrich Himmler, 10 July 1942

Heinrich Himmler possessed a fourteenth century psyche trapped in a twentieth century body. To the *Reichsführer-SS*, the German invasion and acquisition of *Lebensraum* in the east was a long-overdue sequel to the conquests of the *Deutsche Ritterorden* – the Teutonic Knights – in Poland and Lithuania some five hundred years before. Himmler, ever the mystic, liked to tell his SS officers:[2]

> Never forget, we are a knightly Order, from which one cannot withdraw, to which one is recruited by blood and within which one remains with body and soul so long as one lives on this earth.

To complete this image of a medieval paladin, the *Reichsführer-SS* bestowed on his officers silver SS *Totenkopf* (Death's Head) rings, ornately engraved SS officer daggers and exquisitely designed ceremonial swords. For the highest of the high, Himmler created a castle at Wewelsberg – a mountain fortress southwest of Paderborn in Westphalia – fit for the new Knights of the Round Table. These select leaders of the SS were entitled to gather in a huge dining room some 100 by 145 feet in size. Seated in twelve high-backed, pigskin-covered chairs adorned with etched silver nametags denoting seniority, the *SS-Obergruppenführer* would listen for hours as "King Heinrich" dispensed his macabre wisdom. Leading down from the dining room was a long flight of stairs, which ended in a dark crypt, known as 'the realm of the dead'. Encased in five feet thick walls, the chamber contained a stone stoop and twelve stone pedestals. Should one of the dozen barons of this black order perish in the service of the *Reich*, his weapons were to be placed on the stoop and set alight. The smoke from the *ersatz* funeral pyre would spiral upward toward four vents carved in the ceiling, so that the assembled SS warlords could watch the fallen warrior's spirit ascend in a single column of smoke to a figurative Valhalla. The fallen hero's ashes would then be placed in one of the urns to remain in perpetuity.

To the officers of the SS, the *Reichsführer-SS* gave much. In return, he took their souls.

• • •

The Stroop report indicated that an average of thirty-one officers participated in the Warsaw Ghetto operation, but it did not, for the most part, reveal the names of those involved. This study has identified 103 SS officers who are believed to have played significant roles in the SS forces and units assigned to suppress the Warsaw Ghetto Uprising. The officers who directed the operation against the Ghetto were an interesting cast of individuals ranging from lieutenants to general officers, combat heroes to mass murderers. Their biographies are presented in this chapter and are organized according to unit. As mentioned in the introduction, the SS personnel records system fell apart in early 1945. Therefore some of the following officers, whose files indicate that they were not killed in action, could have actually died during the last days of the *Reich* – their deaths never annotated in Berlin.

HIGHER SS AND POLICE LEADER & SS AND POLICE LEADER WARSAW

Six officers have been identified as serving with the Higher SS and Police Leader "East" and the SS and Police Leader Warsaw offices as having played notable roles in the quelling of the Warsaw Ghetto Uprising.

FRIEDRICH-WILHELM KRÜGER

SS-Obergruppenführer Friedrich-Wilhelm Krüger served as the Higher SS and Police Leader "East" from 4 October 1939 to 9 November 1943. Krüger was born 8 May 1894 in Strasbourg, Alsace, the younger brother of future *SS-Obergruppenführer* Walter Krüger. He served as a first lieutenant in World War I with the 25th Infantry Regiment and was awarded the Iron Cross 1st and 2nd Class as well as winning the Wound Badge in Silver for being wounded on several occasions. He joined the Nazi Party on 15 November 1929 with a membership number of 171199. Krüger was a very early member of the SS, joining as an *SS-Untersturmführer* on 1 December 1931 with an SS number of only 6123. Krüger then left the SS and joined the SA. He reported to Himmler concerning the potential revolt of the Brown Shirts, which led to the infamous "Night of the Long Knives" as Hitler and Himmler crushed the SA power base once and for all. Krüger rejoined the SS and was rewarded with a direct promotion to *SS-Obergruppenführer* achieved on 25 January 1935![3] He then became the inspector of all border and watch guard units before joining the SS Main Office.[4]

On 4 October 1939, *SS-Obergruppenführer* Friedrich-Wilhelm Krüger began his reign of office but the road was a rocky one. In addition to constantly fighting with Governor General Hans Frank, Krüger was a target for the Polish resistance as well. On 20 April 1943 the Polish Home Army attempted to assassinate the Higher SS and Police Leader. A resistance fighter threw a bomb at Krüger's automobile as it drove through the streets of Kraków, but the *SS-Obergruppenführer* was not seriously hurt.[5]

After serving as the Higher SS and Police Leader in the General Government, Krüger transferred for a short time to the personal staff of the *Reichsführer-SS* before moving to the 6th SS Division "*Nord*" on 20 May 1944 where he remained with the division for three months. He was awarded the Knight's Cross of the Iron Cross on 30 September 1944 as commander of the 6th SS Division "*Nord*," a part of the 20th Mountain Army in Finland.[6] Himmler then elevated Krüger to the position of commanding general for the Vth SS Mountain Corps, a unit he commanded from 26 August 1944 to March 1945.

In addition to winning the Knight's Cross, Friedrich-Wilhelm Krüger also received the Golden Party Badge in 1939. He was awarded the Clasp to the Iron Cross 2nd Class in June 1943. The timing of this award would indicate it was for service connected with the Warsaw Ghetto Uprising. Krüger obviously knew what was going on in the Ghetto Uprising as he received daily reports from Stroop. Krüger also made a personal visit to the Ghetto on 2 May 1943 to see the fighting first hand. Krüger did not survive the war. He committed suicide on 10 May 1945 in Austria to avoid falling into allied captivity.

MAX JESUITER

SS-Sturmbannführer Max Jesuiter, born in Stettin, Pomerania (now Szczecin, Poland) on 25 August 1897, served as the Chief of Staff to the SS and Police Leader, Warsaw during the Ghetto Uprising. During World War I, Jesuiter fought in several infantry regiments and won the Iron Cross 2nd Class in addition to being wounded in action. He entered the Nazi Party on 1 June 1931 (membership number 551161). On 16 January 1932 he joined the SS and received SS number 35007. Max Jesuiter was married with no children. Jesuiter was promoted to *SS-Untersturmführer* on 9 November 1934, to *SS-Obersturmführer* on 15 September 1935, to *SS-Hauptsturmführer* on 13 September 1936 and *SS-Sturmbannführer* on 9 November 1938. He received a War Service Cross 2nd Class in 1941 and a War Service Cross 1st Class in 1943, most likely for the Ghetto Uprising operation. His personnel file also indicates the award of a Clasp to the Iron Cross 2nd Class (given in lieu of an Iron Cross when the recipient had already won the award in World War I) and an Infantry Assault Badge. The clasp was for Jesuiter's role in crushing the Warsaw Uprising in 1944. He was promoted to *SS-Obersturmbannführer* on 20 April 1944.[7] Some of Max Jesuiter's post-war testimony – provided for another trial – reveals a little of how he thought:[8]

> As to the teletype of 21 April 1943: In this teletype message, on the first page, there is talk of screaming Jews who came out of burning houses and who were supposed to have been removed immediately. I believe that the word "removed" in this sense is simultaneous to "liquidated." If questioned, I cannot say in detail what brought me to this conviction. It also was not in our general use of the language that the word "removed" meant a killing. Therefore, I can only assume that these people had been killed. With regard to additional captured 5,200 Jews mentioned in the next paragraph of this teletype and who were taken to the railway station, it must be assumed that they went to a camp. On the second page of this teletype there is mention of 150 Jews, bandits who were taken care of in war fashion. Here it must be assumed that these people actually lost their lives in connection with resistance efforts.

In the report of 22 April 1943 there is mention of Jews who came out of the houses in large numbers and were liquidated immediately. The additional 5,300 Jews mentioned – according to the wording of the teletype – after they were captured alive, were transported away, which means, taken to some camp.

Concerning the use of language in these teletype messages, it can be said in general that the word "*erfasst*" [caught, taken] merely means that these Jewish people were caught alive (maybe that they voluntarily gave themselves up, maybe that they were hauled out of their quarters by force, or maybe that they were driven out by smoke or smoke candles.) The word "*erfasst*" does not give a clue what happened to these people afterwards. On the other side, if there is mention in such messages that the Jews were gathered for transfer it must be assumed that they were actually transported away. In other instances Stroop says distinctly that Jews were "*erschossen*" [shot] or "*liquidiert*" [liquidated]. In this connection, one exception is the already earlier mentioned word "*ausgesiedelt*" [transferred] where it is only possible to make assumptions about the true fate of these people.

At other times, Max Jesuiter appeared to suffer from the same case of amnesia that many other Nazi witnesses suffered when discussing the Warsaw Ghetto Uprising. The following relates to his memory concerning one of the Police battalions:[9]

> I have no recollection about this unit, their leader and the ways and means of their activity in the Ghetto. When I am being confronted with the name of B, I only dimly remember this name, but no longer have a clearer recollection of this person. I think I remember that B was an older man. As far as I remember, he also was not very active.

Given his close association with the production of the Stroop Report, Max Jesuiter served in one of the most key positions during the Ghetto Uprising. He survived the war.

KARL KALESCHKE

Born 19 February 1895 in Dobrin, *SS-Untersturmführer* Karl Kaleschke served as the Adjutant to the SS and Police Leader, Warsaw during the Ghetto Uprising. Kaleschke served with the 61st Infantry Regiment in World War I and won an Iron Cross 2nd Class. He was also wounded during the conflict. He entered the police in 1922 and was married in 1925. His SS number of 290196 indicates he entered this organization in 1937. Karl Kaleschke joined the Nazi Party on 1 January 1940 with membership number 7906104. He was promoted to *SS-Untersturmführer* on 20 April 1939 while serving in the SD Main Office in Berlin. Kaleschke also served with the *Gestapo* in Köslin (now Koszalin, Poland).[10]

Karl Kaleschke played a key role during the fight against the Jews in 1943. He survived the war. In February 1946 the prosecution for the International Military Tribunal at Nürnberg obtained an affidavit from Kaleschke that was used as evidence against Ernst Kaltenbrunner, the successor to Reinhard Heydrich as head of the RSHA in Berlin. A portion of the statement reads:[11]

> My name is Karl Kaleschke. I was adjutant to Dr. von Sammern-Frankenegg from November 1942 until April 1943, while he was SS and Police Leader of Warsaw. I then became adjutant to SS and Police Leader Stroop until August 1943. The action against the Warsaw Ghetto was planned while von Sammern-Frankenegg was SS and Police Leader. General Stroop took over the command on the day of the commencement of the action. The function of the Security Police during the action against the Warsaw Ghetto was to accompany the SS troops. A certain number of SS troops were assigned to the task to clear a certain street. With every SS group there were from four to six Security Policemen, because they knew the Ghetto very well. These Security Policemen were under Dr. Hahn, Commander of the Security Police of Warsaw. Hahn received his orders not from the SS and Police Leader of Warsaw, but directly from [Ernst] Kaltenbrunner in Berlin. This applies not only to the Ghetto action but also to all matters. Dr. Hahn frequently came to our office and told the SS and Police Leader that he had received such and such an order from Kaltenbrunner, about the contents of which he wanted to inform the SS and Police Leader only. He would not do this for every order but only for certain ones . . . I remember the case of 300 foreign Jews who had been collected in the Polski Hotel by the Security Police. At the end of the Ghetto action, Kaltenbrunner ordered the Security Police to transport these people. During my time in Warsaw the Security Police were in charge of matters concerning the underground movement. The Security Police handled these matters independently of the SS and Police Leader, and received their orders from Kaltenbrunner in Berlin.

Kaleschke's testimony was extremely damaging to Ernst Kaltenbrunner, who was hanged in October 1946.

DR. FERDINAND VON SAMMERN-FRANKENEGG

SS-Oberführer Dr. Ferdinand von Sammern-Frankenegg served as the SS and Police Leader for Warsaw through the first day of the Ghetto Uprising. He was born in Grieskirchen in Upper Austria on 17 March 1897. During World War I he served in the 1st *Kaiserschützen* Regiment and the 9th *Feldjäger* Battalion as a mountain infantry lieutenant. He was a prisoner of war from November 1918 to September 1919 in Italy. Von Sammern received a law degree from the University of Innsbruck. He joined the SS on 1 December 1932 and received a membership number of 292792. On 1 March 1933 he joined the German Nazi Party (Party number 1456955); he had previously joined the Austrian Nazi Party on 1 June 1932. Von Sammern was promoted to *SS-Untersturmführer* on 20 April 1935, to *SS-Obersturmführer* on 9 November 1936 to *SS-Hauptsturmführer* 20 April 1937 and to *SS-Sturmbannführer* on 9 November 1937. He skipped the rank of *SS-Obersturmbannführer* and was promoted directly to *SS-Standartenführer* on 17 March 1938.

Von Sammern served as commander of various SS districts in Germany before the war. Promoted to *SS-Oberführer* on 30 January 1941, he assumed duties as the SS and Police Leader for Warsaw on 22 July 1942. He remained in this position until 20 April 1943 when he was basically relieved of duties.[12] However, von Sammern was a protégé of fellow Austrian Dr. Ernst Kaltenbrunner who ensured that the relief did not permanently ruin von Sammern's career.[13] Himmler once described von Sammern as "from the cavalry, very pleasant, but in no way suited to his functions."[14] Von Sammern then became Heinrich Himmler's representative to the Senior Commander of German Troops in Croatia. On 15 July 1943 von Sammern assumed duties as the SS and Police Leader "Essegg." He received an Iron Cross 2nd Class in 1943.

Von Sammern was promoted to *SS-Brigadeführer* on 20 April 1944. He was killed in action during an artillery barrage near Banja Luka, Yugoslavia on 20 September 1944 while visiting German and Cossack troops fighting Tito's partisans. He was posthumously awarded an Iron Cross 1st Class.[15] Von Sammern-Frankenegg not only planned the German operation to clear the Ghetto, but also oversaw the mass deportations to Treblinka the previous year. He would have undoubtedly been brought to trial after the war had he survived.

JÜRGEN STROOP

Jürgen Stroop, the one German officer who will be forever linked with the Warsaw Ghetto Uprising, assumed command of the Ghetto operation on 19 April 1943. This was the first day of the action, although Heinrich Himmler did not appoint him to the position of SS and Police Leader Warsaw until 29 June 1943. He was born Josef Stroop on 26 September 1895 in Detmold, but later changed his name in honor of his deceased son. During World War I, Stroop served in several infantry regiments at the front and won an Iron Cross 2nd Class. He was also wounded in action. Stroop joined the SS on 1 July 1932 and received SS number 44611. He was admitted into the Nazi Party shortly thereafter on 1 September 1932 (Party number 1292297). Stroop was promoted to *SS-Hauptsturmführer* on 8 March 1934, to *SS-Sturmbannführer* on 20 April 1935 and to *SS-Obersturmbannführer* on 20 April 1936. During the 1930s he attended various leadership courses and commanded several General SS units in Germany proper. He was promoted to *SS-Standartenführer* on 12 September 1937 and to *SS-Oberführer* on 10 September 1939.

From 7 July to 15 September 1941 Jürgen Stroop served in combat on the eastern front with the 3rd SS *Totenkopf* Infantry Regiment of the SS Division "*Totenkopf*." During the fighting he was awarded a Clasp to the Iron Cross 2nd Class and an Infantry Assault Badge in Bronze. Stroop was then promoted to *SS-Brigadeführer* on 16 September 1942 and assigned as an Inspector of the *Sipo* and SD of the Higher SS and Police Leader for Russia-South where he helped secure a key logistical route through October 1942. He then briefly commanded SS garrisons at Kherson before becoming SS and Police Leader Lemberg (now Lvov, Ukraine) in February 1943. From that position he moved to Warsaw on 18 April 1943. Former *SS-Hauptsturmführer* Georg Michalsen, who temporarily served under Stroop during the Ghetto Uprising, had this insight about the man:[16]

> [*Accusation*] The witness [Max] Jesuiter stated that Stroop had an outspoken hatred against Jews. If it had gone according to Stroop, not one train with Jews would have left Warsaw, but Stroop would have liquidated all Jews right there.
>
> [*Michalsen*] I consider this description as valid. I also was under the impression that Stroop was negatively disposed towards a transfer of the Jews and under the circumstances only bent to higher pressures. I also stated that it never happened before Stroop's time that houses were burnt down. But as soon as Stroop arrived, and that was even on his first day, houses were set on fire. I have witnessed myself how people jumped from burning houses. Most probably they died.

After the Ghetto Uprising, *SS-Obergruppenführer* Friedrich-Wilhelm Krüger awarded an Iron Cross 1st Class to Stroop on 18 June 1943 for the action at a gala reception in Warsaw's Lazienki Park. Krüger, Stroop and other leading personalities in Warsaw drank, sang and rode horses to commemorate the event.[17] Stroop then formally assumed the position of SS and Police Leader "Warsaw." He remained in this position until 8 September 1943 when he was named as Higher SS and Police Leader for Greece. Stroop held this post for one month to 4 October 1943. Promoted to *SS-Gruppenführer* on 9 November 1943, Stroop assumed command of *SS-Oberabschnitt* "Rhein-Westmark" in Germany. He held this position until 24 March 1945.[18]

An American court, in a trial lasting from 10 January 1947 to 21 March 1947, convicted Stroop and twenty-two other defendants of complicity in the deaths of downed Allied airmen in the Rhein-Westmark district and sentenced him to death, despite the fact that he had provided testimony used to help convict Ernst Kaltenbrunner. The sentence was not carried out, however, and Stroop was instead extradited to Poland where he stood trial in 1951 for war crimes concerning the Warsaw Ghetto. Once again he was convicted and sentenced to death. He was hanged in Warsaw – some reports state that the execution site was at the former Ghetto – on 8 September 1951.[19] A second date given for his execution is 6 March 1952.[20] Another date given for his death is 9 July 1952.

THEODOR VAN EUPEN

SS-Hauptsturmführer Theodor van Eupen served as the commandant of the Treblinka labor camp during the period of the Ghetto Uprising. He was born 24 April 1907 in Düsseldorf. He joined the SS on 1 October 1930 with an SS number of 4528. Shortly thereafter, on 1 January 1931, van Eupen joined the Nazi Party (membership number 431838.) Van Eupen was promoted to *SS-Untersturmführer* on 15 September 1935, to *SS-Obersturmführer* on 13 September 1936 and to *SS-Hauptsturmführer* on 12 September 1937. He appears to have served as the adjutant for the SS and Police Leader Warsaw in 1940; he then assumed the duties of commandant at the Jewish labor camp at Lemberg. He then moved to Treblinka. The Treblinka labor camp, which was located two kilometers from the Treblinka extermination camp, served as a forced labor compound.

Van Eupen was reported to be present at the January 1943 deportations in Warsaw in some type of supervisory role. I believe it is very possible that he may have visited the April-May deportations as well. Upon leaving Treblinka, van Eupen served under *SS-Brigadeführer* Dr. Günther Merk in SS Special Staff Jedrzejów. During the war he won an Iron Cross 2nd Class. Theodor van Eupen was killed in action by partisans near Jedrzejowo, Poland on 11 December 1944.[21]

• • •

OPERATION REINHARD

This study has identified eight officers who visited Warsaw or who were detailed from the headquarters of *Operation Reinhard*, located in Lublin, to temporarily assist the SS forces in Warsaw before and during the Ghetto Uprising.

ODILO GLOBOCNIK

SS-Gruppenführer Odilo Globocnik, the SS and Police Leader of Lublin and the leader of *Operation Reinhard*, was born in Trieste 21 April 1904. He entered the Nazi Party on 1 January 1931 and received a Party number of 412938. The following year he joined the SS on 1 September 1932 (SS number 292776). An Austrian, he had received a prison sentence in 1933 for the murder of a Viennese Jew.[22] On his release, he served as the *Gauleiter* for Vienna from May 1938 to January 1939. On 12 March 1938 he was elevated to *SS-Standartenführer*. However, he continued his criminal activities and in 1939 the Nazi Party stripped him of all honors for illegal speculation in foreign currency. Globocnik served as an *SS-Unterscharführer* in the *Waffen-SS* regiment "*Germania*" during the Polish Campaign and won an Iron Cross 2nd Class.[23] Heinrich Himmler pardoned his old friend – Himmler referred to him familiarly as "Globus" (Globe) – and installed him as the highest SS authority in the Lublin district on 9 November 1939.[24] In Poland, Globocnik frequently circumvented the head of the General Government, Governor General Hans Frank, as he developed extensive SS economic enterprises in the Lublin area. Commencing in May 1942, he organized the *Operation Reinhard* death camps at Belzec, Sobibór and Treblinka. Globocnik was elevated to *SS-Gruppenführer* on 9 November 1942.[25]

Walter Bellwidt, the commander of the 3rd SS Panzergrenadier Replacement and Training Battalion, testified after the war that he had seen Globocnik in Warsaw, during the Ghetto Uprising, arguing with Jürgen Stroop.[26] We can only speculate as to the topic; he may have been in conflict over Stroop's actions, which placed SS assets in Warsaw in danger of being destroyed in the fighting. In late 1943 Globocnik went to Italy as the Higher SS and Police Leader for the Adriatic Coast. On 17 September 1944, Heinrich Himmler awarded the Anti-Partisan Badge in Silver to Globocnik. On 4 May 1945 he fled with his adjutant to Kötschach in Carinthia, Austria to avoid capture. On 31 May 1945 at 0400 hours a British patrol captured Globocnik along with Ernst Lerch, Herman Höfle and Georg Michalsen, all members of his *Operation Reinhard* staff. At 1130 hours that day Odilo Globocnik swallowed a cyanide capsule and died within seconds.[27] He was buried in an unmarked grave, which was then flattened by tanks; its location remains unknown to this day.[28]

After the war, Ernst Lerch, Globocnik's colleague, described the man behind *Operation Reinhard* in this manner:[29]

> Globocnik had two souls: one sincere and pleasing one; he really was sociable and fun loving, even witty, and then there was another, completely reversed aspect – the harshness and unbending behavior in his work. The orders, which came from above, were executed in each particular case; an order could not be discussed. He had the extraordinary ability, sometimes like that of a priest, to obey these orders.

Globocnik's biographer, Siegfried J. Pucher, characterized the SS officer as dutiful towards the authorities above him and authoritarian towards those below him. His attitude towards National Socialism was "ecstatic" from the beginning; Globocnik was not only convinced in the correctness of the cause; he was a deep believer. He often raved to his fiancée that "he would be in good standing" once National Socialism would take power. Several sources confirmed that Globocnik consumed large quantities of alcohol.[30] A complex individual, Globocnik would have undoubtedly faced the hangman's noose after the war in either Yugoslavia or Poland had he not committed suicide.

OTTO HANTKE

SS-Untersturmführer Otto Hantke was assigned to the SS and Police Leader for Lublin but was detailed to assist the SS forces at Warsaw during the Ghetto Uprising. He was born 21 January 1907 in Katscher, Silesia (now Kietrz/Racibórz, Poland). Hantke served as the commandant of the Jewish labor camp at Budzyn, where the prisoners were employed at a Heinkel aircraft factory.[31] Hantke also served as the second commandant of the Poniatowa labor camp, replacing *SS-Obersturmführer* Gottlieb Hering.[32] He was probably in Warsaw during the time of the Ghetto Uprising to coordinate the deportation of Jews to his labor camp. On 26 July 1974, a Hamburg court sentenced Otto Hantke to life imprisonment for the mass deportations of Jews from Warsaw, and other locations, to the Treblinka extermination camp.[33]

HERMANN HÖFLE

SS-Sturmbannführer Hermann Höfle served as the deputy commander of *Operation Reinhard*, under Odilo Globocnik, during the Ghetto Uprising. Höfle was born 19 June 1911 in Salzburg, Austria. He entered the SS in 1936 (SS number 307469) also joined the Nazi Party (Party number 6341873). Höfle was promoted to *SS-Untersturmführer* on 12 February 1937. He skipped the next officer grade and was promoted to *SS-Hauptsturmführer* on 17 March 1938 and to *SS-Sturmbannführer* on 21 July 1942. Höfle was in charge of the Main Department (*Hauptabteilung*) of *Operation Reinhard*, and as such, he was in charge of the manpower and organization of the operation. Additionally, Höfle coordinated the deportations of Jews from the General Government to the three major extermination camps. In July 1942, Höfle visited Warsaw to conduct just such coordination.

Höfle probably would not have visited Warsaw at the same time that Globocnik did (one of them usually remained in Lublin), but very likely did visit the Ghetto Uprising to offer his expertise concerning deportations, at some point, based on his role in *Operation Reinhard*. He survived the war, and although captured by the British with Odilo Globocnik in May 1945, managed to avoid judicial proceedings until he was arrested in Salzburg, Austria in January 1961. He committed suicide in 1962 while in custody.

FRANZ KONRAD

SS-Obersturmführer Franz Konrad served with the SS Main Economic Office as the business manager for the SS Eastern Industries Ltd. (*Ostindustrie gmbH*) founded by the WVHA in Warsaw during the period of the Ghetto Uprising. Born on 1 March 1906 at Liesing near Vienna, Austria, he had business experience before entering the SS. His SS number of 46204 suggests he entered the organization in July 1932, while his Nazi Party number of 1085499 indicates he joined the party at roughly the same time. Konrad was promoted to *SS-Untersturmführer* on 30 January 1939 and to *SS-Obersturmführer* on 1 July 1941.[34] He served in the SS Cavalry Brigade from July 1941 to 15 May 1942 on the eastern front as the food and rationed supplies officer.[35] While with this unit, he received an Iron Cross 2nd Class. He then transferred to the SS Inspectorate for Cavalry and Vehicles where he served for one year. He appears to have arrived in Warsaw on 5 April 1943. During the Ghetto Uprising, Konrad commanded the *Werterfassung*, an SS enterprise devoted to collecting, classifying, sorting and storing all transportable Jewish property left behind in the deserted apartments and buildings of the Ghetto. After the Ghetto Uprising, he was promoted to *SS-Hauptsturmführer* on 9 November 1944. That year he was also awarded a War Service Cross First Class with Swords.[36]

Konrad survived the war but stood trial with Jürgen Stroop in Warsaw. He was found guilty by the Polish Supreme National Court in 1951 of committing multiple murders in the Warsaw Ghetto and of assisting in the suppression of the Ghetto Uprising and was sentenced to death. He was executed in 1951 or 1952.

ERNST LERCH

SS-Sturmbannführer Ernst Lerch served as the adjutant to SSPF Odilo Globocnik in Lublin and is reported to have visited Warsaw during the Ghetto Uprising in an advisory capacity. Lerch was born 19 November 1914 at Klagenfurt, Austria. He joined the SS on 1 March 1934 with SS number 309700. He had already entered the Nazi Party on 1 December 1932 (Party number 1327396). Lerch was promoted to *SS-Untersturmführer* on 9 November 1936, to *SS-Obersturmführer* on 9 November 1937 and to *SS-Hauptsturmführer* on 12 March 1938. Lerch served in the German Army during the Polish Campaign in 1939. He returned to full-time SS duties in February 1940 and served in the RSHA until September 1941. From Berlin he went to the General Government and to Lublin. Lerch was promoted to *SS-Sturmbannführer* on 21 July 1942.[37] Lerch was not well liked by the other officers assigned to *Operation Reinhard*. He operated the radio link between Globocnik and Himmler and also served as the "gate guard" for admittance to Globocnik's presence.[38]

At the conclusion of *Operation Reinhard*, Odilo Globocnik requested that several members of his staff transfer with him to the office of the Higher SS and Police Leader, Adriatic Coast. Ernst Lerch was one of those men reassigned; he had proved a key cog in the destruction machine at Lublin, winning the War Service Cross 1st Class on 1 September 1943. Lerch was wounded in action on 17 October 1944.[39] He was captured with Odilo Globocnik by British troops in May 1945. Ernst Lerch died in Klagenfurt in 1997.[40]

GEORG MICHALSEN

SS-Hauptsturmführer Georg Michalsen was assigned to the SS and Police Leader for Lublin and *Operation Reinhard* but was detailed to assist the SS forces at Warsaw during the Ghetto Uprising. Michalsen was born 13 September 1906 at Wenrin, Upper Silesia. He joined the SS on with SS number 29337 and entered the Nazi Party on 1 November 1928 (Party number 103613). Michalsen, whose last name is also listed as Michalczyk in his personnel file, was promoted to *SS-Untersturmführer* on 9 November 1934 and to *SS-Obersturmführer* on 30 January 1937. He won an Iron Cross 2nd Class and a War Service Cross 2nd Class during the war. He was promoted to *SS-Hauptsturmführer* on 30 January 1942. The following typewritten letter in his personnel file from *SS-Gruppenführer* Odilo Globocnik describes his activities during the war:[41]

> Dear *SS-Obergruppenführer* Herff,
>
> I am very unhappy about your letter of 23 January 1945 regarding Michalsen, because here I have not only a faithful comrade, but also an excellent performer. During his four years of service with me, Michalsen has fulfilled the following functions [Globocnik added in handwriting: 'among others']:
>
> 1. In Lublin Michalsen established and led ethnic German units.
> 2. Michalsen has participated in Operation "R" [*Operation Reinhard*] in an independent and decisive position and, for instance, has decisively influenced the difficult battles in Warsaw, as well as cleansing Bialystok in five days.
> 3. Here he is the SS and Police Commander of the Province Trieste and is the leader of several thousand men, a few *Reich* Germans, but for the most part ethnic Germans, with absolute success.
> 4. In addition, he has now become the Commander of the Slovenian Assault Regiment.
> 5. For his courageous engagement with bandits in Istria he has received the Iron Cross 2nd Class and the Anti-Partisan Badge. With his capabilities for engagement, Michalsen has fulfilled all prerequisites of a commander.

Georg Michalsen described his own activities during the Warsaw Ghetto Uprising in legal proceedings after the war. Michalsen stated:[42]

> [*Michalsen*] I can make the following statements regarding the prior history of the Stroop mission and the intention to transfer the enterprises to the camps in the district of Lublin: with the ending of the actions of the summer of 1942, my relations to Warsaw had been discontinued. I was most delighted that this matter came to an end for me, and after my return to Lublin, I contacted *SS-Hauptsturmführer* von Mohrenschildt to get away from the Commando Höfle. And it did occur that I got to the administrative office of the *Reichskommissar*. Despite all that, I received the order from Globocnik to take care of the transfer of the Warsaw enterprises to the district of Lublin. Globocnik had a great personal interest in taking over these enterprises in his district because he had great economic interests. I cannot tell with certainty whether this was around October of 1942, but I believe that it was the right time. In any case, as far as I remember, it was still in 1942, namely towards the end of the year. Globocnik ordered me to find suitable quarters. I cannot remember today if I got this order personally. In any case, I was present when the camp at Poniatowa was selected. It is possible that Globocnik himself came along, but I do not remember this. When we were there to inspect the camp at Poniatowa, it was completely empty, and only one team of guards was present which protected the camp. This camp belonged to the *Wehrmacht* . . .
>
> On the following day, which was the second day of the action, Stroop commanded that I should refrain from any involvement because it was only a disturbance be-

cause of the "stupid firms" (or a similar derogatory expression). On the following day the wire came from Kraków that I was ordered back to Lublin. Stroop initiated this recall. As early as on the second day of the action I telephoned Globocnik and told him that I practically was de-commissioned here, and whether I should come back. Globocnik gave me the order to stay [in Warsaw.] On the next morning, which was the third day of the action, he [Globocnik] came to Warsaw by car and negotiated with Stroop. I was not present during this conference and, therefore, do not know what was discussed during that between Stroop and Globocnik. After that I went back to Lublin with Globocnik, but not in the same car; it was the same day, meaning the third day of the action.

It is correct that at the beginning of the Stroop action I still took care of a transfer of Többens Jews to Poniatowa. Which means that one more transfer of the firm of Többens to Poniatowa left Warsaw. As far as I remember, this was on the second day of the action, meaning on April 20. If H. states that this transfer to Poniatowa only left on 21 April, this is also possible. It must have been during the morning because in the afternoon of that day I had already driven back to Lublin. I do no longer remember the details about this transport. At that time there was great confusion among the Jews. Many Jews were inspired by the work of the resistance and by the fighting and it was not that simple to get them together. When H. maintains that I led this action while wearing a steel helmet, with a whip and machine pistol, this is not true. I had left my steel helmet in Lublin and had arrived in Warsaw with my hat. I did not get myself a steel helmet there. At the same time, I only had a pistol, not a machine pistol. More so, I did not have any justification for carrying a whip. I do no longer know if the transfer of the Jews went around the Ghetto to a transfer camp. I also cannot state if I accompanied the transport to the transfer place. I don't think I went along to it. I did not take part in further transports from Warsaw. Of special note is the fact that I was not a participant in the transport of the Jews of the Schultz firm to Trawniki. If such a transport took place, then possibly [*SS-Oberscharführer*] Bartetzko was involved.

[*Question*] Where you ever at the transfer area during the first three days of the Stroop Action?

[*Michalsen*] During those days everything was so chaotic and I was at so many places in the Ghetto that I don't remember where. As a torture, Stroop sent me here and there, especially to the factories with the order to make sure that the Jews of the firm had to line up for roll calls. Real work in that sense was not possible because of the fighting and the large upheaval. When [*SS-Oberscharführer*] Slany and I left Warsaw by car on 21 April, we could still see burning buildings and dark clouds over the Ghetto.

If Jesuiter says or states his suspicion that the people from Lublin organized the whole transport of the Jews from Warsaw, I cannot make a statement about this. I myself did not have such an order. However, I consider it possible that some people of Globocnik's staff in Lublin had gone to Warsaw with the order to supervise the transport of able Jews and to process it. I know that, besides the Jews who were destined for Poniatowa and Trawniki, a number of Jews were taken to Lublin and there apportioned to various camps. In this way, labor forces for the German armament factories were taken to Lublin. When I am being told that Mohwinkel was in Warsaw during the Stroop Action, I now seem to remember that Mohwinkel had something to do with the transport and selection of Jews for Lublin, especially for the DAW [*Deutsche Ausrüstungswerke*].

Basically it was Globocnik's endeavor to only take real labor forces into these camps which then could become pure and exclusive labor camps. Women, children and sick people were not to be taken into these camps, as long as they were not laborers themselves. In Globocnik's plans, these should not be transferred but remain in Warsaw for the time being so that they then would be captured in the last final cleansing of the Warsaw Ghetto and transported off to Treblinka. When I was asked what was to happen to the people who were transported off to Treblinka, I can only say that Globocnik did not tell me explicitly that they were sent to Treblinka for *liquidation*, he did not say that, but it was just inferred in the general circumstances.

This plan as Globocnik envisioned it did not get realized. The firms insisted that all people who were in their factories would be taken to the camps. The firms assumed that no selections would take place, but that all Jews of their factories would be transferred without exception. At the end, Globocnik had to agree to this attitude by the firms. As a fact, such selections among the members of the firms' labor force were no longer made before they were transferred. Globocnik still did not like it, and I remember that at a later time he mockingly remarked that in both camps there were too many women. Globocnik also made fun about the kindergarten in Poniatowa – this happened during an inspection of the Camp Poniatowa. At this inspection by Globocnik, Lerch was also present.

Michalsen, by his own testimony, was present in Warsaw during the Ghetto Uprising at least through 21 April. After *Operation Reinhard* terminated later in 1943, Michalsen went with Globocnik to Trieste where he fought partisans. Unlike many of the *Operation Reinhard* officers, he survived the war. Georg Michalsen was sentenced to twelve years imprisonment by a Hamburg court on 25 July 1974 for mass deportations of Jews to Treblinka and labor camps.[43] He was subsequently released and died in the early 1990s.[44]

REINHOLD VON MOHRENSCHILDT

SS-Hauptsturmführer Reinhold von Mohrenschildt was assigned to the SS and Police Leader for Lublin but was detailed to assist the SS forces at Warsaw during the Ghetto Uprising. Von Mohrenschildt was born 8 November 1915 at Leifling, Austria. He joined the SS with an SS number of 292779. Von Mohrenschildt was promoted to *SS-Hauptsturmführer* on 21 July 1942.[45] Von Mohrenschildt served as the local leader of the *Reich* Office for the Consolidation of German Nationhood (*Reichskommissariat für die Festigung des Deutschen Volkstums*) in Lublin.[46] This office was responsible for a variety of functions including the program of resettlement of *Volksdeutsche* (ethnic Germans), the expropriation and displacement of Slavs in occupied territories and the consignment of Jews and other racial undesirables to forced labor and extermination camps.[47] Von Mohrenschildt played an advisory role in quelling the Ghetto Uprising. He survived the war.

KARL HEINRICH MOHWINKEL

Karl Mohwinkel was born on 25 December 1911 in Celle. Before the war, he served in the 2nd SS Death's Head Riding Regiment. On 26 July 1974, a Hamburg court sentenced Karl Heinrich Mohwinkel to life imprisonment for the mass deportations of Jews to the Majdanek concentration camp.[48]

• • •

COMMANDER OF THE SECURITY POLICE AND THE SECURITY SERVICE – KdS

Fifty-two officers have been identified as serving with the KdS Warsaw, the principal Nazi organization that maintained order within the city, during the period of the Warsaw Ghetto Uprising and the events leading to it.[49]

RUDOLF ALBANBAUER

SS-Obersturmführer Rudolf Albanbauer served as the leader of Section III D (Finance) of Department III, the Security Service, in the KdS for Warsaw during the Ghetto Uprising. Albanbauer was born in Munich on 14 November 1913. He entered the SS on 6 November 1933 (SS number 142045) and the Nazi Party on 1 May 1937 (Party number 5152369). He was promoted to *SS-Untersturmführer* on 10 September 1939 and to *SS-Obersturmführer* on 30 January 1942.[50] He survived the war. Rudolf Albanbauer died on 3 March 1977 in Munich.[51]

FRANZ AVRIL

SS-Untersturmführer Franz Avril was assigned to Section III C (Culture, Religion and Propaganda) of Department III, the Security Service, in the KdS for Warsaw at the time of the Ghetto Uprising. He was born 27 October 1911 in Kaiserslautern; at the age of eighteen, Avril joined the SS on 1 March 1930 (SS number 67687). On 1 May 1933, he entered the Nazi Party with membership number 3070110. Avril spent thirteen years as an enlisted man. Prior to his duties in Warsaw, Avril was assigned to *Einsatzgruppe IV* during the Polish Campaign in 1939. Franz Avril was promoted from *SS-Hauptscharführer* to *SS-Untersturmführer* on 20 April 1943, Hitler's birthday and one day into the Ghetto Uprising.[52] He is believed to have survived the war.

NORBERT GRAF BERGH-TRIPS

SS-Obersturmführer Norbert Graf Bergh-Trips served in Department IV, the *Gestapo*, in various functions, of the KdS during the Ghetto Uprising. Born 18 January 1912 in Graz, Austria, he entered the SS on 2 June 1937 with SS number 281072. Bergh-Trips, an aristocrat, was promoted to *SS-Untersturmführer* on 20 April 1940 and to *SS-Obersturmführer* on 29 January 1941. In 1940, he served at the RSHA in Berlin; Bergh-Trips also worked in the *Gestapo* office at Vienna. He served in the Austrian Army from 1933 to 1934 and entered the Police in 1937. Norbert Graf Bergh-Trips had frequent disciplinary problems in the SS; in 1943 he was sentenced to fourteen days house arrest for misappropriating a vehicle, and to three months arrest for misuse of his office.[53]

Wladyslaw Bartoszewski, in his book *Warsaw Death Ring 1939-1944*, states that Bergh-Trips directed numerous executions of prisoners in the Ghetto as well as on the other streets of Warsaw.[54] For a period, he was also the commandant of Pawiak Prison. After the Ghetto Uprising, Bergh-Trips remained in Warsaw. He received an Iron Cross 2nd Class in 1944, most likely for his role in the Warsaw Uprising in August and September of that year.[55] Norbert Graf Bergh-Trips survived the war. He was called as a witness in 1973 in Germany for proceedings against former SS personnel at Warsaw.[56]

KARL BIEDENKAPP

SS-Obersturmführer Karl Biedenkapp served in the pay office (*Zahlstelle*) of the KdS in Warsaw. Biedenkapp was born in Solms-Ilsdorf on 16 November 1900. A career police officer,

Biedenkapp was an honorary SS officer (SS number 51632). His surviving personnel record reflects no other information.[57] He appears to have been assigned to Warsaw in November 1941.

WOLFGANG BIRKNER

SS-Hauptsturmführer Wolfgang Birkner served as a leader of Section IV A 4 (Personal Security) in Department IV, the *Gestapo*, of the KdS Warsaw during the Ghetto Uprising. He also operated a special unit, Section IV N, with its own network of informers and spies that collected information of interest to the whole branch.[58] Birkner was born in Breslau, Silesia (now Wroclaw, Poland) on 27 October 1913. He joined the SS on 30 July 1934 (SS number 265793) and the Nazi Party on 1 April 1935 (Party number 3601309.) While an enlisted soldier, Birkner served in the SS Regiment *Leibstandarte Adolf Hitler*. He was promoted to *SS-Untersturmführer* on 2 July 1938, to *SS-Obersturmführer* on 30 January 1942 and to *SS-Hauptsturmführer* on 20 April 1943. In the late 1930s, he served in the *Gestapo* at Halle. At the beginning of the war he was assigned to the SD Main Office in Berlin and then to the *Gestapo* office at Schneidemühl. From 3 July to 11 August 1941 he served with *Einsatzgruppe z. b .V.*, a unit headed by Dr. Eberhard Schöngarth, that killed some 10,000 Jews and other "undesirables" in eastern Poland and western Byelorussia. He received a War Service Cross 2nd Class in 1942. Wolfgang Birkner appears to have survived the war.[59]

JOHANNES BÖHM

SS-Obersturmführer Johannes Böhm served with Section IV B 4 (Jewish Affairs), Department IV, *Gestapo*, of the Security Police and Security Service in Warsaw during the Ghetto Uprising. Born 17 February 1912 in Dresden, he entered the Nazi party on 1 November 1932 with party membership number 1377591. Böhm joined the SS one year later on 14 March 1933 as member number 133828. A career police official, Böhm was married. He was promoted to *SS-Untersturmführer* on 4 February 1939 and to *SS-Obersturmführer* on 1 September 1940. From 3 July to 11 August 1941 he served with *Einsatzgruppe z. b. V.*, as the leader of *Teilkommando Böhm*, in eastern Poland and western Byelorussia. After the Ghetto Uprising, Böhm was promoted to *SS-Hauptsturmführer* on 9 November 1943. His personnel record does not reflect any awards or decorations.[60]

Böhm is thought to have survived the war. He probably played an extensive role in the suppression of the Ghetto Uprising based on his duty position.

ALFRED BÖHMER

SS-Untersturmführer Alfred Böhmer served in Department V (*Kripo*) of the KdS Warsaw during the Ghetto Uprising. Born 24 February 1894 in Dresden, Böhmer fought in World War I in the 177th Infantry Regiment, winning the Iron Cross 2nd Class for bravery during which he was wounded four times. He entered the Police in 1919. In 1939, he entered the SS and received SS number 369624. On 1 May 1937, Böhmer entered the Nazi Party (Party number 4953508). Before transferring to Warsaw, Böhmer served in the *Kripo* office at Dresden. After the Ghetto Uprising, he was promoted to *SS-Obersturmführer* on 9 November 1944. There is no indication that Böhmer did not survive the war.[61]

KARL GEORG BRANDT

SS-Obersturmführer Karl Georg Brandt worked for Johannes Böhm in Section IV B 4 (Jewish Affairs), Department IV, *Gestapo*, of the KdS Warsaw. Brandt was born on 5 November 1898 in Karlsmarkt/Brieg in Silesia (now Karlovice/Brzeg, Poland). He entered the Nazi Party on 1 May 1937. Prior to the war he served in the Criminal Police in Bielefeld.[62] Little else is known about this officer, but many Jews in Warsaw said that Brandt "was the true lord of the Ghetto."[63] He served as one of the directors of the deportation operation and seems to have remained in the *Gestapo* in Warsaw through the Warsaw Uprising. Brandt was reported killed during the fighting at Posen (now Poznan, Poland) on 16 February 1945.[64] Other sources indicate that Brandt possibly survived the war.[65]

ULRICH BREITENFELDT

SS-Obersturmführer Ulrich Breitenfeldt served in both Section I B (Training and Education) and Section II A (Police Organization and Regulations) of the KdS for Warsaw. Breitenfeldt was born 21 January 1913 in Berlin-Steglitz. In 1931 Breitenfeldt served in the SA. He entered the SS on 1 November 1932 with SS number 51038. Shortly thereafter, on 1 May 1933, he entered the Nazi Party with Party number 3474424. Breitenfeldt was promoted to *SS-Untersturmführer* on 9 November 1938 and to *SS-Obersturmführer* on 9 November 1942.[66] Breitenfeldt reported for duty just as the Ghetto Uprising was ending, so it is unlikely that he played any major role in the operation. He is believed to have survived the war.

ARTHUR FÜSSEL

SS-Hauptsturmführer Arthur Füssel served as the head of Department I/II, Administration and Law, of the KdS for Warsaw during the Ghetto Uprising. He was born on 21 November 1893. Füssel's personnel file is extremely abbreviated. He appears to have been an honorary SS officer (SS number 50963) which allowed him to wear the uniform while on duty.[67] Füssel was assigned to Warsaw in September 1941. He was designated a *Polizeirat* in December 1942. Arthur Füssel was killed in action in August 1944 during the Warsaw Uprising.

HARRY GEISLER

SS-Sturmbannführer Harry Geisler was assigned as the leader of Department V, Criminal Police (*Kripo*), in the KdS Warsaw during the Ghetto Uprising. Geisler was born 14 July 1899 in Rixdorf. He entered police service in Berlin in November 1925 and was promoted to *Kriminal-Kommisar* on 1 October 1928, to *Kriminal-Rat* on 1 January 1936 and to *Kriminal-Direktor* on 1 April 1941. He joined the Nazi Party on 1 May 1933 (Party number 2580313). Geisler was an honorary *SS-Sturmbannführer* (SS number 50905) and so may have worn the SS uniform on many occasions.[68] Geisler was made a *Regierungsrat* in March 1943. He appears to have survived the war.

WERNER GRABERT

SS-Obersturmführer Werner Grabert was assigned to Section II C (Finance), Department I/II, Administration and Law, in the KdS for Warsaw and served as the commandant of Pawiak Prison during the Ghetto Uprising. Grabert was born 9 July 1905 in Berlin. A career law enforcement officer, Grabert entered the Police in 1927 and served with the *Schutzpolizei* in Berlin for the next nine years. He entered the Nazi Party on 1 October 1939 (Party number 7218859). Grabert served in the RSHA in Berlin before moving to Warsaw in January 1943. With an SS number of 424206, he was promoted to *SS-Untersturmführer* on 20 April 1942 and to *SS-Obersturmführer* on 9 November 1942. Grabert's personnel file indicates a high probability that he survived the war.[69]

WERNER GRAHN

SS-Untersturmführer Werner Grahn served in Section IV E (Counter-Intelligence), Department IV, *Gestapo*, of the KdS for Warsaw. One of the older SS officers at Warsaw, he was born 5 January 1884 in Livenko, Russia. Grahn served in World War I and won an Iron Cross 2nd Class in that conflict. After the war, he briefly served with the *Reinhardt Brigade Freikorps*. A career police officer, Grahn entered the SS on 20 November 1936 with SS number 280102. Six months later, he joined the Nazi Party (Party number 5333178). Before serving in Warsaw, Werner Grahn was assigned to the Hamburg police. Grahn would have made a good counter-intelligence officer from the standpoint of foreign languages; he spoke five. Grahn was promoted to *SS-Obersturmführer* on 21 June 1944.[70] He is believed to have survived the war.

GUSTAV GRAMBOW

SS-Untersturmführer Gustav Grambow served in Section IV A 1 (Communists, Prisoners of War [excluding Polish officers] and Radio Offenses) of Department IV, *Gestapo*, of the KdS Warsaw. Grambow was born 8 December 1894 in Gehmkendorf. He fought in World War I as a member of the 4th Guard Field Artillery Regiment. During this war, he won an Iron Cross 2nd Class and was wounded in action. After the conflict he served briefly with *Freikorps Potsdam*. Grambow served with the Berlin Protective Police from 1919 to 1926. He joined the SS on 5 March 1932 (SS number 36660). Two months later, he entered the Nazi Party with party number 1103533. Gustav Grambow was promoted to *SS-Untersturmführer* on 20 April 1937. During the pre-war period, he was assigned to the *Gestapo* at Potsdam and to the Main SD Office in Berlin.[71] He is believed to have survived the war.

RICHARD GRUDNO

SS-Obersturmführer Richard Grudno was assigned to Section II C (Finance), Department I/II, Administration and Law, in the KdS for Warsaw during the Ghetto Uprising. Grudno was born 7 August 1897 in Königsberg, East Prussia (now Kaliningrad, Russian Federation). An honorary SS officer, he held membership number 51737. Grudno was designated a *Polizei-Inspector* in July 1941 in Warsaw. Nothing else is known about this officer.[72]

DR. LUDWIG HAHN

SS-Obersturmbannführer Dr. Ludwig Hahn served as the Commander of the Security Police and Security Service, KdS, in Warsaw during the Ghetto Uprising. Born 23 January 1908 in Eitzen/Uelzen, he was a lawyer by profession. He entered the Nazi Party on 1 February 1930 (Party number 194463). Hahn joined the SS on 21 April 1933 and received SS number 65823. Married with three children, he attended the University of Jena and Göttingen. He was promoted to *SS-Untersturmführer* on 20 April 1936, to *SS-Obersturmführer* on 30 January 1938, to *SS-Hauptsturmführer* on 1 August 1938 and *SS-Sturmbannführer* on 26 September 1938. During these years he served in the Security Service Main Office (*Reichssicherheitshauptamt*) in Berlin. Prior to assuming duties in Warsaw, Hahn led *Einsatzkommando 1* of *Einsatzgruppe I* during the Polish Campaign in 1939. His personnel file reflects an award of the Iron Cross 2nd Class in 1940, most likely for his work in this *Einsatzkommando*. Hahn also served as the Commander of Security Police and Security Service in Kraków for a brief period. He assumed duties in Warsaw on 1 August 1941. He was promoted to *SS-Obersturmbannführer* on 9 November 1941.

Hahn played one of the most significant roles in the suppression of the Ghetto Uprising as well as supervising the deportation of Warsaw's Jews to Treblinka. After the war, Jürgen Stroop commented favorably on Hahn's ability:[73]

> Dr. Hahn was my main source of strength. I called him several times a day. It was Hahn . . . who mapped things out for me.

Hahn received both the War Service Cross 2nd and 1st Class in 1943 most likely for his role during the fighting. Hahn was designated a *Regierungs-Direktor* in March 1944. He was promoted to *SS-Standartenführer* on 20 April 1944 and won an Iron Cross 1st Class on 9 October 1944 for his part in quelling the Warsaw Uprising.[74] In December 1944 he served with an *Einsatzkommando* in the Moselle region of France. From there he was briefly assigned to Army Group Vistula and then to the SS staff at Dresden. The end of the war saw Ludwig Hahn as a senior Sipo and SD commander in Westphalia. He survived the war, going into hiding under an assumed name, later served as an insurance agent and practiced law in Hamburg. He was arrested in 1961 but released. In 1965 he was once again arrested but released due to reasons of ill health. On 5 June 1973, a Hamburg court sentenced Hahn to twelve years imprisonment for various murders of Jews in Pawiak Prison from 1942 to 1944.[75] He was sentenced by another Hamburg court on 4 July 1975 to life imprisonment for the deportation of at least 230,000 Jews from the Warsaw Ghetto to Treblinka in 1942.[76]

WILHELM HAMMERMEISTER

SS-Untersturmführer Wilhelm Hammermeister was assigned to Section IV A 2 (Sabotage, Forged Passports And Passes, Shootings and Explosions And Air Drops) in Department IV, the *Gestapo*, of the KdS Warsaw during the Ghetto Uprising. Born 24 August 1901 in Grünkirchen, Hammermeister entered the Police in 1923 and served in Police Regiment General Göring from 1933 to 1934. Hammermeister joined the SS in 1937 with membership number 290713. He was promoted to *SS-Untersturmführer* on 20 April 1939. Two years later, Hammermeister entered the Nazi Party on 11 January 1941 (Party number 8288057).[77] Wilhelm Hammermeister is believed to have survived the war.

HUGO HAMPEL

SS-Untersturmführer Hugo Hampel served as the leader for Section III B (Nationality and Race) of Department III, the Security Service, in the KdS for Warsaw during the Ghetto Uprising. Born 3 March 1912 in Tomaschow, Poland, Hampel served in the Polish Army from 1933 to 1935. He entered the SS in 1938 (SS number 392207) and served in *Einsatzgruppe VI* during the Polish Campaign in 1939. Hampel also served at the RSHA in Berlin and may have served in *Einsatzgruppe D* in Russia as well. He was promoted to *SS-Untersturmführer* on 20 April 1941 and to *SS-Obersturmführer* on 30 January 1944. He arrived in Warsaw on 21 April 1942.[78] Hugo Hampel appears to have survived the war.

KARL HEINE

SS-Obersturmführer Karl Heine was assigned to Section III D (Finance) of Department III, the Security Service, in the KdS for Warsaw during the Ghetto Uprising. Heine was born 17 November 1893 in Elversberg. He fought in World War I as an infantryman in the 166th Infantry Regiment. Following that conflict, he entered the work force as a bank official in Saarbrücken. Karl Heine joined the Nazi Party on 1 May 1933 (Party number 2709590), and shortly thereafter spent two years in the SA. On 1 July 1936 Heine entered the SS (SS number 280281). Karl Heine was promoted to *SS-Untersturmführer* on 20 April 1940 and to *SS-Obersturmführer* on 9 November 1942. Karl Heine appears to have served in Warsaw for most of the war and to have survived the hostility.[79]

KARL HELLER

SS-Obersturmführer Karl Heller served as the leader of Section IV E S, a Special Commando, of Department IV, the *Gestapo*, in the KdS for Warsaw during the Ghetto Uprising. Born in Hintermühlen on 3 June 1908, he began a career in the Police in 1928. On 1 May 1938 Heller entered the Nazi Party (Party number 6966598). Two years later, on 1 May 1940, he joined the SS with SS number 383971. Heller became an officer soon in his SS career; he was promoted to *SS-Untersturmführer* on 1 December 1940. During this period, he served in the SD main office in Berlin. He was promoted to *SS-Obersturmführer* on 1 March 1941. Heller was promoted to *SS-Hauptsturmführer* on 30 January 1945. During the War he received the War Service Cross 1st and 2nd Class.[80] He appears to have survived the war.

ERICH HERBERHOLZ

SS-Hauptsturmführer Erich Herberholz was assigned to an unspecified position in the KdS for Warsaw during the period surrounding the Ghetto Uprising. Herberholz was born 23 November 1908 in Berlin. Herberholz enlisted in the Nazi Party on 26 November 1926 (Party number 48030) and received a Golden Party Badge for his early commitment to the Party. A relatively early member of the SS as well, he joined this organization on 1 October 1931 (SS number 19412). Erich Herberholz was promoted to *SS-Untersturmführer* on 30 January 1938, to *SS-Obersturmführer* on 20 April 1939 and to *SS-Hauptsturmführer* on 9 November 1940. During the war he was awarded an Iron Cross 2nd Class and was wounded in action.[81] He was assigned to Warsaw in October 1942. Herberholz is believed to have survived the war.

GOTTLIEB HÖHMANN

SS-Hauptsturmführer Gottlieb Höhmann was assigned as the deputy for Department IV, the *Gestapo*, in the KdS Warsaw during the Ghetto Uprising. Höhmann also served as section leader for Section IV A (hostile activities and sabotage.) He hailed from Remscheid where he was born on 7 January 1907. His SS number of 353228 indicates he joined the organization in 1938. Höhmann had joined the Nazi Party on 23 October 1930 with membership number 360034. He spent six semesters at a university; he was married with one son. He served as a detective with the Criminal Police in Münster and later served with the *Gestapo* in Düsseldorf. Gottlieb Höhmann was promoted to *SS-Untersturmführer* on 20 April 1940, while he was assigned to the SD Main Office and to *SS-Obersturmführer* on 9 November 1940. During the late 1941 – early 1942 time frame Höhmann served with *Einsatzgruppe C* in the Ukraine and was promoted to *SS-Hauptsturmführer* on 9 November 1941. He is believed to have arrived in Warsaw in 1942.[82] He was designated a *Kriminal-Rat* in November 1942 and a *Polizei-Inspektor* in February 1943. For a short period in 1942, Höhmann also served as the commandant of Pawiak Prison.

Gottlieb Höhmann likely played a significant role in the Ghetto Uprising. He is thought to have survived the war.

KARL JEPSEN

SS-Untersturmführer Karl Jepsen was assigned to Section III D (Finance) of Department III, the Security Service, in the KdS for Warsaw during the Ghetto Uprising. Jepsen was born 31 May 1914 in Rendsburg. He joined the SS at age eighteen on 1 May 1933 (SS number 81302). Five years later, on 1 November 1938, Karl Jepsen entered the Nazi Party with Party number 6042864. Jepsen became an *SS-Untersturmführer* on 9 November 1941.[83] Little else is known about this officer; he is believed to have survived the war.

WILFRIED JOPKE

SS-Obersturmführer Wilfried Jopke served as the leader of Section IV E (Counter-Intelligence) in Department IV, the *Gestapo*, of the KdS Warsaw during the Ghetto Uprising. Jopke was born in Ohlau, Silesia (now Olawa, Poland) on 15 July 1906. He entered the SS on 30 January 1938 (SS number 290777), with a direct appointment to *SS-Obersturmführer*, and the Nazi Party on 1 March 1932 (Party number 1025570). Jopke served at the RSHA in Berlin during the late 1930s and then transferred to the *Gestapo* at Breslau. He reported for duty in Warsaw on 6 January 1940 and was designated a *Kriminal-Kommissar* on 1 March 1940. Jopke was promoted to *SS-Hauptsturmführer* on 30 January 1944. He appears to have survived the war.[84]

DR. HERBERT JUNG

SS-Obersturmführer Dr. Herbert Jung served as an assistant in Department I/II, Administration and Law, in the KdS for Warsaw during the Ghetto Uprising. Additionally, for a short period in 1942, he served as the commandant of Pawiak Prison. Jung was born 10 April 1908 in Erdesbach. He entered the SS on 12 July 1940 (SS number 375072) having joined the Nazi Party on 1 May 1933 (Party number 3269169). Jung was promoted to *SS-Untersturmführer* on 1 October 1940 and to *SS-Obersturmführer* on 20 April 1943. Dr. Herbert Jung received a War Service cross 2nd Class in 1943.[85] The *Befehlsblatt des Chefs der Sicherheitspolizei und des SD*, a professional information bulletin of the Security Service, published weekly in Berlin, indicates that Jung was killed in Warsaw in June 1944.[86] Stefan Korbonski, a prominent member of the Polish resistance movement, gives the date of death for Jung as 12 June 1944 and states that he was killed in the Zoliborz area of Warsaw.[87]

DR. ERNST KAH

SS-Sturmbannführer Dr. Ernst Kah served as the Deputy Commander of the KdS and the leader of Department III, the Security Service, in Warsaw during the Ghetto Uprising. Born in Baden-Baden on 20 June 1899, he served in the 170th Infantry Regiment during World War I and won the Iron Cross 2nd Class. After the war, Kah attended the Universities of Heidelberg, Tübingen and Freiburg and received a law degree. He joined the Nazi Party on 1 September 1932 with membership number 1298873. On 1 August 1937 Kah entered the SS with SS number 290543. His initial service was with the SD Main Office in Berlin; he then served in the Security Police in Munich. He was promoted to *SS-Untersturmführer* on 1 May 1938, to *SS-Obersturmführer* on 20 April 1939 and to *SS-Hauptsturmführer* on 9 November 1939. During the Polish Campaign in 1939 he served with *Einsatzgruppe IV*. He then assumed his duties with the Security Police and Security Service in Warsaw. Kah was promoted to *SS-Sturmbannführer* on 1 August 1940. During October 1941, Ernst Kah served as the acting KdS for Warsaw and probably held this position several times during the occupation. In December 1941 he was named leader of Department III. After the Ghetto Uprising, he was promoted to *SS-Obersturmbannführer* on 9 November 1943. The following is a portion of one of his efficiency reports during the war:[88]

> During the Polish campaign, Dr. Kah has excelled as the leader of an *Einsatzkommando* through his clear understanding of the situations and clever leadership of the men. In the practical work in the field of economics in the government, he has shown outstanding knowledge of the subject. He seems worthy of being promoted to *SS-Sturmbannführer*. Dr. Kah was a soldier at the front during the World War [World War I] and is a Lieutenant in the Reserve.

Dr. Ernst Kah played a key role in the German suppression of the Ghetto Uprising. Jürgen Stroop elaborated after the war on Kah's talents and importance:[89]

> It was different with Dr. Kah. *He* contacted *me* in the Ghetto whenever I was in trouble. The man must have been psychic. In moments of doubt, there he'd be, by phone or wireless, telling me what I needed to know, and then pretending it'd been my decision. It was Hahn and Kah . . . who mapped things out for me.

Dr. Ernst Kah survived the war. He died 19 February 1967 in Braunschweig.[90]

JAKOB LECHNER

SS-Hauptsturmführer Jakob Lechner served as a leader of Section IV A 5 (Ciphers) in Department IV, the *Gestapo*, of the KdS Warsaw during the Ghetto Uprising. An Austrian, he was born 31 May 1911 at Kitzbühel. He joined the Nazi Party on 4 May 1933 (Party number 6345064). He had an SS number of 386645. Before serving in Warsaw, Lechner worked at the RSHA in Berlin. In February 1942 he was designated a *Kriminal-Kommissar* in Warsaw. Jakob Lechner survived the Ghetto Uprising but not the war. The Polish underground targeted Lechner for death and assassinated him at 0700 hours on 5 October 1943 in the city.[91]

WILLY LUBENSKY

SS-Untersturmführer Willy Lubensky worked in the Counterfeit Section of Department V, the Criminal Police, in the KdS Warsaw, during and after the Warsaw Ghetto Uprising. Lubensky was born in Magdeburg on 23 October 1895. He won an Iron Cross 2nd Class in World War I while serving with the 17th Reserve Infantry Regiment. Immediately after the conflict, he served for one year in a *Freikorps*. Lubensky then joined the Police in 1921; for many years he served in the Police in Berlin. On 1 March 1933, Willy Lubensky joined the Nazi Party with Party number 1485663. Some four years later, he entered the SS on 9 November 1937 (SS number 290401). Lubensky was promoted to *SS-Untersturmführer* on 9 November 1938. Lubensky survived the Ghetto Uprising but was killed in action on 4 August 1944 during the Warsaw Uprising.[92]

ERICH MERTEN

SS-Untersturmführer Erich Merten served in Section IV E 1, General Counter-Intelligence, of Department IV, the *Gestapo*, in the KdS for Warsaw during the Ghetto Uprising. Merten was born on 28 October 1901 in Hennickendorf. An honorary SS officer, he was given SS number 50936 for administrative purposes. Not much is known about this officer. He appears to have been a career Police officer. He was brought before a court-martial in February 1944 on a charge of involuntary manslaughter but was found not guilty.[93] He was awarded a War Service Cross 1st Class in September 1943. Erich Merten appears to have survived the war.

KURT MÜLDNER

SS-Untersturmführer Kurt Müldner served in an undetermined position in the KdS for Warsaw during the Ghetto Uprising. Müldner was born on 15 November 1902. Another honorary SS officer, he was given SS number 51774 for administrative purposes. Müldner's personnel file consists of only one card. Like many other honorary SS officers, he appears to have been a career Police officer.[94] Kurt Müldner appears to have survived the war.

KARL MÜLLER

SS-Hauptsturmführer Karl Müller served as the leader for Section III A (Administration and Law) of Department III, the Security Service, in the KdS for Warsaw during the Ghetto Uprising. Müller was born in Braunschweig on 6 November 1903. He entered the SS in 1932 (SS number 38663) and the Nazi Party on 1 August 1930 (Party number 280582.) He was promoted to *SS-Untersturmführer* on 13 September 1936, to *SS-Obersturmführer* on 30 January 1938 and to *SS-Hauptsturmführer* on 20 April 1939. He began the war assigned to the SD Main Office in Berlin.[95] He arrived in Warsaw in October 1942.

Karl Müller did not survive the war. His personnel file indicates that he was killed in action in Warsaw on 2 August 1944 during the Warsaw Uprising.[96]

WILHELM MUNK

SS-Untersturmführer Wilhelm Munk served as the leader of the 6th *Kommissariat*, Hotel and Travel Registration, in Department V, the Criminal Police, in the KdS for Warsaw during the Ghetto Uprising. Munk was born on 27 February 1892. An honorary SS officer, he was given SS number 51411 for administrative purposes. Nothing else is known about this officer.[97] Wilhelm Munk appears to have survived the war.

OTTO OERTWIG

SS-Hauptsturmführer Otto Oertwig was assigned to Section II D (Technical Matters) in Department I/II, Administration and Law, of the KdS for Warsaw during the Ghetto Uprising. Oertwig was born 1 August 1906 in Berlin. On 1 April 1930, he joined the Nazi Party (Party number 222279). Otto Oertwig then entered the SA and served in this organization for two years. On 1 November 1932, Oertwig joined the SS and received SS number 53869. From 30 May 1938 to 6 June 1939, he served in the Condor Legion, the German *Luftwaffe* contingent that assisted *Generalissimo* Francisco Franco and his Spanish Nationalist forces during the Spanish Civil War. He received the Spanish Cross military decoration for his contributions.[98] During his service in Spain Oertwig was promoted directly to the grade of *SS-Hauptsturmführer*. He may have served as a *Gestapo* officer at that time. Oertwig survived the Warsaw Ghetto Uprising. He was killed in action on 1 August 1944 during the first day of the Warsaw Uprising.[99]

ALFRED OTTO

SS-Untersturmführer Alfred Otto served as a desk officer in Section IV A 3 c (Principal Resistance Organizations and Secret Political Organizations) in Department IV, the *Gestapo*, of the KdS Warsaw during the Ghetto Uprising. Otto was born in Lódz on 12 March 1900. He joined the SS on 1 November 1931 (SS number 35334) and the Nazi Party on the same day (Party number 711150). Otto was promoted to *SS-Untersturmführer* on 10 September 1939. He worked at the RSHA in Berlin and the *Gestapo* at Schneidemühl before his assignment to Warsaw. Otto received both a War Service Cross 2nd and 1st Class during the war.[100] Heinrich Himmler personally commended him for outstanding leadership in October 1941. He is believed to have survived the conflict.

ALFRED PAGEL

SS-Untersturmführer Alfred Pagel was assigned to the headquarters element of the KdS for Warsaw during the Ghetto Uprising. Born in Kolberg (now Kolobrzeg, Poland) on the Baltic Sea on 5 October 1899, he served with the 22nd Fusilier Regiment in World War I. After the war Pagel served briefly with a *Freikorps*. He entered the SS on 15 March 1933 with SS number 218619. Less than two months later, on 1 May 1933, he also entered the Nazi Party (Party number 1854035). During the campaign against Poland in 1939, he served with *Einsatzgruppe IV* as an *SS-Hauptscharführer*. He then assumed his duties with the Security Police and Security Service in Warsaw. Pagel was promoted to *SS-Untersturmführer* on 30 January 1943. During the war he received a War Service Cross 2nd Class.[101] Alfred Pagel appears to have survived the war.

ARTHUR POTRATZ

SS-Hauptsturmführer Arthur Potratz served as the deputy leader of Department III, the Security Service, in Warsaw during the Ghetto Uprising. He was born 27 August 1906 in Regelnitzen, East Prussia. Potratz joined the Nazi Party on 1 August 1931 (Party number 601144) and entered the SS one month later on 1 September 1931 (SS number 36795). He was promoted to *SS-Untersturmführer* on 20 April 1937, to *SS-Obersturmführer* on 9 November 1939 and to *SS-Hauptsturmführer* on 30 January 1941. Potratz was assigned to Warsaw in April 1941 and awarded a War Service Cross 2nd Class during the war.[102] Arthur Potratz appears to have survived the war.

ERICH RESCHKE

SS-Untersturmführer Erich Reschke served as the leader of Section IV E 1 (General Counter-Intelligence, Desertion, and Monitoring of Foreign Correspondence) in Department IV, the *Gestapo*, of the KdS Warsaw during the Ghetto Uprising. Reschke was born 25 March 1896 in Zbiczno. He fought in World War I as an enlisted soldier in the 61st Infantry Regiment; he was wounded in action and also won an Iron Cross 2nd Class. Reschke entered the SS in 1938 (SS number 353244) and the Nazi Party on 1 April 1933 (Party number 1645347.)[103]

Erich Reschke was promoted to *SS-Untersturmführer* on 20 April 1940. He was assigned to the RSHA in Berlin and also the *Gestapo* at Schneidemühl. From 3 July to 11 August 1941 he served with *Einsatzgruppe z. b. V.* in eastern Poland and western Byelorussia. From that assignment he most likely went to Warsaw. After the Warsaw Ghetto Uprising, he was promoted to *SS-Obersturmführer* on 21 June 1943. His personnel file indicates that he probably survived the war.[104]

GEORG RICHTER

SS-Hauptsturmführer Georg Richter served in Department V (*Kripo*) of the KdS Warsaw during the Ghetto Uprising. He was born 12 December 1900 at Graba/Saalfeld. Richter entered the Nazi Party on 1 December 1931 with membership number 859753. He later entered the SS and received SS number 337656. Before Warsaw Richter served at the RSHA in Berlin and in the SD office at Mannheim. He was promoted to *SS-Untersturmführer* on 1 July 1939, to *SS-Obersturmführer* on 20 April 1941 and to *SS-Hauptsturmführer* on 9 November 1942. He arrived in Warsaw on 1 December 1942 and assumed duties in the *Kripo* section.[105]

Georg Richter received an Iron Cross 2nd Class on 16 December 1943 after the Ghetto Uprising but for undocumented reasons. *SS-Hauptsturmführer* Georg Richter was killed in action on 2 August 1944 during the first days of the 1944 Warsaw Uprising.[106]

HEINZ SCHNARTENDORFF

SS-Obersturmführer Heinz Schnartendorff served as the leader of Section III C (Culture, Religion and Propaganda) of Department III, the Security Service, in the KdS for Warsaw during the Ghetto Uprising. He was born 15 March 1911 at Stralsund. He entered the SS on 1 November 1933 (SS number 179191) and the Nazi Party on 1 April 1933 (Party number 1826160). Schnartendorff was promoted to *SS-Untersturmführer* on 20 April 1940 and to *SS-Obersturmführer* on 30 January 1943. Before serving in Warsaw, he was assigned to the SD in

Stettin.[107] He reported to Warsaw in October 1941.

SS-Obersturmführer Heinz Schnartendorff was killed in action on 2 August 1944 during the 1944 Warsaw Uprising.[108]

HUGO SCHWARZE

SS-Untersturmführer Hugo Schwarze was assigned to Section I D (Internal Discipline) in Department I, Administration and Law of the KdS in Warsaw. Not much is recorded about this officer; he was born 9 December 1896, was admitted to the SS as an honorary SS officer (SS number 50895) and appears to have been a career Police officer.[109]

EUGEN SCHWEIZER

SS-Hauptsturmführer Eugen Schweizer served as the general deputy to Arthur Füssel in Department I/II, Administration and Law, in the KdS for Warsaw during the Ghetto Uprising. Schweizer was born 28 March 1908 in Mühlheim/Main. He entered the SS on 1 November 1933 with membership number 149044 having joined the Nazi Party on 1 April 1933 (Party number 1732151). Schweizer was promoted to *SS-Obersturmführer* on 9 November 1938 and to *SS-Hauptsturmführer* on 30 January 1942. Before arriving in Warsaw, he served with the SD in Stuttgart. His personnel file shows that he probably survived the war.[110]

ALFRED SEILER

SS-Untersturmführer Alfred Seiler was assigned to Section IV E S (Special Commando Spilker) in Department IV, the *Gestapo*, in the KdS Warsaw during the Ghetto Uprising. Seiler was born in Kiel on 30 November 1910. Too young to have served in World War I, he became a mason. He joined the SA in 1929 and served with that organization for seven years. He also joined the Nazi Party on 1 September 1939 and received Party number 148240. Seiler entered the Police in 1934. His SS number of 350774 would indicate that he joined the SS in late 1938, but the exact date is not annotated in his personnel file. Seiler was promoted to *SS-Untersturmführer* on 1 June 1940 and was assigned to the SD Main Office in Berlin at that time. Prior to service in Warsaw, Seiler served with the *Gestapo* at Lódz (renamed Litzmannstadt by the Germans).[111] He was killed in action on 2 March 1945.[112]

ALFRED SPILKER

SS-Obersturmführer Alfred Spilker served in Department IV, the *Gestapo*, within the KdS in Warsaw during the destruction of the Warsaw Ghetto. In this organization, he oversaw a special police intelligence unit, known as *Sonderkommando Spilker* (Special Commando Spilker), whose mission was to identify and actually infiltrate the command centers of the Polish underground.[113] Spilker hailed from Niederbecken where he was born on 1 January 1908. Spilker joined the Nazi Party on 1 December 1930 with membership number 383086. He entered the SS three years later on 28 May 1933 with SS number 165148. Spilker earned the rank of *SS-Untersturmführer* on 9 November 1938. On 30 January 1941 he was promoted to *SS-Obersturmführer*. Spilker received public recognition for his services in September 1941 in the *Befehlsblatt des Chefs der Sicherheitspolizei und des SD*. After the Ghetto Uprising, Alfred Spilker was promoted to *SS-Hauptsturmführer* and was also designated a *Kriminal-Rat* in July 1943. His short personnel file reflects no decorations or awards during his career.[114]

Spilker obviously played a significant role in the Warsaw drama. He is believed to have survived the war.

ERICH SPRUCH

SS-Hauptsturmführer Erich Spruch served as the leader of the Criminal Matters section (*Kriminaldirektion*) within Department V, the Criminal Police, of the KdS Warsaw during the Ghetto Uprising. Spruch was born 15 June 1898. He was an honorary SS officer (SS number 51607 for administrative purposes). Spruch appears to have been a career Police officer but like most honorary SS officers, his personnel file consists of a single information card.[115] Spruch was assigned to Warsaw in January 1942. He was temporarily detailed from Warsaw to Radom in October 1942, but returned to Warsaw in January 1943.

DR. GERHARD STABENOW

SS-Untersturmführer Dr. Gerhard Stabenow served in the KdS office in Warsaw during the Ghetto Uprising. Born 26 January 1906 in Halle, he attended a university and received a law degree. He joined the SS on 1 November 1936 (SS number 350066) and the Nazi Party on 1 May 1937 (Party number 447473). Stabenow was promoted to *SS-Untersturmführer* on 9 November 1940. Dr. Gerhard Stabenow was present in the KdS during the Ghetto Uprising, but we do not know his exact role in suppressing it.[116]

WALTER STAMM

SS-Sturmbannführer Walter Stamm served as the leader of Department IV, the *Gestapo*, of the KdS Warsaw. He was born 25 November 1904 in Braunschweig. He joined the SS on 15 May 1936 with SS number 290041 and entered the Nazi Party on 1 May 1933 with party number 3472486. Stamm was promoted to *SS-Untersturmführer* on 11 September 1938 and *SS-Obersturmführer* the same day! Stamm served with *Einsatzgruppe IV* during the Polish campaign. A lawyer, he served for several years in Kraków in various SS positions. He was assigned to Warsaw in 1941 and was designated a *Kriminal-Rat* in April 1941. Heinrich Himmler personally commended him for outstanding leadership in October 1941. Stamm made *SS-Hauptsturmführer* on 1 September 1942. He was promoted to *SS-Sturmbannführer* on 20 April 1943. Stamm received a War Service Cross 1st Class on 1 September 1943.[117] He is believed to have survived the war.

GUSTAV STEINMETZ

SS-Obersturmführer Gustav Steinmetz was assigned to Section II C (Finance) in Department I/II, Administration and Law, of the KdS Warsaw during the Ghetto Uprising. Steinmetz was born in Ostrowo on 28 March 1912. A watchmaker by trade, he joined the Nazi Party on 8 July 1932 (Party number 1871744). Shortly thereafter, he entered the SS on 28 August 1932 (SS number 51844). He served in the *Leibstandarte SS Adolf Hitler* regiment from 1933 to 1937. He entered the SD and served with *Einsatzgruppe IV* during the Polish Campaign in 1939. He was promoted to *SS-Untersturmführer* on 9 November 1940 and to *SS-Obersturmführer* on 9 November 1942. During the war, Steinmetz received a War Service Cross 2nd Class for unspecified achievement.[118] He appears to have survived the war.

WALDEMAR STERK

SS-Untersturmführer Waldemar Sterk was assigned to the KdS Warsaw in an unspecified position during the Ghetto Uprising. Sterk was born in Halberstadt on 12 June 1899. During World War I, he fought in the 51st Infantry Regiment and won an Iron Cross 2nd Class. From 1918 to 1920 Sterk was held in a French prisoner of war camp. He joined the Police in 1920. Waldemar Sterk entered the SS on 26 October 1935 (SS number 272333) – he had previously been a member of the SA for a year – and joined the Nazi Party on 1 May 1937 (Party number 4583252). He was promoted to *SS-Untersturmführer* on 9 November 1938. During the Polish Campaign in 1939, Sterk served with *Einsatzgruppe IV*. He transferred to the Warsaw KdS in October 1939 and remained there for the next four years. After the Ghetto Uprising, Sterk was designated a *Polizei-Inspektor* in August 1943 and promoted to *SS-Obersturmführer* on 30 January 1944.[119] He appears to have survived the war.

ULRICH STERN

SS-Obersturmführer Ulrich Stern served as a desk officer in Section IV A 3 c (Principal Resistance Organizations and Secret Political Organizations) in Department IV, the *Gestapo*, of the KdS Warsaw during the Ghetto Uprising. Stern was born in Schrotz/Deutsche Krone (now Walcz, Poland) on 2 January 1892. He won an Iron Cross 2nd Class in World War I. Stern joined the SS on 1 March 1933 (SS number 173574) and the Nazi Party on 1 May 1937 (Party number 5277901). He was promoted to *SS-Untersturmführer* on 9 November 1938 and to *SS-Obersturmführer* on 1 September 1942. Before arriving in Warsaw, Stern served with the *Gestapo* at Schneidemühl.[120] After arriving in Warsaw, he was designated a *Polizeirat* in September 1941. Heinrich Himmler personally commended him for outstanding leadership in October 1941. Ulrich Stern is thought to have survived the war.

ALFRED STRUNZ

SS-Obersturmführer Alfred Strunz served as the deputy chief to Department V, Criminal Police (*Kripo*) of the KdS Warsaw. Strunz was born 15 November 1891 in Zwickau. During World War I Strunz won an Iron Cross 2nd Class and was wounded in action serving with the 21st Uhlan Regiment. After the war, he entered the Police. He joined the SS in 1939 (SS number 390508) and the Nazi Party on 1 May 1933 (Party number 2975970). Alfred Strunz was assigned to the RSHA in Berlin and the *Gestapo* in Prague before going to Warsaw. He was promoted to *SS-Untersturmführer* on 20 April 1943, to *SS-Obersturmführer* on 21 June 1943 and to *SS-Hauptsturmführer* on 9 November 1943. Nothing in Strunz's personnel file indicates that he did not survive the war.[121]

WILHELM TEWES

SS-Obersturmführer Wilhelm Tewes served in Department V, Criminal Police (*Kripo*) of the KdS Warsaw during the Ghetto Uprising. Born 6 January 1905 in Neesen/Minden, he entered the SS on 4 January 1939 with membership number 385399. On 1 May 1937 Tewes joined the Nazi Party (Party number 443823). Since 1924 he had served as a career policeman. Tewes worked in the RSHA after joining the SD. He was promoted to *SS-Untersturmführer* on 15 December 1940 and *SS-Obersturmführer* on 20 April 1942. Tewes was assigned to Warsaw in December 1942. After the Ghetto Uprising, Wilhelm Tewes was promoted to *SS-Hauptsturmführer* on 20 April 1944.[122] He is believed to have survived the war.

WERNER WEITZE

SS-Untersturmführer Werner Weitze was assigned to Section II C (Finance) in Department I/II, Administration and Law, of the KdS Warsaw during the Ghetto Uprising. Weitze was born in Breslau on 2 February 1915. A Police officer, he entered the SS on 1 April 1934 (SS number 107433) and then entered the Nazi Party on 1 May 1937 (Party number 5216406). Weitze arrived in Warsaw in June 1941. He was promoted *to SS-Untersturmführer* on 1 September 1942 at the same time he was designated a *Polizei-Inspector*. After the Ghetto Uprising, Weitze was promoted to *SS-Obersturmführer* on 21 June 1943.[123] He appears to have survived the war.

PAUL WERNER

SS-Hauptsturmführer Paul Werner served as the leader of Section IV B (Religious Bodies, Masonic Organizations and Jewish Affairs) in Department IV, the *Gestapo*, of the KdS Warsaw during the Ghetto Uprising. Werner was born 5 September 1890 in Draggas/Schwetz. He entered the SS on 25 January 1937 (SS number 280216) and the Nazi Party on 1 September 1932 (Party number 1293714). He was promoted to *SS-Untersturmführer* on 9 November 1938, to *SS-Obersturmführer* on 9 November 1942 and to *SS-Hauptsturmführer* on 30 January 1943. Before his assignment to Warsaw, Werner served with the *Gestapo* at Köslin. He received a War Service Cross 2nd Class during the war for unspecified reasons.[124] Werner left Warsaw in May 1944 for duties at Stettin. He is believed to have survived the conflict.

OTTO WETTSTÄDT

SS-Untersturmführer Otto Wettstädt was assigned in an unknown capacity to the KdS Warsaw during the Ghetto Uprising. Born 9 April 1909 in Hamburg, he served in the SA from 1929 to 1932 and again from late 1933 to 1934. He then entered the SS on 1 November 1934 with SS number 107371. Three years later, on 1 May 1937, Wettstädt joined the Nazi Party (Party number 5085068). Wettstädt was promoted to *SS-Untersturmführer* on 9 November 1942. During the war, he received a War Service Cross 2nd Class.[125] Otto Wettstädt is believed to have survived the conflict.

WALTER WITOSSEK

SS-Obersturmführer Walter Witossek served as the leader for Section IV A 2 (Sabotage, Forged Passports And Passes, Shootings and Explosions And Air Drops) in Department IV, the *Gestapo*, of the KdS Warsaw during the Ghetto Uprising. Witossek was born 3 February 1901 in Dresden. He entered the SS on 20 August 1938 (SS number 308126) and the Nazi Party on 1 May 1933 (Party number 2453184). Witossek was promoted to *SS-Untersturmführer* on 28 May 1940, to *SS-Obersturmführer* on 20 April 1941 and to *SS-Hauptsturmführer* on 20 April 1944. Before coming to Warsaw, Witossek was assigned to the *Kripo* in Dresden.[126] He arrived in Warsaw in July 1942.

Walter Witossek won an Iron Cross 2nd Class in 1943, very likely for service during the Ghetto Uprising. He received an Iron Cross 1st Class in 1944, quite possibly for the fighting during the Warsaw Uprising in August and September of that year.[127] He was reported to have directed numerous executions of prisoners in the Ghetto as well as in other parts of Warsaw.[128] Walter Witossek is believed to have survived the war.

• • •

22nd and 23rd SS POLICE REGIMENTS

This study has identified seven officers who served in various components of the 22nd and 23rd SS Police Regiments during the Warsaw Ghetto Uprising.

RUDOLPH HARING

Oberst der Schutzpolizei Rudolph Haring served as the *Kommandeur der Ordnungspolizei* (KdO) and the commander of the 22nd SS Police Regiment during the Ghetto Uprising. He does not appear to have ever been a member of the SS. Haring served in Warsaw until 15 July 1944. After serving in Warsaw, Haring commanded the 2nd Police Regiment and then the 25th SS Police Regiment.[129]

OTTO BUNDKE

SS-Sturmbannführer Otto Bundke served as the commander of the 3rd Battalion, 23rd Police Regiment at the Ghetto Uprising. He was born at Zudny, near Posen, on 5 September 1897. Bundke fought in World War I as a member of the 47th Infantry Regiment and later the 58th Infantry Regiment. He won both the Iron Cross 2nd Class and 1st Class during this conflict. A career policeman since 1920, he joined the Nazi Party on 1 May 1933 with membership number 3471565. On 1 May 1939 he entered the SS as member 323311 with a direct commission to *SS-Hauptsturmführer*. Bundke was promoted to *SS-Sturmbannführer* on 30 January 1940.[130] He received a War Service Cross 1st Class with Swords on 14 February 1944 for his participation against the Ghetto Uprising.[131] The following is a portion of the award recommendation:[132]

> Major Bundke, as commander of the 3rd Battalion, 23rd SS Police Regiment, took part in the final pacification action in the former Jewish residential district, and through his own acts and outstanding leadership ability, was able to produce tangible achievements. After the withdrawal of *Waffen-SS* troops [16 May 1943] the battalion was forced to carry out all assignments alone. The enemy, having become aware of the diminution of [our] forces, sent their gangs to once more attack. With this intensified fighting by the well-armed, well-led bands, it became necessary to combat resistance nests concealed among the ruins, cellars and underground channels.
>
> Major Bundke's accomplishments consisted in effectively absorbing compiled intelligence material in leading liquidation actions against the remaining bands. During a number of assaults Bundke himself assumed command, serving his soldiers as a model of daring. He was in the midst of fire in every battle. After the final liquidation of the nests of rebellion, he took upon himself the responsi-

bility for security in the former Jewish residential district and was deployed in a series of major actions in metropolitan Warsaw. He has also performed notable achievements in recent months in carrying out special assignments [executions] . . .

Bundke directly assisted in the quelling of the Ghetto Uprising. He is believed to have survived the war.

MAX EDERER

SS-Hauptsturmführer Max Ederer served with German Police forces during the Ghetto Uprising. Born 19 October 1897 in Munich, he was a combat veteran of World War I serving in the 4th Bavarian Foot Artillery Regiment where he won an Iron Cross 2nd Class. Ederer was a very early member of the SS joining 11 May 1925 with membership number 423. He was also an early entrant into the Nazi Party and boasted Party number 3986. He was a winner of the Nazi "Blood Order" and the Golden Party Badge for this early service.[133] Ederer was promoted to *SS-Untersturmführer* on 9 November 1932, to *SS-Obersturmführer* on 9 November 1933 and *SS-Hauptsturmführer* on 20 April 1935.[134] He definitely played a key role in the suppression of the Warsaw Ghetto Uprising. The following is an award recommendation for Ederer for his actions:[135]

> During the campaign in the former Jewish residential district of Warsaw in July 1943, Captain Ederer personally participated in an armed struggle with nine armed Jewish bandits and caused these Jews to be rendered harmless. In June 1943 while battling and overwhelming a bandit's nest in the former Jewish residential district in Warsaw, Ederer distinguished himself in combating the Jewish-Bolshevik outlaws.

Max Ederer is believed to have survived the war.

DR. FRITZ KNAIPP

SS-Hauptsturmführer Dr. Fritz Knaipp served as a doctor for the 3rd Battalion, 22nd SS Police Regiment during the Ghetto Uprising. Knaipp was born in Weinzödl near Graz, Austria on 10 July 1902. He joined the SS with a direct promotion to *SS-Hauptsturmführer* on 1 January 1940 and the Nazi Party on 1 March 1938. Knaipp served with the 4th SS Division "*Polizei*" from 15 November 1940 to 15 August 1941.[136]

Dr. Knaipp probably attended to casualties in the 3rd Battalion, 22nd Police Regiment during the Ghetto Uprising. He is believed to have survived the war.

KARL SCHÖPPE

SS-Sturmbannführer Karl Schöppe served with the 3rd Battalion, 22nd SS Police Regiment (probably as the battalion commander or executive officer) during the Ghetto Uprising. Schöppe was born in Katscher, Upper Silesia on 2 July 1905. He entered the Police in 1926 and served in this profession thereafter. On 1 April 1933 Schöppe entered the Nazi Party with membership number 1786066. In his youth he attended a university and studied law but did not receive his degree. He joined the SS with a direct commission to *SS-Hauptsturmführer* on 1 October 1941 (SS Number 401370). Schöppe was promoted to *SS-Sturmbannführer* on 20 April 1942. He played an important role in quelling the Ghetto Uprising as evidenced by the award of a War Service Cross 1st Class with Swords – directly from Heinrich Himmler – on 15 July 1943 for his actions during this operation. Karl Schöppe was promoted to *SS-Obersturmbannführer* on 14 August 1944. There is no evidence to suggest that Karl Schöppe did not survive the war.[137]

ERWIN STERNAGEL

Major of Police Erwin Sternagel is believed to have served as the commander of the 1st Battalion, 22nd SS Police Regiment during the Ghetto Uprising. He was born 17 December 1902 in Breslau. Sternagel joined the SS on 1 May 1939 with SS number 323888 and the Nazi Party on 1 August 1932 with Party number 1257743. He joined the Police in 1922 and served in the Stade police force before the war.[138] Stroop placed Sternagel in charge of operations on the second day of the operation, which indicates he played a key role in the suppression of the Ghetto Uprising. The following post-war testimony is reported to be that of Erwin Sternagel as he explained his role in the fighting:[139]

> On the eve of the beginning of the Ghetto action I was ordered to the Commander of the Order Police. Through him I learned about the intended cleansing of the Ghetto. The purpose of this action should be to transfer the industrial concerns in the Ghetto to Lublin and to cleanse the Ghetto from Jews. For this reason, foreign [non-German] units closed off the Ghetto, namely from the outside. I received the order to check the closing during the night before the action. To satisfy this order, I controlled the outer borders up to the morning hours and found that they were in order, with the exception of a few discrepancies, which I could take care of.
>
> During the early morning hours, I met SS units as they were marching up to the southern gate, and they had about two or three armored scouting cars along with them. I continued my drive to my office and reported to the commander of the Order Police the execution of my order. It

was only in the afternoon that I received a new command, which as far as I remember contained that I should report to the commander of the Order Police at the southern gate of the Ghetto. There I met several leading gentlemen who had assembled for a conference. I remember that, besides *SS-Brigadeführer* Stroop, several unit leaders of the SS and the Police were present. Whether the commander of the Security Police, Dr. Hahn, whom I never met in a recognized way, also attended this conference is something that I cannot say. During this conference Stroop informed us that he was ordered by the *Reichsführer-SS* to conduct the Ghetto action by having released the current SS and Police leaders. He emphasized that at the beginning of the action the SS had suffered heavy losses and that it should now be studied how to continue the action. The conference ended with the decision that the Ghetto be split up into sections and that these should be searched thoroughly.

Out of my battalion only the reserves were engaged in this whole action. The remaining forces of the battalion could not be withdrawn from guard duty.

According to the order given to me by the commander of the Order Police, my first duty was to secure the exterior closing off of the Ghetto. For this purpose a room in a house at the southwestern gate was made available to me. From the site of this gate, the daily allocations and mobilization of the various search troops in the Ghetto took place. The troops consisted of soldiers of the SS units with their unit leaders. These were allocated to members of the Security Police who were familiar with the situation in the Ghetto.

I have not participated in any shooting or personally witnessed any, but I did know that Stroop himself shot blindly into a group of captured Jews only because some were laughing while being transported off. In addition, SS people were supposed to have shot with rifles at Jews who were standing on the roofs and balconies of burning buildings. I heard nothing about mass executions, but I assume that I would have heard about it if they had occurred.

[*Question*] *What happened to Jews who were captured and what happened to the confiscated goods of value?*

According to the reports by the search troops, captured Jews were taken to the freight train station near the northern exit. As far as I know, they were transported to Lublin. Captured objects were gathered by the SD and thrown into boxes, which had been made available for this purpose. No lists were kept of these, according to Stroop's instructions. As I was told, the boxes were taken to the office of the SS and Police Chief.

In the late 1940s, Sternagel was reported to have taken up residence in Marburg/Lahn, Germany.[140]

OSKAR ZISENIS

SS-Hauptsturmführer Oskar Zisenis served in an unknown capacity in the Police forces at the Ghetto Uprising. He was born in Potsdam on 21 February 1910. In 1931 and 1932 he was a member of the *Sturmabteilung* (SA), the brown-shirted political strong-arm of the Nazis. Zisenis entered the SS and the Nazi Party on 1 April 1932 (SS number 56906, Party number 1119865). He entered Police service in 1936. Zisenis appears to have been promoted from the enlisted ranks directly to *SS-Obersturmführer* (skipping *SS-Untersturmführer*) on 20 April 1940. He was promoted to *SS-Hauptsturmführer* on 20 April 1942. During the war, he was awarded both the War Service Cross 2nd and 1st Class with Swords.[141] Oskar Zisenis is believed to have survived the war.

• • •

3rd SS PANZERGRENADIER TRAINING AND REPLACEMENT BATTALION

Twenty-three *Waffen-SS* officers appear to have served in the 3rd SS Panzergrenadier Training and Replacement Battalion during the time of the Ghetto Uprising.

HEINRICH AMBERG

SS-Obersturmführer Heinrich Amberg served as the commander for the 4th Company during the time of the Ghetto Uprising. Born 2 March 1911 in Schleswig, he entered the SS on 25 June 1933 with an SS number of 90987. Amberg joined the Nazi Party on 1 May 1937. He was promoted to *SS-Untersturmführer* on 20 April 1938 and served in the 50th *SS-Standarte* before the war. On 20 April 1940, Amberg transferred to the SS Death's Head Replacement Battalion 1 where he remained for eighteen months. During this period he was promoted to *SS-Obersturmführer* on 9 November 1941.

On 18 November 1941 Heinrich Amberg reported to the 3rd SS Division "*Totenkopf*" on the eastern front. While with the division he won the Infantry Assault Badge, Iron Cross 1st and 2nd Class and the Demyansk Shield for the heavy fighting at this area. He was also wounded in action. On 1 July 1942 (probably due to this wound) Amberg transferred to the 3rd SS Panzergrenadier Training and Replacement Battalion and assumed command of the 4th Company. Amberg received his final promotion to *SS-Hauptsturmführer* on 21 June 1943 and remained with this unit until 6 December 1943 when he transferred to the 5th SS Division "*Wiking*."[142] It is possible, based on an examination of his personnel file, that he received a War

Service Cross 2nd Class with Swords for his participation in the Ghetto Uprising, but this is not a certainty. Heinrich Amberg appears to have survived the war.[143]

HANS ARTMANN

In April 1943, *SS-Obersturmführer* Hans Artmann was a member of the battalion staff. Artmann was born in Kohlstetten near Regensburg on 16 October 1914. Not a member of the Nazi Party, he entered the SS on 1 November 1935 and received membership number 391867. Before the war, he served at the Dachau concentration camp. He was promoted to *SS-Untersturmführer* on 20 April 1941 and reported to the 1st SS *Totenkopf* Infantry Regiment the same day. He served with this regiment during *Operation Barbarossa* until 4 September 1941. During this period of front-line service, Artmann received an Infantry Assault Badge and an Iron Cross 2nd Class; he was also wounded in action. *SS-Untersturmführer* Artmann reported to the battalion in Warsaw in September 1941; he was subsequently promoted to *SS-Obersturmführer* on 30 January 1942. He remained in the unit until 14 October 1943. His personnel file reflects a War Service Cross 2nd Class with Swords issued in 1943; it could have been for service in the Ghetto Uprising, but again we cannot be certain of this.

On 14 October 1943, Hans Artmann returned to the 3rd SS Division "*Totenkopf*" but remained with this unit only until 16 February 1944. During this short period it appears that he was wounded in action twice and as a result returned to Warsaw with the battalion. On 9 November 1944 Artmann received his final promotion to *SS-Hauptsturmführer*; he transferred shortly thereafter to the staff of the *Reichsführer-SS*.[144]

WALTER BELLWIDT

During the Warsaw Ghetto Uprising, *SS-Obersturmbannführer* Walter Bellwidt served as the battalion commander of the 3rd SS Panzergrenadier Training and Replacement Battalion. Born 5 May 1900 in Frankfurt am Main, he served in the 63rd Field Artillery Regiment in World War I. Bellwidt joined the Nazi Party on 1 August 1930 (membership number 271609) and was an early entrant of the SS with membership number 15770; he assumed the rank of *SS-Untersturmführer* on 30 April 1933. On 15 June 1934 Bellwidt was promoted to *SS-Obersturmführer*; he was promoted yet again on 15 September 1935 to *SS-Hauptsturmführer*. Walter Bellwidt served with the *SS-Totenkopf-Standarten* (Death's Head units) *Brandenburg* and *Thüringen*; he was the battalion commander of the 1st Battalion of the SS Death's Head Regiment *Thüringen* at the Buchenwald concentration camp from 1938 to 1940. On 30 January 1939, the SS promoted Bellwidt to the rank of *SS-Sturmbannführer*.

Walter Bellwidt transferred to the 14th SS Death's Head Regiment on 10 November 1940; he transferred to the 3rd SS Panzergrenadier Training and Replacement Battalion on 1 July 1941 and appears to have remained with the unit for the duration of the war. Bellwidt received his final promotion on 30 January 1943 to *SS-Obersturmbannführer*. He received an Iron Cross 2nd Class in 1940; on 27 June 1944 Heinrich Himmler ordered that Bellwidt receive a War Service Cross 1st Class for his actions during the *Grosseinsatz Warschau* (Large Action Warsaw). The following is an efficiency report, dated June 1944, for Walter Bellwidt as a battalion commander:[145]

> Open decent character, balanced personality. Due to his cheerful disposition, he seems to have the tendency to take things lighter. Impulsive, well-intentioned, maybe a little soft and lazy.
>
> Intelligent, quick comprehension. Physically strong. Quite good knowledge of the service and efforts. Sufficient tactical nature.
>
> Winning, pleasant character. Polite towards superiors, and a very comrade-like, caring and warm leader.
>
> Solid philosophic attitude, free and convincing presentation full of temperament.
>
> Proven in front of the enemy, winner of Iron Cross 2nd Class. Civilian pilot. The current service position is being fulfilled.
>
> Suitable for next higher service position after a training course and renewed testing at the front.

It is clear that *SS-Obersturmbannführer* Walter Bellwidt played a major role in the German suppression of the Warsaw Ghetto Uprising. He survived the war. The following is a portion of his testimony in a post-war trial – not his own; he does not appear to have been tried for any complicity – in Germany:[146]

> During the spring of 1943 I was the battalion commander with the rank of *SS-Obersturmbannführer* of the 3rd SS Panzergrenadier Training and Replacement Battalion in Warsaw. At the beginning of the action against the Jews, a conference took place with SS and Police Chief von Sammern-Frankenegg. Today I cannot state with certainty that other persons participated in the talks. This conference took place a few days before the later start of the uprising.
>
> During this conference the police chief explained to us that the Ghetto had become a factor of insecurity of the first degree, an oversight about which had been completely lost. It was not know whether the number of inhabitants was 30,000, 50,000 or 70,000 persons. Among these inhabitants were not only Jews, but also German deserters,

Polish resistance fighters, black marketeers, swindlers and criminals. Therefore, it was planned to clear out from the complete Ghetto all living and dead and to transfer them to Lublin. Not one word was said about a liquidation of the Ghetto. He stated that this action had to be accomplished according to a command from higher authorities. I do not remember who had given this command. He stated that he did not have available sufficient forces to accomplish this comprehensive action. He had at his disposal 1,000 men of the Polish police force, whom he would only use as an outer ring. In addition he had a police battalion, but now I do not remember its size. He continued by saying that he relied on my battalion and also on the SS Cavalry Replacement Detachment. He explained that we (my battalion) should help in cleaning out the houses and apartments and to make sure that after the clean-up, these places were not again occupied; all other things, namely the transportation and other details, would be taken care of by the Security Service. I do not recall at this time if *SS-Sturmbannführer* Plänk [the commander of the cavalry unit] also took part in this conference. As this order was announced, I refused that my battalion would take part in this action, whereby I stated that it was my task to train the field reserve for the 3rd SS Division "*Totenkopf*" and not to dispense police functions.

Although I understood the task, which I was supposed to take over, I wanted to keep my battalion out of any action against Jews and for that reason I gave the above justification. To that, von Sammern responded that if I did not want to engage my troops, he would get orders from Berlin. After that, I received the order from Berlin (from the Main Operational Office of the *Waffen-SS*, I do not recall the person who gave the order) to make my troops available for this mission for three days, but only trained personnel, meaning no recruits.

On the day in question when the cleansing was to start, we assembled in an open space in the "large Ghetto" (the "small one" had already been cleaned out, but without participation of my troops), at the entrance to the Ghetto. This was early in the morning. In this assembly, there were also the other units, as well as approximately 180 Ukrainians. There were discussions between Plänk and me during this morning – whom of the two of us should clean up the respective streets. At the beginning of the mission, neither Stroop, whom I did not yet know, nor von Sammern-Frankenegg was present. At the beginning of the mission, each battalion commander was in command of his battalion. At that point there was no unifying higher commander.

After my troops had advanced about thirty or forty meters – we had not yet cleaned up anything – there was heavy fire from the roofs, the cellars, windows and everywhere. We had casualties of at least thirty or forty dead and wounded. After that, I gave the order to collect [the wounded] and retreat. Nobody was prepared for this attack. At the point when my troops retreated, von Sammern and Stroop appeared. It was the time when I met Stroop for the first time. I think von Sammern introduced me to Stroop. Stroop explained to the assembled commanders that he had received the exclusive order (I even believe he said "directly from Himmler") to "lead the cleansing action of the Ghetto." Stroop said to me: "I can see that you are not well disposed towards this police action." He made me understand that my involvement was haphazard. He said: "I am going to create a command staff for these actions under the leadership of a police lieutenant colonel." I have forgotten the name of that man.

I think his name was Sternagel. After that raiding parties were formed. The formation of these raiding parties was accomplished by this lieutenant colonel. Also the engagement of the raiding parties was under the leadership of this lieutenant colonel. The mission on this first day was the first and only command that I ever received during the whole time of the Ghetto Uprising. I also no longer received orders for particular other actions. In the time following, I went into the Ghetto, but not every day. I never went into the Ghetto at night. I had no connection whatsoever with the command post of the police lieutenant colonel. However, Stroop ordered me to report to him from time to time, which I also did. After Stroop had realized that this concerned organized resistance, he went to the commanding General of the *Wehrmacht* and demanded heavy weapons. My people only had the normal infantry equipment, consisting of machine-guns, hand grenades and the like. During the ensuing period I did no longer tried to keep my troops from getting engaged because I had already received the order twice to take part in it, once by von Sammern directly and the second time from Berlin. Because of the organized resistance, the limit of three days of engagement for my battalion had been nullified and was prolonged to the end of the mission. The *Wehrmacht* then made heavy weapons available, namely a platoon of tanks, a platoon of artillery, a platoon of anti-aircraft guns, a platoon of pioneers and a platoon of flame throwers. With the help of the military support the systematic cleansing of the Ghetto could be accomplished. Prisoners who were captured were taken away. It is also possible that they were shot, but I did not see it. All the while during this whole mission it never entered my mind that this action was aimed at destruction and liquidation of the Jews. This was not mentioned with one word. I also want to mention that Stroop again and again stressed, "I am the only one who is responsible, no matter what happens." One morning I noticed that the police chief of Lublin by the name of Globocnik was fighting with Stroop about something. This was at the office of the lieutenant colonel. I did not know what it was all about. In my opinion, it was a fight about competence.

I did see that women and children and also men, who were driven from the houses in the Ghetto, were searched and had things taken away, but I never saw that they were shot. I personally did not participate in any shooting, neither as a bystander, nor did I give the order to shoot. I personally have not shot anybody. In fact, I did not even fight with a weapon. After the Ghetto action as over, I was awarded the War Service Cross 1st Class. I was ashamed to accept this award. To this day I do not know for what I received this award. Stroop at that time appeared with the Iron Cross 1st Class. I do not know today when and for what he received it.

WALTER BIERMANN

SS-Obersturmführer Walter Biermann was assigned as the commander of the 5th Company, 3rd SS Panzergrenadier Training and Replacement Battalion, at the time of the Ghetto Uprising. He was born in Hamburg on 10 May 1916; he entered the SS on 1 October 1936 and received a membership number of 352532. Biermann was promoted to the officer ranks, *SS-Untersturmführer* on 20 April 1941 and served with the 1st SS *Totenkopf* Infantry Regiment until 18 September 1941. During his time in combat in Russia, Biermann won an Iron Cross 2nd Class and an Infantry Assault Badge. He was seriously wounded in the head on 13 July 1941. Biermann then served in the 1st SS *Totenkopf* Infantry Replacement Battalion for one month (probably as part of his recuperation from wounds) and then returned to the 3rd SS Division "*Totenkopf*" and served as an infantry platoon leader until 1 August 1942. He was promoted during this stint to *SS-Obersturmführer* on 21 June 1942 based on a strong recommendation from his battalion and regimental commanders.

On that date Biermann received orders to report to the 3rd SS Panzergrenadier Training and Replacement Battalion. He remained with the battalion in Warsaw until 5 December 1943. Biermann then transferred to the reconnaissance battalion of the 16th SS Division "*Reichsführer-SS*" where it appears he served for the rest of the war.[147] The following is an efficiency report, from October 1944, that *SS-Obersturmführer* Biermann received as a company commander from his detachment commander, *SS-Sturmbannführer* Walter Reder:[148]

> Biermann has a conflicting character and strongly needs supervision and instruction. As soon as he works independently, he tends to become superficial and has strong personal interests.
>
> His softness has not yet been reigned in and there are missions when he fulfills his tasks, but where severity is needed, he is not resistant enough to bear the physical and moral exertions.
>
> To a large part, this may be connected with his severe head wounds.
>
> At this time, he does not completely fulfill the demands of a company leader at the front.

Walter Biermann received no decorations for his part in the quelling of the Ghetto Uprising. Five men of his company were wounded in action during the fighting so we do know that at least elements of his unit took part. It appears that Walter Biermann survived the war.[149]

ALBERT BONNET

SS-Obersturmführer Albert Bonnet served as the 1st Platoon Leader, 2nd Company, of the 3rd SS Panzergrenadier Training and Replacement Battalion during the Warsaw Ghetto Uprising. Born 5 October 1908 in Kassel, he entered the SS on 17 August 1931 and received membership number 42818. Bonnet had previously joined the Nazi Party on 1 April 1931 (membership number 484290). Albert Bonnet was promoted to *SS-Untersturmführer* on 20 April 1934. He was assigned to the 3rd SS Division "*Totenkopf*" from 18 November 1941 to 1 October 1942. During this front-line service he earned the Iron Cross 2nd Class. In October 1942 Bonnet transferred to the 3rd SS Panzergrenadier Training and Replacement Battalion and served in Warsaw until 15 October 1943.

While in Warsaw, Bonnet was promoted to *SS-Obersturmführer* on 9 November 1942. In October 1943, Albert Bonnet went back to front-line service with the 13th SS Division "*Handschar*," a unit composed primarily of Muslims (with German officers) and designed to fight partisans in Yugoslavia.[150] He was seriously wounded and died at Osijek, Yugoslavia on 15 October 1944. It appears that he received a posthumous promotion to *SS-Hauptsturmführer*. Given that the 2nd Company lost five troops killed and wounded during the Ghetto Uprising (on different days of action), it is likely that Albert Bonnet had an active roll in the fighting.[151] *Waffen-SS* platoon leaders fought alongside their men.

ALFRED ECKERT

SS-Obersturmführer Alfred Eckert served as the battalion adjutant of the 3rd SS Panzergrenadier Training and Replacement Battalion at the time of the Ghetto action. Born on 12 September 1910 in Boxtal am Main, Alfred Eckert received SS number 218390 when he entered the SS on 1 June 1933. Four years later, he joined the Nazi Party (membership number 5257390). Eckert served as an enlisted solder until his promotion to *SS-Untersturmführer* on 1 June 1941. He deployed to the Russian front on 18 November 1941 with the 10th Company, 1st *Totenkopf* Infantry Regiment, 3rd SS Division "*Totenkopf*" as a platoon leader and remained with this unit until 26 February 1942. Eckert's personnel file indicates he was involved in an accident at the front and broke a rib, which resulted in some internal bleeding.

On 27 April 1942 Alfred Eckert transferred to the 3rd SS Panzergrenadier Training and Replacement Battalion and assumed duties as the battalion adjutant. Eckert was promoted to *SS-Obersturmführer* on 30 January 1943. He remained in Warsaw until 16 November 1943 when he was assigned to two training courses which prepared him for his final assignment with the 5th SS Division "*Wiking*." The following is an efficiency report that covers the period he was in the battalion:[152]

> From 15 November 1942, *SS-Obersturmführer* Eckert has been Battalion Adjutant. From 5 December 1941 to 27 April 1942 he took part in the Eastern Campaign and served as the first platoon leader. According to his company leader, he has proven to be excellent in this service post and has led his platoon with great circumspection and success.
>
> Since joining the battalion as adjutant, he has earned my complete recognition. His attitude is serious and that of a soldier, his character is indisputable. He is solid as far as ideology is concerned.

Eckert reported to the 5th SS Division on 20 December 1943. He was reported missing in action on 17 February 1944 when the "*Wiking*" Division was overwhelmed at the Tscherkassy Pocket encirclement in southern Russia.

SS-Obersturmführer Eckert received a War Service Cross most likely for his service in the 3rd SS Panzergrenadier Training and Replacement Battalion, but we cannot be certain of this. What is clearer is that as the battalion adjutant, Eckert would have likely visited the soldiers of the battalion as they participated in the operation and, therefore, played an active role in the action.[153]

KURT GRAHOFER

SS-Untersturmführer Kurt Grahofer filled the position of 1st Platoon Leader, 3rd Company, 3rd SS Panzergrenadier Training and Replacement Battalion during the battle. Grahofer hailed from Rekawinkel where he was born 7 February 1921. He joined the SS on 15 November 1940 and received a membership number of 423603. He does not appear to have ever joined the Nazi Party. Grahofer served as an enlisted man until his promotion to *SS-Untersturmführer* on 21 June 1942. On this date he was serving at the front with the 3rd SS Division "*Totenkopf*." On 1 July 1942 he returned to Germany and an assignment with the SS Death's Head Infantry Replacement Battalion 1, which then moved to Warsaw and became the 3rd Battalion. He remained with the unit after the Ghetto Uprising until 4 April 1944 when he was assigned to SS *Jäger* Battalion 500, a special commando unit that fought partisans in central Russia. Kurt Grahofer was killed in action 30 July 1944.

Grahofer was seconded to a Hitler Youth training camp from 22 April 1943 to 30 May 1943. He therefore was not in Warsaw for most of the Ghetto Uprising and must be considered to have been a minor player in the action.[154]

HEINZ KLIPPEL

SS-Obersturmführer Heinz Klippel was the battalion administration officer from 1942 to 1944. Relatively older than his fellow battalion officers, Klippel was born 13 February 1905 in Berlin. He served as an enlisted man in the SS from his entrance into the organization on 1 April 1935 (membership number 269859) to his promotion to *SS-Untersturmführer* on 1 January 1941. Klippel received party number 5274348 when he joined the Nazi Party on 1 May 1937. From 8 April 1941 to 18 February 1942 he served with an artillery unit in the 6th SS Division "*Nord*" but may have not seen actual front-line service. He reported to the 3rd SS Panzergrenadier Training and Replacement Battalion on 18 February 1942 and shortly thereafter, on 20 April 1942, was promoted to *SS-Obersturmführer*. He received his final promotion, to *SS-Hauptsturmführer*, on 21 June 1944.

As battalion administration officer, Klippel would probably have played no role in the actual fighting, although he may have visited the Ghetto on occasion. In 1944 his battalion commander had the following comments about him in an officer efficiency report:[155]

> Klippel is the administrative officer of the battalion. He has a truthful, decent and well-founded character, with a calm, clear demeanor. His conscientiousness, circumspection, delight in responsibility and a marked sense of duty make him excel. With good mental facilities, he possesses a clear talent for understanding and has a concrete way of expressing himself. He is in good physical condition; he makes a great, easily approachable appearance. In

his duty as administrative leader, Klippel demonstrates sufficient knowledge. In matters of organization and administration, paired with his own conscientiousness, he was able to earn the fullest confidence of his superiors. Klippel shows particular interest in the training of the new administrative personnel. He always showed great interest and drive in the matters of the service troops. The appearance of the above-named is that of a proud soldier. His behavior towards his superiors and comrades is correct and tactful; he is positive and energetic towards the men under him. His conduct both within and outside of the service is immaculate. His world outlook is well grounded and he possesses good knowledge. Klippel fully fulfills his current duties as administrative leader of the battalion.

SS-Obersturmführer Heinz Klippel is believed to have survived the war.

KARL KNÖRZER

Karl Knörzer held the rank of *SS-Obersturmführer* as the commander of the Convalescence Company of the 3rd SS Panzergrenadier Training and Replacement Battalion during the Ghetto Uprising. Born 23 November 1919 in Adelstätten near Schwäbisch-Gmünd, he entered the SS on 4 April 1938 with a membership number of 319463, but he does not appear to have ever joined the Nazi Party. Knörzer joined the officer ranks as an *SS-Untersturmführer* on 30 January 1942 and immediately reported to the 3rd SS Panzergrenadier Training and Replacement Battalion. He achieved his final rank of *SS-Obersturmführer* on 9 November 1943. His personnel records show no service with any other unit, nor do they show any decorations.[156] However, another source indicates that Knörzer was wounded in action on 21 October 1941 while serving in Russia with the SS Division "*Totenkopf*."[157]

While Knörzer may have visited the Ghetto fighting out of individual curiosity, his duty position would not have put him at the scene of the fighting. His file indicates a good possibility that he survived the war.

WILHELM LINNENLÜCKE

SS-Untersturmführer Wilhelm Linnenlücke was a new officer when the Ghetto Uprising commenced having been promoted to this rank on 10 March 1943. Linnenlücke hailed from Isenstedt, born there on 13 November 1917. He joined the SS on 20 June 1936 (membership number 287123). Wilhelm Linnenlücke served in combat as an enlisted soldier and received an Iron Cross 2nd Class an Infantry Assault Badge and was wounded in action. This front-line service was most likely with the 3rd SS Division "*Totenkopf*", although there is no mention of a specific unit in his personnel file. As an enlisted soldier before the war he appears to have been assigned to the *SS-Totenkopfstandarte Oberbayern*, a unit which furnished concentration camp guards for Dachau.

Linnenlücke was also seconded to a Hitler Youth training camp from 22 April 1943 to 30 May 1943. Not in Warsaw for most of the Ghetto Uprising, he must be considered a minor player in the action and may have never been present during the fighting. He was promoted to *SS-Obersturmführer* on 20 April 1944. Wilhelm Linnenlücke appears to have survived the war.[158]

DR. FRANK MÜLLER

SS-Obersturmführer Dr. Frank Müller was the battalion physician for the 3rd SS Panzergrenadier Training and Replacement Battalion during the Ghetto Uprising. Born 27 December 1911 in Chemnitz, his SS number of 277223 indicates that he entered the organization in 1935 although the exact date is not recorded in his file. Like many physicians in Germany, he joined the Nazi Party, receiving membership number 4306864 on 1 May 1937.[159] As an enlisted soldier he served as a physician at the Dachau concentration camp in June and July of 1941. He was then assigned at the SS Disciplinary camp at Danzig-Matzkau (a penal camp for SS personnel) before reporting to the 3rd SS Panzergrenadier Training and Replacement Battalion on 2 March 1943. While at Danzig, he was promoted to *SS-Untersturmführer* on 9 November 1941 and *SS-Obersturmführer* on 9 November 1942. He remained in Warsaw until late 1943 or early 1944 when he transferred to the Vth SS Corps.

Müller received a War Service Cross 2nd Class with Swords in 1943. This award may have been in recognition for his work in the Ghetto Uprising. Given that twenty-two personnel from his battalion were reported wounded during the fighting, it is highly likely that Müller was present at the Warsaw Ghetto administering medical aid to the troops. Dr. Frank Müller appears to have survived the war.[160]

GÜNTHER MUSSBACH

SS-Obersturmführer Günther Mussbach served as the Company Commander, 3rd Company, 3rd SS Panzergrenadier Training and Replacement Battalion during the Ghetto Uprising. He was born 30 November 1917 in Kiel. Shortly after his twentieth birthday, he entered the SS (1 November 1937; membership number 353087). Mussbach was promoted to *SS-Untersturmführer* on 20 April 1940. Mussbach served with the 3rd SS Division "*Totenkopf*" from 1 September 1941 to 1 May 1942 and won the Iron Cross 2nd Class and the Infantry Assault Badge for action in Russia. He reported to the 3rd SS Panzergrenadier Training and Replacement Battalion on 1 May

1942 (having been promoted to *SS-Obersturmführer* on 20 April 1942) and remained in Warsaw until 14 October 1943. On this date he transferred to the 14th SS Division "*Galizien*."[161] Mussbach was reported missing in action and believed killed on 20 July 1944 when the division was surrounded and virtually annihilated by the Soviet 1st Ukrainian Front at the Brody encirclement on the eastern front.[162]

From Stroop's casualty list we can pinpoint that the 3rd Company was at the fighting on 13 and 14 May, at the very least. The unit was most likely involved other days when they had no casualties as well. Therefore, Günther Mussbach should be considered to have taken part in the action.

WALTER NOACK

Born 14 December 1915 in Dresden, *SS-Obersturmführer* Walter Noack served as the Headquarters Company Commander, 3rd SS Panzergrenadier Training and Replacement Battalion during the Ghetto Uprising. Noack entered the SS on 2 November 1934 with membership number 277124. He was promoted to *SS-Untersturmführer* on 9 November 1939 and served in the 3rd SS Division "*Totenkopf*" (1st SS *Totenkopf* Infantry Regiment) until 1 December 1941. While in combat with this unit in Russia, he received the Iron Cross 2nd Class and the Infantry Assault Badge. He was also promoted during this tour to *SS-Obersturmführer* on 20 April 1941. He was wounded in action. Noack then served in various replacement units before joining the 3rd SS Panzergrenadier Training and Replacement Battalion on 4 February 1943. He remained in Warsaw until 16 November 1943 when he transferred to the SS Main Leadership Office in Berlin.[163]

While in the battalion, Walter Noack was promoted to *SS-Hauptsturmführer* on 21 June 1943. He also received a War Service Cross 2nd Class with Swords while in the battalion, most likely for service during the Ghetto Uprising. It is likely that he participated in the fighting. It is also likely that Walter Noack survived the war.

HEINRICH OHLMEIER

SS-Obersturmführer Heinrich Ohlmeier was assigned as the 2nd Company Commander, 3rd SS Panzergrenadier Training and Replacement Battalion during the Ghetto Uprising. Ohlmeier was born 4 November 1912 in Blankenese. He joined the Nazi Party on 1 May 1933 (party number 3036587) and entered the SS in late 1938 (number 313351). Heinrich Ohlmeier was promoted to *SS-Untersturmführer* on 20 April 1940 and *SS-Obersturmführer* on 9 November 1941. He served in the 3rd SS Division "*Totenkopf*" from 18 November 1941 to 1 May 1942 when he was assigned to the 3rd SS Panzergrenadier Training and Replacement Battalion. In combat with the *Totenkopf*, he won the Iron Cross 1st and 2nd Class, the Infantry Assault Badge and was wounded in action. In Warsaw, Ohlmeier was promoted to *SS-Hauptsturmführer* on 4 November 1943. On 3 July 1944 Heinrich Ohlmeier was reassigned to the 5th SS Division "*Wiking*."[164]

Based on the casualty reports, the 2nd Company was definitely fighting in the Ghetto on 19 April, 20 April and 8 May. It is quite likely that Ohlmeier was with his troops on those days. Additionally, his personnel file indicates he was awarded a War Service Cross in 1943 while with the battalion. It is likely that this award was related to his service at the Ghetto Uprising. It appears that Heinrich Ohlmeier survived the war.

HANNS RÖGER

SS-Untersturmführer Hanns Röger was born at Ulm-Söflingen on 16 February 1912. He entered the SS on 10 March 1934 with membership number 291078. He was also a member of the Nazi Party (4002359). Röger was elevated to *SS-Untersturmführer* on 21 December 1942. Prior to that date he appears to have won the Iron Cross 2nd Class and Infantry Assault Badge, with the 3rd SS Division "*Totenkopf*" (1st SS *Totenkopf* Infantry Regiment). At some point in the war (but not at Warsaw), he also won an Iron Cross 1st Class.[165]

During the Ghetto Uprising, Röger served as the 1st Platoon Leader, 4th Company, 3rd SS Panzergrenadier Training and Replacement Battalion. Given involvement of the 4th Company in the fighting, there seems to be a reasonable chance that Hanns Röger was in the Ghetto. He also appears to have survived the war.

WERNER SCHMIDT

SS-Untersturmführer Werner Schmidt was assigned as the 1st Platoon Leader, 1st Company, 3rd SS Panzergrenadier Training and Replacement Battalion during the liquidation of the Warsaw Ghetto. He was born 25 April 1896 in Solingen. Schmidt entered the Nazi Party on 1 May 1933 (membership number unknown). He had an interesting career pattern, not joining the SS until 1 January 1942 (SS number 414935). Schmidt came into the organization as an *SS-Untersturmführer*. During 1942 he served with SS Battle Group Jeckeln and the Higher SS and Police Leader for the Caucasus. He reported to the 3rd SS Panzergrenadier Training and Replacement Battalion on 28 April 1943 but only stayed with the unit until 20 May 1943 when he was assigned to a holding camp for ethnic Germans. He was promoted to *SS-Obersturmführer* on 1 July 1943 and to *SS-Hauptsturmführer* on 30 January 1944. From September 1943 to January 1945 Schmidt served with the Estonian Legion, an SS combat unit. During the war, but not at Warsaw, he won the Iron Cross 1st and 2nd Class and was wounded in action several times.[166]

Werner Schmidt probably survived the war. There is no strong indicator that he actively participated in the Warsaw action given his extremely short stay in the battalion, although the 1st Company certainly was in the fight.

EWALD-EDUARD SCHRAMM

SS-Hauptsturmführer Ewald-Eduard Schramm served as the battalion executive officer – the second in command of the unit – of the 3rd SS Panzergrenadier Training and Replacement Battalion during the fighting in Warsaw. Schramm was born at Drzonowoki near Kulm, West Prussia (now Chelmno, Poland) on 22 October 1894. He served in World War I in the 16th Jäger Battalion. He entered the Nazi Party on 11 March 1932 with membership number 1177054. On 1 April 1940 Schramm entered the SS (SS number 357103) with the rank of *SS-Untersturmführer*. On 30 January 1941 he was promoted to *SS-Obersturmführer*; eighteen months later on 21 June 1942 he was promoted to *SS-Hauptsturmführer*. Before coming to Warsaw, Schramm was assigned to the SS Main Leadership Office in Berlin. He served in the battalion from 16 April 1943 to 22 February 1944 when he transferred to the 6th SS Division "*Nord*." It appears he finished the war with another replacement unit. Schramm achieved his final rank of *SS-Sturmbannführer* on 30 January 1945. He received a War Service Cross 2nd Class with Swords the same day.[167]

Schramm arrived in the unit only a few days before the Ghetto Uprising began. The battalion commander could have left him in the garrison to run the normal training activities for the battalion, or he could have brought him into the Warsaw Ghetto during the operation to give him needed combat experience. We do not know what option he took, but we are reasonably certain that Ewald-Eduard Schramm survived the war.

WILHELM SPRENGER

SS-Untersturmführer Wilhelm Sprenger served on the battalion staff during the Ghetto Uprising. Born 19 October 1910 in Schwochow near Pyritz, Pomerania (now Pyrzyce, Poland), he entered the SS on 14 September 1933 as an enlisted man. He entered the Nazi Party four years later on 1 May 1937 with membership number 5638649. He served as an enlisted man, probably with the 6th SS Division "*Nord*" in 1941, and won an Iron Cross 2nd Class. He was also wounded in action that year. Sprenger was promoted to *SS-Untersturmführer* on 20 April 1942 and was assigned to the 3rd SS Panzergrenadier Training and Replacement Battalion. He served with the battalion until 29 May 1943. On this date, Wilhelm Sprenger was reassigned to the 4th SS Division "*Polizei*."[168] He appears to have served with this division for the rest of the war. He was promoted to *SS-Obersturmführer* on 9 November 1943.[169]

It is difficult to determine what role Wilhelm Sprenger had with respect to the Ghetto Uprising. He is believed to have survived the war.

HERBERT TAEGE

SS-Untersturmführer Herbert Taege served in an unknown capacity in the 3rd SS Panzergrenadier Training and Replacement Battalion during the fighting in Warsaw. Born 27 September 1921 in Magdeburg, Taege joined the SS in 1938 and received membership number 379356. He was also a member of the Nazi Party (number 7145619). As an enlisted soldier, he served in the 3rd SS Division "*Totenkopf*" and was wounded in action. In 1942 he served in the guard battalion at the Dachau concentration camp. Herbert Taege was promoted to *SS-Untersturmführer* on 10 March 1943 and reported to Warsaw on 1 April 1943. He remained with the battalion for only one month. On 1 May 1943 Herbert Taege was reassigned to the SS Panzer Training and Replacement Regiment.[170]

As with Wilhelm Sprenger, it is difficult to determine Taege's role in the Ghetto Uprising. Herbert Taege is believed to have survived the war.

HERBERT WEBERMEIER

SS-Obersturmführer Herbert Webermeier served as the battalion lawyer in the 3rd SS Panzergrenadier Training and Replacement Battalion during the Warsaw Ghetto Uprising. Webermeier was born in Barmen on 4 January 1906. He entered the SS on 1 March 1933 (SS number 134887). On 1 May 1933 Webermeier joined the Nazi Party with membership number 1947443. On 9 November 1940 he was promoted to *SS-Untersturmführer* and on 30 January 1942 was elevated to *SS-Obersturmführer*. He joined the battalion the same day and remained in Warsaw until 6 December 1943.

His next assignment was with the 5th SS Division "*Wiking*" where he served as the Headquarters Company Commander for the 10th SS Grenadier Regiment. During the war he received the Iron Cross 2nd Class and the War Service Cross 2nd Class. He was also wounded in action. On 9 November 1944 Webermeier was promoted to *SS-Hauptsturmführer*. Herbert Webermeier appears to have survived the war.[171] While he may have visited the Ghetto during the Ghetto Uprising, his role as the battalion legal advisor would not indicate that he played any major role in the fighting.

SIEGFRIED WERNER

SS-Obersturmführer Siegfried Werner served as the company commander for the 1st Company, 3rd SS Panzergrenadier Training and Replacement Battalion during the Warsaw Ghetto Uprising. Born 4 March 1918 at Rehhof, West Prussia, he entered the SS on 1 April 1937 (SS number 323836). He was also a member of the Nazi Party (Party number 3442662). Werner was assigned to the *Leibstandarte Adolf Hitler* SS Regiment from 1937 to 1939. He was commissioned as an *SS-Untersturmführer* on 20 April 1939. He then transferred to the SS Division "*Totenkopf*" and remained with that unit for several years. We do not know when Werner arrived in Warsaw, but he remained there until 17 May 1943 when he transferred to the 9th SS Division "*Hohenstaufen*."

Given that Werner was about to transfer out of the battalion, he may have been in the process of clearing the unit at the same time as the Ghetto Uprising, and therefore may not have played much of an active role in the fighting. Werner has no existing SS officer personnel file.[172]

ERICH WOYWOTH

SS-Untersturmführer Erich Woywoth served as the musical platoon leader for the 3rd SS Panzergrenadier Training and Replacement Battalion during the Warsaw Ghetto Uprising. He was born 3 January 1884 in Stendal. He fought in World War I winning an Iron Cross 2nd Class during the conflict. Erich Woywoth entered the Nazi Party on 1 May 1931 with membership number 572551. Four years later he joined the SS on 15 October 1935 (SS number 276165). Woywoth was assigned to the battalion on 10 January 1942 and served in Warsaw until 7 March 1944. From there he served one month at the Buchenwald concentration camp and served at the Gross-Rosen concentration camp from 18 April 1944 to early 1945. While at the camp he was promoted to *SS-Obersturmführer* on 20 April 1944.[173]

As the music platoon leader, while he may have visited the Ghetto during the Ghetto Uprising, his duty position clearly indicates that he did not play any major role. He is believed to have survived the war.

MARTIN WÜNSCHE

SS-Obersturmführer Martin Wünsche was assigned as the company executive officer for the Headquarters Company, 3rd SS Panzergrenadier Training and Replacement Battalion during the Warsaw Ghetto Uprising. Wünsche was born in Grossschönau on 12 June 1912. He entered the Nazi Party on 1 May 1937 (Party number 4430472). His SS membership number of 236271 indicates he probably joined this organization in 1932. Wünsche was promoted to *SS-Untersturmführer* on 20 April 1940 and served with the 3rd SS Division "*Totenkopf*" from 15 December 1941 to 1 May 1942. During his service on the eastern front, he received the Iron Cross 2nd Class and the Demyansk Shield, and was wounded by grenade fragments in both legs.

Wünsche joined the battalion in May 1942, was promoted to *SS-Obersturmführer* on 9 November 1942, and served in Warsaw until 20 April 1944. During this period of service he attended several training schools but was present during the entire Ghetto Uprising. He served with the 11th SS Division "*Nordland*" from 20 April 1944 to 8 June 1944 when he was reassigned to the 20th SS Division.[174] On 30 January 1945 Wünsche was promoted to *SS-Hauptsturmführer*.

He is believed to have survived the war. It is likely that Martin Wünsche visited the fighting during the Ghetto Uprising, but we cannot ascertain his exact role.

• • •

SS CAVALRY REPLACEMENT DETACHMENT

Six *Waffen-SS* officers have been identified as serving with the SS Cavalry Replacement Detachment during the time of the Ghetto Uprising.

EGON BIRKIGT

SS-Hauptsturmführer Egon Birkigt served as a troop commander with the SS Cavalry Replacement Detachment during the Ghetto Uprising. Birkigt was born in Berlin-Charlottenburg on 24 June 1910. He entered the SS on 1 March 1933 with SS number 156643. Before the war, he served with various SS mounted units. He was promoted to *SS-Untersturmführer* on 9 November 1936, to *SS-Obersturmführer* on 25 July 1937 and to *SS-Hauptsturmführer* on 25 July 1938. He arrived in Warsaw on 15 March 1943 and remained in the city until 1 February 1944 when he reported to the front lines with the 8th SS Cavalry Division "*Florian Geyer*." In August of that year he returned to the replacement detachment.[175]

Birkigt won an Iron Cross 2nd Class during the war. As a troop commander, he undoubtedly visited the fighting in the Ghetto and may have taken an active role as well. He is believed to have survived the war.

FRED CONRAD

SS-Obersturmführer Fred Conrad served with the SS Cavalry Replacement Detachment in an unknown capacity during the Ghetto Uprising. Conrad was born 24 March 1919 in Dresden. He entered the SS on 1 July 1937 with a membership number of 378451. As an enlisted soldier, he fought in the campaigns in Poland, France and the Balkans as well as Russia. Such a record of service would indicate he was assigned to the *SS Leibstandarte Adolf Hitler* Regiment, but this is not annotated in his file.[176] He then served in the 1st Squadron of the 2nd SS Cavalry Regiment where he served in late 1941 as the car platoon leader.[177] Conrad was promoted to *SS-Untersturmführer* on 30 January 1942. On that date he was serving with the SS Cavalry Brigade in Russia. He continued to serve with this unit until 1 May 1942 when he was assigned to the replacement detachment. Conrad was highly decorated, winning the Infantry Assault Badge and both the Iron Cross 2nd and 1st Class. He was also wounded in action.

Conrad was promoted to *SS-Obersturmführer* on 20 April 1943. He remained with the detachment until 1 January 1944 when he was assigned to the personal staff of the *Reichsführer-SS*. Promoted to *SS-Hauptsturmführer* on 1 April 1944, he went to his final assignment on 3 March 1945 with the 37th SS Division *"Lützow."*[178] He is believed to have survived the war. The degree of his participation in the Ghetto Uprising is unknown. However, he was an extremely combat-experienced soldier who would have had a steadying influence on the troops. The following is an extract from an efficiency report for him written in December 1943:[179]

> Good over-all military knowledge.
> Particularly interested in the cavalry and in riding, with good talent.
> Presentation clear and understandable.
> Dutiful, acts after good consideration and in a professional manner, secure judgment.
> Intellectually very vivid, physically well trained.
> A spirited young leader with a pleasant demeanor.
> Healthy ambition, calm and balanced nature.
> Spotless attitude, agile appearance.
> Suitable as: Ordnance officer in the higher staff.

Fred Conrad is believed to have survived the war.

HANS DEHMKE

SS-Untersturmführer Hans Dehmke served in the SS Cavalry Replacement Detachment until he was killed in action during the Ghetto Uprising on 22 April 1943. We know nothing else about this officer; he has no personnel file at the National Archives nor does he appear to have ever applied to marry through the SS Race and Settlement Office (*Rasse-und Siedlungshauptamt*).

RUDOLF MAEKER

SS-Hauptsturmführer Rudolf Maeker held the position of 3rd Troop Commander with the SS Cavalry Replacement Detachment during the Ghetto Uprising. Maeker was born 19 May 1916 in Oels, Silesia (now Oleznica, Poland). He entered the SS on 2 November 1933 with an SS number of 194860. He was also a member of the Nazi Party joining on 1 May 1937 (Party number 4330146). Rudolf Maeker was promoted to *SS-Untersturmführer* on 9 November 1938 and to *SS-Obersturmführer* on 1 July 1940. During the Polish Campaign in 1939 he won both the Iron Cross 2nd and 1st Class while in the *SS Verfügungstruppe*. From 1941 to 15 March 1943 he served with the SS Cavalry Brigade and then came to the detachment in Warsaw. He was promoted to *SS-Hauptsturmführer* on 6 March 1942. On 24 May 1942 Maeker was awarded the German Cross in Gold. The supporting citation read:[180]

> In the Poland Campaign, *SS-Obersturmführer* Maeker has excelled through his outstanding courage and received the Iron Cross 2nd Class. In the Western Campaign, Maeker also proved himself through special bravery, cold-bloodedness and unwavering action. For outstanding military accomplishments in the Battle of Flanders, he was awarded the Iron Cross 1st Class. During the Russia Campaign, Maeker was first the ordnance officer of the brigade and later squadron leader. Through several exceptional deeds of bravery Maeker has excelled again.
>
> **24 June 1941**. As leader of an advance detachment, Maeker, through courageous advancing, reached the Narew Crossing near Wiczna. By seizing the crossroads 4 kilometers from Narew, he made the assault on Strekowa-Gora possible. Due to his courage, the regiment on the flank of the 87th Infantry Division could successfully execute its mission.
>
> **28 June 1941**. At the assault on a bunker-like fortification at the railway station of Monki, Maeker showed particular cold-bloodedness. He had an anti-tank gun brought in to break the bitter resistance of the enemy in the fortification.
>
> **23 January 1942**. As squadron chief, fighting in front of his men, Maeker took Karpowa, which was heavily defended by positions in the fields. With special courage he pushed his crew more and more forward. With that, Maeker fulfilled his orders whereby the intended assault created a no-man's land. Besides a high percentage of dead and wounded of the enemy, the troops captured six guns, four heavy machine-guns and several light and heavy mortars.
>
> **8 February 1942**. Breaking in and taking of the town of Swinino. Over and above the given order, Maeker made the independent decision and cleansed the area north-easterly of Swinino and with that, took the pressure off the rifle units of the 1st Panzer Division. For this deed which was executed with unheard-of courage, M. received the personal recognition of the Commander of the 1st Panzer Division, Major General Krüger [no relation to Friedrich-Wilhelm Krüger].

15 February 1942. In front of his squadron, which consisted of thirty men, Maeker, with weapon in hand and with outstanding bravery, defeated nine bunkers in the forest at close range. This made it possible for the left flank of the brigade, which was heading towards Ersowo, to be free from enemy fire.

21 February 1942. Staged a feint assault on Mantrowkie, which enabled an assault and penetration of the 1st and 2nd SS Cavalry Regiments of this town. On a completely visible terrain, Maeker brought his unit into such a starting position that the enemy had to expect a severe German assault from this side. Through this diversion which was executed with extreme bravery, the assault by the bulk of the brigade led to a decisive success.

22 February 1942. When the frontal assault on Kotschereschki by the 2nd SS Cavalry Regiment was unsuccessful, a battle group led by Maeker was ordered in. Through clever leadership and exemplary cold-bloodedness, Maeker led the battle group to success. The village was taken.

25 February 1942. Maeker received the order to defend with a reinforced squadron against an enemy attack on the village of Gusewo, which was occupied by the 102nd Infantry Division. After nine hours of fighting, the enemy – about six-fold stronger – broke into the first houses of the village. A possible withdrawal of friendly troops to give up the village was stopped through Maeker's personal merciless and cold-blooded action. This resulted in the village remaining in our own hands. During this act of courage, Maeker was wounded – shot through the shoulder.

SS-Obersturmführer Maeker has acted in critical situations during several engagements in such an outstandingly courageous and cold-blooded fashion that he is worthy of being awarded the German Cross in Gold.

Clearly, Rudolf Maeker was a front-line soldier of the first order. After serving in Warsaw, he was assigned as an aide-de-camp on 25 February 1944 to Field Marshal Walter Model. Maeker received his final promotion on 20 April 1944 to *SS-Sturmbannführer*. Rudolf Maeker probably played an important role in the Ghetto Uprising given his extensive combat experience. He is believed to have survived the war.

WILLI PLÄNK

SS-Hauptsturmführer Wilhelm Plänk served as the detachment commander with the SS Cavalry Replacement Detachment during the Ghetto Uprising. Plänk hailed from Ratingen, where he was born on 16 January 1911. Plänk entered the SS on 15 February 1933 (SS number 124751) and the Nazi Party on 1 May 1933 (Party number 3477629). He was promoted to *SS-Untersturmführer* on 20 April 1936, to *SS-Obersturmführer* on 12 September 1937 and to *SS-Hauptsturmführer* on 10 September 1939. He served in several SS cavalry assignments at the beginning of the war to include the SS Cavalry Brigade from 1 September 1941 to 20 March 1942. He received both the Iron Cross 2nd and 1st Class and also both classes of the War Service Cross with Swords. After the Ghetto Uprising he was promoted to *SS-Sturmbannführer* on 21 June 1943 and to *SS-Obersturmbannführer* on 9 November 1944.[181] He remained with the detachment for the duration of the war and was awarded the German Cross in Gold on 27 January 1945.[182]

SS-Hauptsturmführer Wilhelm Plänk obviously played a key role in quelling the Ghetto Uprising given the large contribution of SS cavalry troops used in the fighting, all of whom belonged to him. He survived the war. The following is his post-war testimony concerning his participation in the Warsaw operation:[183]

> As I have already mentioned during the investigation, *SS-Hauptsturmführer* D., who up to that time was the leader of the SS Cavalry Replacement Detachment, told me on my arrival in Warsaw that shortly before – probably a few days before – that he had been summoned to the SS- and Police Chief von Sammern-Frankenegg. He [von Sammern] had told him that for an anticipated military mission in the Ghetto forces of the *Waffen-SS* were needed.
>
> As it was, we as *Waffen-SS* were not under the jurisdiction of the SS and Police Leader and he had no power to command us whatsoever. However, in certain emergency situations he could requisition forces from the *Waffen-SS*, but at the same time he had to obtain the permission for this from the Main Operational Office of the *Waffen-SS* in Berlin. Up to the time the decision from the Main Operational Office of the *Waffen-SS* arrived, a certain temporary command power of the SS and Police Leader over these requested units of the *Waffen-SS* was appropriate in view of the emergency situation. According to what *SS-Hauptsturmführer* D. told me, the requisitioning of forces of the *Waffen-SS* via the SS and Police Leader was based on a message which the SS and Police Leader had received from the Security Service. How this played out in detail is something I do not know personally. I can only imagine the following: that the Security Service intended to evacuate the Ghetto and now learned through agents that significant resistance was to be expected, that this informa-

tion was transmitted to the SS and Police Leader and that consequently the demand for fighting troops resulted.

Immediately after my arrival, I tried by cable, wireless and telephone to reach the Main Operational Office of the *Waffen-SS* in Berlin to cancel the availability of the troops in my unit. The reason for my protest in Berlin was that the members of the unit were completely untrained recruits. While my efforts with Berlin were still going on, the confirmation of the demand for forces arrived from Berlin through the SS and Police Leader. After that, I immediately drove to Berlin and made a personal appearance at the Main Operational Office of the *Waffen-SS*. For that I had a certain amount of help because as for more than a year previously I had been working in this office and I knew the appropriate people and was also familiar to whom in particular I had to turn to. My first presentation in Berlin had only negative results. About the same time, the Higher SS and Police Leader in Kraków, Krüger, got involved; besides his function as Higher SS and Police Leader, he also was a General of the *Waffen-SS* and Police. In view of his rank of General of the *Waffen-SS* he practically could have given me commands which otherwise in his function as Chief of the SS and Police he could not do.

After my first unsuccessful intervention in Berlin, *SS-Untersturmführer* Dehmke was killed in action. As it has been read to me from the Stroop report that Dehmke – according to Stroop's statement – was killed on 22 April 1943, I consider that as correct. I don't know with certainty whether I was already back in Warsaw when he died, but I definitely attended his funeral. In addition, a number of young men from my unit had been wounded while fighting in the Ghetto. These two factors gave me further arguments to make another presentation in Berlin. I again drove to Berlin and again tried to negotiate the cancellation of this order. This time my intervention was not rejected, and I was assured that the matter would be studied. Based on this study, the requisitioning of my people was canceled. Although it is being presented to me that the Stroop Report indicates that up to and including 13 May 1943 members of the SS Cavalry Detachment were named as wounded soldiers of this mission, I personally think that the availability of members of my unit had already been canceled at an earlier date. If the date of 13 May as mentioned by Stroop is correct, it may have been possible that members of my unit – as they were released from action – were returned one by one and that the soldier [Johann Balogh], who was wounded on 13 May 1943, belonged to the rest of the forces.

I can make the following statement about the kind of mission of these men: The SS Cavalry Replacement Detachment was not engaged as a whole or that those parts that were returned were fighting as a whole unit. However, small troops were formed to which a part of the men of my unit were apportioned. These troops were in each case under the leadership of an officer of Stroop's staff. I can no longer remember names of the members of this staff. I do remember a police officer that in my opinion had the rank of a lieutenant colonel. I do not think that this was Major Schöppe whose name was mentioned to me above. Also the name of Major Bundke is completely unknown to me. I also do not know the name of the Adjutant of Stroop but am now told that it was Kaleschke. I do know the name Jesuiter of the staff of Stroop, but Jesuiter was not a military leader, at least in my opinion. I am mentioning him in this connection because I was mostly at my office and, therefore, did not have any connection with the members of Stroop's staff. My personal involvement in this whole mission was that from time to time I made visits to the Ghetto to look after members of my unit and to try to prevent them getting involved in military action. This was due to their completel lack of military training; this would have been senseless. In addition, these visits served the purpose to find new ideas and arguments for further confrontations in Berlin against the involvement of my people. During those visits in the Ghetto I saw how Jews were hauled out of the houses and led to the railway station where they were put on trains. It was said at that time that they would first be taken to a camp and from there would be resettled in the eastern territory. At that time I neither had concrete knowledge nor knew from hearsay that the expression "*Umsiedlung*" [resettlement] was a code and that these people were actually taken to extermination camps and killed there. I did not see shootings of Jews in the Ghetto except during the fighting. I cannot say which other units took part in this mission. I do know that Ukrainians and also policemen were there, but I am not in a position to name the exact troop designation of these units. I did know at that time that members of Bellwidt's unit were taking part in it. Whether and to what extent the Security Police took part in this action is something that I also cannot tell.

KURT PÖNISCH

SS-Obersturmführer Kurt Pönisch served in the SS Cavalry Replacement Detachment in an unknown capacity during the Ghetto Uprising. Pönisch was born 18 April 1906 in Lommatzsch. He joined the SS on 13 March 1933 with SS number 134176. He enrolled in the Nazi Party on 1 May 1933

(Party number unknown). He was promoted to *SS-Untersturmführer* on 9 November 1941 and served in the SS Division "*Das Reich*" until 14 January 1942.[184] On that date he transferred to the SS Main Leadership Office in Berlin. He reported to the detachment in Warsaw on 15 April 1942. Pönisch received a War Service Cross 2nd Class with Swords; he was promoted to *SS-Obersturmführer* on 30 January 1943.[185]

Pönisch's role in the suppression of the Ghetto Uprising is unclear. He is believed to have survived the war.

• • •

1ST GUARD BATTALION, TRAWNIKI LABOR CAMP "TRAWNIKI MEN"

JOHANN SCHWARZENBACHER

SS-Untersturmführer Herbert Schwarzenbacher served as the battalion commander for the detachment of Ukrainians known as the "Trawniki Men" who deployed from Trawniki to help quash the Ghetto Uprising. He was born 3 January 1909 in Munich. He joined the SS on 15 November 1932 with SS number 171669. Schwarzenbacher also entered the Nazi Party on 1 May 1933 with Party number 1930269. As an enlisted man he was assigned to the SS and Police Leader in Lublin and served as a company commander at Trawniki in 1941. He was promoted to *SS-Untersturmführer* on 31 January 1942 and assumed command of the 1st Guard Battalion at the camp. He deployed the unit to Warsaw on 19 April 1943 and remained there until 19 June 1943. That summer he appears to have served as the commandant of the SS Labor Camp Poniatowa as well. On 9 November 1943 Schwarzenbacher received an Iron Cross 1st Class for his overall performance in *Operation Reinhard*. Following his service in the General Government, Schwarzenbacher transferred with Odilo Globocnik to the Higher SS and Police Leader Adriatic Coast. He was promoted to *SS-Obersturmführer* on 30 January 1944. Again, he served as a guard battalion commander. Schwarzenbacher was killed in action by partisans on 2 June 1944. At 2000 hours that day his vehicle was ambushed on the road from Senosecchia and Storje near Trieste.[186] The casualty report in his personnel file states he was wounded in both legs and shot several times in the head, a classic case of partisans "finishing off" a wounded target.[187]

• • •

GERMAN ARMY

SIEGFRIED HAENICKE

General of Infantry Siegfried Haenicke was in overall command of all German Army units in the entire General Government during the period of the Ghetto Uprising. Haenicke was born on 8 September 1878 in Konstanz. He entered the Imperial German Army in 1897 as an infantry lieutenant. He served in World War I, winning both the Iron Cross 2nd and 1st Class; he was also wounded in action.[188] Haenicke rose through the ranks and was promoted to lieutenant colonel in 1925, to colonel in 1929 and to major general in 1932. He retired later that year. Siegfried Haenicke was recalled to duty in 1939 and placed in command of the 61st Infantry Division. From April to June 1942 Haenicke commanded the XXXVIIIth Corps; he was also promoted to General of Infantry at this time.[189]

Haenicke replaced General Curt Freiherr von Gienanth and undoubtedly knew that the reasons behind von Gienanth's sacking could be applied to him if he was not careful. Haenicke was probably kept appraised of the status of the Ghetto Uprising; there is no evidence that he either visited Warsaw during this time or issued any orders to German Army units during the fight. Haenicke was taken into custody by the Russians on 20 July 1945 and incarcerated in a prisoner of war camp at Mühlberg/Elbe. He died there on 19 February 1946.[190]

FRITZ ROSSUM

All Army units in the Warsaw area committed to assist in quelling the Ghetto Uprising did so at the order of Major General Fritz Rossum, the German Army Commandant of Warsaw, who had operational ownership of the Army formations there. Rossum was born in Aachen on 26 December 1887. He served in World War I but was released from the Army in 1920. He then joined the Police and rejoined the Army on 1 August 1935 with the rank of lieutenant colonel. Rossum was promoted to colonel in 1937 and began World War II as the commander of the 92nd Infantry Regiment. He then became Commandant of Metz in 1940 and was promoted to major general before moving to Warsaw. In late 1943 Rossum assumed duties as chief of all prisoner of war camps in *Wehrkreis X* (Army District 10). He was promoted to lieutenant general on 1 December 1943. Fritz Rossum survived the war and went into retirement in Düsseldorf.[191]

OFFICERS IN THE GERMAN ARMAMENTS OFFICE

A Colonel Freter headed the German Armaments Office in Warsaw. Additional officers in this section included Major Pechstein, Captain Hassler and Captain Deidert.[192] These officers most likely had no level of participation in the Ghetto Uprising itself; they probably provided information that supported continued use of Jewish labor in the armaments and war-related industries in the city. Little information can be found on the careers of these men. Albert Speer mentions that in the fall of 1944 the SS initiated court-martial proceedings against Colonel Freter but that the action was dropped in December 1944.[193] The officers in the Warsaw Armaments Office were in a difficult situation. After the war, at the trial of former *SS-Gruppenführer* Karl Wolff, Hassler testified that in July 1942 he had asked Colonel Freter whether it was true that the Jews in Warsaw were being killed. Freter is reported to have refused to directly answer the question. Instead, Freter informed Hassler that he had three alternatives. He could publicly state his opinion on the issue and then his life would be destroyed. Second, he could report that he was ill and attempt to leave Warsaw. Third, Hassler could remain in the Armaments Command in Warsaw and assist him in doing whatever was still possible to help the Jews.[194] Whatever that was, it wasn't much.

OFFICERS IN THE RAILROAD ARMORED TRAIN REPLACEMENT DETACHMENT 1

As mentioned previously, Major Ernst Naumann was in command of the detachment in Rembertow during period of the fighting at the Ghetto. His adjutant was First Lieutenant (*Oberleutnant*) Hermann Imm. Captain Werner Franke served as the operations officer and acting commander, whenever Naumann was absent from his duties. The detachment supply officer was First Lieutenant Hans Feuerlein; the detachment paymaster was Eberhard Steinweg. On 10 March 1943, First Lieutenant Rudolf Opitz, previously the commander of Armored Train 3 from March 1942 to March 1943, assumed command of a march company, designed to escort finished replacements to the front. First Lieutenant Grabke commanded a replacement company as did Captain Eduard Seele (who had previously commanded Armored Train 28 from June to December 1941.) First Lieutenant Johannes Crasselt commanded the First Training Company (Infantry, Engineers and Radiomen) and First Lieutenant Gustav Gelhaar commanded the Second Training Company (Artillery, *Flak* and *Panzer*). First Lieutenat Hermann Hoppe appears to have been the senior Engineer officer assigned to the detachment. Other officers in the detachment included a Dr. Jerg, Erwin Trzaska, Willi Leggewie and Rudolf Oppenhorst.[195]

This study found no documentation corroborating Stroop's account that two detachment officers were on location during the Warsaw Ghetto fight. There is nothing to suggest that Stroop was not accurate though; I believe that two detachment officers probably were there. It is possible that Naumann, Franke, Crasselt may have had a reason to visit their soldiers who were in action. Hermann Hoppe is the most likely candidate to have been with the troops, but we cannot say with certainty that he was.

Ernst Naumann commanded the unit until 30 April 1945. The following day he assumed command of Railway Armored Train Regimental Staff 3, an organization that supervised the armored trains assigned to Army Group Center. He survived the war. Werner Franke assumed command of Armored Train 70 in September 1943 and commanded this organization until the train was destroyed in combat on 4 April 1944 with the Soviet Army. He then assumed command of Armored Train 76 and commanded this unit from November 1944 to 15 April 1945. Soviet fighter-bombers destroyed this train on that date, but Franke also survived the war. Hans Feuerlein commanded Armored Train 206 at the very end of the war; he too is believed to have survived the conflict. Hermann Hoppe commanded Armored Train 67 from September 1943 to August 1944. Soviet forces destroyed his train on 28 August 1944 but it appears that Hoppe survived. Johannes Crasselt was not so fortunate. He assumed command of Armored Train 78 on 6 February 1945. On 27 March 1945 Soviet aircraft bombed the train in Hungary, killing Crasselt. Gustav Gelhaar also met his fate the same day. Gelhaar had assumed command of Armored Train 79 in February 1945. On 27 March 1945, Soviet ground forces blocked the way of this train in Hungary and attacked. Gelhaar and most of his crew were killed; the remainder went into Soviet captivity.[196]

Notes:

[1] Peter Padfield, *Himmler: Reichsführer-SS*. (New York: Henry Holt and Company, 1990), p. 390. Comment made to Rudolf Höss at Auschwitz-Birkenau.

[2] Ibid., p. 139.

[3] Personalakt Friedrich-Wilhelm Krüger, Washington, D.C: National Archives Microfilm Publication A3343, Records of SS Officers from the Berlin Document Center, Roll SSO-218A.

[4] Mark C. Yerger, *Riding East: The SS Cavalry Brigade in Poland and Russia 1939-1942*. (Atglen, PA: Schiffer Publishing, 1996.), p. 32.

[5] Tadeusz Bielecki and Leszek Szymanski, *Warsaw Aflame: The 1933-1945 Years*. (Los Angeles: Polamerica Press, 1973), p. 98.

[6] Jost Schneider, *Their Honor Was Loyalty! An Illustrated and Documentary History of the Knight's Cross Holders of the Waffen-SS and Police 1940-1945*. (San Jose, CA: R. James Bender Publishing, 1977), p. 201.

The 6th SS Division *"Nord"* was created 28 February 1941 as *SS Kampfgruppe "Nord"* in Norway. In September 1941 the unit reached division status as *SS Division "Nord"*. In September 1942 the unit became the *SS Gebirgs Division "Nord"* due to its mountain configuration. On 22 October 1943 the unit was renamed as the *6th SS Gebirgs Division "Nord"*. The division fought in Finland, Norway, France and Germany.

[7] Personalakt Max Jesuiter, Washington, D.C: National Archives Microfilm Publication A3343, Records of SS Officers from the Berlin Document Center, Roll SSO-138A.

[8] Wolfgang Scheffler and Helge Grabnitz, *Der Ghetto-Aufstand Warschau 1943*, pp. 186-187.

[9] Ibid. pp. 188-189.

[10] Personalakt Karl Kaleschke, Washington, D.C: National Archives Microfilm Publication A3343, Records of SS Officers from the Berlin Document Center, Roll SSO-149A.

[11] International Military Tribunal, *Trial of the Major War Criminals Before the International Military Tribunal, Nürnberg, 14 November 1945 - 1 October 1946. Volume XI, Proceedings, 8 April 1946 – 17 April 1946*. (Nuremberg, Germany, 1947), p. 352.

[12] Personalakt Dr. Ferdinand von Sammern-Frankenegg, Washington, D.C: National Archives Microfilm Publication A3343, Records of SS Officers from the Berlin Document Center, Roll SSO-060B.

[13] Nikolaus von Preradovich, *Oesterreichs Höhere SS-Führer*. (Berg am See, FRG: Kurt Vowinckel-verlag, 1987.), pp. 205-211.

[14] Gerald Reitlinger, *The Final Solution: The Attempt to Exterminate the Jews of Europe, 1939-1945*. (Northvale, N.J.: Jason Aronson, Inc., 1987), p. 271.

[15] Personalakt Dr. Ferdinand von Sammern-Frankenegg, Washington, D.C: National Archives Microfilm Publication A3343, Records of SS Officers from the Berlin Document Center, Roll SSO-060B.

[16] Wolfgang Scheffler and Helge Grabnitz, *Der Ghetto-Aufstand Warschau 1943*, pp. 196-197.

[17] Peter Padfield, *Himmler*, p. 451.

[18] Personalakt Jürgen Stroop, Washington, D.C: National Archives Microfilm Publication A3343, Records of SS Officers from the Berlin Document Center, Roll SSO-167B.

[19] Ruth Bettina Birn, *Die Höheren SS- und Polizeiführer: Himmler's Vertreter im Reich und in den besetzten Gebieten*. (Düsseldorf, FRG: Droste, 1986), p. 347.

[20] Mark C. Yerger, *Allgemeine-SS: The Commands, Units and Leaders of the General SS*. (Atglen, PA: Schiffer Publishing, 1997), p. 36.

[21] Personalakt Theodor van Eupen, Washington, D.C: National Archives Microfilm Publication A3343, Records of SS Officers from the Berlin Document Center, Roll SSO-192.

[22] Ruth Bettina Birn, *Die Höheren SS- und Polizeiführer: Himmler's Vertreter im Reich und in den besetzten Gebieten*, p. 334.

[23] The SS initially established a rank system in August 1929 and modified the structure on four additional occasions. These ranks belonged to the *Allgemeine-SS* – the General SS – the overall body of the SS, distinct from the *Waffen-SS*. Officers who also belonged to the *Waffen-SS* – SS field troops, could have a separate rank in that organization. Therefore, a colonel in the *Allgemeine-SS*, who volunteered for front-line service in the *Waffen-SS*, might only be a captain in that organization, or in Globocnik's case a sergeant. Not all *Allgemeine-SS* officers were in the *Waffen-SS*.

[24] Peter Padfield, *Himmler*, p. 371.

[25] Karl Höffkes, *Hitlers politische Generale: Die Gauleiter des Dritten Reiches*. (Tübingen, FRG: Grabert Verlag, 1986), pp. 93-94.

[26] Wolfgang Scheffler and Helge Grabnitz, *Der Ghetto-Aufstand Warschau 1943*, p. 228.

[27] Siegfried J. Pucher, *"In der Bewegung führend tätig", Odilo Globocnik – Kämpfer für den "Anschluss" Vollstrecker des Holocaust*. (Klagenfurt/Celovec, Slovenia: Drava Verlag, 1997), pp. 141-143.

[28] Karl Höffkes, *Hitlers politische Generale: Die Gauleiter des Dritten Reiches*, pp. 93-94.

[29] Siegfried J. Pucher, *"In der Bewegung führend tätig", Odilo Globocnik – Kämpfer für den "Anschluss" Vollstrecker des Holocaust*, p. 160.

[30] Ibid., pp. 160-161.

[31] 28 January 1999 letter to the author from Michael Tregenza, Holocaust historian and guide at the Majdanek concentration camp in Lublin.

[32] Hering was not directly involved in the Warsaw operation but was a significant figure in *Operation Reinhard*. See: *The Camp Men: The SS Officers Who Ran the Nazi Concentration Camp System* for more information on this officer.

[33] C.F. Rüter & D.W. de Mildt, *Die Westdeutschen Strafverfahren wegen Nationalsozialistischer Tötungsverbrechen 1945 - 1997*. (Amsterdam: Holland University Press, 1998), p. 192.

[34] Personalakt Franz Konrad, Washington, D.C: National Archives Microfilm Publication A3343, Records of SS Officers from the Berlin Document Center, Roll SSO-198A.

[35] Mark C. Yerger, *Riding East: The SS Cavalry Brigade in Poland and Russia 1939-1942*, p. 150.

[36] Personalakt Franz Konrad, Washington, D.C: National Archives Microfilm Publication A3343, Records of SS Officers from the Berlin Document Center, Roll SSO-198A.

[37] Personalakt Ernst Lerch, Washington, D.C: National Archives Microfilm Publication A3343, Records of SS Officers from the Berlin Document Center, Roll SSO-256A.

[38] 28 January 1999 letter to the author from Michael Tregenza, Holocaust historian and guide at the Majdanek concentration camp in Lublin.

[39] Personalakt Ernst Lerch, Washington, D.C: National Archives Microfilm Publication A3343, Records of SS Officers from the Berlin Document Center, Roll SSO-256A.

[40] 28 January 1999 letter to the author from Michael Tregenza, Holocaust historian and guide at the Majdanek concentration camp in Lublin.

[41] Personalakt Georg Michalsen, Washington, D.C: National Archives Microfilm Publication A3343, Records of SS Officers from the Berlin Document Center, Roll SSO-315A.

[42] Wolfgang Scheffler and Helge Grabnitz, *Der Ghetto-Aufstand Warschau 1943*, pp. 190-200.

[43] C.F. Rüter & D.W. de Mildt, *Die Westdeutschen Strafverfahren wegen Nationalsozialistischer Tötungsverbrechen 1945-1997*, p. 192.

[44] 28 January 1999 letter to the author from Michael Tregenza, Holocaust historian and guide at the Majdanek concentration camp in Lublin.

[45] Personalakt Reinhold von Mohrenschildt, Washington, D.C: National Archives Microfilm Publication A3343, Records of SS Officers from the Berlin Document Center, Roll SSO-323A.

[46] Siegfried J. Pucher, *"In der Bewegung führend tätig", Odilo Globocnik – Kämpfer für den "Anschluss" Vollstrecker des Holocaust*, p. 401.

[47] Louis L. Snyder, *Encyclopedia of the Third Reich*. (New York: McGraw-Hill, 1976), p. 285.

[48] C.F. Rüter & D.W. de Mildt, *Die Westdeutschen Strafverfahren wegen Nationalsozialistischer Tötungsverbrechen 1945-1997*, p. 192.

[49] *SS-Hauptsturmführer* Dr. Gerd Bomeier is not included in this total, because it is unclear if he actually was assigned to Warsaw during the Ghetto Uprising, or after it. Bomeier is listed as the district SS physician during 1943 and 1944, but his previous service with the SS Police Division may have extended past 15 May 1943. Dr. Bomeier was born 15 December 1911 in Harburg-Wilhelmshaven. He entered the SS on 20 May 1933 (SS number 93031) and the Nazi Party on 1 June 1933 (Party number 3160497). Bomeier was promoted to *SS-Untersturmführer* on 30 January 1938, to *SS-Obersturmführer* on 11 November 1938 and to *SS-Hauptsturmführer* on 30 January 1939. While serving with the SS Police Division, he was wounded in action and received the Iron Cross 1st and 2nd Class, as well as the Infantry Assault Badge. He is listed in his personnel file as serving with the HSSPF in the General Government in 1944. His file also reflects that Bomeier was killed in action on 13 August 1944. The 1944 *Dienstaltersliste der Waffen-SS, Stand vom 1. Juli 1944* lists Bomeier as a reserve *SS-Sturmbannführer*. Source: Personalakt Dr. Gerd Bomeier, Washington, D.C: National Archives Microfilm Publication A3343, Records of SS Officers from the Berlin Document Center, Roll SSO-089.

The following officers have been identified as serving in the KdS Warsaw during the 1940-1941 time period, but they departed Warsaw well before the Ghetto Uprising (this is a partial list only):

Rank	Name	Date of Birth	Birthplace	SS Number
SS-Untersturmführer	Otto Doberschütz	23 November 1913	Leipzig	210343
SS-Untersturmführer	Erich Engels	11 September 1909	Tecklenburg	290989
SS-Untersturmführer	Helmut Heiss	17 March 1913	Innsbruck, Austria	281036
SS-Untersturmführer	Walter Klaus	7 November 1911	Westeregeln	160145
SS-Untersturmführer	Fritz Kunze	16 April 1912	Waldenburg	188650
SS-Untersturmführer	Walter Leiber	30 March 1913	Neukirchen	270459
SS-Untersturmführer	Gerhard Rehbein	6 July 1912	Dresden	245440
SS-Obersturmführer	Helmut Fromm	26 November 1908	Hanau	101675
SS-Obersturmführer	Heinz Gehrmann	24 July 1910	Könitz	75024
SS-Obersturmführer	Walter Knoll	23 September 1897	Reppen	367236
SS-Obersturmführer	Gerhard Köhler	12 August 1909	Taucka/Leipzig	17988
SS-Obersturmführer	Harald Wiesmann	22 April 1909	Krefeld	127557
SS-Obersturmführer	Hans-Werner Lopass	23 March 1896	Demmin	20072
SS-Hauptsturmführer	Alfred Bartelt	14 December 1905	Gnesen	322114
SS-Hauptsturmführer	Adolf Bonifer	23 November 1908	Darmstadt	107487
SS-Hauptsturmführer	Hans Fleischmann	18 November 1913	Heimersheim	331999
SS-Hauptsturmführer	Helmuth Gohl	16 July 1905	Essingen	267369
SS-Hauptsturmführer	Walter von Kielpinski	29 April 1909	Chemnitz	107278
SS-Sturmbannführer	Günter Rausch	19 May 1909	Sondershausen	17852
SS-Sturmbannführer	Dr. Helmut Tanzmann	18 January 1907	Oschatz	290002

[50] Personalakt Rudolf Albanbauer, Washington, D.C: National Archives Microfilm Publication A3343, Records of SS Officers from the Berlin Document Center, Roll SSO-004.

[51] Letter to the author from the Munich cemetery bureau, 22 September 1999. Albanbauer is buried in the Munich *Nordfriedhof.*

[52] Personalakt Franz Avril, Washington, D.C: National Archives Microfilm Publication A3343, Records of SS Officers from the Berlin Document Center, Roll SSO-022.

[53] Personalakt Norbert Graf Bergh-Trips, Washington, D.C: National Archives Microfilm Publication A3343, Records of SS Officers from the Berlin Document Center, Roll SSO-059.

[54] Wladyslaw Bartoszewski, *Warsaw Death Ring, 1939-1944.* (Warsaw: Interpress Publishers, 1968), p. 341.

[55] Personalakt Norbert Graf Bergh-Trips, Washington, D.C: National Archives Microfilm Publication A3343, Records of SS Officers from the Berlin Document Center, Roll SSO-059.

[56] Conversation with Professor D.W. de Mildt (C.F. Rüter & D.W. de Mildt, *Die Westdeutschen Strafverfahren Wegen Nationalsozialistischer Tötungsverbrechen 1945-1997*), 26 August 1999.

[57] Personalakt Karl Biedenkapp, Washington, D.C: National Archives Microfilm Publication A3343, Records of SS Officers from the Berlin Document Center, Roll SSO-067.

[58] Wladyslaw Bartoszewski, *Warsaw Death Ring, 1939-1944*, p. 339.

[59] Personalakt Wolfgang Birkner, Washington, D.C: National Archives Microfilm Publication A3343, Records of SS Officers from the Berlin Document Center, Roll SSO-072.

[60] Personalakt Johannes Böhm, Washington, D.C: National Archives Microfilm Publication A3343, Records of SS Officers from the Berlin Document Center, Roll SSO-082.

[61] Personalakt Alfred Böhmer, Washington, D.C: National Archives Microfilm Publication A3343, Records of SS Officers from the Berlin Document Center, Roll SSO-083

[62] Josef Wulf, *Das Dritte Reich und seine Vollstrecker: Die Liquidation von 500000 Juden im Ghetto Warschau.* (Berlin-Grunewald: Arani Verlags Gmbh, 1961), pp. 299-303.

[63] Israel Gutman, *The Jews of Warsaw, 1939-1943: Ghetto, Underground, Revolt.* (Bloomington: Indiana University Press, 1982), p. 207.

[64] Dan Kurzman, *The Bravest Battle: The Twenty-eight Days of the Warsaw Ghetto Uprising.* (New York: G. P. Putnam's Sons, 1976), p. 347.

[65] Jaroslaw M. Rymkiewicz, *The Final Station: Umschlagplatz.* Translated by Nina Taylor. (New York: Farrar, Straus and Giroux, 1994), p. 79.

[66] Personalakt Ulrich Breitenfeldt, Washington, D.C: National Archives Microfilm Publication A3343, Records of SS Officers from the Berlin Document Center, Roll SSO-103.

[67] Personalakt Arthur Füssel, Washington, D.C: National Archives Microfilm Publication A3343, Records of SS Officers from the Berlin Document Center, Roll SSO-229.

[68] Personalakt Harry Geisler, Washington, D.C: National Archives Microfilm Publication A3343, Records of SS Officers from the Berlin Document Center, Roll SSO-007A.

[69] Personalakt Werner Grabert, Washington, D.C: National Archives Microfilm Publication A3343, Records of SS Officers from the Berlin Document Center, Roll SSO-026A.

[70] Personalakt Werner Grahn, Washington, D.C: National Archives Microfilm Publication A3343, Records of SS Officers from the Berlin Document Center, Roll SSO-027A.

[71] Personalakt Gustav Grambow, Washington, D.C: National Archives Microfilm Publication A3343, Records of SS Officers from the Berlin Document Center, Roll SSO-027A.

[72] Personalakt Richard Grudno, Washington, D.C: National Archives Microfilm Publication A3343, Records of SS Officers from the Berlin Document Center, Roll SSO-039A.

[73] Kazimierz Moczarski, *Conversations with an Executioner.* Edited by Mariana Fitzpatrick. (Englewood Cliffs, New Jersey), p.142.

[74] Personalakt Dr. Ludwig Hahn, Washington, D.C: National Archives Microfilm Publication A3343, Records of SS Officers from the Berlin Document Center, Roll SSO-053A.

[75] C.F. Rüter & D.W. de Mildt, *Die Westdeutschen Strafverfahren wegen Nationalsozialistischer Tötungsverbrechen 1945 - 1997*, p. 189.

[76] Ibid., p. 194.

[77] Personalakt Wilhelm Hammermeister, Washington, D.C: National Archives Microfilm Publication A3343, Records of SS Officers from the Berlin Document Center, Roll SSO-058A.

[78] Personalakt Hugo Hampel, Washington, D.C: National Archives Microfilm Publication A3343, Records of SS Officers from the Berlin Document Center, Roll SSO-059A.

[79] Personalakt Karl Heine, Washington, D.C: National Archives Microfilm Publication A3343, Records of SS Officers from the Berlin Document Center, Roll SSO-077A.

[80] Personalakt Karl Heller, Washington, D.C: National Archives Microfilm Publication A3343, Records of SS Officers from the Berlin Document Center, Roll SSO-081A.

[81] Personalakt Erich Herberholz, Washington, D.C: National Archives Microfilm Publication A3343, Records of SS Officers from the Berlin Document Center, Roll SSO-089A.

[82] Personalakt Gottlieb Höhmann, Washington, D.C: National Archives Microfilm Publication A3343, Records of SS Officers from the Berlin Document Center, Roll SSO-103A.

[83] Personalakt Karl Jepsen, Washington, D.C: National Archives Microfilm Publication A3343, Records of SS Officers from the Berlin Document Center, Roll SSO-138A.

[84] Personalakt Wilfried Jopke, Washington, D.C: National Archives Microfilm Publication A3343, Records of SS Officers from the Berlin Document Center, Roll SSO-141A.

[85] Personalakt Dr. Herbert Jung, Washington, D.C: National Archives Microfilm Publication A3343, Records of SS Officers from the Berlin Document Center, Roll SSO-143A.

[86] By the resistance but not so stated in the German publication.

[87] Stefan Korbonski, *The Polish Underground State: A Guide to the Underground 1939-1945.* Translated by Marta Erdman. (New York: Hippocrene Books, 1978), p. 86.

[88] Personalakt Dr. Ernst Kah, Washington, D.C: National Archives Microfilm Publication A3343, Records of SS Officers from the Berlin Document Center, Roll SSO-147A.

[89] Kazimierz Moczarski, *Conversations with an Executioner*, p.142.

[90] Letter to the author from the city administration in Baden-Baden, 24 September 1999.

[91] Personalakt Jakob Lechner, Washington, D.C: National Archives Microfilm Publication A3343, Records of SS Officers from the Berlin Document Center, Roll SSO-248A. Lechner's file is severely burned and is therefore missing many details of his life and career.

[92] Personalakt Willy Lubensky, Washington, D.C: National Archives Microfilm Publication A3343, Records of SS Officers from the Berlin Document Center, Roll SSO-279A.

[93] Personalakt Erich Merten, Washington, D.C: National Archives Microfilm Publication A3343, Records of SS Officers from the Berlin Document Center, Roll SSO-310A.

[94] Personalakt Kurt Müldner, Washington, D.C: National Archives Microfilm Publication A3343, Records of SS Officers from the Berlin Document Center, Roll SSO-327A.

[95] Personalakt Karl Müller, Washington, D.C: National Archives Microfilm Publication A3343, Records of SS Officers from the Berlin Document Center, Roll SSO-334A.

[96] Ibid.

[97] Personalakt Wilhelm Munk, Washington, D.C: National Archives Microfilm Publication A3343, Records of SS Officers from the Berlin Document Center, Roll SSO-340A.

[98] Hitler detailed the Condor Legion, a unit of the *Luftwaffe* with ground forces as well, for special duty during the Spanish Civil War. Their mission was to support *Generalissimo* Francisco Franco and his Spanish Nationalist forces. The *Luftwaffe* contingent was the largest element and consisted of *flak* troops, bomber units, fighter units and reconnaissance elements. The Army contingent was much smaller; initially composed of roughly a battalion comprised of a headquarters staff, two line companies and a field maintenance company. Over nineteen thousand German personnel rotated through the Condor Legion from September 1936 to May 1939. Several hundred German soldiers were killed in action or died in accidents or of illness.

[99] Personalakt Otto Oertwig, Washington, D.C: National Archives Microfilm Publication A3343, Records of SS Officers from the Berlin Document Center, Roll SSO-355A.

[100] Personalakt Alfred Otto, Washington, D.C: National Archives Microfilm Publication A3343, Records of SS Officers from the Berlin Document Center, Roll SSO-361A.

[101] Personalakt Alfred Pagel, Washington, D.C: National Archives Microfilm Publication A3343, Records of SS Officers from the Berlin Document Center, Roll SSO-363A.

[102] Personalakt Arthur Potratz, Washington, D.C: National Archives Microfilm Publication A3343, Records of SS Officers from the Berlin Document Center, Roll SSO-390A.

[103] Personalakt Erich Reschke, Washington, D.C: National Archives Microfilm Publication A3343, Records of SS Officers from the Berlin Document Center, Roll SSO-024B.

[104] Ibid.

[105] Personalakt Georg Richter, Washington, D.C: National Archives Microfilm Publication A3343, Records of SS Officers from the Berlin Document Center, Roll SSO-026B.

[106] Ibid.

[107] Personalakt Heinz Schnartendorff, Washington, D.C: National Archives Microfilm Publication A3343, Records of SS Officers from the Berlin Document Center, Roll SSO-091B.

[108] Ibid.

[109] Personalakt Hugo Schwarze, Washington, D.C: National Archives Microfilm Publication A3343, Records of SS Officers from the Berlin Document Center, Roll SSO-123B.

[110] Personalakt Eugen Schweizer, Washington, D.C: National Archives Microfilm Publication A3343, Records of SS Officers from the Berlin Document Center, Roll SSO-125B.

[111] Personalakt Alfred Seiler, Washington, D.C: National Archives Microfilm Publication A3343, Records of SS Officers from the Berlin Document Center, Roll SSO-131B.

[112] Letter to the author from the office of the Oberbürgermeister of Kiel, 27 October 1999.

[113] Wladyslaw Bartoszewski, *Warsaw Death Ring, 1939-1944*, p. 340.

[114] Personalakt Alfred Spilker, Washington, D.C: National Archives Microfilm Publication A3343, Records of SS Officers from the Berlin Document Center, Roll SSO-146B.

[115] Personalakt Erich Spruch, Washington, D.C: National Archives Microfilm Publication A3343, Records of SS Officers from the Berlin Document Center, Roll SSO-147B.

[116] Personalakt Dr. Gerhard Stabenow, Washington, D.C: National Archives Microfilm Publication A3343, Records of SS Officers from the Berlin Document Center, Roll SSO-147B.

[117] Personalakt Walter Stamm, Washington, D.C: National Archives Microfilm Publication A3343, Records of SS Officers from the Berlin Document Center, Roll SSO-149B.

[118] Personalakt Gustav Steinmetz, Washington, D.C: National Archives Microfilm Publication A3343, Records of SS Officers from the Berlin Document Center, Roll SSO-156B.

[119] Personalakt Waldemar Sterk, Washington, D.C: National Archives Microfilm Publication A3343, Records of SS Officers from the Berlin Document Center, Roll SSO-158B.

[120] Personalakt Ulrich Stern, Washington, D.C: National Archives Microfilm Publication A3343, Records of SS Officers from the Berlin Document Center, Roll SSO-158B.

[121] Personalakt Alfred Strunz, Washington, D.C: National Archives Microfilm Publication A3343, Records of SS Officers from the Berlin Document Center, Roll SSO-167B.

[122] Personalakt Wilhelm Tewes, Washington, D.C: National Archives Microfilm Publication A3343, Records of SS Officers from the Berlin Document Center, Roll SSO-176B.

[123] Personalakt Werner Weitze, Washington, D.C: National Archives Microfilm Publication A3343, Records of SS Officers from the Berlin Document Center, Roll SSO-233B.

[124] Personalakt Paul Werner, Washington, D.C: National Archives Microfilm Publication A3343, Records of SS Officers from the Berlin Document Center, Roll SSO-237B.

[125] Personalakt Otto Wettstädt, Washington, D.C: National Archives Microfilm Publication A3343, Records of SS Officers from the Berlin Document Center, Roll SSO-240B.

[126] Personalakt Walter Witossek, Washington, D.C: National Archives Microfilm Publication A3343, Records of SS Officers from the Berlin Document Center, Roll SSO-001C.

[127] Ibid.

[128] Wladyslaw Bartoszewski, *Warsaw Death Ring, 1939-1944*, p. 341.

[129] Kurt Mehner, *Die Waffen-SS und Polizei, 1939-1945*. (Norderstedt, Germany: Militär-Verlag Klaus D. Patzwall, 1995), pp. 323-324.

[130] Personalakt Otto Bundke, Washington, D.C: National Archives Microfilm Publication A3343, Records of SS Officers from the Berlin Document Center, Roll SSO-121.

[131] Josef Wulf, *Das Dritte Reich und seine Vollstrecker: Die Liquidation von 500000 Juden im Ghetto Warschau*, pp. 304-306.

[132] Bernard Mark, *The Extermination and the Resistance of the Polish Jews during 1939-1944*. (Warsaw: Jewish Historical Institute, 1955), pp. 168-169.

[133] The Nazi Party's highest decoration for service, "The Decoration of 9 November 1923" (*Ehrenzeichen vom 9. November 1923*) was also known as the "Blood Order" (*Blutorden*). Hitler created this decoration in March 1934 to commemorate the failed "Beer Hall" Putsch (attempted overthrow of the Bavarian government) on 9 November 1923 in Munich. Eligibility was initially limited to persons who had participated in the events of November 9th and who were known as "Old Comrades." In 1938 eligibility was expanded to include persons who had rendered outstanding service to the party in the 1920s and had received a Weimar court death sentence – and who had subsequently served at least one year in jail – or who had been severely wounded or killed in party service. Sources: LTC John R. Angolia, *For Führer and Fatherland, Military, Political and Civil Awards of the Third Reich, Volumes 1 & 2*. (San Jose, CA: R. James Bender Publishing, 1976) and French MacLean, "The Unknown Generals – German Corps Commanders in World War II." (Masters Thesis, United States Army Command and General Staff College, 1988).

Another Nazi service award was the Golden Party Badge (*Goldenes Parteiabzeichen*). Hitler created this award in October 1933. To receive this award an individual must have had uninterrupted service in the Nazi Party since 27 February 1925 and who held Nazi Party membership numbers 1 to 100,000. As of 1 December 1938, some 1,626 SS officers had a NSDAP number below 100,000. The earlier an individual joined the party, the lower the party number he would receive – the award was designed to recognize the early service of the first party members who joined before it became fashionable to do so. When both criteria were placed in effect, it was found that 22,282 – and not 100,000 – persons actually qualified for the award. Sources: LTC John R. Angolia, *For Führer and Fatherland, Military, Political and Civil Awards of the Third Reich, Volumes 1 & 2*. (San Jose, CA: R. James Bender Publishing, 1976) and *Dienstaltersliste der Schutzstaffel der N.S.D.A.P., Stand vom 1.December 1938*. Berlin: Personalkanzlei des Reichsführers-SS, 1939.

[134] Personalakt Max Ederer, Washington, D.C: National Archives Microfilm Publication A3343, Records of SS Officers from the Berlin Document Center, Roll SSO-173.

[135] Bernard Mark, *The Extermination and the Resistance of the Polish Jews during 1939 - 1944*, pp. 169-170.

[136] Personalakt Dr. Friedrich Knaipp, Washington, D.C: National Archives Microfilm Publication A3343, Records of SS Officers from the Berlin Document Center, Roll SSO-184A.

[137] Personalakt Karl Schöppe, Washington, D.C: National Archives Microfilm Publication A3343, Records of SS Officers from the Berlin Document Center, Roll SSO-097B.

[138] Personalakt Erwin Sternagel, Washington, D.C: National Archives Microfilm Publication A3343, Records of SS Officers from the Berlin Document Center, Roll SSO-158B.

[139] Wolfgang Scheffler and Helge Grabnitz, *Der Ghetto-Aufstand Warschau 1943*, pp. 260-262. The testimony is annotated as coming from the witness E. S. Given the tone of the testimony as that of a Police officer in the 1st Battalion, 22nd SS Police Regiment and the initials, I believe this account is definitely from Erwin Sternagel. He talks about "my battalion" instead of "our" battalion. This is exactly how battalion commanders talk.

[140] Dan Kurzman, *The Bravest Battle: The Twenty-eight Days of the Warsaw Ghetto Uprising*, p. 347.

[141] Personalakt Oskar Zisenis, Washington, D.C: National Archives Microfilm Publication A3343, Records of SS Officers from the Berlin Document Center, Roll SSO-024C.

[142] The 5th SS Division "*Wiking*" was formed 20 November 20 1940 as the *SS Division "Germania"* but was quickly renamed the *SS Division "Wiking"*. On 9 November 1942 the division was renamed the *SS Panzergrenadier Division "Wiking"*. On 22 October 1943 the unit was renamed the *5th SS Panzer Division "Wiking."* The unit fought in Russia, Hungary and Austria.

[143] Personalakt Heinrich Amberg, Washington, D.C: National Archives Microfilm Publication A3343, Records of SS Officers from the Berlin Document Center, Roll SSO-012.

[144] Personalakt Hans Artmann, Washington, D.C: National Archives Microfilm Publication A3343, Records of SS Officers from the Berlin Document Center, Roll SSO-018.

[145] Personalakt Walter Bellwidt, Washington, D.C: National Archives Microfilm Publication A3343, Records of SS Officers from the Berlin Document Center, Roll SSO-055.

[146] Wolfgang Scheffler and Helge Grabnitz, *Der Ghetto-Aufstand Warschau 1943*, pp. 225-229.

[147] The 16th SS Division "*Reichsführer-SS*" was formed on 3 October 1943 from the *SS Sturmbrigade "Reichsführer SS"* and received the name *16th SS Panzergrenadier Division "Reichsführer-SS"*. The unit fought in Italy and Austria.

[148] Personalakt Walter Biermann, Washington, D.C: National Archives Microfilm Publication A3343, Records of SS Officers from the Berlin Document Center, Roll SSO-069.

[149] The author attempted to ascertain the whereabouts of Biermann from the city administration of Frankfurt, his hometown. Their reply suggested knowledge of him but indicated that they would only release information to a close relative.

[150] The 13th SS Division "*Handschar*" was created on 1 March 1943 primarily of Bosnian Muslims and was originally titled the *Kroatische SS Freiwilligen Division* (Croatian SS Volunteer Division). On 2 July 1943 the name was changed to *Kroatische SS Freiwilligen Gebirgs Division*. On 22 October 1943 the SS again changed the unit designation to that of the *13th SS Freiwilligen bosnische herzogowische Gebirgs Division (Kroatien)*. In June 1944 this name was formalized to *the 13th Waffen Gebirgs Division der SS "Handschar" (Kroatien Nr. 1)*. The unit fought partisans in Croatia and also served in Hungary.

[151] Personalakt Albert Bonnet, Washington, D.C: National Archives Microfilm Publication A3343, Records of SS Officers from the Berlin Document Center, Roll SSO-090.

[152] Personalakt Alfred Eckert, Washington, D.C: National Archives Microfilm Publication A3343, Records of SS Officers from the Berlin Document Center, Roll SSO-171.

[153] Ibid.

[154] Personalakt Kurt Grahofer, Washington, D.C: National Archives Microfilm Publication A3343, Records of SS Officers from the Berlin Document Center, Roll SSO-027A.

[155] Personalakt Heinz Klippel, Washington, D.C: National Archives Microfilm Publication A3343, Records of SS Officers from the Berlin Document Center, Roll SSO-181A.

[156] Personalakt Karl Knörzer, Washington, D.C: National Archives Microfilm Publication A3343, Records of SS Officers from the Berlin Document Center, Roll SSO-187A.

[157] Josef Wulf, *Das Dritte Reich und seine Vollstrecker: Die Liquidation von 500000 Juden im Ghetto Warschau*, pp. 307-308.

[158] Personalakt Wilhelm Linnenlücke, Washington, D.C: National Archives Microfilm Publication A3343, Records of SS Officers from the Berlin Document Center, Roll SSO-266A.

[159] More than 38,000 – nearly half of all physicians in the country – joined the Nazi Party. Source: French MacLean, *The Camp Men: The SS Officers Who Ran the Nazi Concentration Camp System*. (Atglen, PA: Schiffer Publishing Co., 1998)

[160] Personalakt Dr. Frank Müller, Washington, D.C: National Archives Microfilm Publication A3343, Records of SS Officers from the Berlin Document Center, Roll SSO-329A.

[161] The 14th SS Division was formed at Debica, Poland in September 1943 as the *14th Galizische SS Freiwilliger Division* of ethnic Germans and Ukrainians from the Galician district. On 22 October 1943 the unit was renamed the *14th Galizische SS Freiwilligen Infanterie Division*. In August 1944 the unit again was redesignated – the *14th Waffen Grenadier Division der SS (galizische Nr. 1)*. This formation fought in Russia, Slovakia and Austria.

[162] Personalakt Günther Mussbach, Washington, D.C: National Archives Microfilm Publication A3343, Records of SS Officers from the Berlin Document Center, Roll SSO-341A.

[163] Personalakt Walter Noack, Washington, D.C: National Archives Microfilm Publication A3343, Records of SS Officers from the Berlin Document Center, Roll SSO-352A.

[164] Personalakt Heinrich Ohlmeier, Washington, D.C: National Archives Microfilm Publication A3343, Records of SS Officers from the Berlin Document Center, Roll SSO-356A.

[165] Personalakt Hanns Röger, Washington, D.C: National Archives Microfilm Publication A3343, Records of SS Officers from the Berlin Document Center, Roll SSO-039B.

[166] Personalakt Werner Schmidt, Washington, D.C: National Archives Microfilm Publication A3343, Records of SS Officers from the Berlin Document Center, Roll SSO-087B.

[167] Personalakt Ewald-Eduard Schramm, Washington, D.C: National Archives Microfilm Publication A3343, Records of SS Officers from the Berlin Document Center, Roll SSO-099B.

[168] The 4th SS Division "*Polizei*" was formed on 9 December 1940 and named *SS-Polizei Division*. The division was renamed the *Polizei Panzergrenadier Division* on 1 June 1943. On 22 October 1943 it became the *4th SS Polizei Panzergrenadier Division*. The unit fought in Russia, Greece, Yugoslavia, Hungary, Pomerania and West Prussia.

[169] Personalakt Wilhelm Sprenger, Washington, D.C: National Archives Microfilm Publication A3343, Records of SS Officers from the Berlin Document Center, Roll SSO-145B.

[170] Personalakt Herbert Taege, Washington, D.C: National Archives Microfilm Publication A3343, Records of SS Officers from the Berlin Document Center, Roll SSO-171B.

[171] Personalakt Herbert Webermeier, Washington, D.C: National Archives Microfilm Publication A3343, Records of SS Officers from the Berlin Document Center, Roll SSO-223B.

[172] Werner does have papers in Microfilm Publication A3343, *Records of SS Personnel from the Berlin Document Center, Series RS – SS Race and Settlement Office* (*RuSHA, Rasse-und Siedlungshauptamt*), Roll G5153. A card in this file shows he may have been killed in action, but we cannot be certain of this.

[173] Personalakt Erich Woywoth, Washington, D.C: National Archives Microfilm Publication A3343, Records of SS Officers from the Berlin Document Center, Roll SSO-014C.

[174] The 11th SS Division "*Nordland*" was formed at Grafenwöhr, Germany in July 1943 as *SS Panzergrenadier Division 11*. On 3 October 1943 the name changed to the *SS Freiwilligen Panzergrenadier Division "Nordland"*; but this was short-lived and the formation became the *11th Freiwilligen Panzergrenadier Division "Nordland"* on 22 October 1943. The unit fought in Croatia, Russia, Courland, Pomerania, the Oder and Berlin.

The 20th SS Division was created on 24 January 1944 as the *20th Estonische SS Freiwilligen Division* from elements of the *3rd Estonische SS Freiwilligen Brigade*. Both units were manned by large contingents of Estonians. In June 1944 the unit was renamed the *20th Waffen Grenadier Division der SS (estonische Nr. 1)*. The unit fought in Estonia and Silesia.

[175] Personalakt Egon Birkigt, Washington, D.C: National Archives Microfilm Publication A3343, Records of SS Officers from the Berlin Document Center, Roll SSO-072.

[176] Personalakt Fred Conrad, Washington, D.C: National Archives Microfilm Publication A3343, Records of SS Officers from the Berlin Document Center, Roll SSO-131.

[177] Mark C. Yerger, *Riding East: The SS Cavalry Brigade in Poland and Russia 1939-1942*, p. 152.

[178] On 20 February 1945 the *37th SS Freiwilligen Kavallerie Division "Lützow"* was formed at Pressburg. It fought in Hungary.

[179] Personalakt Fred Conrad, Washington, D.C: National Archives Microfilm Publication A3343, Records of SS Officers from the Berlin Document Center, Roll SSO-131.

[180] Personalakt Rudolph Maeker, Washington, D.C: National Archives Microfilm Publication A3343, Records of SS Officers from the Berlin Document Center, Roll SSO-288A.

[181] Personalakt Wilhelm Plänk, Washington, D.C: National Archives Microfilm Publication A3343, Records of SS Officers from the Berlin Document Center, Roll SSO-382A.

[182] Mark C. Yerger, *Riding East: The SS Cavalry Brigade in Poland and Russia 1939-1942*, p. 71.

[183] Wolfgang Scheffler and Helge Grabnitz, *Der Ghetto-Aufstand Warschau 1943*, pp. 241-244.

[184] The 2nd SS Division "*Das Reich*" was originally formed 1 April 1940 as the *SS Division Verfügungstruppe* which, in turn, became the *SS Division (motorized) "Reich"* on 21 December 1940. The unit received a further name change on 15 October 1942 to *SS Division (motorized) "Das Reich"*. On 9 November 1942 the division was subsequently renamed *SS Panzergrenadier Division "Das Reich"*. On 22 October 1943 the division acquired its final designation *2nd SS Panzer Division "Das Reich"*. *Das Reich* served in the Netherlands, France, the Balkans, Russia, Normandy, the Ardennes, Hungary and Bohemia.

[185] Personalakt Kurt Pönisch, Washington, D.C: National Archives Microfilm Publication A3343, Records of SS Officers from the Berlin Document Center, Roll SSO-386A.

[186] Many of the SS personnel involved in *Operation Reinhard* were transferred in the fall of 1943 to the Dalmatian coast to operate a holding center for Jews enroute to Auschwitz and to exterminate Italian and Yugoslav partisans in the area.

[187] Personalakt Johann Schwarzenbacher, Washington, D.C: National Archives Microfilm Publication A3343, Records of SS Officers from the Berlin Document Center, Roll SSO-123B.

Officers assigned to the camps associated with *Operation Reinhard* – Belzec, Sobibór and Treblinka – were over six times as likely to have later been killed in action than those assigned to other concentration camps. Perhaps the high battlefield fatality rate of these officers is within the norm and that the many absent personnel files for these men are simply the result of human error (either during the war by SS clerks or after the conflict in the preservation of the records within the archival system.) There are three plausible explanations for what may have happened. First, there is a possibility that nothing untoward occurred; the increased fatalities just happened. War is a dangerous occurrence – World War II was especially bloody – and under this sequel these men simply were a few of the many victims. The second possibility is that the SS hierarchy deliberately placed the men in a particularly dangerous and confusing theater of operations and let events happen on their own. This would indicate a realization on the part of Odilo Globocnik, and even perhaps Heinrich Himmler, that the fewer of these *Operation Reinhard* men that survived, the better. In a brutal partisan warfare, such as that in Yugoslavia, both sides seldom took prisoners of war. A captive German officer would meet a quick death and would be in no position to bargain information he possessed to gain better treatment in confinement, which was at least theoretically possible if captured by conventional forces. Finally, the third possibility is that the SS, in some way, actually took active measures to silence some of their own. A plan of this nature would have been approved only at the highest levels, and even then probably never in writing. The fact that every *Operation Reinhard* officer was not killed does not decrease the possibility of this alternative; perhaps senior SS leaders had a plan to eliminate the officers over a lengthy period of time to preclude suspicion on the part of the survivors. I believe that the second possibility is the most likely – that senior SS officials placed the men in particularly lethal environments where the likelihood of becoming a living prisoner of war was low and the probability of combat death was high. For a more detailed discussion see *The Camp Men: The SS Officers Who Ran the Nazi Concentration Camp System*, by the author.

[188] *Rangliste des Deutschen Reichsheeres, Nach dem Stande vom 1. Mai 1929*. (Berlin: E.S. Mittler & Sohn, 1929), p. 112.

[189] Wolf Keilig, *Die Generale des Heeres*. (Friedberg, FRG: Podzun-Pallas-Verlag, 1983), p. 122.

[190] Ibid., p. 122.

[191] Ibid., p. 284.

[192] Helge Grabitz and Wolfgang Scheffler, *Letzte Spuren: Ghetto Warschau, SS-Arbeitslager Trawniki, Aktion Erntefest, Fotos und Dokumente über Opfer des Endlösungswahns im Spiegel der historischen Ereignisse*. (Berlin: Edition Hentrich, 1988), p. 158.

[193] Albert Speer, *Infiltration*. (New York: MacMillan Publishing, 1981), pp.267-268.

[194] Ibid., p. 361.

[195] Wolfgang Sowodny, *Die Panzerzüge des Deutschen Reiches, 1904-1945*. (Freiburg, Germany: Eisenbahn Kurier Verlag, 1996), pp. 80-83.

[196] Ibid., pp. 417-426.

7

THE TROOPS

"There are no fighters in the SS better than we are. There are none more daring and none harder than we are. Germany could not hold on for a single day without us."[1]

- Theodor Eicke, 1937

In the beginning, Heinrich Himmler wanted only men who stood five feet, eleven inches or taller. In the beginning, he wanted blond-haired and blue-eyed men. In the beginning, he wanted men who could prove that they had several generations of Aryan blood running through their veins – because Nordic blood was the best blood on the earth. In the beginning, Heinrich Himmler could afford to reject nine of ten candidates to the SS. But as the war progressed, the *Reichsführer-SS* found that he had to lower his standards. By 1943, with the Russians moving west, in perhaps a horrible repetition of Genghis Khan and his Asiatic hordes, Heinrich Himmler did not need blond gods. He did not need men who could quote Friedrich Nietzsche – or any other German philosopher; he just needed men who could pull a trigger.

• • •

The following chapter outlines biographical information concerning enlisted soldiers who are believed to have been present in Warsaw during the period of the Ghetto Uprising. The Stroop Report indicates that upwards of some 2,000 troops may have taken part in the operation. This work has identified 954 enlisted personnel as potential participants in the German operation at the Warsaw Ghetto in the following organizations:

145 – KdS Warsaw
2 – SSPF Lublin
17 – 1st Guard Battalion, Trawniki Labor Camp
42 – 22nd SS Police Regiment
10 – 23rd SS Police Regiment
35 – SS Cavalry Field Replacement Detachment
703 – 3rd SS *Panzergrenadier* Training and Replacement Battalion

As mentioned in the introduction, the naming of an enlisted soldier in this chapter does not mean that he committed any atrocities or war crimes in conjunction with the operation. It means that I believe the soldier was present for duty in the city of Warsaw during the Ghetto Uprising. Therefore, it is very likely that he could have been involved in some aspect of the operation, based on the fact that he was a member of a formation that actively operated in the Ghetto operation. The men could have been present inside the Warsaw Ghetto itself, could have pulled cordon security duty just outside the Ghetto wall or could have served in a support role (cooks, drivers, arms room, supply, mechanics, etc.) Those troops in the Security Police, subordinate to the KdS Warsaw, or the Trawniki guard detachment were generally used to conduct more of the "dirty work" as were many of the police troops. Those soldiers in the cavalry and panzer grenadier replacement units conducted more traditional military functions. However, any of these men, should they still be alive, could probably contribute valuable additional historical information on the operation.

The soldiers of the 3rd SS Division *"Totenkopf,"* many of who had returned to the 3rd SS Panzergrenadier Replacement and Training Battalion as instructors, had an impressive reputation in combat. Dr. Charles W. Sydnor, Jr., in his work, *Soldiers of Destruction: The SS Death's Head Division, 1933-1945,* perhaps best summarizes the fighting qualities of these soldiers. Sydnor states:[2]

> The SS man's ability to remain calm in the face of disaster, his willingness to fight on against impossible odds, his lust for killing Russians, and most important, his readiness to perish rather than retreat and appear weaker than his racial enemy were all qualities that proved crucial throughout the war in retrieving hopeless situations; they became hallmarks of the *Totenkopfdivision's* performance wherever it fought.

This assessment, however, did not apply to all the troops in the division. Beginning in late 1941, *SS-Gruppenführer* Theodor Eicke, the *Totenkopf* commander, vehemently complained that the replacements that the division had received were markedly inferior to those whose places they filled. Eicke summarized his complaints as follows:[3]

- inexperienced reservist officers who were assigned to the division;
- poor physical quality, laziness and political ignorance of arriving enlisted replacements;
- susceptibility of ethnic German recruits to illness and cowardice;
- lack of political training and National Socialist indoctrination.

The troops of the SS Cavalry Replacement Detachment possessed similar traits to those associated with the *Totenkopf.* The cavalry soldiers of the detachment's parent formation, the SS Cavalry Division, had been assigned to extensive anti-partisan duty on the Russian front since June 1941. In that month, both existing SS cavalry regiments were assigned to the *Kommandostab "Reichsführer-SS",* which was then detailed to the area of operations of the XXXXIInd Army Corps. In August 1941, Himmler combined the two cavalry regiments into the SS Cavalry Brigade (*SS-Kavallerie-Brigade*).[4] At least one post-war source states that the *Waffen-SS* Cavalry Brigade conducted *Einsatzkommando*-type operations in Russia. From 29 July through 12 August 1941, the unit conducted operations in the Pripjet marshes region near Pinsk. *SS-Standartenführer* Hermann Fegelein, the brigade commander, reported that 14,178 looters, 1,001 partisans and 699 Red Army soldiers were executed. A reported eight thousand Jewish males were killed; the women and children were reportedly driven into the marshes. During the entire Pinsk operation at least eleven thousand Jews were executed.[5]

In the summary of the Stroop Report, Jürgen Stroop provides a hint that the SS soldiers became more proficient at their gruesome work as the operation progressed. Stroop recounted that:[6]

> The longer the resistance lasted, the tougher became the men of the *Waffen-SS*, Police and Army who fulfilled their duty here indefatigably in faithful comradeship and stood together as models and examples of soldiers. Their duty hours often lasted from early morning until late at night. At night, search patrols with rags wound around their feet, remained at the heels of the Jews and left them no respite. Not infrequently, they caught and killed Jews who used the night hours for supplementing their stores from abandoned bunkers and for contacting neighboring groups or for exchanging the latest news with them.

To be sure, Stroop was writing his report to present himself in the most favorable light. His pride in his men's handiwork certainly has a degree of obscenity to it. However, if we analyze the description further in a dispassionate manner – if it is possible to do that – we can discern that the German soldiers at the Warsaw Ghetto did increase their proficiency as the fight wore on. As we have seen, they retreated on the first day. But by the end of the operation, they were conducting sophisticated night patrols with methods of increased stealth for that time.

The conduct of the *Waffen SS* during the quelling of the Ghetto Uprising was probably reflective of both Dr. Sydnor and Theodor Eicke's views as well as the practical experience gained by the men as the fighting continued. Some of the troops were undoubtedly fanatical veterans, while others were new recruits who ran at the first shots on 19 April 1943.

COMBAT ACHIEVEMENTS

These identified troops at Warsaw possessed a wealth of previous combat experience. At the very least – we cannot be exact because most SS enlisted personnel files were never captured by the Allies (unlike the SS officer files that were) – some 216 of these enlisted men served in combat prior to the Warsaw Ghetto operation. In examining the troops that were at Warsaw in April 1943 we find that at least forty had received the Iron Cross 1st or 2nd Class for front-line combat during the war. At the outbreak of World War II the German Armed Forces re-instituted the Iron Cross 1st Class and 2nd Class (the award had been in existence over one hundred years.) Hitler stated that the Iron Cross 2nd Class would reward a single act of bravery in combat beyond the normal requirements of duty.

It could be awarded to all members of the Armed Forces or to civilians serving with the military. The Iron Cross 1st Class, also re-instituted on 1 September 1939, was usually awarded for an additional three to five significant acts of valor.[7] Recommendations for both classes of award went first from the soldier's company commander to battalion commander to regiment commander, with the approval authority resting with the division commander.[8]

Many of the enlisted participants in the operation received awards for their actions. *SS-Rottenführer* Josef Blösche was one of these men. His award citation reads as follows:

> For several months, Blösche has been engaged in the accomplishment of the resettlement of the Jews from the Ghetto. After the conclusion of the resettlement, he was mainly active in guard duty and overseeing the Jews in the Ghetto. At the beginning of the action of 19 April 1945 Blösche succeeded repeatedly to capture armed Jews, i.e., to locate smaller bunkers in which Jews had been hiding for some time and to clean them out. Since the beginning of the action of 19 April 1943 he was engaged as a particularly good expert about the geography of the place and then, fearlessly, repeatedly broke armed resistance. His accomplishments and his ever-ready willingness must be stressed in particular.

At least sixty-three enlisted personnel assigned to units combating the Warsaw Ghetto Uprising had previously been wounded in combat. Many others had additional combat awards. Most of the infantrymen who had seen service on the Russian front (members of the 3rd SS Panzergrenadier Replacement and Training Battalion) possessed the Infantry Assault Badge (*Infanterie-Sturmabzeichen*). Instituted in 1939, it was presented to single out the highly hazardous combat achievement of officers and men of the infantry and mountain infantry. Criteria for the Infantry Assault Badge specified that the soldier take part in at least three infantry assaults, armed reconnaissance, hand-to-hand combat or participate in the restoration of the main line of defense on three different days.[9]

While hundreds of other German soldiers in the fighting were raw recruits, the many combat veterans provided a great degree of tactical expertise, which only increased the odds in their favor. Despite this edge, there appears to have been some instances of disorganization. Several enlisted soldiers testified after the war on their experiences in the Warsaw Ghetto. The following comes from a soldier in the engineer commando from the Armored Train Replacement Detachment in Rembertow:[10]

> I am familiar with the cleaning out of the Warsaw Ghetto because I personally was there one day during that time. As I have already stated, I was in the 2nd Company of the Infantry Trainers. I was very surprised when one day – as I remember, as the only man from my company – I was taken away and ordered to a 10.5cm howitzer. About ten men arrived, who had all come from the Artillery, now we found out that we were supposed to go to Warsaw that same morning. I believe that a lieutenant was in charge of this mission.
>
> We then were ordered for action in the Ghetto. We took our howitzers to a street within the Ghetto where we got our howitzers into position and practically waited all day for further orders. We did not send one shot off.

The following is testimony from Erich Waclawik of the 3rd Battalion, 22nd SS Police Regiment. Waclawik was wounded in action on 23 April 1943:[11]

> At the time from April 19th on, the [3rd] Battalion of the 22nd [SS Police] Regiment was taken to Warsaw for action in the Ghetto. Before the mission – it was on a Monday – I had to report to some Police comrades at the SS and Police Chief's office. On that day I was ordered to guard the Ghetto wall from the outside. On that day nothing special happened at the wall. Due to the shootings, which had started in the Ghetto, the police companies were called in. We started our engagement in the morning hours of 19 April 1943. On the other days, we were allowed to occupy our place at other times of the day. Commandos were established, consisting of three to four men. It was the task of these commandos to search the apartments and cellars for Jewish persons. The Jews found were taken to the command post and gathered there. I don't remember where the command post was. It was at an entrance to the Ghetto. The troops, which I belonged to, did not take any Jews. The houses, which we searched, were already empty because the Jews had already left their apartments. Therefore, I did not encounter any resistance anywhere. Each troop had to comb through certain house complexes. When we had completed these orders, we had to report back to the group leader. When it was necessary, we were allocated new building complexes.
>
> On Good Friday, 23 April 1943, I was taken with Group Leader T. and his group (strength of the commando was 1 officer and 8 troops) on a truck (crew and policemen) to a site outside of the Ghetto. According to the statements of an ethnic German, Jews were supposed to be hidden in a bakery in Warsaw. We searched the building, especially the rooms in the basement. Indeed, two Jewish women were found in the bakery. The Jewish women, as well as the owner of the bakery, who was Polish, were

taken and put on the truck. To guard these people I personally sat with them on the truck on the rear bench. After that, we were supposed to search other houses where Jews were supposed to be hidden. As far as I remember, it was the Senatorska Street. We reached the street. Whether Jews were found in this house is something I do no longer remember today. When the house was being searched, I stayed on the truck with another comrade. This was Comrade H [probably Oskar Hexel]. While we were guarding the prisoners on the truck, suddenly I heard an attack behind me. The tarpaulin was lifted up. When I turned around, I saw two men who threw an object into the vehicle. Because of that, I immediately released the safety on my rifle to be able to defend the captured people and myself. Immediately I felt a bang and a pressure wave, the vehicle was in flames. I sought safety and jumped from the vehicle. I do not know what happened to the captured people. As far as I know, the driver of the vehicle was standing somewhere away from the truck. I also did not see Comrade H [Hexel had his lower right leg seriously wounded; it had to be later amputated.] anymore. I then ran into the direction of the fleeing men. On that path, I collapsed due to my wounds. I was not able to take my rifle from the truck. But I did draw my pistol. Because of my wounds, I was taken to the field hospital.

• • •

The following pages detail the more important personal and career information of 954 SS enlisted personnel who either have been positively identified as having taken part in the quelling of the Warsaw Ghetto Uprising or who were likely there. Most *Waffen-SS* and Police personnel are listed with last name, first name, rank, date of birth and place of birth. The personnel of the KdS, the major apparatus of destruction in the city, are outlined in greater detail in the footnotes. To help standardize the information, the following data-field explanations are provided:

Last Name – self-explanatory. This does not account for any individual who may have changed his last name after the war.

First Name – self-explanatory; includes any academic titles such as "Dr."

Date of Birth – self-explanatory. The final authority for this information came from the National Archives microfilm collection of the Berlin Document Center collection of SS enlisted personnel files.

Place of Birth – for personnel born inside Germany, the town or city is listed. For those born outside of Germany, the country is included as well. A few of the very small towns could actually have been in Austria but were not so annotated in the file.

SS Rank – denotes the rank an individual had during the Ghetto Uprising (not necessarily the highest rank that individual held later in the war). Some enlisted personnel at the Warsaw Ghetto later became officers.

SS Number – denotes the number each SS man received upon entering the organization. The lower the number, the earlier the individual entered the SS.

Unit – indicates the unit an individual served with during the operation at the Ghetto.

Footnotes – This category includes known decorations, incidents of being wounded in action (to include being wounded during the Ghetto Uprising), ultimate fate, etc.

TABLE 2

KdS WARSAW – ENLISTED PERSONNEL

Last Name	First Name	Rank	Date of Birth	Place of Birth
Albers[12]	August	SS-Scharführer	9 March 1910	Wangeroode
Arzt[13]	Fritz	SS-Rottenführer	25 September 1909	Reichenbach
Bäcker[14]	Hans	SS-Oberscharführer	4 August 1913	Munich
Bässler[15]	Fritz	SS-Hauptscharführer	2 March 1913	Rachlin
Ballhause[16]	Werner	SS-Oberscharführer	27 March 1903	Berlin
Barton[17]	Franz	Kriminal Angestellter		
Bartz[18]	Paul	SS-Sturmscharführer	25 October 1898	Kolmar/Posen
Baumgartner[19]	Josef	SS-Sturmscharführer	25 December 1919	Salzburg
Baumstark[20]	Albert	SS-Rottenführer	9 March 1912	Bühl/Baden
Beresniewicz[21]	Josef	SS-Rottenführer	27 May 1908	Bialystok, Russia
Bertram[22]	Karl	SS-Oberscharführer	7 August 1909	Schlierstein
Bindernagel[23]	Otto	SS-Sturmscharführer	5 October 1910	Zepernick
Birkholz[24]	Otto	SS-Sturmscharführer	4 August 1912	Bochum
Blösche[25]	Josef Oskar	SS-Rottenführer	5 February 1912	Friedland
Böhnke[26]	Alfred	SS-Oberscharführer	22 December 1912	Königsberg
Breger[27]	Martin	SS-Oberscharführer	9 September 1909	Behlkow
Brockmann[28]	Karl	SS-Unterscharführer	5 November 1909	Hehlen
Brümmel[29]	Erich	SS-Oberscharführer	11 September 1911	Plümenhagen
Budde[30]	Ignas	Kriminal Sekretär		
Bürkl[31]	Franz	SS-Scharführer		
Czeratzki[32]	Hermann	SS-Sturmscharführer	13 March 1893	
Czorny[33]	Ewald	SS-Scharführer	15 August 1913	
Damitz[34]	Alfred	SS-Sturmscharführer	9 September 1900	Zechendorf
Denzel[35]	Georg	SS-Oberscharführer	11 September 1913	Burlafingen
Dereser[36]	Fritz	SS-Oberscharführer	4 June 1909	Kornwestheim
Diehm[37]	Otto	SS-Oberscharführer	5 March 1909	Crailsheim
Drath[38]	Paul	SS-Oberscharführer	9 December 1899	
Ebert[39]	Otto	SS-Sturmscharführer		
Edler[40]	Bruno	SS-Sturmscharführer		
Ehnert[41]	Paul	SS-Oberscharführer		
Eibisch[42]	Max	SS-Sturmscharführer	21 December 1908	Plauen
Engels[43]	Kurt	SS-Oberscharführer	3 August 1915	Cologne
Fahner[44]	Gustav	SS-Oberscharführer	9 May 1911	Opladen
Fahrenberger[45]	Rudolf	SS-Oberscharführer	22 February 1910	Hochheim/Erfurt
Folta[46]	Georg	SS-Hauptscharführer	31 July 1909	Langendorf
Fuss[47]	Heinrich	SS-Hauptscharführer	10 January 1907	Königsberg
Glöckner[48]	Rudolf	SS-Oberscharführer		
Griesche[49]	Bruno	SS-Oberscharführer	22 February 1899	Kutschkau
Hämmerli[50]	Heinrich	SS-Hauptscharführer	29 December 1906	Salder
Hahn[51]	Erich	SS-Oberscharführer	26 June 1911	Templin
Hanisch[52]	Eduard	SS-Rottenführer	26 July 1907	Zackerzewo
Harbusch[53]	Heinrich	SS-Oberscharführer	10 April 1903	Beisefurth
Hartmann[54]	Erwin	SS-Hauptscharführer	26 September 1907	Nieder-Linda
Hiersemann[55]	Paul Gerhard	SS-Sturmscharführer	11 October 1902	Dresden

Höhmann[56]	Wilhelm	SS-Hauptscharführer	24 June 1908	Frankfurt/Oder
Hörmann[57]	Paul	SS-Hauptsturmführer	14 June 1914	Amendingen
Hörnig[58]	Kurt	SS-Sturmscharführer	9 April 1907	Gottesberg/Silesia
Hundt[59]	Herbert	SS-Oberscharführer	12 November 1912	Breslau
Jahnke[60]	Paul	SS-Sturmscharführer		
Jahns[61]	Horst	SS-Sturmscharführer	18 November 1913	Schneidemühl
Janz[62]	Witold	SS-Rottenführer		
Jung[63]	Viktor	SS-Unterscharführer	23 September 1911	Riga, Russia
Junghart[64]	Otto	SS-Scharführer	12 January 1909	
Kaiser[65]	Ernst	SS-Sturmscharführer		
Kamm[66]	August	SS-Sturmscharführer	18 April 1906	Feuchtwangen
Kelm[67]	Kurt	SS-Oberscharführer	9 February 1911	Dopiewiec/Posen
Klaustermeyer[68]	Karl-Heinrich	SS-Oberscharführer	22 February 1914	Bünde
Kleist[69]	Hermann	SS-Sturmscharführer		
Klinkmann[70]	Henry	SS-Scharführer	24 April 1910	
Knak[71]	Erwin	SS-Sturmscharführer		
Knodelseder[72]	Karl	SS-Rottenführer	3 September 1907	Haslach
Köhler[73]	Hugo	SS-Sturmscharführer	26 June 1911	Gosswitz
Köhler[74]	Wilhelm	SS-Oberscharführer	12 May 1901	Holzminden
Koglin[75]	Walter	SS-Oberscharführer	25 November 1913	Porst/Köslin
Kohls[76]	Friedrich	SS-Sturmscharführer		
Kolbe[77]	Herbert	SS-Sturmscharführer	11 April 1905	Neundorf
Kolberg[78]	Josef	SS-Sturmscharführer	15 July 1900	Deuthen
Kosmala[79]	Rudolf	SS-Sturmscharführer	31 October 1901	
Kracht[80]	Erich	SS-Oberscharführer	30 May 1914	Hoppenrade
Kraft[81]	Heinrich	Kriminal Sekretär		
Krausshaar[82]	Max	SS-Oberscharführer	20 June 1908	Gaildorf
Kreisel[83]	Walter	SS-Rottenführer	22 October 1905	Auerbach
Kressner[84]	Werner	SS-Oberscharführer	13 May 1914	Schwiebus
Krömer[85]	Wilhelm	SS-Scharführer	6 December 1908	Beuthen
Krooss[86]	Heinrich	SS-Rottenführer	22 May 1906	Dortmund
Lange[87]	Friedrich	SS-Sturmscharführer		
Langer[88]	Edmund	SS-Scharführer	29 October 1914	Beuthen
Lempik[89]	Friedrich	SS-Hauptscharführer	2 October 1906	Chropaczew
Liedtke[90]	Reinhold	SS-Rottenführer	12 August 1918	Kempa
Lindner[91]	August	SS-Oberscharführer	9 November 1905	Bochum
Lorenz[92]	Max	SS-Sturmscharführer	30 June 1890	Klingenthal
Lotholz	Edmund	SS-Rottenführer	1 November 1904	
Lubinetzkyj[93]	Wolodymar	SS-Oberscharführer	28 October 1903	Medyka
Mechert[94]	Wilhelm	SS-Rottenführer	22 August 1909	Bütow/Pomerania
Melzer[95]	Hans	SS-Hauptscharführer	3 May 1918	Thorn
Mende[96]	Gerhard	SS-Oberscharführer	22 July 1911	Oppeln (now (Opole, Poland)
Merkel[97]	Helmut	SS-Oberscharführer	9 November 1913	Zella-Mehlis
Meusert[98]	Franz	SS-Oberscharführer	27 July 1908	Fahr am Main
Meyer[99]	Fritz	SS-Oberscharführer		
Mielke[100]	Alfred	SS-Sturmmann	21 April 1908	Dortmund
Mischke[101]	Karl	SS-Oberscharführer	29 September 1899	Kicker
Möller[102]	Otto	SS-Sturmscharführer	6 October 1905	Seligenthal
Mohr[103]	Hans			

Müller[104]	Georg	SS-Sturmscharführer	31 December 1909	Munich
Müller[105]	Karl	SS-Hauptscharführer		
Münkwitz[106]	Werner	SS-Sturmscharführer	8 January 1910	
Naporra[107]	Kurt	SS-Hauptscharführer	28 October 1905	Berlin
Nicolaus[108]	Kurt	SS-Oberscharführer	30 November 1910	Antonienhütte
Nieratschker[109]	Hugo	SS-Scharführer	18 June 1909	
Ogorrek[110]	Johann	SS-Hauptscharführer	4 July 1895	Klein-Strelitz
Orf[111]	Helmut	SS-Scharführer	1 May 1916	Schleusingen
Pautz[112]	Robert	SS-Sturmscharführer		
Perlbach[113]	Wilhelm	SS-Oberscharführer	25 September 1911	Köslin
Peter[114]	Heinz	SS-Oberscharführer		
Piecyk[115]	Alfons	SS-Rottenführer	15 October 1909	Königshütte (now Chorzów, Poland)
Pietsch		Polizei Oberinspektor		
Rättig[116]	Arthur	SS-Unterscharführer		
Ragoss[117]	Waldemar	SS-Rottenführer	30 August 1908	Rehden
Raths[118]	Gerhard	SS-Unterscharführer	30 September 1913	
Reichow[119]	Waldemar	SS-Oberscharführer	14 May 1908	Stolpmünde (now Ustka, Poland)
Renzel[120]	Wilhelm	SS-Rottenführer	22 November 1908	Segelhorst
Ress[121]	Lothar	SS-Oberscharführer	19 June 1908	Kegenfeldt
Richter[122]	Rudolf	SS-Sturmscharführer		
Riemann[123]	Karl	SS-Sturmscharführer		
Rudolph[124]	Willi	SS-Sturmscharführer	14 November 1891	Potsdam
Roeser[125]	Lothar	SS-Rottenführer	12 June 1910	Sitzendorf
Rückert[126]	Georg	SS-Rottenführer		
Rührnschopf[127]	Fritz	SS-Rottenführer	21 August 1910	Weissenburg
Schimmann[128]	Hermann	SS-Sturmscharführer	16 April 1908	Mülheim/Ruhr
Schlader[129]	Eduard	SS-Oberscharführer	2 October 1906	Doblen, Russia
Schmidt[130]	Herbert	SS-Hauptscharführer	24 December 1900	Liegnitz (now Legnica, Poland)
Schöneborn[131]	Arthur	SS-Unterscharführer	20 August 1905	Elberfeld
Schramm[132]	Friedrich	SS-Sturmscharführer	29 January 1910	Vienna, Austria
Schröckenstein[133]	Heinrich	SS-Rottenführer	6 April 1909	Ybbs, Austria
Schubert[134]	Arno	SS-Rottenführer	18 October 1907	Lichta/Rudolfstadt
Schuchardt[135]	Alfred	SS-Sturmscharführer	22 October 1903	Nordheim
Schween[136]	Walter	SS-Sturmscharführer		
Schweitzer[137]	Konrad	SS-Rottenführer	24 August 1910	Bebra
Shary[138]	Fritz	SS-Scharführer	27 April 1913	Kattowitz (now Katowice, Poland)
Soden[139]	Helmut	SS-Oberscharführer		
Stahlhut[140]	Siegfried	SS-Sturmscharführer	17 September 1897	Berlin
Stegner[141]	Konstantin	SS-Unterscharführer		
Steinebrunner[142]	Alfred	SS-Oberscharführer		
Steinmetz[143]	Wilhelm	SS-Sturmscharführer	26 July 1900	Frankfurt
Stephan[144]	Otto	SS-Hauptscharführer	22 March 1899	Berlin
Stippler[145]	Wilhelm	SS-Oberscharführer		
Stoffel[146]	Willy	SS-Hauptscharführer	13 May 1916	Wiesbaden
Stoll[147]	Walter	SS-Hauptscharführer	27 January 1909	Berlin
Theiss[148]	Heinrich	SS-Sturmscharführer	1 June 1912	Flensungen

Uebel[149]	Gerhard	SS-Hauptscharführer	30 October 1908	Plauen
Verch[150]	Paul	SS-Scharführer	26 March 1907	Schneidemühl
Vogel[151]	Kurt	SS-Hauptscharführer	20 June 1902	Greifenhagen
Vogt[152]	Max	SS-Sturmscharführer		
Vorpahl[153]	Karl	SS-Rottenführer		
Walottek[154]	Eugen	SS-Scharführer	18 August 1911	Schoppinitz
Weiler[155]	Friedrich	Kriminal Angestellter		
Weise[156]	Günter	SS-Oberscharführer	25 June 1914	Frankfurt/Oder
Werner[157]	Roman	Kriminal Sekretär		
Wiener[158]	Hans	SS-Oberscharführer		
Wild[159]	Adolf	SS-Sturmscharführer	16 December 1905	Reistenhausen
Witze	Karl	SS-Scharführer		
Wulfes[160]	Otto	SS-Unterscharführer	13 June 1912	Hehm/Holstein
Zwerina[161]	Josef	SS-Rottenführer	8 November 1925	Ungarschütz

TABLE 3

3rd SS TRAINING & REPLACEMENT BATTALION ENLISTED PERSONNEL

Last Name	First Name	Rank	Date of Birth	Place of Birth
Abicht	Emil	SS-Panzergrenadier	4 August 1909	
Ackermann[162]	Ernst	SS-Panzergrenadier	10 February 1925	
Adrat	Erich	SS-Unterscharführer	15 February 1912	
Ahrend	Otto	SS-Unterscharführer	30 April 1911	
Ahrens	Karl	SS-Panzergrenadier	9 September 1909	
Akermann	Wilhelm	SS-Unterscharführer	15 March 1911	
Alf	Friedrich	SS-Panzergrenadier	13 February 1925	
Algermissen[163]	Bernhard	SS-Schütze	15 June 1925	
Alt[164]	Robert	SS-Rottenführer	30 December 1909	Hattenheim
Ambros	Alois	SS-Panzergrenadier	3 April 1925	
Anselm[165]	Eugen	SS-Schütze	20 October 1898	Gut Döbrin, Ukraine
Antzok[166]	Alfons	SS-Sturmmann	23 July 1919	Martinau
Arfsten	Jakob	SS-Unterscharführer	23 April 1908	Föhr
Arlt[167]	Leonhard	SS-Rottenführer	1 January 1923	Engenhausen
Arps[168]	August	SS-Panzergrenadier	14 November 1909	Wennemannswisch
Aschinger[169]	Albert	SS-Rottenführer	4 July 1911	Pforzheim
Asimus	Kurt	SS-Freiwilliger	4 May 1943	
Autenrieth[170]	Hermann	SS-Hauptscharführer	2 December 1911	Esslingen
Baarck[171]	Wilhelm	SS-Rottenführer	26 April 1921	Klein Rönnau
Bach	Friedrich	SS-Sturmmann	2 June 1923	
Bachler	Adolf	SS-Panzergrenadier	10 May 1909	Jenbach/Tirol
Bachmann	Fritz	SS-Sturmmann	26 September 1898	
Bade	Jürgen	SS-Panzergrenadier	9 August 1908	Neuhof/Ribnitz
Baldt[172]	Alfred	SS-Panzergrenadier	15 September 1906	
Ball[173]	Otto	SS-Unterscharführer	10 August 1905	Gaggenau
Balz	Otto	SS-Panzergrenadier	22 August 1912	
Barde	Robert	SS-Schütze	9 February 1912	
Baron	Helmut	SS-Sturmmann	10 March 1921	Königshütte

Barth	Walter	SS-Panzergrenadier	16 October 1907	
Barth	Wilhelm		21 May 1903	
Barwasser	Karl	SS-Unterscharführer	28 October 1919	Nassau
Baumann	Hans	SS-Unterscharführer	12 December 1920	
Baumgartl[174]	Rudolf	SS-Rottenführer	22 November 1907	
Becker[175]	Karl	SS-Panzergrenadier	16 November 1909	
Becker	Willi	SS-Panzergrenadier	16 July 1925	
Beeker	Konrad	SS-Schütze	7 October 1925	
Behrendt	Hans	SS-Panzergrenadier	28 September 1909	
Bender	Hermann	SS-Unterscharführer	12 May 1911	
Berens	Josef	SS-Panzergrenadier	14 July 1925	
Bichler	Lorenz	SS-Panzergrenadier	21 October 1924	Percha/Bavaria
Bietz	Heinrich	SS-Panzergrenadier	26 February 1906	
Birk	Josef	SS-Panzergrenadier	2 September 1908	
Bitzer	Wilhelm	SS-Scharführer	8 December 1909	Werden/Ruhr
Blaas[176]	Hugo	SS-Schütze	1 July 1906	Davoe, Switzerland
Blaseio[177]	Bruno	SS-Unterscharführer	21 September 1911	Horst/Emschen
Bleicher[178]	Johann	SS-Rottenführer	4 April 1908	
Bobrowski	Ernst	SS-Rottenführer	7 December 1905	Neuheim
Bodmann	Herbert	SS-Panzergrenadier	27 November 1925	Essen
Boeck	Peter	SS-Panzergrenadier	21 September 1906	Dirnhausen
Boeckmann[179]	Siegfried	SS-Panzergrenadier	14 October 1912	Hannover
Boes	Walter	SS-Panzergrenadier	7 August 1925	
Boettcher[180]	Emanuel	SS-Sturmmann	10 May 1907	Tarutone, Bessarabia
Boland	Alfons	SS-Panzergrenadier	12 May 1909	
Bomski	Franz	SS-Schütze	22 December 1905	
Braeutigam[181]	Franz	SS-Unterscharführer	4 April 1912	Paderborn
Branden, von der	Ludwig	SS-Schütze	14 August 1920	
Braun	Anton	SS-Schütze	20 July 1925	
Braun	Josef	SS-Panzergrenadier	30 December 1925	
Braun	Otto	SS-Rottenführer	16 February 1921	Echterdingen
Braun	Robert	SS-Rottenführer	16 November 1921	Reimsbach
Braunschweiger[182]	Ernst	SS-Rottenführer	3 April 1921	Augsberg
Brede	Otto	SS-Oberschütze	6 May 1910	Adlig Brühlsdorf
Brill	Wilhelm	SS-Panzergrenadier	3 March 1907	Limbach/Saar
Broscheck	Arno	SS-Sturmmann	29 April 1922	
Brosda	Walter	SS-Panzergrenadier	4 March 1922	
Brüggemann	Otto	SS-Grenadier	5 April 1910	Scharringhausen
Brusch	Fritz	SS-Unterscharführer		
Buchenau[183]	Werner	SS-Panzergrenadier	20 May 1906	
Bühl[184]	Ulrich	SS-Oberscharführer	19 May 1922	Freising
Büttner	Martin	SS-Oberscharführer		
Buhrmester	Erich	SS-Panzergrenadier	6 March 1925	Minden
Burchardt[185]	Werner	SS-Panzergrenadier	6 November 1906	
Burmann	Johannes	SS-Schütze	17 July 1914	Hage
Buschmann	Kurt	SS-Unterscharführer	31 March 1912	Bochum
Buskies	Ernst	SS-Schütze	8 November 1924	
Busse	Otto		13 July 1906	
Buxel[186]	Gerd	SS-Sturmmann	21 December 1923	Hamburg
Cada[187]	Adolf	SS-Panzergrenadier	4 July 1912	Vienna, Austria

Cafuta	Otto	SS-Rottenführer	10 March 1910	
Callesen	Carl	SS-Sturmmann	9 June 1908	
Carl	Robert	SS-Panzergrenadier	22 November 1913	Dingsleben
Cermak	Leonhard	SS-Panzergrenadier	6 March 1908	
Charstensen	Peter	SS-Panzergrenadier	14 March 1908	
Coellen[188]	Wilhelm	SS-Panzergrenadier	18 January 1909	
Cordts	Erich	SS-Sturmmann	15 February 1924	Wremen
Cornitzius	Karl	SS-Panzergrenadier	11 August 1909	
Czabon	Johannes	SS-Panzergrenadier	28 January 1914	
Czwielung[189]	Friedrich	SS-Panzergrenadier	5 April 1907	
Dahlhaus	Bernhard	SS-Schütze	17 January 1923	
Dahms	Albert		8 November 1908	
Dangl	Benno	SS-Panzergrenadier	28 February 1925	
Dannhauer[190]	Gerhard	SS-Panzergrenadier	13 May 1925	Halle/Westfalen
Danziger	Helmut	SS-Unterscharführer	4 July 1921	Neutitschein
Darschinger	Josef	SS-Panzergrenadier	6 August 1925	
Daul	Eugen	SS-Unterscharführer	30 July 1908	
Decher[191]	Ernst	SS-Panzergrenadier	12 November 1908	
Degen	Hermann	SS-Panzergrenadier	13 March 1906	Munich
Delp	Werner	SS-Sturmmann	16 November 1919	Hamburg
Derflinger[192]	Karl	SS-Unterscharführer	16 January 1919	Gleink
Derichs[193]	Karl	SS-Hauptscharführer	20 January 1916	Kaldenkirchen
Dethloff	Hans	SS-Panzergrenadier	7 January 1908	
Detzer	Walter	SS-Panzergrenadier	10 October 1924	Magdeburg
Deutmann	Georg	SS-Panzergrenadier	20 August 1925	
Diebold	Alfred	SS-Rottenführer	22 May 1909	Neckarau
Diederich	Eduard	SS-Panzergrenadier	6 July 1906	
Diehm	Karl	SS-Rottenführer	7 March 1910	
Dittmer[194]	Kurt	SS-Panzergrenadier	11 June 1925	Minden
Doeppe[195]	Otto	SS-Panzergrenadier	1 November 1924	
Domas	Wilhelm	SS-Panzergrenadier	5 November 1925	Jülich
Dorn[196]	Friedrich	SS-Hauptscharführer	21 September 1913	Grossenbuch
Draexler	Franz	SS-Grenadier	8 June 1924	
Dreibrodt	Paul	SS-Schütze	20 February 1907	
Drinhaus	Alois	SS-Panzergrenadier	26 Match 1925	
Droste	Hermann	SS-Panzergrenadier	27 August 1925	
Dürr	Hubert	SS-Schütze	3 November 1924	Feldkirch, Austria
Düsterwald[197]	Josef	SS-Panzergrenadier	29 May 1922	
Dumfart[198]	Rudolf	SS-Unterscharführer	7 April 1920	Linz, Austria
Dunkl	Ludwig	SS-Sturmmann	17 March 1902	
Ehm	Wilhelm	SS-Rottenführer	20 November 1907	
Ehrensberger	Georg	SS-Schütze	10 March 1907	Alfeld
Eichhorn[199]	Kurt	SS-Hauptscharführer	21 July 1912	Plaün
Eisel	Georg	SS-Panzergrenadier	27 August 1908	
Elley	Jürgen	SS-Panzerobergrenadier	16 January 1911	
Emmert	Josef	SS-Schütze	22 April 1906	
Engelschall	Robert	SS-Unterscharführer	16 April 1922	
Enzbrunner[200]	Martin	SS-Unterscharführer	9 January 1922	Fürstenzell
Ernst	Albert	SS-Oberscharführer	1 June 1910	
Ertner	Theodor	SS-Sturmmann	16 September 1908	

Esser	Josef	SS-Rottenführer	9 November 1903	
Ethheber	Konrad	SS-Panzergrenadier	28 October 1907	
Exner	Max	SS-Panzergrenadier	25 December 1912	
Falk	Bartholomäus	SS-Panzergrenadier	24 August 1911	Gleissenberg
Feder	Fritz	SS-Unterscharführer	23 August 1908	Pirmasens
Fenk[201]	Martin	SS-Panzergrenadier	12 April 1908	
Ferrenberg	Jakob	SS-Panzergrenadier	3 June 1907	
Fischer	August	SS-Panzergrenadier	30 January 1910	
Fischer[202]	Georg	SS-Hauptscharführer	10 September 1917	Degendorf
Fischer	Karl	SS-Unterscharführer	16 December 1902	Marienbad
Fister[203]	Hans	SS-Rottenführer	22 June 1921	
Fitzner	Adam	SS-Schütze	22 December 1910	Gadowo/Konin
Fleischmann[204]	Franz	SS-Panzergrenadier	23 August 1925	Stengelheim
Fleischmann[205]	Mathias	SS-Rottenführer	25 June 1921	Irritz
Flötgen	Bernhard	SS-Panzergrenadier	18 November 1925	
Folkerts	Riek	SS-Panzergrenadier	1 January 1911	
Forster[206]	Hans	SS-Unterscharführer	31 May 1914	Eslarn
Forster	Heinrich	SS-Panzergrenadier	12 December 1925	
Frankenfeld	Rudi	SS-Panzergrenadier	14 November 1925	
Fratzke	Hugo-Karl	SS-Sturmmann	12 December 1905	Bromberg (now Bydgoszcz, Poland)
Frenz	Ernst	SS-Panzergrenadier	9 April 1908	
Frey	Emil	SS-Schütze	24 November 1925	
Friedrich	Oskar	SS-Panzergrenadier	11 December 1925	
Friemann	Günter	SS-Schütze	30 August 1925	
Friesen	Arthur	SS-Schütze	24 June 1907	Mühlhausen/East Prussia
Fritsch	Richard	SS-Sturmmann	29 August 1911	Zauritz/Grottkau
Fritz	Gerhard	SS-Panzergrenadier	25 April 1924	
Fritz	Otto	SS-Panzergrenadier	28 October 1905	Schulitz
Fröhlich	Fridolin	SS-Unterscharführer	2 March 1913	Iphofen
Fröse	Wilhelm	SS-Schütze	12 August 1908	
Fuchs	Josef	SS-Oberschütze	6 November 1922	
Gäde[207]	Fritz	SS-Unterscharführer	25 November 1912	Kloetze
Gall	Richard	SS-Panzergrenadier	18 December 1910	
Gallein	Hans	SS-Panzergrenadier	29 April 1925	
Gangnus	Konstantin	SS-Sturmmann	11 February 1920	
Gasteiger	Max	SS-Panzergrenadier	13 April 1908	Munich
Genant[208]	Karl	SS-Panzergrenadier	31 July 1907	
Gerken	Johann	SS-Panzergrenadier	24 November 1906	
Gertner[209]	Franz	SS-Hauptscharführer	27 November 1914	Zehdenik
Geweth	Peter	SS-Panzergrenadier	17 October 1911	Penzberg/Bavaria
Giese	Wolfgang	SS-Schütze	27 July 1925	Schwerin
Gieseler[210]	Ewald	SS-Rottenführer	3 January 1924	Hönnersum
Gille	Fritz	SS-Panzergrenadier	12 December 1906	
Göbel	Hans	SS-Sturmmann	25 July 1912	Bärenstein
Göllner	Richard	SS-Rottenführer	3 February 1923	Pressburg
Goldbach	Wilhelm	SS-Unterscharführer	5 December 1919	Riesa
Gräfenstein	Willi	SS-Schütze	25 August 1906	Ellinghausen
Greimel[211]	Josef	SS-Rottenführer	23 March 1909	Lassing
Grell	Waldemar	SS-Panzergrenadier	18 September 1911	

Grentz[212]	Herbert	SS-Sturmmann	18 September 1922	Berlin
Grimminger	Rudolf	SS-Rottenführer	14 October 1922	Wetzgau
Gruber	Franz	SS-Unterscharführer	21 September 1903	
Gründl	Hermann	SS-Panzergrenadier	27 December 1925	
Güthinger	Robert	SS-Rottenführer	4 July 1907	Stuttgart
Gützlaff	Friedrich	SS-Panzergrenadier	5 March 1909	
Guralski	Ernst	SS-Panzergrenadier	2 July 1925	
Haag[213]	Otto	SS-Schütze	1 July 1921	Palanka/Hungary
Haas[214]	Franz	SS-Schütze	4 January 1923	Bawanischte
Haase	Ernst	SS-Panzergrenadier	26 March 1906	
Hackenberger	Willi	SS-Sturmmann	23 November 1924	Reimsbach/Saar
Häusler	Willi	SS-Panzergrenadier	30 December 1907	
Hagensen	Max	SS-Panzergrenadier	8 September 1926	
Hahn	Eugen	SS-Rottenführer	8 May 1909	Kirchheim
Hamm[215]	Josef	SS-Unterscharführer	29 February 1904	Füssen
Hansen	Friedrich	SS-Panzergrenadier	28 November 1925	
Hansen	Hans	SS-Grenadier		
Hanusen	Gustav	SS-Sturmmann	30 March 1907	
Harfeld[216]	Hans	SS-Panzerobergrenadier	12 May 1924	Hamburg
Harste	Karl	SS-Rottenführer		
Hartmann	Hans	SS-Unterscharführer		
Haschke[217]	Kurt	SS-Rottenführer	19 October 1921	Breslau
Haubenwallner[218]	Ferdinand	SS-Panzergrenadier	27 May 1916	Strallegg
Hauber	Karl	SS-Panzergrenadier	4 April 1909	
Hauguth	Karl	SS-Panzergrenadier	28 January 1911	Eger
Haupt	Jakob	SS-Panzergrenadier	13 May 1906	
Hausa[219]	Alfons	SS-Panzergrenadier	10 May 1912	Groslogisch
Hauschele	Hermann	SS-Oberscharführer		
Haushalter[220]	Heinz	SS-Sturmmann	12 May 1924	Einbeck
Heese[221]	Erich	SS-Rottenführer	13 October 1923	Tarnowke
Heiden	Günter von der	SS-Schütze	8 December 1925	
Heinen[222]	Jakob	SS-Rottenführer	26 November 1922	Beles
Heinol	Josef	SS-Sturmmann	27 January 1921	
Heins	Ernst	SS-Rottenführer	9 August 1903	
Heitmann[223]	Robert	SS-Panzergrenadier	1 June 1925	Münster
Hennig[224]	Arnold	SS-Unterscharführer	11 July 1908	Riga, Russia
Herold	Karl	SS-Rottenführer		
Hertel	Siegfried	SS-Unterscharführer	28 October 1917	
Hessenauer[225]		SS-Rottenführer		
Hetzler	Kurt	SS-Panzergrenadier	11 February 1906	
Heuer	Albert	SS-Rottenführer		
Heuschele[226]	Hermann	SS-Oberscharführer	17 January 1917	Frankenbach
Heymann	Peter	SS-Panzergrenadier	28 August 1925	
Hilscher[227]	Rudolf	SS-Unterscharführer	17 April 1910	
Hinz	Helmut	SS-Panzergrenadier	27 April 1925	
Hinz	Wilhelm	SS-Rottenführer		
Höffler	Franz	SS-Rottenführer	2 February 1925	Ostern, Rumania
Höring	Hermann	SS-Grenadier	29 January 1910	
Hoffmann[228]	Eugen	SS-Rottenführer	30 December 1923	Warsaw, Poland
Hofmann[229]	Theo	SS-Oberscharführer	22 March 1910	Nürnberg

Hohenberger[230]	Albin	SS-Oberscharführer	9 April 1915	Eng/Franconia
Hohl	Anton	SS-Panzergrenadier	2 December 1910	
Hohmann	Alfons	SS-Panzergrenadier	19 July 1922	
Hohmeyer	Helmut	SS-Panzergrenadier	27 October 1925	
Holl	Josef	SS-Schütze	5 August 1923	
Holzer	Anton	SS-Panzergrenadier	7 September 1925	Freising
Holzer	Ludwig	SS-Sturmmann	5 December 1904	
Hopp	Rudolf	SS-Panzergrenadier	13 October 1906	Braunschweig
Hornung[231]	Fritz	SS-Oberscharführer	21 November 1918	Hagen
Horstmeier	Helmut	SS-Panzergrenadier	24 May 1925	
Huber	Ernst	SS-Panzergrenadier	24 February 1925	
Hubrich	Wilhelm	SS-Panzergrenadier	17 April 1925	Rheinbach
Hübner	Karl-Heinz	SS-Rottenführer	19 March 1922	
Hund	Alfred	SS-Panzergrenadier	6 June 1910	Immenstaad
Huth	Fridolin	SS-Panzergrenadier	19 July 1906	
Immler	Luitpold	SS-Panzergrenadier	12 March 1925	
Ingo	Wilhelm	SS-Sturmmann	20 December 1913	
Jäger	Paul	SS-Panzergrenadier	14 January 1925	
Jäncke	Artur	SS-Panzergrenadier	30 November 1909	
Jahn	Gustav	SS-Panzergrenadier	11 June 1906	
Jahnke	Rudolf	SS-Panzergrenadier	10 August 1908	
Jahr	Ewald	SS-Schütze	2 April 1905	Zempelburg
Jahr	Oskar	SS-Sturmmann	27 December 1912	Zempelburg
Jakubowski	Anton	SS-Panzergrenadier	9 December 1910	
Jendro	Otto	SS-Rottenführer	7 May 1921	Wohlsdorf
Jene	Karl	SS-Panzergrenadier	3 November 1911	
Jeske	Arthur	SS-Sturmmann	6 November 1906	Lodz
Jettenberger	Ludwig	SS-Rottenführer	18 February 1908	Augsburg
Jörissen	Wilhelm	SS-Schütze	25 August 1924	
Johannsen	Johannes	SS-Sturmmann	15 April 1923	Tondern
Josten[232]	Peter	SS-Rottenführer	25 August 1905	Aachen
Jucknat[233]	Oswald	SS-Unterscharführer	9 June 1909	Berlin
Jung[234]	Walter	SS-Rottenführer	20 March 1921	Oberbieber
Kaboth	Erwin	SS-Panzergrenadier	22 June 1907	
Kästner	Helmut	SS-Panzergrenadier	23 October 1925	
Kaiser	Wolfgang	SS-Panzerobergrenadier		
Kalinowski	Anton	SS-Panzergrenadier	27 April 1920	
Kallrath[235]	Heinrich	SS-Schütze	6 February 1920	Warden/Aachen
Kammerer	Eugen	SS-Panzergrenadier	13 November 1906	
Kammerer	Josef	SS-Panzergrenadier	21 February 1925	
Kandula	Johann	SS-Freiwilliger	30 June 1916	
Kapitza[236]	Klemens	SS-Panzergrenadier	22 November 1924	
Kaprolat	Otto	SS-Schütze	18 April 1915	
Keller	Josef	SS-Panzergrenadier	30 June 1925	
Kellner		SS-Oberscharführer		
Kemesch	Michael	SS-Schütze	22 January 1922	Marienfeld/Banat
Kessler[237]	Franz	SS-Unterscharführer	7 November 1919	Porstendorf
Kessler	Karl	SS-Panzergrenadier	6 March 1906	
Kiermeier	Johann	SS-Panzergrenadier	12 January 1922	
Kind		SS-Rottenführer		

Kirchner	Walter	SS-Rottenführer	15 April 1921	
Kirschner	Paul	SS-Sturmmann	6 February 1911	Kroschen
Klagges	Josef	SS-Panzergrenadier	22 July 1925	
Klein	Wilhelm	SS-Panzergrenadier	23 February 1907	
Kleiner[238]	Johann	SS-Panzergrenadier	10 January 1925	Haging
Kleuters	Anton	SS-Schütze	13 December 1924	
Kleuver	Hans	SS-Unterscharführer	10 May 1912	Troisdorf
Klippel	Willi	SS-Panzergrenadier	27 May 1921	
Klix	Gerhard	SS-Schütze	2 August 1924	
Klösters[239]	Paul	SS-Panzergrenadier	13 August 1925	Kleve
Klöver[240]	Eggo	SS-Hauptscharführer	23 January 1917	Elisabethfehn
Kloss	Herbert	SS-Sturmmann	2 September 1923	
Knaack	Paul	SS-Panzergrenadier	6 September 1907	
Knappe[241]	Walter	SS-Rottenführer	6 April 1924	Liegnitz
Koch	Adam	SS-Schütze	21 June 1921	
Koch	Franz	SS-Panzergrenadier	24 October 1921	
Koch	Josef	SS-Panzergrenadier	1 September 1923	
Koch[242]	Michael	SS-Rottenführer	24 February 1921	Laserfeld
König	Karl	SS-Panzergrenadier	18 November 1908	Wuppertal
Köpke	Hermann	SS-Panzergrenadier	20 March 1906	
Kohler[243]	Julius	SS-Unterscharführer	21 January 1912	Tuttlingen
Kohllöffel	Artur	SS-Panzergrenadier	4 May 1922	Piesteritz
Kolb[244]	Georg	SS-Mann	31 March 1908	
Kolb	Hans	SS-Unterscharführer		
Konow[245]	Ernst	SS-Schütze	22 January 1910	
Kopperschmidt[246]	Hans	SS-Unterscharführer	23 March 1922	Neustrelitz
Kosarz[247]	Franz	SS-Panzergrenadier	6 January 1924	
Koschmieder	Karl	SS-Panzergrenadier	29 April 1914	
Krämer	Heinrich	SS-Panzergrenadier	25 November 1906	
Kramer	Gustav	SS-Panzergrenadier		
Krause	Albert	SS-Schütze	10 January 1921	
Krause	Walter	SS-Panzergrenadier	11 April 1909	
Krauth[248]	Eugen	SS-Unterscharführer	13 October 1907	Eberbach
Kreitmeier[249]	Lorenz	SS-Panzergrenadier	15 January 1925	Petershausen
Krenzel	Günter	SS-Panzergrenadier	13 March 1925	
Kries	Wilhelm	SS-Panzergrenadier	9 January 1907	
Kroplewski[250]	Sigmund	SS-Panzergrenadier	6 December 1910	Rowijewski, Ukraine
Krull	Wilhelm	SS-Schütze	20 November 1924	
Kühn	Karl	SS-Sturmmann	5 July 1911	Ripalke/Rippin
Kuhlmann	Franz-Josef	SS-Panzergrenadier	18 September 1925	
Kuisl	Alois	SS-Panzergrenadier	5 March 1925	Buttenwiesen
Kulnat	Gerhard	SS-Panzergrenadier	14 November 1925	
Kunkel	Jakob	SS-Panzergrenadier	8 October 1906	
Kurz	Eduard	SS-Panzergrenadier	24 September 1911	
Kurzthaler	Armin	SS-Panzergrenadier	18 April 1924	
Labenbacher	Anton	SS-Schütze	2 March 1924	Münichhofen
Lange[251]	Erich	SS-Panzergrenadier	10 February 1907	Goehren
Langenbacher	Emil	SS-Panzergrenadier	25 September 1906	
Langenkamp[252]	Herbert	SS-Unterscharführer	15 December 1913	Wuppertal-Barmen
Langer	Ernst	SS-Unterscharführer		

Latsch[253]	Heinrich	SS-Rottenführer	12 September 1911	Hackenbruch
Lausch	Julius	SS-Sturmmann	16 May 1913	Kieselstädt
Lautenschlager	Willi	SS-Unterscharführer		
Lehman	Heinz	SS-Sturmmann	16 February 1912	
Leinmüller[254]	Rudolf	SS-Rottenführer	5 March 1909	Gutenstein, Austria
Lent	Franz van	SS-Schütze	10 October 1925	
Lenz	Otto	SS-Rottenführer	4 September 1922	Kamenz/Silesia
Leonhard	Richard	SS-Panzergrenadier	14 November 1922	Burgstaden
Lerchl[255]	Lorenz	SS-Oberscharführer	25 November 1915	Bachenhausen
Lieber	Richard	SS-Panzergrenadier	2 December 1912	
Liesegang	Günter	SS-Panzergrenadier	28 June 1922	
Linkowski	Willi	SS-Panzergrenadier	14 June 1908	
Lipke	Kunibert	SS-Sturmmann	24 May 1909	
Lipkowski	Heinrich	SS-Panzergrenadier	4 February 1925	
Lochner	Hans	SS-Unterscharführer	26 May 1906	Auschowitz
Lönne	Helmut	SS-Panzergrenadier	27 July 1925	
Lönnecke	Friedrich	SS-Panzergrenadier	20 June 1925	
Löwer	Friedrich	SS-Panzergrenadier	21 October 1907	
Lommler	Hermann	SS-Panzergrenadier	14 October 1907	
Look[256]	Hans	SS-Rottenführer	10 June 1917	Zempelburg
Lüdtke[257]	Franz	SS-Unterscharführer	22 October 1920	Selesen
Lünse[258]	Walter	SS-Unterscharführer	29 December 1910	Liebgarten
Lungwitz	Walter	SS-Panzergrenadier	27 January 1910	
Lustig	Franz	SS-Unterscharführer	25 July 1907	Leipertilz/Iglau
Luther[259]	Walter	SS-Unterscharführer	30 June 1913	Bromberg
Maassmann	Heinrich	SS-Schütze	5 April 1923	
Mach	Max	SS-Panzergrenadier	10 October 1914	
Macha[260]	Alfred	SS-Unterscharführer	14 February 1919	Hindenburg
Maier	Jakob	SS-Panzergrenadier	25 April 1907	
Malle[261]	Valentin	SS-Panzergrenadier	13 February 1913	Klagenfurt, Austria
Malohn	Josef	SS-Unterscharführer	29 August 1908	
Mansfeld	Erich	SS-Panzergrenadier	18 October 1919	
Maquine	Peter	SS-Sturmmann	26 April 1922	
Marquardt	Werner	SS-Panzergrenadier	22 August 1912	Leipzig
Masuch	Andreas	SS-Panzergrenadier	19 January 1907	
Matthes[262]	Gerhard	SS-Schütze	30 November 1922	Triebes
Matthews	Reinhold	SS-Panzergrenadier	15 February 1906	Güntergost
Maul	Martin	SS-Panzerobergrenadier	1 September 1909	Bad Wörishofen
Maul	Walter	SS-Panzergrenadier	20 April 1909	
Mauthe	Freiedrich	SS-Schütze	21 January 1905	
May	Erich	SS-Hauptscharführer		
May	Kurt	SS-Sturmmann	30 December 1919	
Mees	Hubert	SS-Panzergrenadier	8 May 1907	
Meier[263]	Arno	SS-Rottenführer	27 October 1907	Dörfels/Coburg
Meier[264]	Ernst	SS-Panzergrenadier	3 June 1909	
Meier	Fritz	SS-Sturmmann	2 February 1907	Dowin
Meier[265]	Heinrich	SS-Panzergrenadier	16 October 1910	Hamburg
Meier	Johann	SS-Panzergrenadier	25 February 1909	Röthenbach
Meine	Georg	SS-Sturmmann	22 April 1908	
Menken	Helmut	SS-Panzergrenadier	26 November 1924	

Merdian	Johann	SS-Panzergrenadier	9 September 1925	
Metz[266]	Alfred	SS-Unterscharführer	19 November 1907	Neviges
Mews	Wilhelm	SS-Oberscharführer		
Meyer[267]	Wilhelm	SS-Rottenführer	11 February 1922	Wiswedel
Meyer[268]	Wilhelm	SS-Sturmmann	29 January 1924	Siedenburg
Miche	Albert	SS-Schütze	19 May 1920	
Michel	Wilhelm	SS-Rottenführer	7 April 1923	
Milla	Toni	SS-Sturmmann	13 March 1922	Silbereck, Hungary
Miller	Alfons	SS-Panzergrenadier	19 March 1908	
Möhlmann[269]	Walter	SS-Panzergrenadier	14 December 1925	Dünne
Mönnig[270]	Oskar	SS-Panzergrenadier	9 November 1921	Wittenberg
Mohr[271]	Erwin	SS-Rottenführer	12 September 1921	Berlin
Mrokron[272]	Stanislaus	SS-Rottenführer	15 November 1920	Gross Schimmendorf
Mühlbacher[273]	Franz	SS-Unterscharführer	15 December 1919	Bad Ischl, Austria
Müller[274]	Alois	SS-Panzergrenadier	8 October 1909	
Müller	Ernst	SS-Panzergrenadier	27 December 1906	
Müller	Max	SS-Panzergrenadier	29 March 1906	
Müller	Rudolf	SS-Rottenführer	1 July 1902	Bridigau
Müller	Valentin	SS-Schütze	14 February 1921	Hungary
Muigg	Gottfried	SS-Panzergrenadier	16 October 1906	
Mutschall[275]	Hans	SS-Schütze	24 August 1919	Tarutino, Bessarabia
Naudascher[276]	Willi	SS-Oberscharführer	28 March 1919	Kippenheim
Naünburg	Otto	SS-Rottenführer	20 May 1905	
Nee[277]	Gerhard	SS-Panzergrenadier	14 June 1925	Bokelermoor
Nenast[278]	Willi	SS-Rottenführer	6 February 1920	
Neuhoff	Günther	SS-Panzergrenadier	24 March 1925	
Neumann	Ernst	SS-Schütze	28 July 1905	
Neuper[279]	Ernst	SS-Sturmmann	22 February 1924	Würzburg
Neusel[280]	Walter	SS-Rottenführer	11 November 1910	Darmstadt
Nibel	Franz	SS-Panzergrenadier	17 January 1912	
Nickolai	Artur	SS-Rottenführer	29 October 1911	
Nieder	Wenzeslas	SS-Panzergrenadier	10 May 1925	Starkertshofen
Niedermaier	Johann	SS-Panzergrenadier	15 November 1925	
Niesenhaus	Josef	SS-Panzergrenadier	18 February 1925	
Niggemann	Heinz	SS-Panzergrenadier	2 June 1923	
Nitzsche[281]	Kurt	SS-Unterscharführer	13 September 1916	Adelwitz
Nolte	Siegfried	SS-Panzergrenadier	21 January 1925	
Nordenholt	Hans	SS-Panzergrenadier	23 December 1922	
Norwaischas[282]	Vinzent	SS-Sturmmann	14 June 1903	Aukschelisken, Russia
Notdurfter	Josef	SS-Unterscharführer		
Numberger[283]	Johann	SS-Panzergrenadier	31 July 1925	
Nuscheler	Hans	SS-Panzergrenadier	5 February 1925	
Oberdahn	Robert	SS-Rottenführer		
Obermüller	Gerhard	SS-Panzergrenadier	28 August 1925	
Obladen	Karl	SS-Panzergrenadier	9 December 1925	
Odenhoven	Eduard	SS-Panzergrenadier	21 December 1925	
Offermann	Anton	SS-Panzergrenadier	16 December 1925	
Ohlrich	Adolf	SS-Rottenführer	11 September 1910	
Ohlrogge	Heinz	SS-Rottenführer	29 May 1922	
Oprotkowitz[284]	Arnold	SS-Schütze	27 September 1924	Treuburg

Otto	Rudolf	SS-Panzergrenadier	13 January 1925	
Overmann[285]	August	SS-Panzergrenadier	3 September 1925	Münster
Pacchiaffo[286]	Hans	SS-Unterscharführer	18 August 1905	Troppau
Pasenau	Ernst	SS-Panzergrenadier	28 May 1906	
Paulsen	Andreas	SS-Panzergrenadier	13 August 1907	
Pauly	Karl	SS-Panzergrenadier	28 July 1925	Oberhausen
Peierer	Felix	SS-Panzergrenadier	11 April 1925	
Perpeet	Ferdinand	SS-Panzergrenadier	4 April 1925	
Petersen	Andreas	SS-Panzergrenadier	6 June 1906	Krusau
Petersen	Christian	SS-Panzerobergrenadier	10 June 1904	
Petersen[287]	Hans	SS-Sturmmann	3 February 1914	Tondern, Denmark
Petersen	Helmut	SS-Panzergrenadier	24 December 1907	
Petruschat[288]	Albert	SS-Schütze	2 October 1916	Wirscham, Russia
Petry[289]	Hans	SS-Sturmmann	10 April 1923	
Petsch[290]	Adolf	SS-Rottenführer	8 May 1906	
Pfabe[291]	Wilhelm	SS-Schütze	15 March 1925	Eschwege/Kassel
Pickenbrock	Josef	SS-Panzergrenadier	30 November 1925	Essen
Piehl	Heinz	SS-Schütze	11 August 1924	
Pietschmann[292]	Wilhelm	SS-Unterscharführer	5 June 1910	Holzhausen
Pischl[293]	Alfred	SS-Unterscharführer	30 January 1922	
Pitsch	Franz	SS-Schütze	29 January 1921	
Pitzer	Willibald	SS-Rottenführer	15 February 1908	Ramsau
Pötzel	Erhard	SS-Unterscharführer		
Polley	Kurt	SS-Panzergrenadier	7 February 1907	
Pomberger	Konrad	SS-Panzergrenadier	22 September 1909	
Portschy[294]	Albert	SS-Unterscharführer	25 March 1914	Unterschützen, Austria
Posch[295]	Joseph	SS-Rottenführer	22 July 1920	Hall, Austria
Poschen	Rudolf	SS-Panzergrenadier	7 July 1925	
Potthoff[296]	Hermann	SS-Rottenführer	28 June 1913	Bremen
Pracht	Anton	SS-Panzergrenadier	6 March 1925	
Praml[297]	Josef	SS-Hauptscharführer	7 January 1905	Haus/Grafenau
Prüter	Werner	SS-Unterscharführer	10 January 1905	Klein Sieman
Puder	Hans	SS-Panzergrenadier	25 November 1911	
Puhl[298]	Walter	SS-Rottenführer	20 September 1920	Saarbrücken
Quispel	Johann	SS-Schütze	30 December 1926	
Raczak	Johann	SS-Grenadier	16 December 1912	
Raddatz[299]	Karl	SS-Schütze	10 April 1904	Gross-Babenz
Rademacher	Kurt	SS-Sturmmann	11 January 1925	Berlin-Lichtenberg
Radl	Friedrich	SS-Panzergrenadier	31 March 1907	
Raeder[300]	Hans	SS-Panzergrenadier	10 October 1916	
Rahn	Franz	SS-Schütze	17 November 1902	Kalenzig
Ranft[301]	Heinrich	SS-Unterscharführer	15 August 1911	Aschaffenburg
Rasmussen[302]	Nikolai	SS-Sturmmann	23 June 1907	Solderup, Denmark
Rausch	Alfred	SS-Unterscharführer	1 November 1920	
Rauscher	Friedrich	SS-Schütze	14 December 1917	
Regus	Johann	SS-Panzergrenadier	23 October 1907	
Reh[303]	Heinz	SS-Sturmmann	28 April 1923	Putzar
Reinhard	Willi	SS-Panzergrenadier	23 September 1912	
Reiter	Herbert	SS-Rottenführer	26 October 1920	
Reith	Richard	SS-Unterscharführer	8 May 1908	Wörrstadt

Renner	Michael	SS-Panzergrenadier	7 August 1925	
Renz	Wenzel	SS-Panzergrenadier	29 November 1906	Greslitz
Rettich[304]	Anton	SS-Rottenführer	11 April 1923	Djakowo
Reuter[305]	Wolfgang	SS-Panzergrenadier	17 September 1925	Hagen
Richter[306]	Horst	SS-Rottenführer	12 November 1922	
Richter	Kurt	SS-Panzergrenadier		
Rick	Heinrich	SS-Panzergrenadier	11 May 1911	
Rickmeyer[307]	Hans	SS-Unterscharführer	2 July 1910	Halle
Rieber[308]	Alois	SS-Sturmmann	17 November 1906	Burladingen
Riedel[309]	Hermann	SS-Rottenführer	23 February 1906	
Riemann[310]	Paul	SS-Rottenführer	16 December 1919	Ineritz
Riemant	Boleslav	SS-Schütze	20 August 1923	
Ringburger	Heinz	SS-Panzergrenadier	26 September 1925	
Ritschl	Friedrich	SS-Panzergrenadier	25 March 1902	
Robbert	Ernst	SS-Panzergrenadier	9 April 1925	
Rödder	Robert	SS-Schütze	27 June 1925	
Röhe	Christian	SS-Panzerobergrenadier	13 March 1924	
Römmer[311]	Kurt	SS-Unterscharführer	28 March 1921	Hamburg
Römmert	Ernst	SS-Panzergrenadier	21 April 1907	
Rompf	Emil	SS-Panzergrenadier	23 February 1906	
Rosenau	Hans	SS-Panzergrenadier	6 March 1907	
Roszkowski	Christian	SS-Panzergrenadier	9 April 1925	
Roth	Leopold	SS-Schütze	7 October 1901	
Rottinghaus	Bernhard	SS-Panzergrenadier	12 December 1911	
Rüter	Karl-Heinz	SS-Panzergrenadier	4 November 1925	
Rupp[312]	Adolf	SS-Panzergrenadier	30 November 1921	Wasserburg
Rzepka	Wladislaus	SS-Panzergrenadier	23 June 1922	
Sammer[313]	Theodor	SS-Panzergrenadier	6 November 1925	Petting/Bavaria
Sandner	Alfons	SS-Panzergrenadier	15 April 1925	
Saür	Josef	SS-Panzergrenadier		
Saupper[314]	Artur	SS-Oberscharführer	6 August 1913	Essen
Schaaf	Friedrich	SS-Panzergrenadier	10 July 1906	
Schache[315]	Herbert	SS-Sturmmann	20 November 1920	Gross Schonewald
Schade[316]	Werner	SS-Schütze	8 May 1924	Johannesburg
Schödler	Josef	SS-Panzergrenadier	17 March 1906	
Schäfer	Rudolf	SS-Unterscharführer	30 March 1901	Berglangenbach
Schätzle[317]	Franz	SS-Unterscharführer	10 December 1909	Tuttlingen
Schanden	Karl	SS-Schütze	19 May 1900	
Scharnowski[318]	Franz	SS-Panzergrenadier	1 August 1908	
Scheer	Klemens	SS-Panzergrenadier	8 May 1925	
Scheffler[319]	Sigismund	SS-Rottenführer	9 April 1919	Ukmerge, Lithuania
Scheidler[320]	Josef	SS-Panzergrenadier	9 June 1910	Rastenhof
Scherübel	Walter	SS-Rottenführer	15 June 1922	
Scheyl	Willi	SS-Panzergrenadier	27 August 1911	
Schier	Rudolf	SS-Panzergrenadier	18 February 1908	
Schilder[321]	Alfred	SS-Schütze	9 February 1909	Ziegenholz
Schillikowski	Hermann	SS-Panzergrenadier	6 July 1925	
Schinkewitz	Erwin	SS-Unterscharführer		
Schlegel	Adalbert	SS-Panzergrenadier	2 September 1911	
Schlegel[322]	Hans	SS-Panzergrenadier	2 January 1908	Fürth

Schlund	Fritz	SS-Grenadier	1 November 1909	
Schmelzer[323]	Fritz	SS-Sturmmann	10 May 1922	Langendreer
Schmidt	Emil	SS-Unterscharführer	4 July 1909	Nürtingen
Schmidt	Ernst	SS-Panzergrenadier	9 May 1912	Berlin
Schmidt	Hans	SS-Obergrenadier	24 February 1912	Duisburg
Schmidt	Walter	SS-Rottenführer		
Schmidt[324]	Walter	SS-Panzergrenadier	13 July 1921	Patzig
Schmidthuysen	Hans	SS-Sturmmann	19 August 1921	
Schmitt	Karl	SS-Panzergrenadier	13 January 1908	
Schmitt	Konrad	SS-Schütze	1 March 1901	
Schmorde	Otto	SS-Panzergrenadier	19 March 1907	
Schneckmann	Werner	SS-Panzergrenadier	7 January 1911	
Schneider[325]	Ernst	SS-Scharführer	3 January 1917	Bad Liebenstein
Schneider	Karl	SS-Panzergrenadier	2 July 1907	Neustadt/Silesia
Schneider[326]	Wilhelm	SS-Panzergrenadier	25 January 1925	Hamborn
Schnellbacher	Ludwig	SS-Panzergrenadier	13 September 1916	Hoechst
Schnepf[327]	Ernst	SS-Unterscharführer	7 April 1901	
Schnur[328]	Karl	SS-Unterscharführer	16 March 1912	Falkenberg
Schöller	Axel		7 March 1907	
Scholz[329]	Friedrich	SS-Panzergrenadier	2 June 1910	Reutlingen
Scholz	Josef	SS-Unterscharführer	1 March 1909	Hohenfluss
Schradi	Willi	SS-Rottenführer	13 July 1908	Offenburg
Schramm	Ewald	SS-Hauptsturmführer	22 October 1894	Drzonowakr
Schrautemeier[330]	Friedrich	SS-Panzergrenadier	6 January 1925	Lippstadt
Schröder	Adolf	SS-Panzergrenadier	14 June 1925	
Schröder	Karl	SS-Panzergrenadier	21 November 1909	
Schröder	Otto	SS-Schütze	24 July 1924	
Schüssler[331]	Heinrich	SS-Unterscharführer	13 January 1912	Kassel
Schuffenhauser	Günter	SS-Rottenführer		
Schuhmacher	Johannes	SS-Rottenführer		
Schulz[332]	Erich	SS-Unterscharführer	25 January 1922	Fliegerhorst
Schulz	Leopold	SS-Panzergrenadier	18 December 1925	
Schulz	Martin		2 February 1912	
Schuster[333]	Arnold	SS-Unterscharführer	29 January 1910	Coswig
Schuster	Paul	SS-Panzergrenadier	10 August 1906	
Schwager[334]	Kurt	SS-Unterscharführer	28 September 1911	Zeitz
Schwarzmüller[335]	Gottfried	SS-Panzergrenadier	31 May 1907	
Schweigard	Max	SS-Panzergrenadier	27 May 1907	
Seeger	Paul	SS-Panzergrenadier	18 May 1908	
Seemann	Karl	SS-Panzergrenadier	24 September 1911	
Seitz	Friedrich	SS-Panzergrenadier	29 July 1906	
Selbach	Paul-Werner	SS-Panzergrenadier	23 October 1925	
Sellenschütter	Hans	SS-Panzergrenadier	19 July 1922	
Seltmann[336]	Lothar von	SS-Schütze	12 January 1917	Graz, Austria
Selzer	Hans	SS-Rottenführer	3 February 1906	
Senger[337]	Paul	SS-Unterscharführer	12 January 1906	Bruchsal
Siding[338]	Eduard	SS-Sturmmann	15 May 1924	Linz, Austria
Siegel[339]	Hans	SS-Rottenführer	21 December 1919	Breslau
Sielaff	Karl	SS-Unterscharführer	5 December 1909	Schidlitz
Simon[340]	Walter	SS-Panzerobergrenadier	30 August 1911	Lüsberg

Singer	Wilhelm	SS-Panzergrenadier	27 May 1908	
Singl	Casimir	SS-Panzergrenadier	15 September 1925	
Söffker[341]	Karl	SS-Unterscharführer	18 January 1920	Klein Wieden
Sommerer[342]	Xaver	SS-Rottenführer	24 December 1908	Freinhausen
Sonntag	Franz	SS-Panzergrenadier	7 June 1908	
Spanner[343]	Fritz	SS-Schütze	25 May 1925	Nürnberg
Spiegler	Gerhard	SS-Rottenführer	14 May 1912	
Splitthoff	Vincenz	SS-Rottenführer	22 October 1919	Magdeburg
Stadelmann[344]	Heinz	SS-Unterscharführer	21 September 1910	Münster
Stahlbusch[345]	Karl	SS-Schütze	4 March 1906	Rummelsburg
Stark	Werner	SS-Sturmmann	16 May 1912	Werdau
Steen[346]	Heinrich	SS-Freiwilliger	16 April 1911	Neukirchen
Stegemann	Alfons	SS-Panzergrenadier	3 July 1925	
Steger	Heinrich	SS-Mann	8 October 1911	Karlsruhe
Steigmeier[347]	Kurt	SS-Schütze	3 March 1925	Heldburg
Stihler	Karl	SS-Oberscharführer	3 May 1912	Anderten
Stöger	Albert	SS-Panzergrenadier	16 October 1925	
Strangmann[348]	Heinrich	SS-Rottenführer	11 October 1909	Bremen
Strassburg[349]	Franz	SS-Oberscharführer	20 April 1911	Eisenach
Strauss	Josef	SS-Rottenführer	9 May 1914	
Strebl	Erich	SS-Sturmmann	24 October 1909	
Streppel[350]	Werner	SS-Panzergrenadier	31 August 1925	Lüdenscheid
Striemann[351]	Helmut	SS-Rottenführer	28 December 1923	Guben
Stürmer	Gustav	SS-Sturmmann		
Stumpp	Albert	SS-Sturmmann	18 September 1907	
Stuwe[352]	Heinz	SS-Panzergrenadier	30 November 1924	
Sude[353]	Karl	SS-Unterscharführer	5 December 1912	Korbach
Tag	Jakob	SS-Panzergrenadier	11 February 1906	
Tanzel	Josef	SS-Schütze	14 March 1906	
Tatenhorst[354]	Bruno	SS-Unterscharführer	24 June 1912	Bielefeld
Tatura	Bernhard	SS-Sturmmann	28 October 1912	
Tauschmann[355]	Karl	SS-Panzergrenadier	29 May 1922	
Tegtmeier	Walter	SS-Unterscharführer	31 January 1902	Hannover
Temme	Karl-Heinz	SS-Panzergrenadier	15 May 1925	
Terp	Jes	SS-Panzergrenadier	30 June 1916	
Theis	Werner	SS-Panzergrenadier	16 May 1925	
Theisen	Johann	SS-Panzergrenadier	13 March 1925	
Theiss	Kurt	SS-Rottenführer	14 October 1911	Lomersheim
Thibaut[356]	Georg	SS-Panzerobergrenadier	27 December 1917	Esqülbecq, Flanders
Thiele	Alfred	SS-Panzergrenadier	9 September 1925	
Thielsen	Gottfried	SS-Panzergrenadier	13 February 1909	Mönklow
Thiemer[357]	Artur	SS-Rottenführer	20 April 1922	Fretzdorf
Tiemann	Helmut	SS-Sturmmann	4 September 1922	
Tillmann	Josef	SS-Panzergrenadier	18 April 1925	
Tippelt	Eduard	SS-Sturmmann	8 January 1909	
Tölle	Josef	SS-Panzergrenadier	11 April 1925	
Tölle	Josef	SS-Panzergrenadier	10 December 1925	
Toma	Johann	SS-Schütze	19 December 1920	
Toppmöller	Albert	SS-Panzergrenadier	8 May 1922	
Traupe	Erich	SS-Oberschütze	7 January 1921	

Treuss	Erich	SS-Panzergrenadier	7 May 1925	
Trippe	Arthur	SS-Rottenführer	26 September 1907	
Tröger	Hermann	SS-Grenadier	3 March 1908	
Trübendörfer	Karl	SS-Unterscharführer	16 May 1912	
Trynes	Nikolaus	SS-Panzergrenadier	27 May 1924	
Türke[358]	Werner	SS-Panzergrenadier	2 August 1908	
Tuffner[359]	Peter	SS-Panzergrenadier	27 February 1924	Hodschagh, Hungary
Üllendahl	Ernst	SS-Unterscharführer	19 July 1912	Duisburg
Uliczka[360]	Erich	SS-Unterscharführer	19 December 1909	Berlin
Ullrich	Wilhelm	SS-Panzergrenadier	16 December 1906	
Unger	Hans	SS-Schütze	13 June 1907	Donauwörth
Upleger	Hans	SS-Panzergrenadier	1 March 1909	
Urban	Otto	SS-Rottenführer	31 July 1908	Pragerhof, Austria
Utzinger[361]	Hans	SS-Sturmmann	5 June 1922	Thaleichweiler
Vanjo	Gebhard	SS-Unterscharführer	27 August 1919	
Veen	Walter van	SS-Freiwilliger	27 October 1925	
Venner[362]	Rudolf	SS-Sturmmann	3 September 1924	Stettin
Vogel	Hans	SS-Oberscharführer	13 September 1909	Nürnberg
Vogel	Wolfram	SS-Schütze	26 April 1924	
Vogten	Wilhelm	SS-Schütze	27 August 1925	
Voigt	Karl-Heinz	SS-Panzergrenadier	5 December 1921	
Voss[363]	Karl-Heinz	SS-Unterscharführer	24 December 1924	Woltersdorf
Voss	Werner	SS-Unterscharführer	1 August 1920	
Vrnak[364]	August	SS-Unterscharführer	26 December 1920	Linz, Austria
Wachter[365]	Thomas	SS-Oberscharführer	12 February 1919	Heinersberg
Wälzel[366]	Karl	SS-Sturmmann	28 February 1924	Marxgrün, Austria
Wagner	Karl	SS-Panzergrenadier	22 May 1912	
Wallner[367]	Simon	SS-Unterscharführer	21 August 1920	St. Johann, Austria
Walter	Gottlieb	SS-Panzergrenadier	21 February 1912	
Walther	Herbert	SS-Panzergrenadier	29 April 1906	
Walz	Ernst	SS-Panzergrenadier	4 June 1906	
Warnecke	Theodor	SS-Panzergrenadier	2 May 1906	
Wartewig[368]	Karl	SS-Unterscharführer	2 October 1911	Eisenach
Wassertheuer[369]	Werner	SS-Sturmmann	10 October 1924	Rattendorf
Weber[370]	Erwin	SS-Unterscharführer	20 June 1912	Strassburg
Weberhake	Wilhelm	SS-Panzergrenadier	8 October 1908	
Wechs	Klaus	SS-Panzergrenadier	25 November 1925	
Weerd	Hermann	SS-Panzergrenadier	30 October 1925	
Wehner[371]	Albin	SS-Unterscharführer	23 May 1908	Motzlar/Eisenach
Weiner	Martin	SS-Unterscharführer	6 August 1909	
Weinert	Adolf	SS-Schütze	14 January 1905	
Weissenborn[372]	Karl-Heinz	SS-Rottenführer	10 February 1922	Derna/Dortmund
Weisser	August	SS-Grenadier	8 June 1911	
Weissflog[373]	Konrad	SS-Unterscharführer	22 July 1922	Schwarzenberg
Welkener	Ernst	SS-Panzergrenadier	18 July 1925	
Wenke[374]	Otto	SS-Sturmmann	8 June 1912	Herne
Wenzel[375]	Hermann	SS-Unterscharführer	26 August 1912	Kottowitz
Werner	Felix	SS-Panzergrenadier	15 October 1911	
Wesemann	Heinrich	SS-Panzergrenadier	8 April 1925	Elbrinxen
Wessling	Karl	SS-Schütze	11 March 1910	

Wiebrock	Walter	SS-Panzergrenadier	8 November 1906	
Wieczorek	Adalbert	SS-Panzergrenadier	3 November 1907	
Wieczorek	Max	SS-Panzergrenadier	12 October 1908	
Wiefel	Werner	SS-Rottenführer	7 November 1921	Arnsbach
Wienholz	Willi	SS-Unterscharführer	27 January 1910	Greifswald
Wiesmann	Leo	SS-Schütze	2 March 1916	
Wiethase	Haralt	SS-Freiwilliger	30 June 1922	
Wild	Wilhelm	SS-Panzergrenadier	7 April 1922	
Wilhelmsen	Christian	SS-Rottenführer	30 April 1903	
Wille[376]	Edwin	SS-Schütze	3 May 1925	Hirtengrün
Wittenberg	Erich	SS-Panzergrenadier	19 April 1907	
Wölfle	Hermann	SS-Panzergrenadier	10 December 1906	
Wölki	Paul	SS-Schütze	12 September 1925	
Wojtakowski[377]	Felix	SS-Schütze	18 April 1911	Wanne-Eickel
Wolf[378]	Johann	SS-Sturmmann	29 September 1905	Ludwigshafen
Wolf[379]	Michael	SS-Panzergrenadier	22 May 1925	Osterholzen
Wollner	Alois	SS-Schütze	26 May 1905	
Wrobel[380]	Alfred	SS-Panzergrenadier	15 February 1922	
Wünnenberg[381]	Erich	SS-Unterscharführer	19 November 1919	Langenberg
Zahn	Hermann	SS-Panzergrenadier	8 January 1924	
Zalto	Franz	SS-Schütze	7 April 1923	
Zander	Karl	SS-Panzergrenadier	28 May 1925	
Zehetbaür[382]	Anton	SS-Schütze	20 June 1902	Amberg
Zezulka	Franz	SS-Panzergrenadier	27 September 1910	
Zimmermann	Ernst	SS-Unterscharführer		
Zintl[383]	Johann	SS-Unterscharführer	17 March 1920	Schöntal, Czecho-slovakia

TABLE 4

SS CAVALRY REPLACEMENT DETACHMENT ENLISTED PERSONNEL

Last Name	First Name	Rank	Date of Birth	Place of Birth
Balogh[384]	Johann	SS-Schütze	24 December 1923	
Böhm[385]	Fritz	SS-Schütze	8 August 1916	
Bordican[386]	Franz	SS-Schütze	11 May 1916	
Haller[387]	Johann	SS-Reiter	12 February 1920	
Hauschildt[388]	Robert	SS-Unterscharführer	19 March 1921	Gadeland
Heit[389]	Anton	SS-Reiter	17 September 1921	
Herbst[390]	Hermann	SS-Schütze	26 April 1925	
Hörnike[391]	Rudolf	SS-Schütze	27 August 1925	
Imgrund[392]	Anton	SS-Reiter	22 September 1922	
Krenzke[393]	Fritz	SS-Rottenführer	1 November 1920	Grosswobiser
Kruse[394]	Heinz	SS-Sturmmann	4 December 1922	Ütersen/Hamburg
Kuding[395]	Andreas	SS-Schütze	25 January 1921	
Kyasch[396]	Otto	SS-Schütze	9 November 1912	
Lebisch[397]	Johann	SS-Reiter	6 June 1921	
Liebig	Erich		25 September 1905	Schreiberhau

Mielke[398]	Hugo	SS-Unterscharführer	9 June 1912	Paderborn
Müller[399]	Anton	SS-Reiter	2 December 1921	
Neugebaür[400]	Johann	SS-Reiter	16 March 1912	
Nissner[401]	Johann	SS-Schütze	23 April 1922	
Overkamp	Anton		4 October 1915	
Poepl[402]	Georg	SS-Reiter	18 January 1924	
Preusse[403]	Wolfgang	SS-Sturmmann	22 July 1922	
Reinke[404]	Oskar	SS-Oberreiter	26 August 1924	
Reitzig[405]	Günther	SS-Reiter	7 January 1924	
Schay[406]	Ludwig	SS-Schütze	30 November 1920	
Schuster[407]	Joseph	SS-Rottenführer	15 March 1920	Kelling
Staab[408]	Willi	SS-Rottenführer	27 September 1920	
Strobel[409]	Franz	SS-Reiter	2 March 1922	
Török[410]	Ludwig	SS-Reiter	8 September 1924	
Tyrek[411]	Johann	SS-Sturmmann	16 February 1920	Berlin-Neukölln
Vogel[412]	Fritz	SS-Unterscharführer	31 October 1920	
Wieck[413]	Fritz	SS-Rottenführer	15 August 1921	Dortmund
Wiesinger[414]	Alexander	SS-Reiter	11 January 1924	
Zechmeister[415]	Gottlieb	SS-Schütze	1 April 1922	
Zechmeister[416]	Karl	SS-Schütze	15 March 1915	

TABLE 5

22nd SS POLICE REGIMENT – ENLISTED PERSONNEL

Last Name	First Name	Rank	Date of Birth	Place of Birth
Adler[417]	Erwin	Zugwachtmeister		
Bauer[418]	Erich			
Bolze[419]	Hans-Joachim	Rottwachtmeister	9 October 1920	
Büthe[420]	Karl	Oberwachtmeister		
Czapp[421]	Alfons	Zugwachtmeister	15 September 1911	
Czesnik[422]	Kurt	Zugwachtmeister	9 November 1909	
Doerner[423]	Wilhelm	Oberwachtmeister		
Duschek[424]	Gustav	Hauptwachtmeister		
Federmann[425]	Ralf	Oberwachtmeister		
Fick[426]	Herbert	Oberwachtmeister		
Fischer[427]	Erich	Zugwachtmeister		
Graf[428]	Moritz	Wachtmeister		
Hartmann[429]	Rudolf	Wachtmeister	8 June 1909	
Heinsohn[430]	Wilhelm	Zugwachtmeister		
Heller[431]	Willy	Wachtmeister		
Hexel[432]	Oskar	Wachtmeister	15 February 1917	Lemberg
Hoelser[433]	Wilhelm	Zugwachtmeister		
Kemen[434]	Theodor	Oberwachtmeister		
Klemm[435]	Wilhelm	Wachtmeister	3 February 1917	
Klingberg[436]	Paul	Zugwachtmeister		
Koglin[437]	Otto	Zugwachtmeister	3 April 1911	
Kreuz[438]	Rudolf	Wachtmeister	25 October 1908	
Lehnhard[439]	Hermann	Oberwachtmeister	29 October 1911	

Linke[440]	Robert	Oberwachtmeister	6 March 1909
Luebzow[441]	Erich	Wachtmeister	
Mueller[442]	Josef	Zugwachtmeister	
Neidhard[443]	Karl	Wachtmeister	14 March 1903
Perschke[444]	Erich	Zugwachtmeister	30 December 1914
Pfleiderer[445]	Hermann	Zugwachtmeister	
Pils[446]	Gerhard	Zugwachtmeister	
Pulfer[447]	Ludwig	Zugwachtmeister	
Riemer[448]	Horst	Oberwachtmeister	10 May 1908
Schaller[449]	Gustav	Wachtmeister	
Schluter[450]	Willi	Oberwachtmeister	
Schreier[451]	Max		16 September 1906
Spalleck[452]	Johannes	Wachtmeister	
Sprotte[453]	Karl	Oberwachtmeister	11 September 1907
Thelen[454]	Stefan	Wachtmeister	
Vogel[455]	Hermann	Wachtmeister	
Waclawik[456]	Erich	Zugwachtmeister	25 April 1910
Wurzbach[457]	Alfred	Zugwachtmeister	
Ziegler[458]	Emil	Wachtmeister	

TABLE 6

23rd SS POLICE REGIMENT – ENLISTED PERSONNEL

Last Name	First Name	Rank	Date of Birth
Dimpfl[459]	Ludwig		16 September 1910
Eggert[460]	Hermann		25 September 1904
Frischhut[461]	Karl		1 August 1902
Guenther[462]	Paul		19 December 1909
Kron[463]	Rudolf		14 June 1902
Luenen[464]	Otto	Wachtmeister	9 December 1905
Michels[465]	Alois		24 July 1911
Mussel[466]	Wilhelm		23 January 1914
Profittlich[467]	Josef		22 March 1903
Vogl[468]	Max		10 October 1903

TABLE 7

1ST GUARD BATTALION, TRAWNIKI LABOR CAMP "TRAWNIKI MEN"

Last Name	First Name	Rank	Date of Birth
Bartetzko[469]	Franz	SS-Oberscharführer	
Dawidenko[470]	Andrej	Wachmann	31 January 1923
Huzulak[471]	Nikolai	Wachmann	16 March 1923
Iwanyschyn[472]	Grigor	Wachmann	1924
Knyhynyzkyn[473]	Iwan	Wachmann	21 July 1923
Kosatschok[474]	Jurko	Wachmann	3 May 1921

Lehnert	Eugen	SS-Unterscharführer	
Mayowski	Sepp	SS-Oberscharführer	23 December 1914
Minenko[475]	Michael	Wachmann	11 February 1921
Napieralla[476]	Josef	SS-Scharführer	
Nestarenko[477]	Paul	Wachmann	17 August 1919
Odartschenko[478]	Borys	Wachmann	11 January 1923
Protschenko[479]	Anrej	Wachmann	1 October 1922
Roschdestwenskyj[480]	Borys	Wachmann	10 April 1914
Schmidt[481]	Emil	Wachmann	2 February 1923
Stark[482]	Willi	Wachmann	4 April 1920
Usik[483]	Wladimir	Wachmann	16 June 1917

Notes:

[1] Tom Segev, *Soldiers of Evil: The Commandants of the Nazi Concentration Camps*. (New York: McGraw-Hill Book Company, 1987), p. 95.

[2] Charles W. Sydnor, Jr., *Soldiers of Destruction: The SS Death's Head Division, 1933-1945*. (Princeton, NJ: Princeton University Press, 1977), p. 196.

[3] Ibid., p. 205.

[4] Mark C. Yerger, *Riding East: The SS Cavalry Brigade in Poland and Russia 1939-1942*. (Atglen, PA: Schiffer Publishing, 1996), pp. 85-93.

[5] French MacLean, *The Field Men: The SS Officers Who Led the Einsatzkommandos - the Nazi Mobile Killing Units*. (Atglen, PA: Schiffer Publishing Co., 1999).

[6] 1061-PS, Summary, p. 9.

[7] Ibid., p. 205.

[8] For non-divisional units assigned to a corps, the corps commander approved receipt of the award. Although the intent was to let an appropriate time pass between the award of the 2nd Class and the 1st Class, this could be compressed to one or two days.

[9] Ibid., pp. 80-81. The regimental commander could authorize the award.

[10] Wolfgang Scheffler and Helge Grabnitz, *Der Ghetto-Aufstand Warschau 1943*. (Munich, Germany: Goldmann Verlag, 1993), p. 382.

[11] Ibid., pp. 360-361.

[12] Pawiak Prison; SS number 214927.

[13] Pawiak Prison; SS number 78772.

[14] Section IV C 1. Sentenced by a Hamburg court on 29 August 1975 to seven years imprisonment for his part in the deportation of at least 230,000 Jews from the Warsaw Ghetto to Treblinka in 1942.

[15] Registrar Section; SS number 308659.

[16] SS number 385047; later promoted to *SS-Untersturmführer*.

[17] Submitted for War Service Cross 2nd Class.

[18] Section IV C 1; served in 85th Infantry Regiment in World War I.

[19] Section V, 6th *Kommissariat*; SS number 491002; promoted to *SS-Untersturmführer* 9 November 1944.

[20] Pawiak Prison; SS number 251351.

[21] Section IV A 3; awarded Iron Cross 1st Class 1 September 1944.

[22] Section I C; awarded Iron Cross 1st Class 1 September 1944.

[23] Section II C; SS number 130634; served in *Gestapo* Potsdam before the war; served in *Leibstandarte Adolf Hitler* Regiment 1934-1936.

[24] Section IV D; SS number 404573.

[25] Department IV; SS number 314655; awarded War Service Cross 2nd Class for service during Ghetto Uprising; executed in East Germany after the war. Nicknamed "Frankenstein" by the Jews in the Ghetto.

[26] Section IV E S; SS number 254911; served in Border Police at the beginning of the war.

[27] Section IV A 3; SS number 372282; served in *Gestapo* Köslin before the war.

[28] Pawiak Prison; SS number 53480; killed in action 11 January 1945 at Posen.

[29] Section II D 3; served in *Gestapo* Köslin before the war.

[30] Submitted for War Service Cross 2nd Class.

[31] Pawiak Prison; arrived in Warsaw in 1941; killed in action 7 September 1943.

[32] Section IV E 3.

[33] Section IV A 1.

[34] Section IV A; served earlier in *Gestapo* Köslin; served in *Schutzpolizei* from 1922 to 1938.

[35] Section IV A 2; killed in action August 1944 in Warsaw Uprising.

[36] Section II D 3; SS number 30336.

[37] Section IV A 3; personally commended by Heinrich Himmler, October 1941.

[38] Section IV A 3; *Volksdeutsch*.

[39] Section IV A 3 a.

[40] Section IV A 3 d.

[41] Killed in action June 1943.

[42] Section II C; SS number 404592; served in Police from 1928.

[43] Section IV A 3.

[44] Section IV E 1; SS number 144295; served in *Schutzpolizei* 1934-1936.

[45] Section II D 3; SS number 114724.

[46] Section IV A S; served in *Landespolizei* 1928-1937; shot twice in lung; served in *Gestapo* Oppeln in 1938; Iron Cross 1st Class for the Warsaw Uprising.

[47] Section IV A 3; served in *Schutzpolizei* Königsberg 1927-1936; served at *Gestapo* Lauenburg in 1937; killed in action January 1944.

[48] Section IV E 3; submitted for War Service Cross 2nd Class.

[49] Section IV E 3; SS number 323723; served in *Einsatzgruppe IV* during Polish Campaign.

[50] Section IV C 2; submitted for War Service Cross 2nd Class; in Police since 1928.

[51] Section IV B; awarded Iron Cross 1st Class 27 September 1944; served in SD Lublin.

[52] Pawiak Prison; awarded Iron Cross 1st Class 27 September 1944.

[53] N-Ost; served in *Kripo* Kassel.

[54] Section IV A 3; in Police since 1927.

[55] Pawiak Prison; in Police since 1924; served in *Gestapo* Chemnitz; killed in action August 1943.

[56] Section IV A 3; SS number 307857; served in *Gestapo* Frankfurt/Oder before the war.

[57] Section I A 2; SS number 120603.

[58] Section IV A 2; served in *Gestapo* Chemnitz before the war.

[59] Section IV D; SS number 367073; served in *Einsatzgruppe IV* during Polish Campaign; served in *Gestapo* Frankfurt/Oder before the war; acquitted by a Hamburg court on 29 August 1975 of assisting in the deportation of at least 230,000 Jews from the Warsaw Ghetto to Treblinka in 1942.

[60] Section IV E 1.

[61] Section I A 2; SS number 158510; promoted to *SS-Untersturmführer* 20 April 1944.

[62] Section II D 3; killed in action August 1944 in the Warsaw Uprising.

[63] Section II C; served in Latvian Army 1933-1934.

[64] N-Ost; SS number 170340; served at SD Kattowitz; father changed last name from Jaworski to Junghart; sentenced to 6 weeks arrest during the war for insubordination.

[65] Section V, 1st *Kommissariat*.

[66] Section II C; SS number 426592; promoted to *SS-Untersturmführer* 30 January 1944; in Police since 1925.

[67] Section IV A 3; SS number 310012; served in SD Frankfurt/Oder

[68] Section IV. On 4 February 1965, a Bielefeld court sentenced him to life imprisonment.

[69] Section IV E 1.
[70] Section IV C 2.
[71] Killed in action August 1944 in the Warsaw Uprising.
[72] Pawiak Prison; promoted to *SS-Rottenführer* 1 November 1942.
[73] Section IV A 3; SS number 288470; promoted to *SS-Untersturmführer* 30 January 1945.
[74] Section II D; SS number 396192; promoted to *SS-Untersturmführer* 9 November 1944.
[75] Section IV A 3; SS number 136265; served in Gestapo Köslin.
[76] Section IV A 3; killed in action August 1944 in Warsaw Uprising.
[77] Section II C; SS number 386714; promoted to *SS-Untersturmführer* 21 June 1944; in Police since 1923.
[78] Section IV E S; last name originally Koslowski; served in Berlin Police.
[79] Section V, 3rd *Kommissariat*; wounded in action 19 April 1943.
[80] Section III A; SS number 272675; promoted to *SS-Untersturmführer* 9 November 1943; awarded Iron Cross 1st Class.
[81] Killed in action April 1944.
[82] N-Ost.
[83] Section IV C 2; SS number 139271; may have served in an *Einsatzkommando* in summer 1942.
[84] Section IV E 1; SS number 375087; wife worked as stenographer in KdS Warsaw.
[85] Section II C 3; SS number 189494; killed in action by Polish resistance, 22 June 1944 in Warsaw.
[86] Pawiak Prison; SS number 192565.
[87] Killed in action August 1944 in the Warsaw Uprising.
[88] Section IV A 3; SS number 170721; served in *Leibstandarte Adolf Hitler* Regiment, 1934-1938; wife died in childbirth in 1944.
[89] Section IV E S; served at *Gestapo* Schneidemühl in 1939.
[90] Section IV A 3; awarded Iron Cross 1st Class 1 September 1944.
[91] Medical Section; awarded Iron Cross 1st Class 27 September 1944.
[92] Section IV A 3 c; SS number 382361; promoted to *SS-Untersturmführer* 14 December 1943.
[93] Promoted to *SS-Untersturmführer* 17 May 1944.
[94] Pawiak Prison; SS number 215356; promoted to *SS-Rottenführer* 1 November 1942.
[95] Section II D; promoted to *SS-Untersturmführer* 10 August 1944.
[96] Section IV B; SS number 91531.
[97] Section II D 2; SS number 67407; served at Buchenwald concentration camp in 1937; awarded Iron Cross 1st Class 1 September 1944.
[98] Section II D; SS number 147549; served at Dachau concentration camp in 1935; served at Sachsenhausen concentration camp in 1937; served in SD Leipzig.
[99] Killed in action August 1944 in Warsaw Uprising.
[100] Section IV A 3; SS number 234253.
[101] SS number 280260; promoted to *SS-Untersturmführer* 21 June 1943.
[102] Section IV A 3; promoted to *SS-Untersturmführer* 1 September 1943.
[103] Submitted for War Service Cross 2nd Class.
[104] Section IV E S; awarded Iron Cross 1st Class 1 September 1944.
[105] Killed in action August 1944 in Warsaw Uprising.
[106] Section IV E 1; served in *Gestapo* Frankfurt/Oder before the war.
[107] Section IV A 3; submitted for War Service Cross 2nd Class.
[108] Section IV A 1; SS number 416456; promoted to SS-*Untersturmführer* 21 June 1943; promoted to *SS-Obersturmführer* 9 November 1943.
[109] Wounded in action 25 April 1943.
[110] Section V, 4th *Kommissariat*; SS number 357233.
[111] Section IV E 3; SS number 293173; acquitted by a Hamburg court on 29 August 1975 of assisting in the deportation of at least 230,000 Jews from the Warsaw Ghetto to Treblinka in 1942.
[112] Section IV A 3 c.
[113] Section IV A 2; SS number 259988.
[114] Section IV E 3; killed in action August 1944 in Warsaw Uprising.
[115] Pawiak Prison; served in Polish army before the war; spoke Polish.
[116] Section IV E S; killed in action May 1944.
[117] Pawiak Prison; *Volksdeutsch*; spoke Polish; in Warsaw since 23 January 1941.
[118] Section III G.
[119] Section IV A 2; SS number 145782; served in SD Potsdam.
[120] Section IV B; SS number 165172; probably served in an *Einsatzkommando* in 1942.
[121] Section IV A 1; SS number 129220.
[122] Section IV E S.
[123] Killed in action September 1943.
[124] Section IV E 1; SS number 56944.
[125] Section IV A 3 a; SS number 240464.
[126] Section IV E 1; killed in action December 1943.
[127] Pawiak Prison; SS number 161258; wounded in action 19 April 1943.
[128] Section IV A 3 d; served in Schutzpolizei 1928-1937; served in SD Frankfurt/Oder.
[129] Section IV E S; *Volksdeutsch*; served in *Gestapo* Elbing spoke Polish.
[130] Section IV A Special Commando; SS number 369532; promoted to *SS-Untersturmführer* 9 November 1944.
[131] Section IV B; SS number 260439.
[132] Section V, 4th *Kommissariat*; SS number 332017; promoted to *SS-Untersturmführer* 9 November 1944.
[133] Section IV E 2.
[134] Pawiak Prison; SS number 97908.
[135] Section III; SS number 490658; killed in action 2 August 1944 in Warsaw Uprising.
[136] Section IV A 1.
[137] Section II C; SS number 67277.
[138] Section IV D; awarded Iron Cross 1st Class 27 September 1944.
[139] Killed in action June 1944.
[140] Section IV A 1; SS number 185458; promoted to *SS-Untersturmführer* 30 January 1945; served in German Navy in World War I.
[141] Pawiak Prison; killed in action August 1944 in Warsaw Uprising.
[142] Pawiak Prison; killed in action August 1944 in Warsaw Uprising.
[143] Section II A 2; SS number 327297; awarded Iron Cross 1st Class 27 September 1944.
[144] Section II D 3; SS number 51174; awarded Iron Cross 1st Class 1 September 1944.
[145] Killed in action January 1944.
[146] Section IV N; SS number 32290; War Service Cross 2nd Class; wife worked for SD Lublin.
[147] Section V, 3rd *Kommissariat*; SS number 386734; served in *Kripo* Stettin.
[148] Served in SD Düsseldorf.
[149] Section IV A 2; submitted for War Service Cross 2nd Class.
[150] Section IV A 3 c; SS number 158498; probably served in *Einsatzgruppe IV* in Polish Campaign.
[151] Section IV A 3; SS number 280113, promoted to *SS Untersturmführer* 21 June 1944; served in Police since 1925.
[152] Section IV A 3 c.
[153] Section IV C 2; SS number 167420.
[154] Section IV E S; probably served in an *Einsatzgruppe* in Polish Campaign.
[155] Submitted for War Service Cross 2nd Class.
[156] Section IV B; served in *Gestapo* Frankfurt/Oder.
[157] Submitted for War Service Cross 2nd Class.
[158] Section IV A 3; killed in action February 1944.
[159] Section IV E 1; submitted for War Service Cross 2nd Class; served in *Gestapo* Neustadt/Weinstrasse.
[160] Pawiak Prison; SS number 91114.
[161] Section IV C 2; spoke Czech.
[162] Served in Natzweiler concentration camp.
[163] Wounded in action 25 November 1943 in eye and head; wounded in action in 1942.
[164] Wounded in action 27 November 1943 in legs; discharged from SS 12 April 1945.
[165] Discharged from SS 30 April 1945.
[166] Killed in action 8 February 1944.
[167] Wounded in action 17 September 1941 in right calf.
[168] Later assigned to 9th SS Division "*Hohenstaufen*".
[169] Wounded in action 4 July 1942.
[170] Served in 1st SS Division "*Leibstandarte Adolf Hitler*"; promoted to *SS-Untersturmführer*.
[171] Wounded in action 22 July 1941.
[172] Wounded in action 13 May 1943.
[173] Wounded in left upper arm, 5 March 1943 vicinity Khar'kov.
[174] Served in Flossenbürg concentration camp.
[175] Classified as sole surviving son.
[176] Wounded in action 24 August 1944; Iron Cross 2nd Class 1944.
[177] Wounded in stomach by grenade fragment 30 September 1941; probably in hospital during Ghetto Uprising.
[178] Served at Mauthausen concentration camp.
[179] Wounded in action 25 April 1943, @1930 hours in left upper ankle.
[180] Served at Dachau concentration camp in 1942; classified as sole surviving son.
[181] Wounded in action 8 July 1941 with 3rd SS Division "*Totenkopf*".
[182] Wounded in right arm 1 September 1941.
[183] Classified as sole surviving son.

[184] Promoted to *SS-Untersturmführer*, 9 November 1944.
[185] Wounded in action 2 May 1943.
[186] Iron Cross 2nd Class; Demyansk Shield.
[187] Released from SS 18 March 1944.
[188] Classified as sole surviving son.
[189] Wounded in action 27 April 1943.
[190] Wounded 9 December 1943 in left lung; Iron Cross 2nd Class; Panzer Battle Badge in Bronze.
[191] Classified as sole surviving son.
[192] Wounded in neck in 1942; wounded again in 1944; Iron Cross 2nd Class; Infantry Assault Badge; Demyansk Shield.
[193] Served at Dachau concentration camp before the war; Iron Cross 1st Class; Infantry Assault Badge; Demyansk Shield; Promoted to *SS-Untersturmführer* 9 November 1943; promoted to *SS-Obersturmführer* 21 June 1944.
[194] Wounded in left leg 20 October 1943; contracted Spotted Fever April 1944.
[195] Wounded in action 13 May 1943.
[196] Lost left eye and badly injured right eye in 1944; Iron Cross 2nd Class; Infantry Assault Badge; Demyansk Shield; promoted to *SS-Untersturmführer* 21 June 1944; promoted to *SS-Obersturmführer* 9 November 1944.
[197] Classified as sole surviving son.
[198] Wounded 3 February 1942; Iron Cross 2nd Class.
[199] Promoted to *SS-Untersturmführer* 21 June 1944.
[200] Wounded 14 May 1943 in right eye by grenade fragment – lost eye; wounded 5 July 1942 in right hand.
[201] Classified as sole surviving son.
[202] Served at Dachau concentration camp before the war.
[203] Missing in action 4 December 1944.
[204] Wounded 25 October 1943 in right shoulder by shrapnel; wounded 10 September 1944 in left shoulder.
[205] Wounded 11 May 1942 in right knee and left shin; killed in action 22 September 1944.
[206] Wounded in action 6 May 1943; hand grenade shrapnel in back; wounded 17 January 1944 in left foot; wounded 11 March 1942 in hand; Iron Cross 1st and 2nd Class, Demyansk Shield.
[207] Wounded 26 May 1942 in lower leg; Iron Cross 1st and 2nd Class; Infantry Assault Badge.
[208] Wounded in action 19 April 1943.
[209] Served at Sachsenburg concentration camp in 1935; served at Buchenwald concentration camp in 1938.
[210] Wounded 20 May 1942 in neck and shoulder by shrapnel.
[211] Released from SS on 29 November 1944.
[212] Wounded 6 June 1942 by shrapnel in right arm.
[213] Died 7 November 1943.
[214] Wounded 13 May 1941 in arm and foot in 3rd SS Division "*Totenkopf*".
[215] Wound Badge Black, Infantry Assault Badge.
[216] Wounded 29 October 1943 in right shoulder.
[217] Wounded 19 September 1943; left leg amputated; Iron Cross 2nd Class, Infantry Assault Badge; Wound Badge Silver.
[218] Killed in action 10 July 1943 at Kursk.
[219] Wounded in action 20 April 1943; wounded 9 September 1943 by shrapnel in back; wounded 13 February 1944 in right arm.
[220] Wounded in action 6 May 1943; wounded in action 10 July 1941.
[221] Wounded in left arm 15 September 1942.
[222] Wounded 17 October 1941 in left thigh; wounded 19 September 1944 in left arm.
[223] Wounded in action 7 October 1943.
[224] Promoted to *SS-Untersturmführer* 16 May 1944; Iron Cross 2nd Class.
[225] On battalion soccer team.
[226] Wounded 11 May 1942 in thigh.
[227] Wounded in both legs 23 July 1944; shot in shoulder 4 August 1944; Iron Cross 2nd Class, Infantry Assault Badge.
[228] Served at Buchenwald concentration camp in 1941.
[229] On battalion soccer team.
[230] Served at Dachau concentration camp 1936.
[231] Served at Dachau concentration camp 1936-1939; wounded twice in 1942 by shell fragments to neck and head; Iron Cross 1st & 2nd Class, Infantry Assault Badge.
[232] Served at Mauthausen concentration camp in 1942.
[233] Wounded in left arm, 1940 in French Campaign; served at Flossenbürg concentration camp in 1941; killed in action 31 July 1943.
[234] Wounded in action before arriving at battalion; Infantry Assault Badge.
[235] Close Combat Bar 1st Class, Wound Badge in Silver.
[236] Wounded in action 8 May 1943.
[237] Caught jaundice in Russia.
[238] Wounded 4 September 1943 in right leg by shrapnel.
[239] Missing in action 29 October 1943.
[240] Served at Dachau concentration camp before the war; served in SS Division "*Totenkopf*" in French Campaign.
[241] Wounded 23 October 1941 in right knee.
[242] Wounded in left hip by shrapnel, 10 August 1942.
[243] Served in SS Division "*Totenkopf*" in French Campaign.
[244] Found unfit for SS service.
[245] Classified as sole surviving son.
[246] Wounded in throat 24 March 1942.
[247] Wounded in action 14 May 1943.
[248] Struck by fever 10 October 1942.
[249] Later served in 1st SS Division "*Leibstandarte Adolf Hitler*"; suffered 2nd degree frostbite 21 February 1944. Cold weather injuries took their toll in the German armed forces throughout World War II. Casualty returns for the German Army in front of Moscow for December 1941 show over 100,000 cases of frostbite. Over 14,000 were classified as "major" and required one or more amputations. About 62,000 were viewed as "moderate" – resulting in total incapacity but not requiring amputation; 36,000 were classified as "light", with the patient able to return to duty in ten days or less. To commemorate the campaign, Adolf Hitler instituted the Eastern Front Medal. The troops referred to the decoration as the *Gefrierfleisch Orden* – the Order of the Frozen Meat. Source: French MacLean, *Quiet Flows the Rhine: German General Officer Casualties in World War II*. (Winnipeg, Canada: J.J. Fedorowicz, 1996).
[250] Not fit for front-line service.
[251] Wounded 31 August 1943 in left elbow.
[252] Wounded in 1941 and 1942; Iron Cross 2nd Class in 1942; served in 17th SS Division "*Götz von Berlichingen*", 1945.
[253] Wounded 30 December 1941 in right arm; caught gonorrhea in July 1943.
[254] Served at Sachsenhausen concentration camp in 1941.
[255] Wounded twice in 1941; received Iron Cross 2nd Class, 1940; killed in action 7 September 1943.
[256] Missing in action 8 February 1944.
[257] Served at Buchenwald concentration camp 1937-1939; Stroop Report: wounded in action 24 April 1943.
[258] Wounded in neck, 11 July 1941.
[259] Served in Polish Army 1935-1937.
[260] Iron Cross 1st and 2nd Class; promoted to *SS-Untersturmführer* 21 December 1944.
[261] Wounded 20 April 1943, gunshot to lower right leg; 3rd SS Division "*Totenkopf*" in 1944.
[262] Wounded 25 September 1941 in left hand.
[263] Served at Dachau concentration camp.
[264] Classified as sole surviving son.
[265] Wounded in action 3 May 1943.
[266] Diagnosed with stomach ulcer, 27 September 1941.
[267] Received Iron Cross 1st and 2nd Class; promoted to *SS-Untersturmführer* 1 October 1944.
[268] Promoted to *SS-Rottenführer* 1 November 1943.
[269] Received Iron Cross 2nd Class and Panzer Badge.
[270] Wounded by shrapnel in throat 28 January 1944; wounded by bomb shrapnel in the hand 8 March 1944.
[271] Wounded 27 September 1941 in left hand.
[272] Wounded in throat 26 March 1942.
[273] Frostbite to both hands 13 March 1942; wounded in arm and ear by grenade shrapnel 9 October 1942; Iron Cross 1st and 2nd Class.
[274] Classified as sole surviving son.
[275] Promoted to *SS-Rottenführer* 30 March 1944.
[276] Served at Dachau concentration camp before the war; Iron Cross 2nd Class; Wound Badge.
[277] Wounded by shrapnel in left arm, 10 September 1944.
[278] Wounded in left eye 12 September 1942; killed in action 12 December 1943.
[279] Promoted to *SS-Unterscharführer* 18 January 1944; promoted to *SS-Scharführer* 1 May 1944; promoted to *SS-Untersturmführer* 1 October 1944.
[280] Assigned to 12th SS Division "*Hitlerjugend*" 23 October 1944; Iron Cross 2nd Class; Infantry Assault Badge; promoted to *SS-Untersturmführer* 16 May 1944.
[281] Served at Sachsenburg and Buchenwald concentration camps; War Service Cross 2nd Class.
[282] Promoted to *SS-Rottenführer* 1 June 1944.
[283] Classified as sole surviving son.
[284] Wounded by shrapnel in the head 12 September 1943.
[285] Killed in action 15 October 1943.
[286] War Service Cross 2nd Class.

[287] Served in 3rd SS Division "*Totenkopf*".
[288] Contracted jaundice 14 August 1943.
[289] Wounded in action 27 April 1943.
[290] Served at Mauthausen concentration camp.
[291] Wounded 12 September 1943; lower right arm amputated; promoted to *SS-Unterscharführer* 1 February 1944; Panzer Assault Badge.
[292] Died 14 October 1944.
[293] On battalion soccer team.
[294] Iron Cross 2nd Class; Infantry Assault Badge; 3rd SS Division "*Totenkopf*".
[295] Wounded in action 14 May 1943; wounded in left arm 13 August 1942; Iron Cross 2nd Class.
[296] Reduced from officer ranks.
[297] Wounded in right arm 9 October 1941.
[298] Assigned to the 12th SS Division "*Hitlerjugend*" 15 July 1944; received Iron Cross 2nd Class, Infantry Assault Badge.
[299] Wounded by shrapnel in foot 10 September 1944.
[300] Wounded in action 14 May 1943.
[301] Promoted to *SS-Oberscharführer* 1 August 1944.
[302] Iron Cross 2nd Class.
[303] Suffered from blood poisoning 20 July 1942; promoted to *SS-Rottenführer* 1 August 1942.
[304] Wounded in right lung 20 October 1941; on battalion soccer team.
[305] Promoted to *SS-Unterscharführer* on 1 September 1944.
[306] Promoted to *SS-Unterscharführer* on 1 January 1945.
[307] Promoted to *SS-Oberscharführer* 1 December 1943.
[308] Wounded in left leg 5 September 1944.
[309] Served at Dachau concentration camp before the war; killed in action 16 August 1944.
[310] Wounded by shrapnel in left arm 17 June 1942.
[311] Promoted to *SS-Untersturmführer* 21 June 1944; wounded 25 August 1944.
[312] Served in 9th SS Division "*Hohenstaufen*," 5 June 1943.
[313] Wounded in hand 12 September 1943.
[314] Killed in action 19 March 1944
[315] Served in 3rd SS Division "*Totenkopf*" 1941; 25th SS Division, 1945.
[316] Wounded in right foot, 24 October 1943.
[317] Promoted to *SS-Oberscharführer* 1 February 1945.
[318] Classified as sole surviving son.
[319] Wounded in the chest 30 September 1941; Infantry Assault Badge.
[320] Wounded and lost his left arm, 10 September 1943; released from SS 21 January 1945.
[321] Served at Flossenbürg concentration camp.
[322] Classified as sole surviving son.
[323] Wounded in right shoulder 30 September 1942; Iron Cross 2nd Class; Infantry Assault Badge.
[324] Wounded in action 28 April 1943.
[325] Served at Dachau concentration camp 1936; 3rd SS Division "*Totenkopf*" 1941; 13th SS Division "*Handschar*" 1943.
[326] Wounded in action 19 April 1943; wounded 21 October 1943 in stomach.
[327] Killed in action 29 May 1944.
[328] Killed in action 8 July 1944.
[329] Wounded in action 19 April 1943.
[330] Wounded in right leg 17 January 1944 by shrapnel; wounded in right elbow 27 July 1944.
[331] Served in 3rd SS Division "*Totenkopf*" 1940.
[332] Wounded in action 8 May 1943 reflected in the Stroop Report; personnel file shows wound from 16 May 1942 instead; Iron Cross 1st and 2nd Class.
[333] Promoted to *SS-Oberscharführer* 1 August 1944; War Service Cross 2nd Class.
[334] Served at Buchenwald concentration camp; promoted to *SS-Oberscharführer* 21 October 1943.
[335] Classified as sole surviving son.
[336] Promoted to *SS-Untersturmführer* 9 November 1944; 20th SS Division 1944-1945; War Service Cross 2nd Class.
[337] Served in 16th SS Division "*Reichsführer-SS*" 1943-1944.
[338] Frostbite 2nd and 3rd degree of both feet 26 December 1941; promoted to *SS-Unterscharführer* 1 February 1945.
[339] Iron Cross 1st and 2nd Class.
[340] Served at Dachau concentration camp, 1938-1939.
[341] Wounded in action in 1941.
[342] Served at Dachau concentration camp in 1942, late 1943 and 1944; classified as sole surviving son.
[343] Wounded in stomach 15 November 1943.
[344] Infantry Assault Badge.
[345] Missing in action 24 March 1944; Iron Cross 2nd Class, Panzer Badge.
[346] Served in 3rd SS Division "*Totenkopf*" in French Campaign.
[347] Wounded by shrapnel left knee, left arm 22 September 1943; wounded by shrapnel 10 October 1944 in hip.
[348] In December 1942 complained of flat feet and rheumatism; Iron Cross 2nd Class, Infantry Assault Badge.
[349] Butcher by trade; promoted to *SS-Hauptscharführer* 1 June 1944.
[350] Served 3rd SS Division "*Totenkopf* 1943; wounded 22 November 1943; left arm amputated.
[351] Wounded 10 May 1942 by shrapnel left shoulder blade; killed in action 19 September 1943; Iron Cross 2nd Class.
[352] Killed in action 13 May 1943.
[353] Wounded 14 September 1941; Iron Cross 2nd Class, Infantry Assault Badge.
[354] Promoted to *SS-Hauptscharführer* 30 January 1945.
[355] Classified as sole surviving son.
[356] Served in 5th SS Division "*Wiking*".
[357] Wounded in both legs 1942; promoted to *SS-Unterscharführer* 1 April 1944.
[358] Classified as sole surviving son.
[359] Wounded 18 November 1941 by shrapnel in left elbow.
[360] Wounded in left eye 4 May 1942.
[361] Promoted to *SS-Rottenführer* 1 October 1944.
[362] Wounded in right shin 4 January 1942; promoted to *SS-Unterscharführer* 1 May 1944.
[363] Wounded 5 March 1943 in lower jaw; 3rd SS Division "*Totenkopf*"; Iron Cross 2nd Class.
[364] Wounded 20 May 1942 by shrapnel in right leg and left arm; 3rd SS Division "*Totenkopf*"; promoted to *SS-Oberscharführer* 1 February 1944.
[365] Wounded in action 14 May 1943; wounded in arm 26 July 1941; Iron Cross 2nd Class, Infantry Assault Badge.
[366] Wounded by shrapnel in left arm 27 November 1941; missing in action 27 March 1944.
[367] Wounded in action 25 July 1941.
[368] Promoted to *SS-Oberscharführer* 1 January 1944.
[369] Transferred from 3rd SS Division "*Totenkopf*" (bad heart); promoted to *SS-Rottenführer* 1 December 1943; Infantry Assault Badge.
[370] Killed in action 26 September 1944.
[371] Contracted malaria November 1941; 3rd SS Division "*Totenkopf*"; Iron Cross 2nd Class; Infantry Assault Badge.
[372] Iron Cross 2nd Class; Infantry Assault Badge; promoted to *SS-Unterscharführer* 1 May 1944.
[373] Wounded in shoulder 25 February 1943; 3rd SS Division "*Totenkopf*"; Iron Cross 2nd Class, Infantry Assault Badge.
[374] Promoted to *SS-Unterscharführer* 20 April 1944.
[375] US Prisoner of War 15 August 1944.
[376] Served 1st SS Division "*Leibstandarte Adolf Hitler;*" killed in action 21 February 1945.
[377] Wound Badge 1 June 1943.
[378] Served in Natzweiler concentration camp in 1942; promoted to *SS-Rottenführer* 1 October 1943.
[379] Iron Cross 2nd Class.
[380] Classified as sole surviving son.
[381] Wounded 14 July 1942 by shrapnel in left leg; Iron Cross 2nd Class.
[382] Wounded by shrapnel in both legs 24 October 1943; frostbite 2nd and 3rd degree in both hands 19 February 1944; 3rd SS Division "*Totenkopf*".
[383] Served in 2nd SS Division "*Das Reich*" in 1942.
[384] Wounded in action 14 May 1943.
[385] Wounded in action 19 April 1943.
[386] Wounded in action 14 May 1943.
[387] Wounded in action 24 April 1943.
[388] Wounded in action 20 April 1943; missing in action 17 January 1945, 8th SS Cavalry Division "*Florian Geyer.*"
[389] Wounded in action 20 April 1943.
[390] Wounded in action 3 May 1943.
[391] Wounded in action 3 May 1943.
[392] Wounded in action 19 April 1943.
[393] Wounded in action 25 April 1943.
[394] Wounded in action 19 April 1943 (pistol shot to lower right stomach); wounded in right arm, 21 February 1942 in SS Cavalry Brigade.
[395] Wounded in action 14 May 1943.
[396] Wounded in action 12 May 1943.
[397] Wounded in action 28 April 1943.
[398] Wounded in action 7 May 1943. Sentenced to life imprisonment in Erfurt in 1960.

[399] Wounded in action 19 April 1943.
[400] Wounded in action 20 April 1943.
[401] Wounded in action 29 April 1943.
[402] Wounded in action 21 April 1943.
[403] Wounded in action 10 May 1943.
[404] Wounded in action 19 April 1943.
[405] Wounded in action 19 April 1943.
[406] Wounded in action 20 April 1943.
[407] Wounded in action 26 April 1943; promoted to *SS-Unterscharführer*, 1 November 1943
[408] Wounded in action 10 May 1943.
[409] Wounded in action 19 April 1943.
[410] Wounded in action 28 April 1943.
[411] Wounded in action 19 April 1943; file shows wounds to shoulder and leg; served in 4th SS Division "*Polizei*" and 8th SS Cavalry Division "*Florian Geyer.*"
[412] Wounded in action 24 April 1943; wounded 5 May 1942 by grenade shrapnel in right foot; promoted to *SS-Obersturmführer* 1 October 1944; Iron Cross 2nd Class, Infantry Assault Badge.
[413] Wounded in action 5 May 1943; died 11 January 1944; posthumously promoted to *SS-Untersturmführer*.
[414] Wounded in action 28 April 1943.
[415] Wounded in action 10 May 1943.
[416] Wounded in action 19 April 1943.
[417] 3rd Battalion, 22nd SS Police Regiment; submitted for War Service Cross 2nd Class.
[418] 22nd SS Police Regiment; awarded War Service Cross 2nd Class.
[419] 3rd Battalion, 22nd SS Police Regiment; killed in action 1 May 1943.
[420] 3rd Battalion, 22nd SS Police Regiment; submitted for War Service Cross 2nd Class.
[421] 1st Battalion, 22nd SS Police Regiment; wounded in action 15 May 1943; survived war; lived in Gelsenkirchen.
[422] 3rd Battalion, 22nd SS Police Regiment; wounded in action 21 April 1943.
[423] 3rd Battalion, 22nd SS Police Regiment; submitted for War Service Cross 2nd Class.
[424] 3rd Battalion, 22nd SS Police Regiment; submitted for War Service Cross 2nd Class.
[425] 3rd Battalion, 22nd SS Police Regiment; submitted for War Service Cross 2nd Class.
[426] 3rd Battalion, 22nd SS Police Regiment; submitted for War Service Cross 2nd Class.
[427] 3rd Battalion, 22nd SS Police Regiment; submitted for War Service Cross 2nd Class.
[428] 3rd Battalion, 22nd SS Police Regiment; submitted for War Service Cross 2nd Class.
[429] 1st Battalion, 22nd SS Police Regiment; killed in action 6 May 1943.
[430] 3rd Battalion, 22nd SS Police Regiment; submitted for War Service Cross 2nd Class.
[431] 3rd Battalion, 22nd SS Police Regiment; submitted for War Service Cross 2nd Class.
[432] 3rd Battalion, 22nd SS Police Regiment; wounded 23 April 1943; right leg amputated below knee; promoted to *SS-Untersturmführer* 21 June 1944; Iron Cross 2nd Class; Wound Badge Silver.
[433] 3rd Battalion, 22nd SS Police Regiment; submitted for War Service Cross 2nd Class.
[434] 22nd SS Police Regiment; submitted for War Service Cross 2nd Class.
[435] 3rd Battalion, 22nd SS Police Regiment; wounded in action 19 April 1943.
[436] 22nd SS Police Regiment; submitted for War Service Cross 2nd Class.
[437] 1st Battalion, 22nd SS Police Regiment; wounded in action 21 April 1943.
[438] 1st Battalion, 22nd SS Police Regiment; wounded in action 19 April 1943.
[439] 22nd SS Police Regiment; submitted for War Service Cross 2nd Class.
[440] 3rd Battalion, 22nd SS Police Regiment; wounded in action 2 May 1943.
[441] 3rd Battalion, 22nd SS Police Regiment; submitted for War Service Cross 2nd Class.
[442] 3rd Battalion, 22nd SS Police Regiment; submitted for War Service Cross 2nd Class.
[443] 3rd Battalion, 22nd SS Police Regiment; wounded in action 23 April 1943.
[444] 1st Battalion, 22nd SS Police Regiment; submitted for War Service Cross 2nd Class; wounded in action 21 April 1943.
[445] 3rd Battalion, 22nd SS Police Regiment; submitted for War Service Cross 2nd Class.
[446] 3rd Battalion, 22nd SS Police Regiment; submitted for War Service Cross 2nd Class.
[447] 3rd Battalion, 22nd SS Police Regiment; submitted for War Service Cross 2nd Class.
[448] 1st Battalion, 22nd SS Police Regiment; killed in action 6 May 1943.
[449] 3rd Battalion, 22nd SS Police Regiment; submitted for War Service Cross 2nd Class.
[450] 3rd Battalion, 22nd SS Police Regiment; submitted for War Service Cross 2nd Class.
[451] 22nd SS Police Regiment; awarded War Service Cross 2nd Class.
[452] 3rd Battalion, 22nd SS Police Regiment; submitted for War Service Cross 2nd Class.
[453] 1st Battalion, 22nd SS Police Regiment; wounded in action 19 April 1943.
[454] 3rd Battalion, 22nd SS Police Regiment; submitted for War Service Cross 2nd Class.
[455] 3rd Battalion, 22nd SS Police Regiment; submitted for War Service Cross 2nd Class.
[456] 3rd Battalion, 22nd SS Police Regiment; wounded in action 23 April 1943.
[457] 3rd Battalion, 22nd SS Police Regiment; submitted for War Service Cross 2nd Class.
[458] 3rd Battalion, 22nd SS Police Regiment; submitted for War Service Cross 2nd Class.
[459] Awarded War Service Cross 2nd Class.
[460] Awarded War Service Cross 2nd Class.
[461] Awarded War Service Cross 2nd Class.
[462] Awarded War Service Cross 2nd Class.
[463] Awarded War Service Cross 2nd Class.
[464] 3rd Company, 23rd SS Police Regiment; wounded in action 13 May 1943.
[465] Awarded War Service Cross 2nd Class.
[466] Awarded War Service Cross 2nd Class.
[467] Awarded War Service Cross 2nd Class.
[468] Awarded War Service Cross 2nd Class.
[469] Killed in action near Kraftborn on 31 January 1945.
[470] Wounded in action 19 April 1943.
[471] Wounded in action 21 April 1943.
[472] Wounded in action 23 April 1943.
[473] Wounded in action 21 April 1943.
[474] Wounded in action 25 April 1943.
[475] Wounded in action 19 April 1943.
[476] Acquitted by a Hamburg court on 3 June 1976 of complicity in the deportation of the Warsaw Ghetto and of murder at Trawniki.
[477] Wounded in action 19 April 1943.
[478] Killed in action 22 April 1943.
[479] Wounded in action 19 April 1943.
[480] Wounded in action 19 April 1943.
[481] Wounded in action 24 April 1943.
[482] Killed in action 22 April 1943.
[483] Wounded in action 27 April 1943.

8

CONCLUSION

"In Warsaw the wrong methods were applied."[1]

- Odilo Globocnik

The preceding study points us in the direction of many interesting conclusions concerning the German participation in quelling the Warsaw Ghetto Uprising. Let us begin with establishing some small findings and then work our way up to grander-scale judgments.

First, let us dispel a few exaggerations. The Warsaw Ghetto Uprising did not signal the beginning of the end for the German armed forces in World War II. It did not turn the tide in the favor of the allies in Europe. It did not cause Hitler to shift massive numbers of troops from the front lines to protect the interior areas of the *Reich*. The average German soldier, even the average *Waffen-SS* soldier, at the front in Russia felt absolutely no impact as a result of the Ghetto Uprising. The supplies traveling through Warsaw toward the front-lines were never disrupted for even one day as a result of the fighting in April and May of 1943. The use of two obsolete Czech tanks and a handful of armored cars did not deprive the front of much-needed armored vehicles. While perhaps a few hundred recruits – and this is debatable – were delayed from reporting to the front by a couple of weeks, the outcome of the upcoming battle at Kursk depended not a whit on this. Having said all this, however, there were ramifications.

Although neither the Jewish resistance nor the Polish resistance perhaps realized it at the time, the German security apparatus did not adhere to the principle of unity of command. The SS and Police Leader for Warsaw was held responsible for everything that happened in the city. That call to accounting cost von Sammern his job. However, it appears that the KdS not only took operational orders from the SSPF, they also received operational instructions straight from Berlin. Jürgen Stroop discussed this dual chain of command after the war in an affidavit:[2]

> *SS-Obersturmbannführer* Dr. Hahn was Commander of the Security Police of Warsaw at that time. Hahn gave the Security Police their orders concerning the tasks in this action. These orders were not given to Hahn by me, but came from Kaltenbrunner in Berlin. As SS and Police Leader of Warsaw I gave no orders to the Security police. All orders came to Hahn from Kaltenbrunner in Berlin. For example, in June or July of the same year [1943], I was together with Hahn in Kaltenbrunner's office and Kaltenbrunner told me that while Hahn and I must work together, all basic orders to the Security Police must come from him in Berlin.

We must certainly take Stroop's statement with a grain of salt. Undoubtedly he was being severely pressured to give highly damaging testimony to be used against Kaltenbrunner at trial. He may have thought that telling the prosecutors what they wanted to hear might save him from the hangman's noose (it didn't.) But clearly, Stroop did not have complete operational control that Himmler intended his Higher SS and Police Leaders and SS and Police Leaders to have. Such was the Byzantine nature of the SS. Dual command structures present many problems. Entities working for different bosses have different agendas, which are often hard to pull together. It is not inconceivable to believe that German anti-resistance efforts were hampered by such an arrangement.

Walter Bellwidt's testimony after the war as the former commander of the 3rd SS Training and Replacement Battalion sheds new light on a variety of points found in the Stroop Report. Of his several pages of testimony, replete with numerous "I do not recall" answers, are four interesting observations:

- Among the Ghetto inhabitants were not only Jews but also German deserters.
- Bellwidt received an order from Berlin to make his troops available for the mission "but only trained personnel, meaning no recruits."
- Bellwidt observed at least thirty to forty dead and wounded during the initial encounter on 19 April.
- Odilo Globocnik was fighting with Stroop about something in Warsaw during the Ghetto Uprising.

The statement made about German deserters is a fascinating one. Just how many German deserters were in the Ghetto? Were they Army, SS or *Luftwaffe*? Did they still have their weapons and ammunition, and if so, did these deserters fight against the German troops? It is likely that these renegades from military service lived in that section known as the "Wild Ghetto," when Stroop's forces overran that area what happened to these men? Unfortunately, none of my research for this book can answer these fascinating questions.

Bellwidt's second point indicates that he sent combat veterans into the fight versus trainees. Most postwar accounts of the Ghetto Uprising indicate the opposite, that the Germans sent many untrained or partially trained recruits into the fight. Bellwidt's statement is not supported by the casualty figures for the battalion. The unit suffered twenty-seven casualties according to Stroop (not including the two from the Soviet air attack.) Twenty-one of these casualties (78%) were men of the *SS-Panzergrenadier* and *SS-Sturmmann* ranks; that is generally to younger soldiers still in training. While Bellwidt may have initially attempted to only commit combat veterans, the casualty figures indicate that he was not successful in this effort. But it is interesting to note that someone in Berlin wanted to commit only more experienced troops. I believe he sent a mixture of both. Examining the battalion's personnel reports, each company not only had inexperienced trainees but also veteran trainers and a non-commissioned officer chain of command. Logically, these mixed squads and platoons would have been committed as units. The troops would have been used to receiving orders from their sergeants, and these experienced non-commissioned officers would have known how to handle emergency situations. The training cadre may have even viewed the Ghetto Uprising as an unforecast practical exercise.

SS-Hauptsturmführer Wilhelm Plänk, the commander of the SS Cavalry Replacement Detachment, also presented interesting observations after the war. Two of Plänk's major assertions were that the men of his unit that were in the fighting were untrained recruits and that they did not fight together as units, i.e., they were distributed as individuals to other formations. Let's look at Plänk's assertions. First, the Stroop Report shows that the SS Cavalry Replacement Detachment had non-commissioned officers wounded in action on 20 April, 24 April and 7 May, with sergeants wounded in action on 25 April, 26 April, 5 May and 10 May. All these men were assumed to be well-trained veterans; Plänk did not just send raw recruits into the action. Second, military logic would favor the use of the SS cavalry troops as integral small units, not as individual replacements. The detachment sent five officers and three hundred and eighty-one men to Stroop on the first day of the operation. In all likelihood these men were employed together as squads and platoons, if not as companies (or troops [*Schwadron*] as they are called in the cavalry.) Sending individual soldiers or pairs of soldiers to different elements out of a formation of almost four hundred would have taken an inordinately long time. Then, in the evening, accounting for all these troops would have been a nightmare for the chain of command. This does not even take into account combat efficiency, the first and foremost consideration of a commander, which dictates that units that live, train and fight together are far more efficient than ad hoc formations put together at the last moment. If Plänk allowed his men to be distributed in penny packets, then he was not half the commander his later record purported him to be. In any case, despite their dislike at being placed under Stroop's command, the two *Waffen-SS* commanders had little option. Max Jesuiter described the relationship in post-war testimony:[3]

> As I reported earlier, conflicts between Stroop and the leaders of the *Waffen-SS* units resulted over the requisitioning of *Waffen-SS* forces. This must have happened as early as the second or third day of the mission. After that Stroop contacted Himmler by teletype and requested 100% commanding power, which he also was granted.

Walter Bellwidt's and Wilhelm Plänk's statements on troops and casualties add more fuel to a fire that will never be extinguished. Just how many Germans became casualties during the Ghetto Uprising? While I believe that the true numbers will never be known, we can conduct some analysis of the various numbers. The following sources show the wide disparity in assessing German losses:

Stroop Report	16 killed	85 wounded
Central Archives of the Polish Ministry of Internal Affairs		
	400 killed	1,000 wounded
Polish underground	86 killed	420 wounded

These numbers obviously vary. What we can say is that the Germans had a better-than-average opportunity to evacuate their wounded to excellent medical facilities in Warsaw, which means that the ratio of killed to wounded was probably not much worse than 1:5. That tends to call into question the estimate by the Central Archives of the Polish Ministry of Internal Affairs, which would have the ratio of killed-to-wounded at 2:5. Interestingly, the Polish underground calculated ratio is also approximately 1:5. Second, during the research for this book, I examined hundreds of individual soldier records, primarily from the 3rd SS Panzergrenadier Training and Replacement Battalion, one of the two largest contributors of forces to the action. According to the Stroop Report, this unit suffered four killed and twenty-three wounded. Of these wounded, one man was burned on the face (he was in one of the tanks when it was set on fire), one received a gunshot wound to the left ankle and three were hit with grenade shrapnel. In no case did any of the hundreds of individual personnel records I examined indicate that a soldier was wounded during the Ghetto Uprising but was not included on Stroop's by-name list of casualties. While the sample of thirteen known wound causes for the attacking Germans at the Ghetto is admittedly small, it would indicate that a high percentage of the wounded became casualties through grenade shrapnel. It is clear that the resistance fighters possessed hundreds of grenades and homemade bombs, it is also possible that the shrapnel came from German-thrown grenades in the close confines of the Ghetto. In any case, soldiers sustaining grenade wounds who have access to prompt, competent medical treatment, clearly available in Warsaw, frequently do not succumb to these wounds.[4] The following table lists the causes for all wounds that are known:

TABLE 8

KNOWN WOUNDS FOR GERMANS AT THE WARSAW GHETTO

Name	Date Wounded	Type of Wound
Friedrich Scholz	19 April 1943	Facial Burns
Johann Tyrek	19 April 1943	Gunshot
Heinz Kruse	19 April 1943	Pistol Shot, Stomach
Valentin Malle	20 April 1943	Gunshot, Lower Leg
Josef Siegert	20 April 1943	Gunshot, Lung
Hans Dehmke (KIA)	22 April 1943	Grenade Shrapnel
Erich Waclawik	23 April 1943	Grenade Shrapnel
Oskar Hexel	23 April 1943	Lower Leg (Amputated)
Siegfried Böckmann	25 April 1943	Gunshot, Upper Ankle
Fritz Krenzke	25 April 1943	Gunshot, Foot
Johann Lebisch	28 April 1943	Grenade Shrapnel, Knee
Hans Forster	6 May 1943	Grenade Shrapnel, Back
Martin Enzbrunner	14 May 1943	Grenade Shrapnel, Face

Hence, I believe that German casualties were probably close to Stroop's numbers, although they could have been a little higher.[5] Stroop submitted his report each day; he knew that a deliberately false report could come back to haunt him. It would be difficult for Stroop to make large changes in the casualty figures after the battle was over, if he had already gone on record each day with different numbers. And as we have seen, Stroop had no idea how long the fighting would last.

While we will never know for sure, there is one explanation for the casualties that supports both the figures in the Stroop Report and those different numbers given by Jewish survivors of the fighting. Stroop's summaries concentrate on German casualties. He mentions a few of the "Trawniki Men" but does not list Latvian or Lithuanian casualties. He may not have received timely reports from these units or he could have thought that Himmler was not interested in what happened to these auxiliary troops. These Latvian and Lithuanian units could have suffered dozens of killed and wounded, exactly the figures that the surviving defenders mentioned in their accounts of the fighting. With the smoke, fire, bullets and explosions constantly occurring, it would have been very easy for the defenders to see enemy troops falling and then making an assumption that these were German troops. Such an explanation could account for many more Nazi casualties than were listed in the Stroop Report. Jürgen Stroop may have been close to the mark, concerning German casualties, but the defenders could be correct on overall enemy casualties if Latvians and Lithuanians are added.

Walter Bellwidt's final comment concerning Odilo Globocnik is interesting because it corroborates Georg Michalsen's testimony that Globocnik visited Warsaw on 21 April 1943. We know that many of Globocnik's *Operation Reinhard* officers were detailed to Warsaw during the deportations in July through September 1942 and again during the Ghetto Uprising; I believe we can now pinpoint with certainty that Odilo Globocnik was in the city. I am convinced that Bellwidt is to be believed; the chief of *Operation Reinhard* appears to have witnessed what transpired in Warsaw, if only for a few hours.

This leads us to a rather obvious question. Why did the Nazis not completely liquidate the Warsaw Ghetto in the summer of 1942 rather than simply deport some 250,000 persons leaving tens of thousands alive? They had the Jews psychologically defeated in September 1942. The resistance was unable at that time to mount any significant defense. Once again, Israel Gutman provides a plausible explanation in *The Jews of Warsaw, 1939-1943: Ghetto, Underground, Revolt.* Gutman lists three major factors that were a part of the German decision to hold off completing the murder operations that summer:[6]

- By 1942 there was a steady intensification of the shortage of manpower harnessed to the German war effort. The armament authorities exerted great pressure to protect their workers, in this case Jews, in their factories.
- The Nazis feared that totally liquidating the Ghetto in one fell swoop would lead to the destruction of existing assets, such as factories, within the Ghetto that the SS wanted to transfer intact to other locations.
- The SS intended to employ some remaining Jews to collect, store and guard abandoned property in preparation for shipment to the *Reich.*

This decision became a miscalculation. Gerald Reitlinger, in his work *The Final Solution: The Attempt to Exterminate the Jews of Europe 1939-1945*, states that:[7]

> . . . in neglecting to make the Warsaw Ghetto a true concentration camp in October 1942, Himmler miscalculated. It is true that this might have meant the combing out of each building separately, but that would have been easier in October than it proved to be in the following April.

Miscalculations abounded at other levels of decision-making as well. Jürgen Stroop violated numerous principles of war in his handling of the quelling of the Ghetto Uprising. An interesting comparison is to review several fundamentals on war as expressed by the noted Chinese military philosopher Sun Tzu, and then to compare Stroop's actions with these standards.

- All warfare is based on deception – Sun Tzu.[8]

Stroop had no deception plan. The Germans almost announced the first day's fight as their troops arrived at the Ghetto entrances several hours before the attack even began and then stood around in full view and just waited until dawn. Stroop thought that by varying the start time each day for his Ghetto sweeps he would fool the Jews. He didn't.

- If you know yourself but not the enemy, for every victory gained you will also suffer a defeat – Sun Tzu.[9]

SS-Brigadeführer Stroop possessed little detailed knowledge of the Jewish resistance forces inside the Ghetto. He seemed amazed that they possessed various weapons and was stunned by their ferocity in fighting. Stroop appears to have been overly concerned on where the Jews were in the Ghetto, not what they could do against his troops. As a result, Nazi forces appear to have frequently been the victims of ambush. Additionally, Stroop does not appear to have had an accurate count of the total number of Jews in the Ghetto. Part of that responsibility lies with others. Dr. Richard Korherr, the chief statistician of the SS, stated in a report that 50,000 Jews remained in the Ghetto as of 31 December 1942.[10] However, Heinrich Himmler, during his trip to Warsaw, was informed on 9 January 1943 that 35,000 Jews remained in the Ghetto, of whom 20,000 were said to be armaments workers.[11] Nevertheless, Himmler wrote to Friedrich Krüger on 20 January 1943 that he believed that there were 40,000 Jews in the Ghetto.[12] All these numbers would subsequently proven to be low. Either the *Gestapo* section in the KdS failed to obtain adequate information concerning the defenders in the Ghetto or Stroop chose not to listen to their reports. Either conclusion is plausible.

- Whoever is first in the field and awaits the coming of the enemy will be fresh for the fight; whoever is second in the field and has to hasten to battle will arrive exhausted – Sun Tzu.[13]

Stroop pulled out his attacking troops each night and sent them back to their barracks; some had to travel twenty kilometers. He generally did this around 2100 hours. Given their transportation time back to their cantonment areas, supper and an accountability formation, the soldiers probably did not get to sleep until 2300 hours. Their leaders most likely awoke them at 0400 hours so they could draw equipment, wash, eat breakfast, hold another formation, load their vehicles and move back to the Ghetto area in time to receive their orders for the day, all before the attacks would begin at 0900 or 1000 hours. After several days of this routine the troops undoubtedly were exhausted. Such a tactic also allowed the Jewish defenders to reoccupy terrain that they had lost during the day. This undoubtedly caused the Germans to fight again and again for the same city block.

• When you surround an army, leave an outlet free. Do not press a desperate foe too hard – Sun Tzu.[14]

Sun Tzu's adage does not mean that the enemy would be allowed to escape, simply to have him believe that there is a road to safety and thus prevent the enemy to fight with a courage born of despair. The Jews knew there was no way out for them; they believed that they would be killed in action or be sent to the gas chambers of Treblinka. Therefore, the resistance had no incentive in survival. Stroop never understood the motivation for Jewish resistance in the Ghetto. Yitzhak Arad states in his "The Armed Jewish Resistance in Eastern Europe" contribution to *The Holocaust and History: The Known, The Unknown, The Disputed and The Reexamined*, that one of the major aims of the Ghetto Uprising was revenge. His support comes from a letter written by Mordechai Anielewicz during the fighting in which he stated:[15]

> The dream of my life has risen to become fact. Self-defense in the Ghetto will have been a reality. Jewish armed resistance and revenge are facts. I have been a witness to the magnificent, heroic fighting of Jewish men in battle.

Stroop underestimated this revenge factor and also did not comprehend just how long the action would take. Dan Kurzman, author of *The Bravest Battle: The Twenty-eight Days of the Warsaw Ghetto Uprising*, presents his own succinct view of why the battle lasted so long. Kurzman states:[16]

> This battle lasted as long as it did because, essentially, there was no room for bargaining on either side. The Germans, led by SS Major General Jürgen Stroop, were bound by Nazi ideology to murder all captured Jews, either on the spot or in death camps. The Jews, most of them led by Mordechai Anielewicz, were bound by a pact of honor to die by their own hands rather than surrender. This was truly a battle to the death. And it took time to root out and kill tens of thousands of people.

While Stroop may have been in ignorance as to the damage a long siege inflicted, higher officials in the government did understand the ramifications of a delayed struggle. Dr. Josef Goebbels maintained an extensive set of diaries from 1942 to the end of the war. He mentioned the Ghetto Uprising on four dates. The first was on 25 April 1943 when Goebbels wrote:[17]

> From a report from the occupied areas I gather that a truly grotesque situation obtains in Warsaw. The Jews tried to leave the Ghetto by subterranean passages. Thereupon these underground passages were flooded. The Ghetto is now under artillery fire. When such conditions prevail in an occupied city, it certainly cannot be said to be pacified. It is high time that we evacuate the Jews just as quickly as possible from the General Government.
>
> In Warsaw conditions are chaotic not only in the Ghetto, but also among sections of the Polish population. It would be a good thing if a new man – a person who could put an end to these difficulties . . . filled the post of governor general.

According to his diary, Goebbels next wrote about the action on 1 May 1943 when he noted:[18]

> The only noteworthy item is the exceedingly serious fights in Warsaw between the police and even a part of our *Wehrmacht* on the one hand and the rebellious Jews on the other. The Jews have actually succeeded in making a defensive position of the Ghetto. Heavy engagements are being fought there which led even the Jewish Supreme Command's issuing daily communiqués. Of course the fun won't last very long. But it shows what is to be expected of the Jews when they are in possession of arms. Unfortunately some of their weapons are good German ones, especially machine-guns. Heaven only knows how they got them. Attempts at assassination and acts of sabotage are occurring in the General Government at far beyond the normal rate.

The third entry by Josef Goebbels in his diary concerning Warsaw occurred on 10 May 1943. Goebbels wrote:[19]

> The fights in the Warsaw Ghetto have largely petered out. I received a secret report on the mysterious questions as to how the Jews got hold of the large supplies of arms with which they defended themselves. For the most part they bought them from our brave allies as they were fleeing homeward and in Warsaw got rid of their weapons for good money. There are soldiers for you!

Goebbels made an interesting remark in his diary on 22 May 1943, which was technically, according to Stroop, after the end of the Ghetto Uprising:[20]

> The battle of the Warsaw Ghetto continues. The Jews are still resisting. On the whole, however, resistance is no longer dangerous and has virtually been broken.

The numbers seem to support the assertion of Josef Goebbels. Stroop reports, and there is little evidence to doubt this portion of his account, that SS forces killed 7,000 Jews in action. Stroop further asserts that an additional 5,000 to 6,000 Jews were killed but that their bodies were never found under the rubble. Stroop sent 6,929 Jews to Treblinka where most died in the gas chambers within hours of arriving at this extermination camp. A quick addition concludes that the Nazis, therefore, killed 13,000 Jews in the Ghetto itself and caused roughly 7,000 to perish shortly after leaving the Ghetto – 20,000 dead in all. Additionally, the Nazis deported 42,136 Jews to several labor camps. Trawniki received 6,000. Poniatowa absorbed another 14,000. And the old airport camp at Lublin took in 22,136. Many of those who went to Lublin later went to Budzyn and the Heinkel factory as slave laborers or to Skarzysko-Kamienna and the Hugo Schneider munitions factory. Other Jews went from Lublin to Auschwitz. After the war, Max Jesuiter elaborated on the killings:[21]

> I am of the opinion that these approximately 7,000 Jews who were killed in the Ghetto also include those Jews who were shot during battle, as also those who were shot outside of the battle scene. Otherwise, Stroop would have had to mention another figure. In my opinion, 7,000 is the total number of Jews who were shot in Warsaw during fighting and outside of the fighting. In this summarizing Teletype it is mentioned that 6,929 Jews were liquidated by their being transported to Treblinka. If I am asked whether I knew that Stroop had gotten an assured confirmation for this, namely that all people who were transported to Treblinka were killed there, I must state that I have never seen or heard about such a confirmation in writing, per teletype or by telephone. I also know nothing about tales and statements by Stroop that he himself had received such a confirmation. I believe much more that it was an irrevocable conviction of Stroop that the people who got to Treblinka also had to go to the gas chambers. At that time this conviction was clear to us. Naturally, this does not preclude that it is possible when by coincidence acute labor shortage was present, people out of these transports were selected for labor. I have no knowledge about this.

And the killings still did not stop. The Warsaw Ghetto Uprising had rocked Heinrich Himmler back on his heels concerning the remaining Jews in the General Government. Sometime in the next several months the *Reichsführer-SS* decided that all the Jews in Hans Frank's empire must be killed. In November 1943 the Germans decided to eliminate the remaining 43,000 Jews at Treblinka, at Trawniki and at Poniatowa in an operation they termed *Erntefest* (Fall Harvest).[22] A soldier in the 1st Battalion, 22nd SS Police Regiment, recalls what transpired:[23]

> During early November/December 1943 the sudden order came from the battalion that every base had to contribute all available forces for a special mission. The 1st Battalion of the 22nd SS Police Regiment gathered in one of the barracks at Lublin. My company leader B. and my platoon commander M. were among them. One morning we were taken by truck to about twenty to fifty kilometers outside of Lublin. Here in the forest there was a Jewish camp. We were informed that the Jews were to be shot. We of the First Company were ordered to close the area off. I think that parts of the other companies belonged to the shooting commandos. I also saw many members of the SS and the SD.
>
> We of the First Company formed a closed-off path from the gate of the camp to the ditch were the shooting took place. The path was about 150 meters long.
>
> The shootings started immediately. In front of the gate to the camp, the Jews had to strip naked and had to proceed to the ditch with raised hands. Here we separated them by sex and shot them. The children were with their mothers. The shootings lasted all day long. I myself was standing in the row of guards near the gate of the camp. In my estimation, the ditch was about 100 meters away. The Jews were shot with machine pistols. The men doing the shooting were policemen of our battalion, but I could not recognize them. I can only say that my superiors were also standing at the ditch.

In the Nazi mind, finally the Warsaw Ghetto was no more. The Jews were gone. More than 1,000 buildings in the Ghetto were destroyed.[24] But the Nazis were wrong. Goebbels, Himmler, Globocnik, Krüger, von Sammern, Stroop, Hahn, Jesuiter and the others believed that they could destroy the Warsaw Ghetto by razing its buildings with fire, artillery and high explosives. They were wrong. The Nazis thought that they could destroy the Warsaw Ghetto by killing its inhabitants in the sewers of the city, in the gas chambers of Treblinka and in the muddy, cold ditches outside of Trawniki and Poniatowa. They were wrong. The Warsaw Ghetto could not be destroyed – could never be destroyed – because it no longer consisted of just buildings, apartments, avenues or streets. It was no longer even men, women and children – the Ghetto had turned into something more. Jürgen Stroop and the SS, supported by German Army troops with tanks, machine-guns, demolition charges and flame-throwers, did not understand the nature of the battle. They were predictable in their attack routes and formations. They allowed the defenders to regroup each night and thus had to fight for the same buildings day after day. The Nazis treated the fighting as a simple hunting exercise and so took their time. However, the Jewish Resistance fought the battle otherwise, and it was the tenacity of the defenders and the extended length of the fight that propelled the Warsaw Ghetto into history. Knowing they were ultimately doomed, the defenders fought not for victory, but for dignity and thereby transformed the fighting in the Warsaw Ghetto into a struggle of legendary proportions.

The Germans won the battle. But the 2,000 officers and men of the dreaded *Gestapo*, *Sicherheitsdienst* and *Waffen-SS* – well-equipped, decorated combat veterans of the eastern front – could not defeat the legend.[25]

Notes:

[1] Gerald Reitlinger, *The Final Solution: The Attempt to Exterminate the Jews of Europe, 1939-1945*. (Northvale, N.J.: Jason Aronson, Inc., 1987), p. 271.

The Germans learned from their experiences, however, and put their new knowledge to work in Warsaw one year later. The Polish Uprising, which began on 1 August 1944, threatened to cut the lines of supply and communication to the German 9th Army fighting further to the east. Colonel General Heinz Guderian, the German Army Chief of Staff, made a request to Hitler that the Army be allowed to put down the revolt and that the city correspondingly be declared part of the army operations zone. Hitler refused Guderian's request and gave the mission to *Reichsführer-SS* Heinrich Himmler as Commander in Chief of the Replacement Army. Himmler, in turn, placed a senior SS general in charge. The Germans used more sophisticated weapons and tactics in the fight for the city than they had in the Ghetto in 1943. On 14 August the Germans introduced thirty-five "Goliaths" in Panzer Detachment 302 and a 38cm storm mortar in Assault Mortar Company 1000. On 18 August they brought in the 60cm mortar "Karl" in Heavy Artillery Battery 638.

The radio-controlled demolition vehicle "Goliath" was a small tracked robot, which weighed about eight hundred pounds, carried an explosive charge of between one hundred sixty and two hundred twenty pounds. The theory behind the weapon was that a remote human operator would guide it to an obstacle or structure that needed to be destroyed – but that was too heavily defended for an open assault by troops. Some models were controlled by signals sent through a wire connected to the vehicle, while others were radio controlled. Once in position, the operator detonated the explosive charge, which destroyed the "Goliath" and the target as well.

The 60cm mortar "Karl" was the biggest German artillery piece to ever be mounted on a self-propelled carriage. Capable of firing a huge explosive projectile with a high trajectory to penetrate underground fortifications, it was initially designed for use against the French Maginot Line. Six weapons were built and used at Brest-Litovsk and Sevastopol earlier in the war. They were initially constructed with 60cm barrels but several were refitted with 54cm pieces to increase the weapon's range. The weapon at 132 tons was actually too heavy to travel far on its self-propelled carriage and would be transported by train, suspended between two special railway cars on a special steel truss. The "Karl" was then detrained and set up in a local firing position. An accompanying special ammunition loader, based on a Mark IV tank chassis and equipped with a 2.5 ton crane, would load the ammunition into the "Karl's" huge loading tray prior to firing.

Himmler also brought special shock troops to quell the city; one was the SS Dirlewanger unit. During the defeat of the 1944 Warsaw Uprising, the Dirlewanger Brigade burned prisoners alive with gasoline, impaled babies on bayonets and stuck them out of windows and hung women upside down from balconies. This was all according to Himmler's design to create sheer violence and terror, which would extinguish the revolt in just a few days. For a more thorough account of the SS at the 1944 Warsaw Uprising see *The Cruel Hunters: SS-Sonderkommando Dirlewanger, Hitler's Most Notorious Anti-partisan Unit*, by the author.

[2] International Military Tribunal, *Trial of the Major War Criminals Before the International Military Tribunal, Nürnberg, 14 November 1945 - 1 October 1946. Volume XI, Proceedings, 8 April 1946 – 17 April 1946*. (Nuremberg, Germany, 1947), p. 355.

[3] Wolfgang Scheffler and Helge Grabnitz, *Der Ghetto-Aufstand Warschau 1943*. (Munich, Germany: Goldmann Verlag, 1993), p. 185.

[4] During World War II, the German Central Archives for Military Medicine analyzed some 3,015,589 wounded soldiers with extremely detailed results. Overall, they found that of every 100 casualties, 24% were killed in action, 30% were seriously wounded and 46% were classified as lightly wounded. This compared to a casualty rate of 13.8% killed and 86.2% wounded in World War I. The archivists believed that the increased death rate was due, in part, to an increase in weapons' lethality; additionally, the greater fluidity of the World War II battlefields made casualty evacuation more difficult than in the more static World War I battlefields. In 1942, the Archives did a study as to the location of war wounds on the human body. They found that of all wounds inflicted on German soldiers 5% were skull wounds, 8% facial wounds, 1.3% throat wounds, 6.3% shoulder wounds, 7.3% chest wounds, 6.3% upper arm wounds, 16.5% lower arm wounds, 3.5% stomach wounds, 10.1% upper leg wounds, 28.3% lower leg wounds and 3.4% back wounds. By 1944 wounds were further categorized as to location on the body (such as direct hit (massive simultaneous multiple wounds), head, chest, stomach, back, throat, legs and arms) with respect to casualties who were fatally wounded, seriously wounded (but survived) and lightly wounded. It was shown that of those patients, who were fatally wounded, 42.61% had received head wounds while only 3.04% had been wounded in the legs. Leg wounds, 28.02%, on the other hand, were the most frequent injury for seriously wounded patients, while arm injuries, 37.77%, were the most frequent type of injury to those patients who were classified as lightly wounded. Source: French MacLean, *Quiet Flows the Rhine: German General Officer Casualties in World War II*. (Winnipeg, Canada: J. J. Fedorowicz Publishing, 1996).

[5] The author tried numerous avenues to secure by-name proof that Stroop omitted casualties from his report. In one instance, I reviewed the weekly *Befehlsblatt des Chefs der Sicherheitspolizei und des SD*, a weekly information sheet published by the RSHA in Berlin, concerning Security Police and SD activities (National Archives, National Archives Microfilm Publication A3345, *Series DS, Miscellaneous Collection*. Washington, D.C: Roll J043). In this source, I found the following KdS personnel listed as dying in Warsaw during April, May and June of 1943:

Kurt Zeidler (April 1943)
Edmund Lotholz (May 1943)
Herbert Schulz (May 1943)
Ewald Lange (May 1943)
Horst Corfel (May 1943)
Paul Ehnert (June 1943)

Edmund Lotholz is listed in the Stroop Report as killed in action but the others are not. Home Army assassins killed Herbert Schulz on 6 May as he walked to the KdS headquarters to work near Mokotowska Street. Ewald Lange was ambushed and killed by members of the Home Army on 22 May at Three Crosses Square. However, I could not find a cause of death for the other three and it could be that they died in some non-Ghetto Uprising related event or accident. Therefore, we cannot conclude with certainty that these three perished as a result of the Ghetto Uprising fighting.

[6] Israel Gutman, *The Jews of Warsaw, 1939-1943: Ghetto, Underground, Revolt*. (Bloomington, IN: Indiana University Press, 1982), pp. 277-278.

[7] Gerald Reitlinger, *The Final Solution: The Attempt to Exterminate the Jews of Europe, 1939-1945*, p. 271.

[8] Lionel Giles, *Sun Tzu on the Art of War*. (London), p. 6.

[9] Ibid., p. 25.

[10] Arno Mayer, *Why Did The Heavens Not Darken?* (New York: Pantheon Books, 1988), p. 401.

[11] Ibid., p. 400.

[12] Israel Gutman, *The Jews of Warsaw, 1939-1943: Ghetto, Underground, Revolt*, p. 307.

[13] Lionel Giles, *Sun Tzu on the Art of War*, p. 42.

[14] Ibid., p. 69.

[15] Michael Berenbaum and Abraham J. Peck, *The Holocaust and History: The Known, The Unknown, The Disputed and The Reexamined*. (Bloomington, Indiana: Indiana University Press, 1998), p. 594.

[16] Dan Kurzman, *The Bravest Battle: The Twenty-eight Days of the Warsaw Ghetto Uprising*. (New York: G.P. Putnam's Sons, 1976), p. 18.

[17] Louis P. Lochner, editor, *The Goebbels Diaries, 1942-1943*. (Garden City, NY: Doubleday & Company, 1948), pp. 343-344.

[18] Ibid., pp. 350-351.

[19] Ibid., p. 364.

[20] Ibid., p. 388.

[21] Wolfgang Scheffler and Helge Grabnitz, *Der Ghetto-Aufstand Warschau 1943*, p. 189.

[22] Thomas Sandkühler, *"Endlösung" in Galizien: Der Judenmord in Ostpolen und die Rettungsinitiativen von Berthold Beitz 1941-1944*. (Bonn, Germany: J.H.W. Dietz, 1996), p. 270.

[23] Wolfgang Scheffler and Helge Grabnitz, *Der Ghetto-Aufstand Warschau 1943*, p. 263.

[24] From a report by Ludwig Fischer. Source: Israel Gutman, *Resistance: The Warsaw Ghetto Uprising*. (Boston: Houghton Mifflin Company, 1994), p. 253.

[25] Hans Frank realized this fact to some extent. In December 1943 he stated the following to a group of *Luftwaffe* officers:

We have in this country one point which is the source of all evil: that is Warsaw. If we had no Warsaw in the General Government, we would not have four-fifths of the difficulties to contend with. Warsaw is, and will continue to be, a hotbed of turbulence, a point from which unrest spreads over the country.

(Source: Tadeusz Bielecki and Leszek Szymanski, Warsaw *Aflame: The 1933-1945 Years*. Los Angeles: Polamerica Press, 1973, p. 30.)

9

EPILOGUE

"A war waged with no regard for morale principles can never be won. There's such a thing as divine justice on earth."[1]

- Admiral Wilhelm Canaris, Chief of German Intelligence

There is one more question that must be answered to complete our look at the SS at Warsaw. What postwar legal price did the Nazis officers and enlisted men pay for the destruction of the Warsaw Ghetto? Certainly the actions in the Ghetto from 1940 to 1942 violated numerous internationally accepted legal codes. The 1942 mass deportations clearly fell into the category of murder and the more generic "crimes against humanity." It could also be argued that the actual destruction of the Ghetto during the 1943 Ghetto Uprising also fell into those genre, as well as into the classification as a war crime. The aforementioned crimes frequently call for the death penalty or, at the least, extensive periods of incarceration.

This study identified some 1,057 officers and enlisted men as serving in Warsaw during this period. Many, if not most, were involved to some degree of participation in the event or in tangential activities concerning the Ghetto. Some could never be prosecuted. Of the 103 SS officers in this study, it appears that eighteen were killed in action between May 1943 and May 1945. An additional three committed suicide at the end of the war or later when they were facing legal proceedings. More may have been killed during the war; the German personnel records contain spotty entries after February 1945, so it is quite possible that more fell in combat. Forty-five enlisted personnel of 954 identified in this study were killed in action during the war. Many more undoubtedly died during the conflict; the SS *Totenkopf* Division, to which many of the enlisted troops were later assigned, had one of the highest casualty rates of any unit in the German armed forces. Considering that perhaps as many as seventy-five or eighty percent of the SS officers and sixty or seventy percent of the enlisted men, who were at Warsaw, survived the conflict, one might think that postwar courts in Germany and Poland would have been busy handling dozens – perhaps hundreds – of cases. Such was not the case.

Six officers from this study, as well as two others, who worked at Treblinka, (see Appendix 5) appear to have been brought to trial for activities related to the Warsaw Ghetto Uprising by authorities in Poland and the Federal Republic of Germany (FRG). The results of these proceedings are shown in the following table:[2]

TABLE 9

SS OFFICERS BROUGHT TO JUSTICE FOR THE DESTRUCTION OF THE WARSAW GHETTO

Name	Trial Date	Location	Sentence
Dr. Ludwig Hahn	1975	Hamburg, FRG	Life
Otto Hantke	1974	Hamburg, FRG	Life
Franz Konrad	1951	Warsaw, Poland	Death
Georg Michalsen	1974	Hamburg, FRG	12 Years
Karl Mohwinkel	1974	Hamburg, FRG	Life
Jürgen Stroop	1951	Warsaw, Poland	Death

Five enlisted personnel, as well as eleven enlisted men at Treblinka, went before the judicial process as well. Trials took place in the Federal Republic of Germany and the German Democratic Republic (GDR). The following table shows the results of these proceedings:[3]

TABLE 10

SS ENLISTED SOLDIERS BROUGHT TO JUSTICE FOR THE DESTRUCTION OF THE WARSAW GHETTO

Name	Trial Date	Location	Sentence
Hans Bäcker	1975	Hamburg, FRG	7 Years
Josef Blösche	1969	Erfurt, GDR	Death
Karl Klaustermeyer	1965	Bielefeld, FRG	Life
Helmut Orf	1975	Hamburg, FRG	6 Years
Hugo Mielke	1960	Erfurt, GDR	Life

It therefore seems that only seven percent of the SS officers who had served at Warsaw and who had survived the war were brought to trial, while the figure is less than one percent for the enlisted SS ranks. There may well ultimately be divine justice, as claimed by Admiral Canaris, the *Wehrmacht's* intelligence chief, earlier in the war. But there certainly does not appear to have been much legal justice in Germany, either sought or obtained, against those involved in the destruction of a large portion of one of the great cities of Europe or for the murder of the hundreds of thousands of people who lived there.

Notes:

[1] Heinz Höhne, *Canaris: Hitler's Master Spy*. (Garden City, NY: Doubleday & Company, 1979), p. 364.

[2] Protected identity source in Germany, who, due to Germany's privacy laws, wishes to remain anonymous.

[3] Ibid.

APPENDICES

APPENDIX 1 – SS, UNIFORMED POLICE AND *KRIPO* RANKS

SS RANK	**POLICE RANK**	
Reichsführer-SS		Reichs Leader
SS-Oberstgruppenführer	Generaloberst der Polizei	General
SS-Obergruppenführer	General der Polizei	Lieutenant General
SS-Gruppenführer	Generalleutnant der Polizei	Major General
SS-Brigadeführer	Generalmajor der Polizei	Brigadier General
SS-Oberführer		Senior Colonel
SS-Standartenführer	Reichskriminaldirektor Regierungs- und Kriminal-Direktor Oberst der Schutzpolizei Oberst der Gendarmerie	Colonel
SS-Obersturmbannführer	Oberregierungs- und Kriminal-Rat Oberstleutnant der Schutzpolizei Oberstleutnant der Gendarmerie	Lieutenant Colonel
SS-Sturmbannführer	Regierungs- und Kriminal-Rat Kriminal-Direktor Kriminal-Rat Major der Schutzpolizei Major der Gendarmerie	Major
SS-Hauptsturmführer	Kriminal-Rat Kriminal-Kommissar Hauptmann der Schutzpolizei Hauptmann der Gendarmerie	Captain
SS-Obersturmführer	Kriminal-Kommissar Kriminal-Inspektor Oberleutnant der Schutzpolizei Revieroberleutnant der Schutzpolizei Oberleutnant der Gendarmerie Bezirksoberleutnant der Gendarmerie	First Lieutenant
SS-Untersturmführer	Kriminalobersekretär Kriminalsekretär Leutnant der Schutzpolizei Revierleutnant der Schutzpolizei Leutnant der Gendarmerie Bezirksleutnant der Gendarmerie	Second Lieutenant

ENLISTED

SS-Sturmscharführer	Kriminalsekretär Meister der Schutzpolizei Meister der Gendarmerie	Master Sergeant
SS-Hauptscharführer	Kriminaloberassistent Hauptwachtmeister der Schutzpolizei Hauptwachtmeister der Gendarmerie	Master Sergeant
SS-Oberscharführer	Kriminalassistent Zugwachtmeister der Schutzpolizei Revieroberwachtmeister der Schutzpolizei Zugwachtmeister der Gendarmerie Bezirksoberwachtmeister der Gendarmerie	Technical Sergeant
SS-Scharführer	Ausserplanmässiger Kriminalassistent Oberwachtmeister der Schutzpolizei Oberwachtmeister der Gendarmerie	Staff Sergeant
SS-Unterscharführer	Kriminalassistenten-anwärter Wachtmeister der Schutzpolizei Wachtmeister der Gendarmerie	Staff Sergeant
SS-Rottenführer	Rottwachtmeister der Schutzpolizei Rottwachtmeister der Gendarmerie	Sergeant
SS-Sturmmann	Unterwachtmeister der Schutzpolizei Unterwachtmeister der Gendarmerie	Corporal
SS-Oberschütze SS-Obergrenadier SS-Panzerobergrenadier SS-Oberreiter	Unterwachtmeister der Schutzpolizei Unterwachtmeister der Gendarmerie	Private First Class
SS-Schütze SS-Grenadier SS-Reiter SS-Panzergrenadier SS-Freiwilliger	Anwärter der Schutzpolizei Anwärter der Gendarmerie	Private

Note: The SS rank of *SS-Stabsscharführer* and and the Police rank of *Kompanie-Hauptwachtmeister* were position titles roughly equivalent to a company first sergeant.

Police general officers, who were also members of the SS, were often referred to as *SS-Brigadeführer und Generalmajor der Polizei, SS-Gruppenführer und Generalleutnant der Polizei or SS-Obergruppenführer und General der Polizei*, etc.

APPENDIX 2 – SS AND POLICE LEADERS 1939-1943 in POLAND

HIGHER SS AND POLICE LEADER "EAST"
HÖHERER SS UND POLIZEIFÜHRER OST (HSSPF)

SS-Obergruppenführer Friedrich-Wilhelm Krüger	4 October 1939 – 9 November 1943

SENIOR COMMANDER OF THE ORDER POLICE "GENERAL GOVERNMENT"
BEFEHLSHABER DER ORDNUNGSPOLIZEI (BdO)

Oberst der Schutzpolizei Emil Horing	1 October 1939 – 25 October 1939
General der Polizei Herbert Becker	25 October 1939 – 31 October 1940
Generalleutnant der Polizei Paul Riege	31 October 1940 – 22 August 1941
Oberst der Gendarmerie Rudolf Müller-Bonigk	22 August 1941 – September 1941
Generalleutnant der Polizei Gerhard Winkler	September 1941 – May 1942
General der Polizei Herbert Becker	May 1942 – August 1943

SENIOR COMMANDER OF THE SECURITY POLICE AND SECURITY SERVICE "GENERAL GOVERNMENT"
BEFEHLSHABER DER SICHERHEITSPOLIZEI UND SICHERHEITSDIENST (BdS)

SS-Brigadeführer Bruno Streckenbach	1 November 1939 – 14 January 1941
SS-Oberführer Eberhard Schöngarth	14 January 1941 – June 1943

SS AND POLICE LEADER "WARSAW"
SS UND POLIZEIFÜHRER WARSCHAU (SSPF)

SS-Gruppenführer Paul Moder	14 November 1939 – 4 August 1941
SS-Oberführer Arpad Wigand	4 August 1941 – 22 July 1942
SS-Oberführer Dr. Ferdinand von Sammern-Frankenegg	22 July 1942 – 19 April 1943
SS-Brigadeführer Jürgen Stroop	19 April 1943 – 13 September 1943

DISTRICT COMMANDER OF THE ORDER POLICE
KOMMANDEUR DER ORDNUNGSPOLIZEI (KdO)

Oberstleutnant der Schutzpolizei Karl Brenner	
Oberstleutnant der Schutzpolizei Joachim Petsch	
Oberst der Schutzpolizei Rudolf Haring	April 1943 – 15 July 1944

DISTRICT COMMANDER OF THE SECURITY POLICE AND SECURITY SERVICE
KOMMANDEUR DER SICHERHEITSPOLIZEI UND SICHERHEITSDIENST (KdS)

SS-Obersturmbannführer Josef Meisinger[1]	March 1940 – 1941
SS-Obersturmbannführer Johannes Müller	1941– 1 August 1941
SS-Obersturmbannführer Dr. Ludwig Hahn	1 August 1941 – 1944

[1] Meisinger was tried before the Polish Supreme National Court and found guilty of crimes against the population of Warsaw on 3 March 1947. He was executed shortly thereafter.

APPENDIX 3 – GERMAN PERSONNEL LOSSES DURING THE WARSAW GHETTO UPRISING

19 APRIL 1943

WOUNDED

SS-Panzergrenadier Friedrich Scholz [Face burned, Molotov cocktail]	5th Company, 3rd SS Panzergrenadier Training and Replacement Battalion
SS-Panzergrenadier Wilhelm Schneider	2nd Company, 3rd SS Panzergrenadier Training and Replacement Battalion
SS-Panzergrenadier Karl Genant	2nd Company, 3rd SS Panzergrenadier Training and Replacement Battalion
SS-Sturmmann Johann Tyrek [Gunshot wound]	SS Cavalry Replacement Detachment
SS-Schütze Fritz Böhm	SS Cavalry Replacement Detachment
SS-Schütze Karl Zechmeister	SS Cavalry Replacement Detachment
SS-Reiter Anton Imgrund	SS Cavalry Replacement Detachment
SS-Sturmmann Heinz Kruse [Pistol shot to lower right stomach]	SS Cavalry Replacement Detachment
SS-Reiter Anton Müller	SS Cavalry Replacement Detachment
SS-Oberreiter Oskar Reinke	SS Cavalry Replacement Detachment
SS-Reiter Günther Reitzig	SS Cavalry Replacement Detachment
SS-Reiter Franz Strobel	SS Cavalry Replacement Detachment
Wachtmeister der Schutzpolizei Wilhelm Klemm	3rd Battalion, 22nd SS Police Regiment
Oberwachtmeister der Schutzpolizei Kurt Sprotte	1st Battalion, 22nd SS Police Regiment
Wachtmeister der Schutzpolizei Rudolf Kreuz	1st Battalion, 22nd SS Police Regiment
SS-Sturmscharführer Rudolf Kosmala	Sicherheitspolizei
SS-Rottenführer Fritz Rührnschopf	Sicherheitspolizei
Wachmann Paul Nestarenko	Trawniki camp
Wachmann Borys Roschdestwenskyj	Trawniki camp
Wachmann Andrej Protschenko	Trawniki camp
Wachmann Andrej Dawidenko	Trawniki camp
Wachmann Michael Minenko	Trawniki camp

20 APRIL 1943

KILLED

SS-Panzergrenadier Paul Jäger	4th Company, 3rd SS Panzergrenadier Training and Replacement Battalion
Gefreiter Joseph Strupp	Light Alarm Flak Battery 3/VIII
Schütze Christian Hohbein	Light Alarm Flak Battery 3/VIII

WOUNDED

SS-Panzergrenadier Valentin Malle [Gunshot wound, lower right leg]	2nd Company, 3rd SS Panzergrenadier Training and Replacement Battalion
SS-Panzergrenadier Alfons Hausa	2nd Company, 3rd SS Panzergrenadier Training and Replacement Battalion
SS-Reiter Anton Heit	SS Cavalry Replacement Detachment
SS-Schütze Ludwig Schay	SS Cavalry Replacement Detachment
SS-Unterscharführer Robert Hauschild	SS Cavalry Replacement Detachment
SS-Reiter Johann Neugebauer	SS Cavalry Replacement Detachment
Feldwebel Josef Siegert [Gunshot through the lung]	Engineer Commando Rembertow
SS-Oberscharführer Sepp Mayowski	Trawniki camp

21 APRIL 1943

WOUNDED

SS-Reiter Georg Pöpl	SS Cavalry Replacement Detachment
Zugwachtmeister der Schutzpolizei Kurt Czesnik	3rd Battalion, 22nd SS Police Regiment
Zugwachtmeister der Schutzpolizei Erich Perschke	1st Battalion, 22nd SS Police Regiment
Zugwachtmeister der Schutzpolizei Otto Koglin	1st Battalion, 22nd SS Police Regiment
Wachmann Nikolai Huzulak	Trawniki camp
Wachmann Iwan Knyhynyzkyn	Trawniki camp

22 APRIL 1943

KILLED

Untersturmführer Hans Dehmke [Hand grenade explosion]	SS Cavalry Replacement Detachment
Wachmann Willi Stark	Trawniki camp
Wachmann Borys Odartschenko	Trawniki camp

23 APRIL 1943

WOUNDED

Zugwachtmeister der Schutzpolizei Erich Waclawik [Grenade shrapnel]	3rd Battalion, 22nd SS Police Regiment
Wachtmeister der Schutzpolizei Karl Neidhard	3rd Battalion, 22nd SS Police Regiment
Wachtmeister der Schutzpolizei Oskar Hexel [Right lower leg; amputated below the knee]	3rd Battalion, 22nd SS Police Regiment
Wachmann Grigor Iwanyschyn	Trawniki camp

24 APRIL 1943

WOUNDED

SS-Unterscharführer Franz Lüdtke	1st Company, 3rd SS Panzergrenadier Training and Replacement Battalion

Lüdtke's name is misspelled as Lüdzke in the Stroop Report. Additionally, Lüdtke's personnel file indicates that he was wounded on 23 April ***1942*** by grenade shrapnel to the left arm and head while serving on the eastern front, **not** in April 1943. It is very possible, even likely, that Lüdtke was not wounded during the Ghetto Uprising but was included in the Stroop Report due to a clerical error.

SS-Unterscharführer Fritz Vogel	SS Cavalry Replacement Detachment
SS-Reiter Johann Haller	SS Cavalry Replacement Detachment
Wachmann Emil Schmidt	Trawniki camp

25 APRIL 1943

WOUNDED

SS-Panzergrenadier Siegfried Böckmann [Gunshot wound, left upper ankle]	1st Company, 3rd SS Panzergrenadier Training and Replacement Battalion
SS-Rottenführer Fritz Krenzke [Gunshot wound, left foot]	SS Cavalry Replacement Detachment
SS-Scharführer Hugo Nieratschker	Sicherheitspolizei
Wachmann Jurko Kosatschok	Trawniki camp

26 APRIL 1943

WOUNDED

SS-Rottenführer Joseph Schuster	SS Cavalry Replacement Detachment

27 APRIL 1943

WOUNDED

SS-Panzergrenadier Friedrich Czwielung	5th Company, 3rd SS Panzergrenadier Training and Replacement Battalion
SS-Sturmmann Hans Petry	5th Company, 3rd SS Panzergrenadier Training and Replacement Battalion
Wachmann Wladimir Stasik	Trawniki camp

28 APRIL 1943

WOUNDED

SS-Panzergrenadier Walter Schmidt	1st Company, 3rd SS Panzergrenadier Training and Replacement Battalion
SS-Reiter Ludwig Török	SS Cavalry Replacement Detachment
SS-Reiter Alexander Wiesinger	SS Cavalry Replacement Detachment
SS-Reiter Johann Lebisch [Shrapnel right knee; leg amputated]	SS Cavalry Replacement Detachment

29 APRIL 1943

WOUNDED

SS-Schütze Johann Nissner	SS Cavalry Replacement Detachment

30 APRIL 1943
NO CASUALTIES REPORTED

1 MAY 1943

KILLED

Rottwachtmeister der Schutzpolizei Hans Bolze — 3rd Battalion, 22nd SS Police Regiment
SS-Rottenführer Edmund Lotholz — Sicherheitspolizei

2 MAY 1943

WOUNDED

SS-Panzergrenadier Werner Burchardt — 1st Company, 3rd SS Panzergrenadier Training and Replacement Battalion
Oberwachtmeister der Schutzpolizei Robert Linke — 3rd Battalion, 22nd SS Police Regiment

3 MAY 1943

WOUNDED

SS-Panzergrenadier Heinrich Meier — 5th Company, 3rd SS Panzergrenadier Training and Replacement Battalion
SS-Schütze Rudolf Hörnicke — SS Cavalry Replacement Detachment
SS-Schütze Hermann Herbst — SS Cavalry Replacement Detachment

4 MAY 1943
NO CASUALTIES REPORTED

5 MAY 1943

WOUNDED

SS-Rottenführer Fritz Wieck — SS Cavalry Replacement Detachment

Fritz Wieck died on 11 January 1944. His personnel file does not indicate the cause of death, but it may have been from complications of this wound.

6 MAY 1943

KILLED

Oberwachtmeister der Schutzpolizei Horst Riemer — 1st Battalion, 22nd SS Police Regiment
Wachtmeister der Schutzpolizei Rudolf Hartmann — 1st Battalion, 22nd SS Police Regiment

WOUNDED

SS-Unterscharführer Hans Forster [Grenade shrapnel in back and arm] — 1st Company, 3rd SS Panzergrenadier Training and Replacement Battalion
SS-Sturmmann Heinz Haushalter — 1st Company, 3rd SS Panzergrenadier Training and Replacement Battalion

7 MAY 1943

WOUNDED

SS-Unterscharführer Hugo Mielke — SS Cavalry Replacement Detachment

8 MAY 1943

KILLED

SS-Panzergrenadier Lorenz Bichler — 2nd Company, 3rd SS Panzergrenadier Training and Replacement Battalion
SS-Panzergrenadier Helmut Hinz — 4th Company, 3rd SS Panzergrenadier Training and Replacement Battalion

WOUNDED

SS-Unterscharführer Erich Schulz — 2nd Company, 3rd SS Panzergrenadier Training and Replacement Battalion
SS-Panzergrenadier Klemens Kapitza — 2nd Company, 3rd SS Panzergrenadier Training and Replacement Battalion
Schütze Otto Kiel — Engineer Commando Rembertow

9 MAY 1943
NO CASUALTIES REPORTED

10 MAY 1943

WOUNDED

SS-Rottenführer Willi Staab	SS Cavalry Replacement Detachment
SS-Schütze Gottlieb Zechmeister	SS Cavalry Replacement Detachment
SS-Sturmmann Wolfgang Preusse	SS Cavalry Replacement Detachment

11 MAY 1943

KILLED

SS-Sturmmann Heinz Lehmann	1st Company, 3rd SS Panzergrenadier Training and Replacement Battalion

12 MAY 1943

WOUNDED

SS-Schütze Otto Kyasch	SS Cavalry Replacement Detachment

13 MAY 1943

KILLED

SS-Panzergrenadier Heinz Stuwe [Air attack]	3rd Company, 3rd SS Panzergrenadier Training and Replacement Battalion
SS-Panzergrenadier Gerhard Fritz [Air attack]	3rd Company, 3rd SS Panzergrenadier Training and Replacement Battalion

WOUNDED

SS-Panzergrenadier Alfred Baldt	5th Company, 3rd SS Panzergrenadier Training and Replacement Battalion
SS-Panzergrenadier Otto Döppe	3rd Company, 3rd SS Panzergrenadier Training and Replacement Battalion
Wachtmeister der Schutzpolizei Otto Luenen	3rd Company, 23rd SS Police Regiment

14 MAY 1943

WOUNDED

SS-Panzergrenadier Franz Kosarz	3rd Company, 3rd SS Panzergrenadier Training and Replacement Battalion
SS-Oberscharführer Thomas Wachter [Grenade shrapnel]	4th Company, 3rd SS Panzergrenadier Training and Replacement Battalion
SS-Unterscharführer Martin Enzbrunner [Grenade shrapnel; lost right eye]	4th Company, 3rd SS Panzergrenadier Training and Replacement Battalion
SS-Panzergrenadier Hans Raeder	4th Company, 3rd SS Panzergrenadier Training and Replacement Battalion
SS-Rottenführer Joseph Posch	4th Company, 3rd SS Panzergrenadier Training and Replacement Battalion
SS-Schütze Johann Balogh	SS Cavalry Replacement Detachment
SS-Schütze Andreas Kuding	SS Cavalry Replacement Detachment
SS-Schütze Franz Bordican	SS Cavalry Replacement Detachment

15 MAY 1943

WOUNDED

Zugwachtmeister der Schutzpolizei Alfons Czapp	1st Battalion, 22nd SS Police Regiment

APPENDIX 4 – DAILY DEPORTATIONS FROM WARSAW TO TREBLINKA DURING *OPERATION REINHARD* 22 JULY – 21 SEPTEMBER 1942

DATE	*VICTIMS*
22 July	6,250
23 July	7,300
24 July	7,400
25 July	7,530
26 July	6,400
27 July	6,320
28 July	5,020
29 July	5,480
30 July	6,430
31 July	6,756
1 August	6,220
2 August	6,276
3 August	6,458
4 August	6,568
5 August	6,623
6 August	10,085
7 August	10,672
8 August	7,304
9 August	6,292
10 August	2,158
11 August	7,725
12 August	4,688
13 August	4,313
14 August	5,168
15 August	3,633

DATE	*VICTIMS*
16 August	4,095
17 August	4,160
18 August	3,926
19-24 August	20,000
25 August	3,002
26 August	est. 3,000
27 August	2,454
28 August	None
29 August	None
30 August	None
31 August	None
1 September	None
2 September	None
3 September	4,609
4 September	1,669
5 September	None
6 September	3,634
7 September	6,840
8 September	13,596
9 September	6,616
10 September	5,199
11 September	est. 5,000
12 September	4,806
21 September	2,196

APPENDIX 5 – SS PERSONNEL AT TREBLINKA

SS-Oberscharführer Max Bialas – conducted roll calls (killed at Treblinka, 1942)

SS-Obersturmführer Dr. Irmfried Eberl – first commandant of Treblinka (suicide 1948)

SS-Oberscharführer Kurt Franz – deputy to Franz Stangl (sentenced 1965, life imprisonment)

SS-Scharführer Erich Fuchs – electrician (sentenced 1966, 4 years)

SS-Unterscharführer August Hingst – cook

SS-Scharführer Josef Hirtreiter – unloaded transport trains (sentenced 1951, life imprisonment)

SS-Unterscharführer Otto Richard Horn – worked at the incinerator (sentenced 1965, acquitted)

SS-Oberscharführer Kurt Küttner – in charge of the Lower Camp (died before trial)

SS-Unterscharführer Erwin Herman Lambert – building team foreman (sentenced 1965, 4 years)

SS-Scharführer Mätzig

SS-Oberscharführer Heinrich Matthes – chief non-commissioned officer at the gas chambers (sentenced 1965, life imprisonment)

SS-Scharführer Willi Mentz – worked in Lazarette (sentenced 1965, life imprisonment)

SS-Scharführer August Miete – in charge of the Lazarette (sentenced 1965, life imprisonment)

SS-Rottenführer Gustav Münzberger – assistant at gas chambers (sentenced 1965, 12 years)

SS-Unterscharführer Franz Albert Rum – moved prisoners through the tube to gas chambers (sentenced 1965, 3 years; but died before imposition of sentence)

SS-Oberscharführer Otto Stadie – sergeant major of the camp (sentenced 1965, 7 years)

SS-Hauptsturmführer Franz Stangl – second commandant of Treblinka (sentenced, died 1971)

SS-Scharführer Franz Suchomel – in charge of "Gold Jews" who sorted jewelry (sentenced 1965, 7 years)

SS-Obersturmführer Richard Thomalla – in charge of the construction of camp

APPENDIX 6 – STROOP REPORT SUMMARY OF RESISTANCE LOSSES AND CAPTURED EQUIPMENT

Stroop Report, 24 May 1943

Addition Number 1 To The Report

Of the 56,065 Jews caught altogether, about 7,000 were destroyed in the former Ghetto during the operation. A further 6,929 Jews were destroyed by transporting them to T. II; the sum total of Jews destroyed is therefore 13,929. Beyond the number of 56,065 is an estimated number of 5,000 to 6,000 Jews destroyed by demolition of the bunkers or by perishing in the flames.

Addition Number 2 To The Report

Altogether 631 bunkers were destroyed

Addition Number 3 To The Report (Items Captured)

7 Polish rifles, 1 Russian rifle, 1 German rifle
59 pistols of various caliber
Several hundred hand-grenades to include Polish-made and hand-made
Several hundred incendiary bottles
Some homemade explosive charges
Some infernal machines with fuses
Large amounts of explosives, ammunition for all caliber of weapons to include machine-gun ammunition

With regard to the catch of arms one must take into consideration that in most cases we were not able to capture the weapons since the Jews and bandits would throw them into holes or hideouts before being captured. The smoke generated in the bunkers also prevented our men from discovering and capturing the weapons. Since we had to destroy the bunkers immediately, we were not in a position to search for weapons later on. The hand-grenades, explosive charges and incendiary bottles were used against the enemy once we captured them.

In addition, we captured 1,240 used uniform tunics (partly adorned with Iron Cross and East Front ribbons), 600 pair of used trousers, various pieces of field equipment, German steel helmets and 108 horses (of which 4 remain in the Ghetto on hearse detail.)

We also captured some 4.4 million zloty. We believe we have moreover some 5 to 6 million more zloty that have not been counted yet. Additionally we captured a considerable amount of foreign currency to include $14,300 in paper money, $9,200 in gold and large amounts of valuables to include rings, bracelets, watches, etc.

Addition Number 4 To The Report

With the exception of eight buildings (Police barracks, hospital and accommodations for working parties) the whole of the former Ghetto is completely destroyed. Where demolitions were not completed, only partition walls are still standing. But the ruins still contain enormous amounts of bricks and scrap material, which could be used elsewhere.

SOURCES

Published Books

Adler, Stanislaw. *In the Warsaw Ghetto: 1940-1943: An Account of an Eyewitness*. Jerusalem: Yad Vashem, 1982.

Ainsztein, Reuben. *The Warsaw Ghetto Revolt*. New York: Holocaust Library, 1979.

Aktion T4, 1939-1945. Berlin, FRG: Hentrich, 1989.

Angolia, LTC John R. *For Führer and Fatherland, Military, Political and Civil Awards of the Third Reich, Volumes 1 & 2*. San Jose, CA: R. James Bender Publishing, 1976.

Arad, Yitzhak. *Belzec, Sobibór, Treblinka: The Operation Reinhard Death Camps*. Bloomington, IN: Indiana University Press, 1987.

Barkai, Meyer. *The Ghetto Fighters*. New York: Tower, 1962.

Bartoszewski, Wladyslaw. *Warsaw Death Ring, 1939-1944*. Warsaw: Interpress Publishers, 1968.

Bayer, Hanns. *Kavallerie-Divisionen der Waffen-SS im Bild*. Osnabrück, FRG: Munin Verlag, 1982.

Bender, Roger James, and Taylor, Hugh Page. *Uniforms, Organization and History of the Waffen-SS, Volumes 1-5*. San Jose, CA: R. James Bender Publishing, 1971.

Berenbaum, Michael and Abraham J. Peck. *The Holocaust and History: The Known, The Unknown, The Disputed and The Reexamined*. Bloomington, Indiana: Indiana University Press, 1998.

Berg, Mary. *Warsaw Ghetto: A Diary*. New York: Fischer, 1945.

Bielecki, Tadeusz and Leszek Szymanski. *Warsaw Aflame: The 1933-1945 Years*. Los Angeles: Polamerica Press, 1973.

Birn, Ruth Bettina. *Die Höheren SS- und Polizeiführer: Himmler's Vertreter im Reich und in den besetzten Gebieten*. Düsseldorf, FRG: Droste, 1986.

Bradley, Dermot, Hildebrand, K.F., Rövekamp, Markus. *Die Generale des Heeres 1921-1945, Band 1: Ab – Bi, Band 2: Bl -Cz, Band 3: Da – Fl, Band 4: Fl – G*. Osnabrück, Germany: Biblio Verlag, 1993.

Buchheim, Hans, Martin Broszat, Hans-Adolf Jacobsen and Helmut Krausnick. *Anatomy of the SS State*. New York: Walker & Company, 1968.

Butler, Rupert. *The Black Angels: A History of the Waffen-SS*. New York: St. Martin's Press, 1979.

Chamberlain, Peter & Chris Ellis. *Pictorial History of Tanks of the World 1915-45*. Harrisburg, PA: Stackpole Books, 1972.

Ciborowski, Adolf and Stanislaw Jankowski. *Warsaw Rebuilt*. Warsaw: Polonia Publishing House, 1962.

Creveld, Martin van. *Fighting Power: German and U.S. Army Performance, 1939-1945*. London: Arms and Armour Press, 1983.

Dienstaltersliste der Schutzstaffel der NSDAP, Stand vom 1. December 1934. Berlin: 1934.

Dienstaltersliste der Schutzstaffel der NSDAP, Stand vom 1. July 1935. Berlin: 1935.

Dienstaltersliste der Schutzstaffel der NSDAP, Stand vom 1. December 1936. Berlin: 1936.

Dienstaltersliste der Schutzstaffel der NSDAP, Stand vom 1. December 1937. Berlin: 1937.

Dienstaltersliste der Schutzstaffel der NSDAP (SS), Stand vom 1. December 1938. Herausgeben von Brün Meyer. Osnabrück, Germany: Biblio-Verlag, 1996.

Dierich, Wolfgang. *Die Verbände der Luftwaffe*. Stuttgart, FRG: Motorbuch Verlag, 1976.

Diroll, Bernd. *Personen-Lexikon der NSDAP, Band 1 – SS-Führer A-B*. Norderstedt, Germany: Verlag Klaus D. Patzwall, 1998.

Donat, Alexander, editor. *The Death Camp Treblinka: A Documentary*. New York: Holocaust Library, 1979.

Edelheit, Abraham J. & Hershel Edelheit. *History of the Holocaust: A Handbook and Dictionary*. Boulder, CO: Westview Press, 1994.

Engelmann, Joachim & Scheibert, Horst. *Deutsche Artillerie 1934-1945*. Limburg, FRG: C.A. Starke, 1974.

Fellgiebel, Walther-Peer. *Die Träger des Ritterkreuzes des Eisernen Kreuzes 1939-1945*. Friedberg, FRG: Podzun-Pallas-Verlag, 1986.

Friedman, Philip, ed. *Martyrs and Fighters*. New York: Praeger, 1954.

Gilbert, Martin. *Atlas of the Holocaust*. London: The Rainbird Publishing Group, 1982.

Giles, Lionel. *Sun Tzu on the Art of War*. London.

Goldhagen, Daniel Jonah. *Hitler's Willing Executioners: Ordinary Germans and the Holocaust*. New York: Vintage Books, 1997.

Graber, G.S. *History of the SS*. New York: David McKay Company, 1978.

Grabitz, Helge and Wolfgang Scheffler. *Letzte Spuren: Ghetto Warschau, SS-Arbeitslager Trawniki, Aktion Erntefest, Fotos und Dokumente über Opfer des Endlösungswahns im Spiegel der historischen Ereignisse*. Berlin: Edition Hentrich, 1988.

Gutman, Israel, editor in chief. *Encyclopedia of the Holcaust*. New York: MacMillan Publishing Company, 1990.

Gutman, Israel. *The Jews of Warsaw, 1939-1943: Ghetto, Underground, Revolt*. Bloomington: Indiana University Press, 1982.

Gutman, Israel. *Resistance: The Warsaw Ghetto Uprising*. Boston: Houghton Mifflin, 1994.

Heydecker, Joe E. *The Warsaw Ghetto: A Photographic Record 1941-1944*. New York: St. Martin Press, 1991.

Hilberg, Raul. *The Destruction of the European Jews*. (Revised and Definitive Edition). New York: Holmes & Meier, 1985.

Hilberg, Raul. *Sonderzüge nach Auschwitz*. Mainz, FRG: Dumjahn Verlag, 1981.

Hilberg, Raul, et. al. *The Warsaw Diary of Adam Czerniakow: Prelude to Doom*. New York: Stein and Day, 1979.

Hildebrand, Karl Friedrich. *Die Generale der deutschen Luftwaffe, 1935-1945, Band 1: A-G, Band 2: H-N, Band 3: O-Z*. Osnabrück, Germany: Biblio Verlag, 1990.

Höffkes, Karl. *Hitlers politische Generale: Die Gauleiter des Dritten Reiches*. Tübingen, FRG: Grabert Verlag, 1986.

Höhne, Heinz. *The Order of the Death's Head: The Story of Hitler's SS*. New York: Coward-McCann, 1985.

International Military Tribunal. *Trial of the Major War Criminals Before the International Military Tribunal, Nürnberg, 14 November 1945 – 1 October 1946. Volume XI, Proceedings, 8 April 1946 – 17 April 1946*. Nuremberg, Germany, 1947.

International Military Tribunal. *Trial of the Major War Criminals Before the International Military Tribunal, Nürnberg, 14 November 1945 – 1 October 1946. Volume XXVI, Documents and Other Material in Evidence, Numbers 405-PS to 1063 (d)-PS*. Buffalo, NY: William S. Hein & Co. Inc., 1995.

Jagielski, Jan & Tomasc Lec. *Nie Zatarte Slady Getta Warszawskiego (The Remnants of the Warsaw Ghetto)*. Warsaw: Zydowski Instytut Historyczny INB, 1997.

Kannapin, Norbert. *Die deutsche Feldpostübersicht, Band I-III*. Osnabrück, FRG: Biblio-Verlag, 1980.

Katsh, Abraham I. *The Warsaw Diary of Chaim A. Kaplan*. Revised edition. New York: Collier, 1973.

Keilig, Wolf. *Die Generale des Heeres*. Friedberg, FRG: Podzun-Pallas Verlag, 1983.

Kermish, Joseph. "The Warsaw Ghetto Uprising in the Light of a Hitherto Unpublished Official German Report" in *Yad Vashem Studies on the European Jewish Catastrophe and Resistance*, Volume IX. Jerusalem: Yad Vashem, 1973.

Kirk, John & Young, Robert. *Great Weapons of World War II*. New York: Bonanza Books, 1961.

Klee, Ernst, Willi Dressen and Volker Riess. *The Good Old Days: The Holocaust as Seen by Its Perpetrators and Bystanders*. New York: Koneck & Koneckt, 1991.

Koch, Horst Adalbert. *Flak. Die Geschichte der Deutschen Flakartillerie und der Einsatz der Luftwaffenhelfer*. Bad Nauheim, FRG: Podzun Verlag, 1965.

Koehl, Robert Lewis. *The Black Corps: The Structure and Power Struggles of the Nazi SS*. Madison, WI: The University of Wisconsin Press, 1983.

Kogon, Eugen, Hermann Langbein and Adalbert Rückerl. *Nazi Mass Murder: A Documentary History of the Use of Poison Gas*. New Haven, CN: Yale University Press, 1993.

Korbonski, Stefan. *The Polish Underground State: A Guide to the Underground 1939-1945*. Translated by Marta Erdman. New York: Hippocrene Books, 1978.

Korczak, Janusz. *The Warsaw Ghetto Memoirs of Janusz Korczak*. Washington, D.C.: University Press of America, 1979.

Krannhals, Hanns von. *Der Warschauer Aufstand 1944*. Frankfurt, FRG: Bernard & Graefe Verlag, 1964.

Krall, Hanna. *Shielding the Flame: An Intimate Conversation with Dr. Marek Edelman, the Last Surviving Leader of the Warsaw Ghetto Uprising*. New York: Holt, 1986.

Kurzman, Dan. *The Bravest Battle: The Twenty-eight Days of the Warsaw Ghetto Uprising*. New York: G.P. Putnam's Sons, 1976.

Landau, Elaine. *Warsaw Ghetto Uprising*. New York: Macmillan, 1992.

Lepre, George. *Himmler's Bosnian Division: The Waffen-SS Handschar Division, 1943-1945*. Atglen, PA: Schiffer, 1997.

Lewin, Abraham. *A Cup of Tears: A Diary of the Warsaw Ghetto*. Oxford: Blackwell, 1989.

Littlejohn, David. *Foreign Legions of the Third Reich. Volume 4: Poland, the Ukraine, Bulgaria, Romania, Free India, Estonia, Latvia, Lithuania, Finland and Russia*. San Jose, CA: R. James Bender Publishing, 1987.

Lochner, Louis P. Editor. *The Goebbels Diaries, 1942-1943*. Garden City, NY: Doubleday & Company, 1948.

Logusz, Michael O. *Galicia Division: The Waffen-SS 14th Grenadier Division 1943-1945*. Atglen, PA: Schiffer Publications, 1997.

Lukas, Richard C. *The Forgotten Holocaust: The Poles Under German Occupation, 1939-1944*. Lexington, KY: The University Press of Kentucky, 1986.

MacLean, French. *The Camp Men: The SS Officers Who Ran the Nazi Concentration Camp System*. Atglen, PA: Schiffer Publishing Co., 1998.

MacLean, French. *The Cruel Hunters: SS-Sonderkommando Dirlewanger, Hitler's Most Notorious Anti-partisan Unit*. Atglen, PA: Schiffer Publishing Co., 1998.

MacLean, French. *The Field Men: The SS Officers Who Led the Einsatzkommandos - the Nazi Mobile Killing Units*. Atglen, PA: Schiffer Publishing Co., 1999.

MacLean, French. *Quiet Flows the Rhine: German General Officer Casualties in World War II*. Winnipeg, Canada: J.J. Fedorowicz, 1996.

Mark, Bernard. *Der Aufstand im Warschauer Ghetto*. Berlin: Dietz Verlag, 1957.

Mark, Bernard. *The Extermination and the Resistance of the Polish Jews during 1939 – 1944*. Warsaw: Jewish Historical Institute, 1955.

Mayer, Arno. *Why Did The Heavens Not Darken?* New York: Pantheon Books, 1988.

Mehner, Kurt. *Die Waffen-SS und Polizei, 1939-1945*. Norderstedt, Germany: Militär-Verlag Klaus D. Patzwall, 1995.

Milton, Sybil and Andrzej Worth, Eds. *The Stroop Report: The Warsaw Ghetto is No More!* New York: Pantheon, 1979.

Moczarski, Kazimierz. *Conversations with an Executioner*. Edited by Mariana Fitzpatrick. Englewood Cliffs, New Jersey.

Mollo, Andrew and Hugh Page Taylor. *Uniforms of the SS: Collected Edition, Volumes 1 to 6*. London: Windrow & Greene, 1997.

Müller-Hillebrand, Burkhart. *Das Heer 1933-1945, Band III: Der Zweifrontenkrieg*. Frankfurt, FRG: E. S. Mittler Verlag & Sohn, 1969.

Munoz, Antonio J., editor. *The German Police*. Reprint of SHAPE G-2 Report, April 1945. New York: Axis Europa, Inc., 1997.

Neufeldt, Hans-Joachim, Huck, Juergen and Tessin, Georg. *Zur Geschichte der Ordnungspolizei, 1936-1945*. Freiburg, FRG: Bundesarchiv, 1957.

Nowak, Jan. *Courier From Warsaw*. Detroit: Wayne State University Press, 1982.

Padfield, Peter. *Himmler*. New York: Henry Holt and Company, 1990.

Pohl, Dieter. *Nationalsozialistische Judenverfolgung in Ostgalizien 1941-1944*. Munich, Germany: Oldenbourg Verlag, 1997.

Poteranski, Waclaw. *The Warsaw Ghetto: on the 25th Anniversary of the Armed Uprising of 1943*. Warsaw: Interpress, 1963.

Preradovich, Nikolaus von. *Die Generale der Waffen-SS*. Berg am See, FRG: Kurt Vowinckel-verlag, 1985.

Preradovich, Nikolaus von. *Oesterreichs Höhere SS-Führer*. Berg am See, FRG: Kurt Vowinckel-verlag, 1987.

Pucher, Siegfried J. *"In der Bewegung führend tätig", Odilo Globocnik – Kämpfer für den "Anschluss" Vollstrecker des Holocaust*. Klagenfurt/Celovec, Slovenia: Drava Verlag, 1997.

Rangliste des Deutschen Reichsheeres, Nach dem Stande vom 1. Mai 1929. Berlin: E.S. Mittler & Sohn, 1929.

Reitlinger, Gerald. *The Final Solution: The Attempt to Exterminate the Jews of Europe, 1939-1945*. Northvale, N.J.: Jason Aronson, Inc., 1987.

Reitlinger, Gerald. *The SS: Alibi of a Nation, 1922-1945*. London: Arms and Armour Press, 1981.

Ringelblum, Emanuel. *Notes from the Warsaw Ghetto: The Journal of Emanuel Ringelblum*. New York: Schocken, 1974.

Roland, Charles G. *Courage Under Siege: Starvation, Disease, and Death in the Warsaw Ghetto*. New York: Oxford University Press, 1992.

Rüter, C.F. and de Mildt, D.W. *Die Westdeutschen Strafverfahren wegen Nationalsozialistischer Tötungsverbrechen 1945 – 1997*. Amsterdam: Holland University Press, 1998.

Rymkiewicz, Jaroslaw M. *The Final Station: Umschlagplatz*. Translated by Nina Taylor. New York: Farrar, Straus and Giroux, 1994.

Sagel-Grande, Dr. Irene; Adelheid L. Rüter-Ehrlermann, Dr. H. H. Fuchs and C. F. Rüter. *Justiz und NS-Verbrechen, Band XXII*. Amsterdam: University Press Amsterdam, 1981.

Sakowska, Ruta. *The Warsaw Ghetto, 1940-1943*. Warsaw: Privately published.

Sandkühler, Thomas. *"Endlösung" in Galizien: Der Judenmord in Ostpolen und die Rettungsinitiativen von Berthold Beitz 1941-1944*. Bonn, Germany: J.H.W. Dietz, 1996.

Scheffler, Wolfgang and Helge Grabnitz. *Der Ghetto-Aufstand Warschau 1943*. Munich, Germany: Goldmann Verlag, 1993.

Schneider, Jost. *Their Honor Was Loyalty! An Illustrated and Documentary History of the Knight's Cross Holders of the Waffen-SS and Police 1940-1945*. San Jose, CA: R. James Bender Publishing, 1977.

Segev, Tom. *Soldiers of Evil: The Commandants of the Nazi Concentration Camps*. New York: McGraw-Hill Book Company, 1987.

Snyder, Louis L. *Encyclopedia of the Third Reich*. New York: McGraw-Hill, 1976.

Sowodny, Wolfgang. *Die Panzerzüge des Deutschen Reiches, 1904-1945*. Freiburg, Germany: Eisenbahn Kurier Verlag, 1996.

Speer, Albert. *Infiltration*. New York: MacMillan Publishing, 1981.

Spielberger, Walter J. and Uwe Feist. *Sturmartillerie: From Assault Guns to Hunting Panther. Armor Series 3*. Fallbrook, CA: Aero Publishers, 1967.

Stein, George H. *The Waffen SS: Hitler's Elite Guard at War*. Ithaca, New York: Cornell University Press, 1966.

Sydnor, Charles W. Jr. *Soldiers of Destruction: The SS Death's Head Division, 1933-1945*. Princeton, NJ: Princeton University Press, 1977.

Tessin, Georg. *Verbände und Truppen der deutschen Wehrmacht und Waffen-SS im Zweiten Weltkrieg 1939-1945, Band I – XVI (4)*. Osnabrück, FRG: Biblio Verlag, 1979.

Treseder, Terry Walton. *Hear, O Israel: A Story of the Warsaw Ghetto*. New York, Atheneum, 1990.

United States Holocaust Memorial Museum. *Historical Atlas of the Holocaust*. New York: Macmillan Publishing USA, 1996.

Vopersal, Wolfgang. *Soldaten, Kämpfer, Kameraden: Marsch und Kämpfe der SS-Totenkopf-Division, Band 2b & 3*. Osnabrück, FRG: Selbstverlag, 1984.

War Department, Military Intelligence Service. *German Anti-aircraft Artillery*, Special Series No. 10. Washington, DC: Government Printing Office, 1943.

War Department, Military Intelligence Service. *German Infantry Weapons*, Special Series No. 14. Washington, DC: Government Printing Office, 1943.

War Department. *Handbook on German Military Forces, 15 March 1945*. Gaithersburg, Maryland: Reprinted by The Military Press, 1970.

War Department. *Handbook on German Military Forces*. Baton Rouge, Louisiana: Reprinted by Louisiana State University Press, 1990.

Warszawskie Getto. Warsaw: Wydawnictwo Interpress, 1988.

Werstein, Irving. *The Uprising of the Warsaw Ghetto, November 1940 – May 1943*. New York: W.W. Norton & Company, 1968.

Wulf, Josef. *Das Dritte Reich und seine Vollstrecker: Die Liquidation von 500000 Juden im Ghetto Warschau*. Berlin-Grünewald: Arani Verlags Gmbh, 1961.

Yerger, Mark C. *Allgemeine-SS: The Commands, Units and Leaders of the General SS*. Atglen, PA: Schiffer Publishing, 1997.

Yerger, Mark C. *Riding East: The SS Cavalry Brigade in Poland and Russia 1939-1942*. Atglen, PA: Schiffer Publishing, 1996.

Zuckerman, Yitzhak. *A Surplus of Memory: Chronicle of the Warsaw Ghetto Uprising*. Berkeley, CA: University of California Press, 1993.

Zylberberg, Michael. *A Warsaw Diary: 1939-1945*. London: Valentine, Mitchell, 1969.

Video Media

British Broadcasting Corporation Television. *The Warsaw Ghetto*. London: 1969. Re-released by Hollywood Home Theater.

Archival Sources

National Archives. *National Archives Microfilm Publication A3343, Records of SS Personnel from the Berlin Document Center, Series SSO – SS Officers*. Washington, D.C.: Rolls SSO-004, 012, 018, 022, 055, 059, 067, 069, 082, 089, 090, 103, 121, 131, 171, 173, 192, 229, 007A, 026A, 027A, 039A, 053A, 058A, 059A, 081A, 089A, 103A, 138A, 143A, 147A, 149A, 181A, 184A, 197A, 198A, 218A, 266A, 279A, 288A, 308A, 310A, 315A, 323A, 327A, 329A, 334A, 340A, 341A, 352A, 355A, 356A, 363A, 382A, 386A, 390A, 024B, 039B, 060B, 087B, 091B, 097B, 099B, 123B, 125B, 131B, 145B, 146B, 147B, 149B, 156B, 158B, 167B, 171B, 223B, 233B, 240B, 241B, 001C, 014C, 024C.

National Archives. National Archives Microfilm Publication A3343, *Records of SS Personnel from the Berlin Document Center, Series SSM – SS Enlisted Men*. Washington, D.C.

National Archives. National Archives Microfilm Publication A3343, *Records of SS Personnel from the Berlin Document Center, Series RS – SS Race and Settlement Office (RuSHA, Rasse-und Siedlungshauptamt)*. Washington, D.C.

National Archives. National Archives Microfilm Publication A3345, *Series DS – Miscellaneous Collection*. Washington, D.C: Roll J043.

National Archives. National Archives Microfilm Publication A3343, *Records of SS Personnel from the Berlin Document Center, Series SS – SS Lists*. Washington, D.C.

National Archives. *National Archives Microfilm Publication T-175, Records of the Reich Leader of the SS and Chief of the German Police (Reichsführer SS und Chef der Deutschen Polizei)*. Washington, D.C.

National Archives. *The Stroop Report*. Washington, D.C.

Unpublished Sources

MacLean, French L., "The Unknown Generals: German Corps Commanders in World War II." (Masters Thesis) United States Army Command and General Staff College, Fort Leavenworth, Kansas, 1988.

PHOTO SECTION

Warsaw Jews walking on Grzybowska Street, 1940. The German sign on the left announces that the area is infected with typhus. (Hans-Joachim Gerke, courtesy of USHMM Photo Archives)

Warsaw Jews walking along a Ghetto street among buildings destroyed during the Polish campaign in 1939. (Hans-Joachim Gerke, courtesy of USHMM Photo Archives)

View of the courtyard of the Krochmalna Street orphanage sometime between 1940 and 1942. (National Museum of American Jewish History, courtesy of USHMM Photo Archives)

Inhabitants of the Warsaw Ghetto attempt to repair a wagon broken down at the intersection of Nowolipki and Karmelicka Streets sometime during the summer of 1941. (Raphael Scharf, courtesy of USHMM Photo Archives)

A German soldier stands guard at an entrance to the Warsaw Ghetto circa 1941. (Hans-Joachim Gerke, courtesy of USHMM Photo Archives)

Street scene of Jews in the Ghetto at the intersection of Karmelicka and Nowolipki Streets. (Raphael Scharf, courtesy of USHMM Photo Archives)

Funeral hearse moving on Leszno Street enroute to the Jewish cemetery during the summer of 1941. (Raphael Scharf, courtesy of USHMM Photo Archives)

Right: A woman escorts a group of children through a rubble-strewn street in the Warsaw Ghetto in the summer of 1941. The buildings were most likely destroyed during the Polish campaign in 1939. (Raphael Scharf, courtesy of USHMM Photo Archives)

A group of Jews walking along a street next to the Ghetto wall sometime in 1941 or 1942. (YIVO Institute for Jewish Research, courtesy of USHMM Photo Archives)

Operation Reinhard – German, Latvian, Lithuanian and Ukrainian auxiliary police and soldiers prepare for a deportation action sometime between July and September 1942. Latvian personnel in the center of the photograph are from the 22nd Latvian, 272nd Latvian or 274th Latvian Police Battalions that were brought in the city for the action. (Archiwum Akt Nowych, courtesy of USHMM Photo Archives)

Operation Reinhard – German troops and Jewish Police during a deportation action sometime between July and September 1942. (Archiwum Akt Nowych, courtesy of USHMM Photo Archives)

Operation Reinhard – German personnel and Jewish Police during a deportation action sometime at the train station of the Umschlagplatz between July and September 1942. (Archiwum Akt Nowych, courtesy of USHMM Photo Archives)

Deutsch

Opposite
Top: Operation Reinhard – A scene from a Nazi documentary film "Between Vistula and Rhine" shows SS troops deporting Jews from the Warsaw Ghetto in 1942. Soldiers are standing next to freight cars. Troops are all enlisted personnel. (Documentary Film Archives, courtesy of USHMM Photo Archives)

Bottom: Operation Reinhard – German personnel at a Warsaw railroad station observe Jewish women being deported in open cattle cars, 1942 or early 1943. Some of the personnel appear to be German Army officers. (YIVO Institute for Jewish Research, courtesy of USHMM Photo Archives)

Operation Reinhard – The end of the line, the Treblinka railroad station, November 1998. (Author photograph)

Operation Reinhard – Most buildings in the village of Treblinka are still log construction even in November 1998. (Author photograph)

Operation Reinhard – Area around the Treblinka railroad station in winter, November 1998. (Author photograph)

Operation Reinhard – View looking from near the Treblinka extermination camp down the spur rail line toward the village of Treblinka, November 1998. (Author photograph)

Operation Reinhard – View of the railroad siding area, in November 1998, at the entrance of the camp. Siding location is commemorated on the right by concrete rail ties. (Author photograph)

Operation Reinhard – Concrete markers at right of photo show rough boundary of the front of the camp, November 1998. (Author photograph)

Left: Operation Reinhard – Close-up of stone markers; some have a name of a city inscribed, others bear no name and represent the hundreds of smaller hamlets that lost Jews to Treblinka. Photo taken in November 1998. (Author photograph)

Operation Reinhard – No actual remnants, such as buildings or barbed wire fence, of the extermination camp remain as the Nazis destroyed the camp in late 1943. Treblinka is memorialized today by irregular-shaped stone markers denoting each city and town from which Jews were deported. The large tower in the center commemorates the deportations from Warsaw. Photo taken in November 1998. (Author photograph)

The Ghetto Uprising – SS troops force Jews to evacuate an apartment building during the suppression of the Ghetto Uprising. Little battle damage can be seen to this building. (Louis Gonda, courtesy of USHMM Photo Archives)

The Ghetto Uprising – A German gun crew, possibly a 100mm gun mentioned in the Stroop Report, prepares to shell the ruins of a building. The two personnel on the right are Police officers. None of the Germans appears to be concerned about possible return fire or snipers. (Louis Gonda, courtesy of USHMM Photo Archives)

The Ghetto Uprising – SS enlisted troops pause to eat during operation. As they are sitting close together and that none is wearing a helmet indicates that the troops are unconcerned about Jewish fire against them. (Louis Gonda, courtesy of USHMM Photo Archives)

The Ghetto Uprising – A woman hangs from a balcony, preparing to drop to the street and the waiting SS. While at least one window is broken, there does not appear to be any damage to the façade from gunfire. (Louis Gonda, courtesy of USHMM Photo Archives)

The Ghetto Uprising – SS, Police and German Army personnel look on as Jews are pulled from an underground bunker on 8 May 1943. Jürgen Stroop is at the rear center of the photograph (M1943 cap and goggles around neck.) Smiling SS officer in the front is an SS-Sturmbannführer, possibly Max Jesuiter. Immediately to the right is an SS-Hauptsturmführer. (Yad Vashem Photo Archives, courtesy of USHMM Photo Archives)

The Ghetto Uprising – An SS-Untersturmführer interrogates a Jewish resistance fighter on 9 May 1943. Collar tab and battle badges indicate that the officer is a combat veteran, likely from the SS Cavalry Replacement Detachment. (Louis Gonda, courtesy of USHMM Photo Archives)

The Ghetto Uprising – Jürgen Stroop (third from right) at the Umschlagplatz with a group of SS and Police officers. Vehicle is a German armored half-track. Officer at the center of the photograph is possibly SS-Sturmbannführer Max Jesuiter. Soldier on far left with Death's Head collar tab, is likely from the 3rd SS Panzergrenadier Training and Replacement Battalion. (Yad Vashem Photo Archives, courtesy of USHMM Photo Archives)

The Ghetto Uprising – A German 20mm gun crew in action during the suppression of the Ghetto Uprising. (Archiwum Akt Nowych, courtesy of USHMM Photo Archives)

The Ghetto Uprising – Smoke rises from a building adjacent to the Ghetto wall during the Uprising. Lack of damage and debris indicates that the photo was taken early in the Uprising. Note solid construction of five-story buildings. (Archiwum Akt Nowych, courtesy of USHMM Photo Archives)

Below: The Ghetto Uprising – Members of an SS/SD detachment rest along a street in Warsaw. Photo is dated 18/19 April 1943, so the officers could be preparing for the operation by conducting a reconnaissance. Lack of helmets and firearms indicates that they do not believe that they will be attacked. (Yad Vashem Photo Archives, courtesy of USHMM Photo Archives)

Opposite
Top: The Ghetto Uprising – Ukrainians from the 1st Guard Battalion, Trawniki Labor Camp "Trawniki Men" march into action during the Uprising. Personnel to the left of the formation are probably SS non-commissioned officers assigned to the unit. Photograph was quite possibly taken by SS-Untersturmführer Herbert Schwarzenbacher, who served as the battalion commander for the detachment of Ukrainians. (Yad Vashem Photo Archives, courtesy of USHMM Photo Archives)

Bottom: The Ghetto Uprising – SS-Brigadeführer Jürgen Stroop, on the left, stands with members of his staff. Officer in the center with a blank, black collar tab is in the SD. Officer second from right is possibly SS-Sturmbannführer Max Jesuiter. (Bildarchiv Preussischer Kulturbesitz, courtesy of USHMM Photo Archives)

The Ghetto Uprising – SS troops comb the ruins of the Warsaw Ghetto sometime between 14 and 16 May 1943. Circular hole with water appears to be a bomb crater rather than one caused by a relatively small caliber artillery shell. German troops appear to be unconcerned about potential fire from the Resistance based on their proximity to one another in an open area. (Bildarchiv Preussischer Kulturbesitz, courtesy of USHMM Photo Archives)

The Ghetto Uprising – Another photo showing Stroop and several key officers. SD officer, almost completely hidden on the far right, is from the KdS. Second from the right, holding gloves, is an SS-Untersturmführer Schwarz. Heavyset officer, third from right is SS-Untersturmführer Karl Brandt. Partially hidden man, fourth from the right, is SS-Untersturmführer Karl Kaleschke. Next to him, with the goggles around his neck, is Jürgen Stroop. Officer to the far left appears to be SS-Obersturmführer Franz Konrad. (Louis Gonda, courtesy of USHMM Photo Archives)

The Ghetto Uprising – Another view of Jews at the Umschlagplatz. Photograph appears to show smoke from burning Ghetto fires. The soldier in the center, armed with a submachine gun, is SS. The soldier to the right appears to be Ukrainian. (Yad Vashem Photo Archives, courtesy of USHMM Photo Archives)

The Ghetto Uprising – A burning building on 3 Muranowska Street sometime in April 1943. Top floor exhibits pockmarks from German small arms fire, probably from rifles. (Zydowski Instytut Historyczny Instytut Naukowo-Badawczy, courtesy of USHMM Photo Archives)

Below: The Ghetto Uprising – Germans assemble a crowd of Jews at the Umschlagplatz during the Ghetto Uprising. Far right soldier appears to have a German "potato-masher" hand grenade stuck in his belt. (Yad Vashem Photo Archives, courtesy of USHMM Photo Archives)

Opposite:
Top: The Ghetto Uprising – German Army enlisted man escorts an elderly Jew past SS personnel. (YIVO Institute for Jewish Research, courtesy of USHMM Photo Archives)

Bottom: The Ghetto Uprising – Germans march captured Jews down Nowolipie Street toward the Umschlagplatz. Lorries in the background are probably in use to transport troops. (Howard Kaplan, courtesy of USHMM Photo Archives)

The Ghetto Uprising – Polish firefighters and SS personnel watch fire consume a building in the Ghetto. (Howard Kaplan, courtesy of USHMM Photo Archives)

The Ghetto Uprising – German Police and SS troops arrest Jews on Nowolipie Street during the Ghetto Uprising. (Howard Kaplan, courtesy of USHMM Photo Archives)

The Stroop Report – The original German caption reads "To the Umschlagplatz." Germans march Jews captured during the Uprising. SS troops appear to be from the SS Cavalry Replacement Detachment based on collar tabs. Soldier on right wears Iron Cross 2nd Class. Column has just left the Ghetto through a gate. (National Archives, courtesy of USHMM Photo Archives)

Opposite
Top: The Stroop Report – The original German caption reads "Jewish rabbis." SS and SD personnel interrogate captured Jews. Soldier with the rifle over his shoulder is believed to be SS-Rottenführer Josef Blösche. (National Archives, courtesy of USHMM Photo Archives)

Bottom: The Stroop Report – The original German caption reads "An assault squad." SS troops walk past a block of burning buildings. (National Archives, courtesy of USHMM Photo Archives)

The Stroop Report – The original German caption reads "Pulled from the bunkers by force." SS and SD personnel guard captured Jews. Soldier with the goggles over his helmet is believed to be SS-Rottenführer Josef Blösche. (National Archives, courtesy of USHMM Photo Archives)

Opposite
Top: The Stroop Report – The original German caption reads "Just pulled from a bunker." SS troops search personnel belongings as a small number of resistance fighters lie on the rubble nearby. Troops do not appear to be concerned about concealed weapons that the defenders could possibly have. (National Archives, courtesy of USHMM Photo Archives)

Bottom: The Stroop Report – The original German caption reads "Jewish traitors." SS officer questions captured Jews. Jürgen Stroop is standing in the center. (National Archives, courtesy of USHMM Photo Archives)

The Stroop Report – The original German caption reads "A bunker is opened." SS troops force Jews to open a bunker on 8 May 1943. (National Archives, courtesy of USHMM Photo Archives)

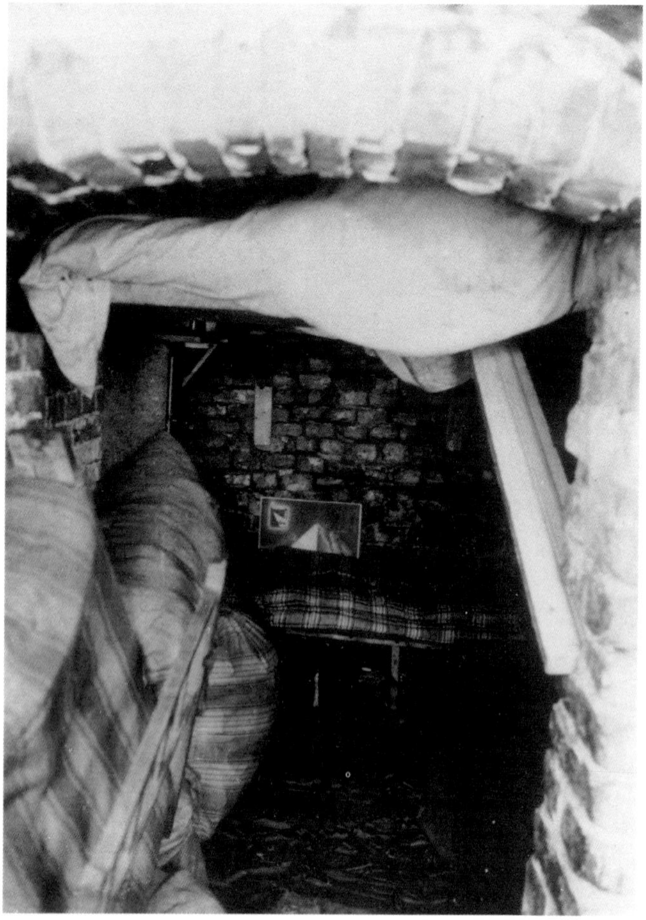

The Stroop Report – The original German caption reads "Pictures of a so-called residential bunker." Sleeping area in a bunker prepared by the Jewish resistance. (National Archives, courtesy of USHMM Photo Archives)

The Stroop Report – The original German caption reads "Securing a street." German Police and SS soldiers man a machine gun during the Ghetto Uprising at an entrance to the Ghetto. (National Archives, courtesy of USHMM Photo Archives)

The Stroop Report – The original German caption reads "Before the search." SS line up captured Jews against the Ghetto wall prior to searching them for weapons. (National Archives, courtesy of USHMM Photo Archives)

The Stroop Report – The original German caption reads "Bandits who jumped." SS troops observe the bodies of Jews who jumped to their deaths from an apartment building on 22 April 1943. (Bildarchiv Preussischer Kulturbesitz, courtesy of USHMM Photo Archives)

The Stroop Report – The original German caption reads "Askaris assigned to the operation." Ukrainians from the 1st Guard Battalion, Trawniki Labor Camp "Trawniki Men" prepare for action during the Uprising. The Germans nicknamed these personnel "Askaris." German officer facing Ukrainians is Jürgen Stroop. (Bildarchiv Preussischer Kulturbesitz, courtesy of USHMM Photo Archives)

The Stroop Report – The original German caption reads "Destruction of a housing block. 100mm German gun has just fired at the upper story of building to the front. Crewmen at left cover their ears. (National Archives, courtesy of USHMM Photo Archives)

The Stroop Report – No original German caption. SS troops search ruined buildings for Jews. (National Archives, courtesy of USHMM Photo Archives)

Below: The Stroop Report – The original German caption reads "These bandits offered resistance." SS troops guard members of the Jewish resistance just captured. (National Archives, courtesy of USHMM Photo Archives)

The Stroop Report – The original German caption reads "Askaris used during the operation." Two Ukrainian troops observe what appears to be recently murdered Jews in a doorway. (National Archives, courtesy of USHMM Photo Archives)

Opposite: The Stroop Report – No original German caption. German soldier stands among the ruins in the Warsaw Ghetto. (National Archives, courtesy of USHMM Photo Archives)

Opposite
Top: The Stroop Report – The original German caption reads "Pulled from a bunker." An SS soldier searches a captured Jewish resistance fighter. This is the only photo known to show German troops at the Ghetto Uprising with fixed bayonets. (National Archives, courtesy of USHMM Photo Archives)

The Stroop Report – The original German caption reads "In the radio car of the command post." German Police man the radio command car. (National Archives, courtesy of USHMM Photo Archives)

The Stroop Report – The original German caption reads "Bandits!" SS troops guard members of the Jewish resistance. SS soldier facing right is an SS-Rottenführer, probably from the SS Cavalry Replacement Detachment. He is a combat veteran with an Iron Cross 2nd Class and a Wound Badge, probably from service on the eastern front. (National Archives, courtesy of USHMM Photo Archives)

The Stroop Report – The original German caption reads "They were also discovered in underground bunkers." SS-Brigadeführer Jürgen Stroop looks on as German soldiers discover the entrance to an underground bunker. (National Archives, courtesy of USHMM Photo Archives)

Hans Frank, Governor General of Poland from 1939 to 1945. He was executed on 16 October 1945. (Lena Fagen, courtesy of USHMM Photo Archives)

Below: Governor General Hans Frank hosts Reichsführer-SS Heinrich Himmler in 1940 at a dinner held at Wewel castle in Kraków. (Muzeum Historii Fotografii, courtesy of USHMM Photo Archives)

Ukrainians greet Governor General Hans Frank on a visit to their town. (Yad Vashem Photo Archives, courtesy of USHMM Photo Archives)

Former SS-Brigadeführer Jürgen Stroop, shown in Wiesbaden in 1945 after his arrest by the U.S. Army. (Peter E. Teil, courtesy of USHMM Photo Archives)

Stroop Report. Command Group in the Warsaw Ghetto. Man leaning on the car on the right is Jürgen Stroop. Other personnel at the vehicle appear to be police. (BAK, 146/2000/8/2)

Stroop Report. Destroyed building of the former Judenrat in the Warsaw Ghetto. (BAK, 146/2000/8/3)

Warsaw Ghetto fires; note the SS man as he wraps a bandana over his face to protect himself from heavy smoke. (BAK, 146/2000/8/4)

SS men with a staff car and motorcycle in thick smoke on a Warsaw Ghetto street during the Ghetto Uprising. Observation was often limited to just a few yards during the fighting. (BAK, 146/2000/8/15)

View of a section of the destroyed Warsaw Ghetto. The picture appears to have been taken shortly after the war. The Nazis later demolished those buildings not destroyed during the Ghetto Uprising and used some of the materials for construction of a temporary concentration camp in the city. (BAK, 183/10/525/10N)

SS men at a gate along the Warsaw Ghetto wall. (BAK, 90/6/29)

Stroop Report. Original caption reads "The Jewish work section leaders of the firm Brauer." SS man assembles Jewish work section leaders of the Brauer armaments works inside the Warsaw Ghetto. (BAK, 85/5/1A)

Stroop Report. Original caption reads "Out of the work shops!" SS troops watch Jews as they depart workshops in the Warsaw Ghetto with their meager belongings. These victims are undoubtedly on their way to the Umschlagplatz. (BAK, 85/5/5A)

Stroop Report. Original caption reads "Smoking out the Jews and bandits." German troops observe burning buildings on a Warsaw Ghetto street. Three have protective gas masks but at least two do not. Some German troops may have tried to use these masks to protect them against heavy smoke. (BAK, 89/100/28A)

Friedrich Wilhelm Krüger (center) at Radom, Poland. On the right is an unidentified SD SS-Untersturmführer; on the left appears to be Hans Frank. Krüger would later win the Knight's Cross of the Iron Cross as a Waffen-SS commander. (BAK, 92/15/21A)

Reinhard Heydrich (right) and Friedrich Wilhelm Krüger (left) at a ski competition at Kitzbühl, Austria in 1941. Heydrich masterminded the Final Solution before his death in June 1942, while Krüger served as the Higher SS and Police Leader for the General Government at the time of the Warsaw Ghetto Uprising. Heydrich wears a SD insignia on his sleeve, a Luftwaffe Pilot's Badge on his lower breast pocket, a Nazi Party Golden Party Badge above that, and an Iron Cross 2nd Class ribbon in his tunic buttonhole. (BAK, 69/43/47)

Defendant Jürgen Stroop in the witness box in Warsaw, July 1951. (Main Commission for the Investigation of Nazi War Crimes)

SS-Gruppenführer Odilo Globocnik, chief of Operation Reinhard, the action that sent hundreds of thousands of Jews in Warsaw to their deaths in 1942. (USHMM Photo Archives)

SS-Sturmbannführer Ernst Lerch, the adjutant to SSPF Odilo Globocnik in Lublin. (National Archives)

SS-Obersturmbannführer Dr. Ludwig Hahn, the Commander of the Security Police and Security Service, KdS, in Warsaw. (National Archives)

SS-Sturmbannführer Dr. Ernst Kah, the Deputy Commander of the KdS and the leader of Department III, the Security Service, in Warsaw. (National Archives)

SS-Sturmbannführer Karl Schöppe, 3rd Battalion, 22nd SS Police Regiment. (National Archives)

SS-Sturmbannführer Walter Stamm, the leader of Department IV, the Gestapo, of the KdS Warsaw. (National Archives)

SS-Hauptsturmführer Erich Herberholz of the KdS for Warsaw. (National Archives)

SS-Oberscharführer Gerhard Mende, Section IV B, KdS Warsaw. (National Archives)

SS-Oberscharführer Rudolf Fahrenberger, Section II D 3 in the KdS for Warsaw. (National Archives)

SS-Rottenführer Josef Blösche, Section IV, the Gestapo, in the KdS for Warsaw. (National Archives)

SS-Sturmscharführer Otto Bindernagel, Section II C (Finance), Department I/II, Administration and Law, in the KdS for Warsaw. (National Archives)

SS-Hauptscharführer Fritz Bässler, Registrar Section, in the KdS for Warsaw. (National Archives)

SS-Sturmscharführer Paul Hiersemann, Pawiak Prison. (National Archives)

SS-Oberscharführer Gustav Fahner, Section IV E 1, the Gestapo, of the KdS for Warsaw. (National Archives)

SS-Obersturmbannführer Walter Bellwidt, the battalion commander of the 3rd SS Panzergrenadier Training and Replacement Battalion. (National Archives)

Narrow street in the Warsaw Ghetto, 1940. Wall at the end of the street marks Ghetto boundary. German attackers in streets of this width would have had no room to maneuver. (Main Commission for the Investigation of Nazi War Crimes)

Jews constructing perimeter Ghetto wall in 1940. (Main Commission for the Investigation of Nazi War Crimes)

Crowded street scene in the Warsaw Ghetto, 1940-1941. The density of the population inside the Ghetto promoted the conditions for rampant disease. (Main Commission for the Investigation of Nazi War Crimes)

Jewish forced labor detachment clears rubble in Warsaw, 1941. (Main Commission for the Investigation of Nazi War Crimes)

Warsaw Ghetto, probably between September 1942 and April 1943. Rubble in the street would have made maneuvering by German tanks and armored cars very difficult. The wall across the street in the background is part of the perimeter wall of the Ghetto. (Main Commission for the Investigation of Nazi War Crimes)

Heavy destruction in the Warsaw Ghetto, April-May 1943. Severe damage to buildings shown is probably from demolition charges, artillery or possibly aerial bombs. (Main Commission for the Investigation of Nazi War Crimes)

SD officer (note all-black collar tab) supervises Jews as they are marched to the Umschlagplatz, April-May 1943. (Main Commission for the Investigation of Nazi War Crimes)

German Army and SS personnel in discussion, Warsaw 1943. The two personnel with submachine guns are from the SD. Partially hidden officer in the center, with hand on hip, is probably Jürgen Stroop. Army officers are probably from the Armaments department. (Main Commission for the Investigation of Nazi War Crimes)

German Army officer (note Army decal on helmet and high black boots) observes destruction of a building in the Warsaw Ghetto, April-May 1943. Officer is probably from one of the Army engineer detachments present at the action and given this type of mission. (Main Commission for the Investigation of Nazi War Crimes)

German anti-aircraft troops move a 20mm gun just outside the Warsaw Ghetto, 1943. (Main Commission for the Investigation of Nazi War Crimes)

SS soldier escorts Jews to the Umschlagplatz, 1943. (Main Commission for the Investigation of Nazi War Crimes)

German tank during a lull in the Warsaw Ghetto, 1943. Vehicle is a captured Czech light tank, Model 38. The Nazis employed at least two such vehicles during the Ghetto Uprising with limited success. (Main Commission for the Investigation of Nazi War Crimes)

German troops pull Jews from an underground bunker, 1943. Soldiers are wearing coveralls. (Main Commission for the Investigation of Nazi War Crimes)

Germans pull a Jewish woman from a bunker. The sitting prisoner appears to be begging for his life; the soldiers, and SS officer in the lower left corner, seem amused. (Main Commission for the Investigation of Nazi War Crimes)

Jürgen Stroop reviews SS troops, Warsaw, 1943. Two soldiers in the center front rank wear the General Assault Badge on their uniform pocket. This is indicative that the soldiers shown are probably from the SS cavalry unit as the infantrymen had a different badge denoting combat service. The two probably received the award for previous service in Russia. (Main Commission for the Investigation of Nazi War Crimes)

Jürgen Stroop (with paper in hands) reviews an order, Warsaw, 1943. SS gurads with submachine guns keep a watch for snipers. (Main Commission for the Investigation of Nazi War Crimes)

Right: German 20mm anti-aircraft gun fires at a building inside the Warsaw Ghetto, 1943. Note rounds exploding on the side of the third floor building directly to the front. The gun crew is close enough to the target to receive accurate enemy fire in return – which happened on at least one occasion. (Main Commission for the Investigation of Nazi War Crimes)

MAP SECTION

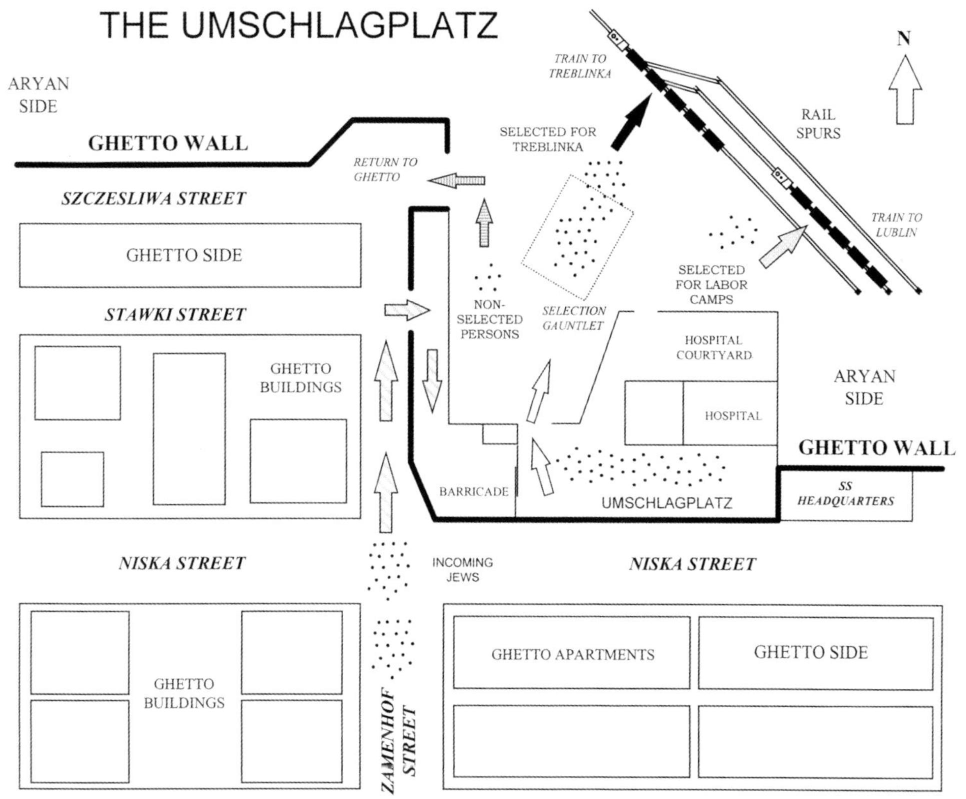
THE UMSCHLAGPLATZ
ARYAN SIDE
GHETTO WALL
SZCZESLIWA STREET
GHETTO SIDE
STAWKI STREET
GHETTO BUILDINGS
NISKA STREET
ZAMENHOF STREET
INCOMING JEWS
RETURN TO GHETTO
NON-SELECTED PERSONS
SELECTION GAUNTLET
SELECTED FOR TREBLINKA
TRAIN TO TREBLINKA
RAIL SPURS
N
TRAIN TO LUBLIN
SELECTED FOR LABOR CAMPS
HOSPITAL COURTYARD
HOSPITAL
ARYAN SIDE
GHETTO WALL
SS HEADQUARTERS
BARRICADE
UMSCHLAGPLATZ
NISKA STREET
GHETTO APARTMENTS
GHETTO SIDE
GHETTO BUILDINGS

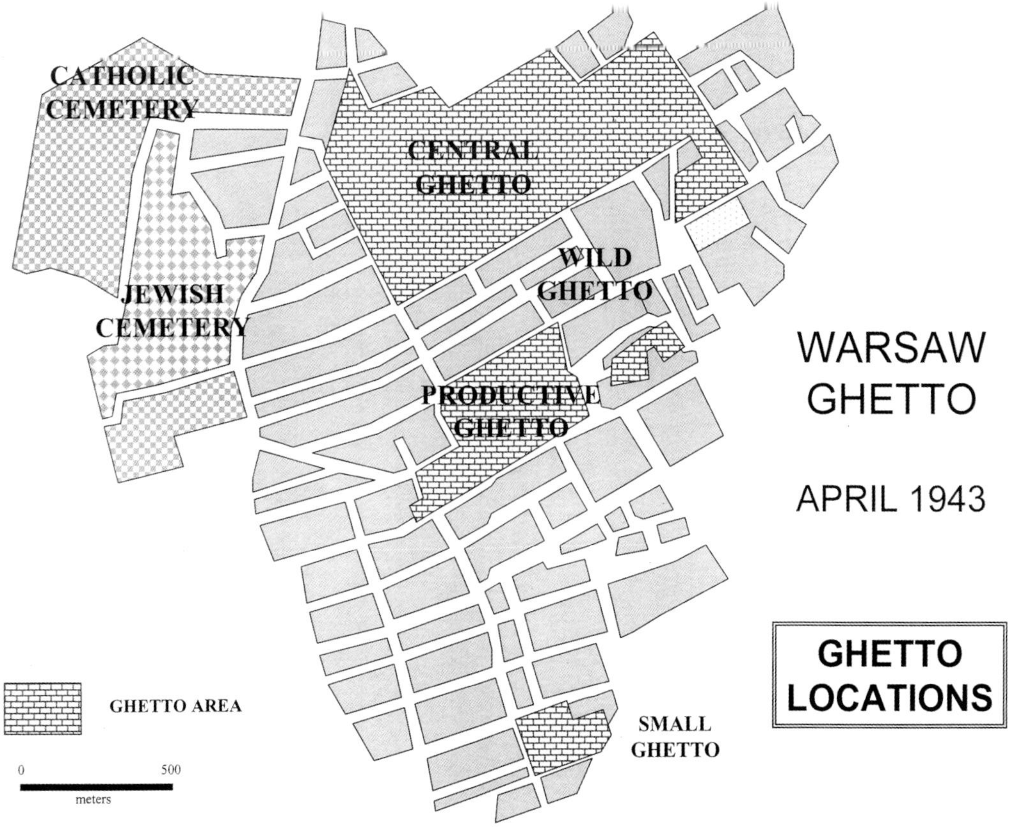
CATHOLIC CEMETERY
JEWISH CEMETERY
CENTRAL GHETTO
WILD GHETTO
PRODUCTIVE GHETTO
SMALL GHETTO
WARSAW GHETTO
APRIL 1943
GHETTO LOCATIONS
GHETTO AREA
0
500
meters

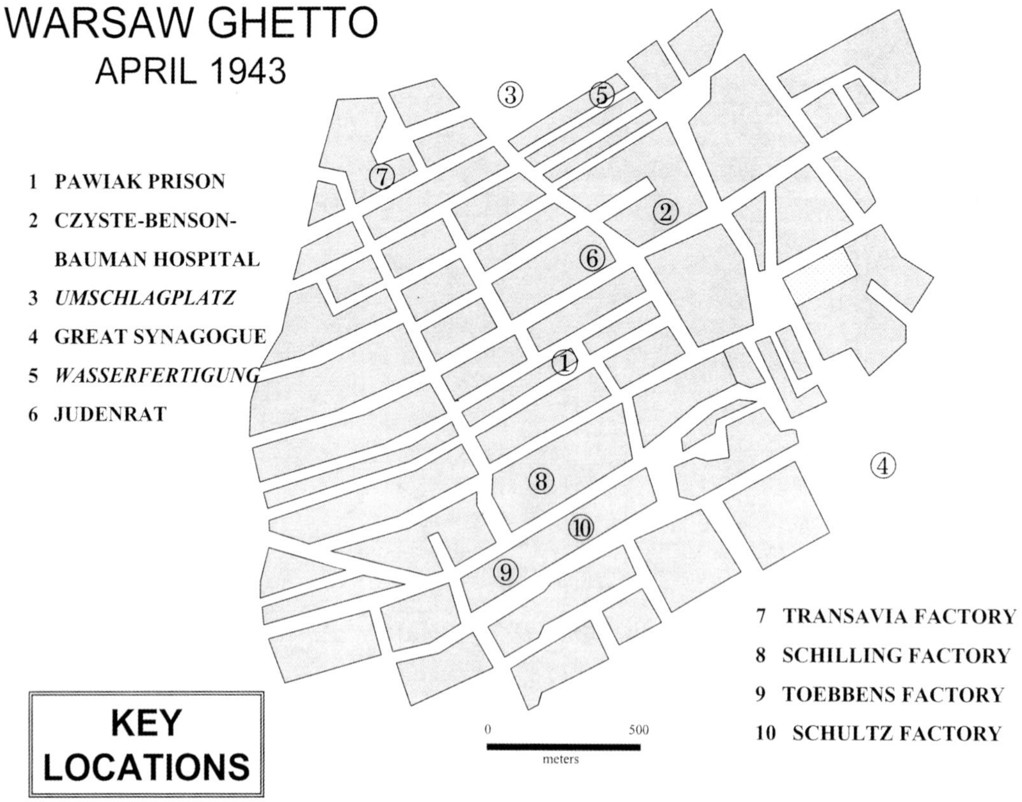
WARSAW GHETTO
APRIL 1943
1 PAWIAK PRISON
2 CZYSTE-BENSON-BAUMAN HOSPITAL
3 *UMSCHLAGPLATZ*
4 GREAT SYNAGOGUE
5 *WASSERFERTIGUNG*
6 JUDENRAT
7 TRANSAVIA FACTORY
8 SCHILLING FACTORY
9 TOEBBENS FACTORY
10 SCHULTZ FACTORY
0
500
meters
KEY LOCATIONS

WARSAW GHETTO
APRIL 1943
BUNKER LOCATIONS
0
500
meters
RESISTANCE DEFENSIVE POSITIONS

WARSAW GHETTO
19 APRIL 1943

1 0600-0630: First German attack; Germans withdraw.

2 0800: Second German attack; Germans withdraw.

3 1000: Germans begin shooting several hundred Jews in courtyard of Judenrat.

4 Germans attack Czyste-Berson-Baumann Hospital.

5 1200-2030: Subsequent German attacks.

6 Continuous fighting in Muranowska Square.

7 1730: Resistance ambushes German column.

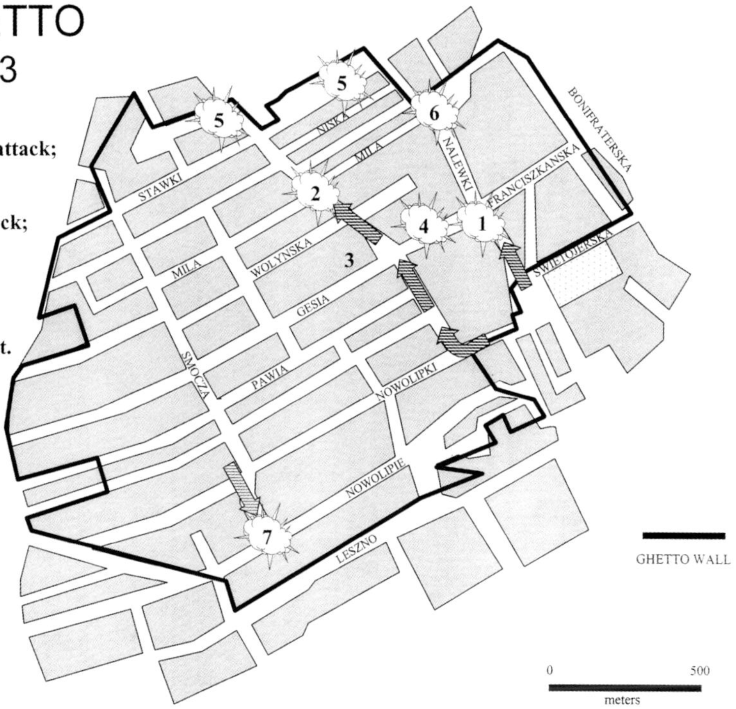

1 1800: Polish Home Army attacks Germans outside Ghetto.

2 1200: Germans control Muranowska Square.

3 1700: Germans attack Brushmaker District.

4 Additional German attacks.

5 Jewish Resistance detonates mine on Walowa Street.

6 German tanks attack Resistance positions on Muranowska Street.

7 Resistance ambushes German columns.

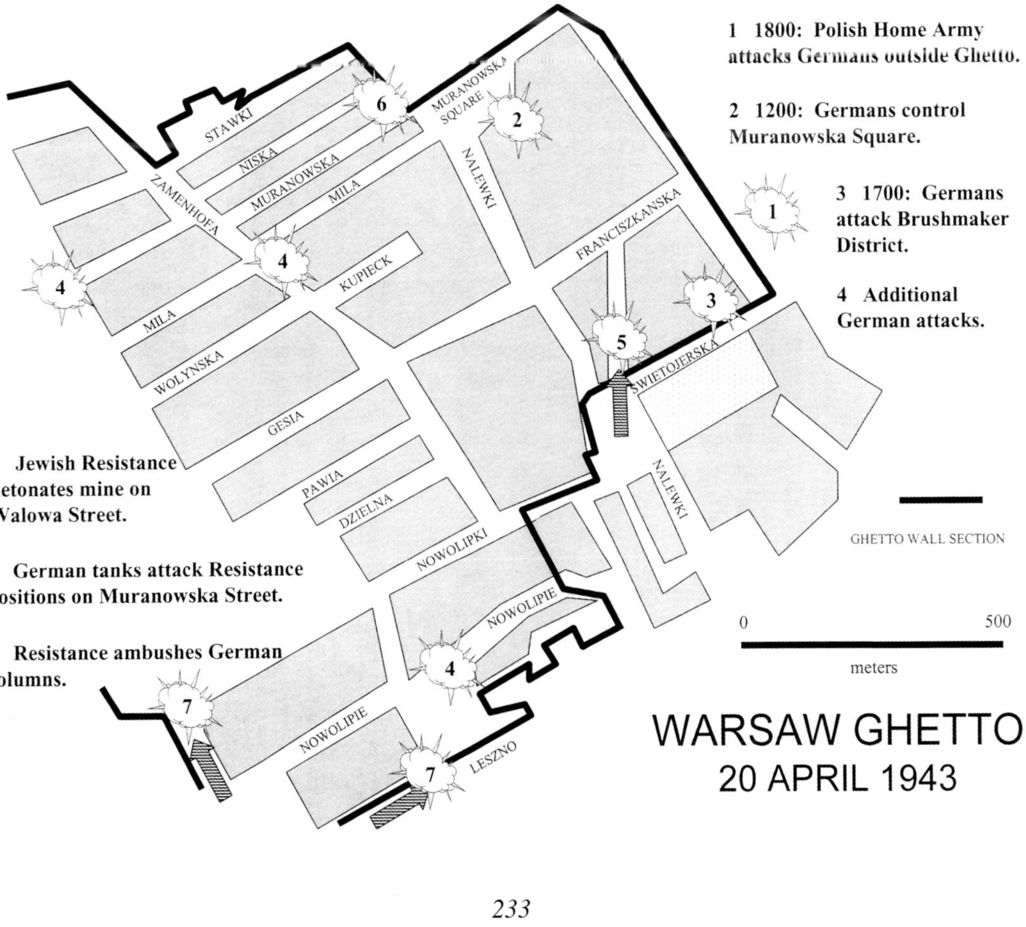

WARSAW GHETTO
20 APRIL 1943

WARSAW GHETTO
21APRIL 1943

1 **0700: Germans begin attacks against Resistance defenses in buildings.**

2 **Germans attack Resistance defenses in bunkers.**

3 **1200: Germans attack Brushmaker District.**

WARSAW GHETTO
22 APRIL 1943

1 **0700: Germans begin attacks against Resistance defenses.**

2 **Resistance regains control of Muranowska Square.**

3 ***SS-Untersturmführer* Dehmke killed by hand grenade explosion.**

4 **Germans machine-gun hostage members of the *Judenrat* at the *Umschlagplatz*.**

5 **Germans emplace machine-gun on roof overlooking Brushmaker District.**

6 **German artillery destroys one of two Resistance machine-guns on a roof on Muranowska Street.**

Germans intentionally set fire to buildings.

WARSAW GHETTO
23 APRIL 1943

1 0700: Germans begin attacks against Resistance defenses.

2 Germans destroy Resistance squad that is enroute to attack a Gestapo headquarters.

3 Germans mount searchlights on roofs overlooking Productive Ghetto.

Germans intentionally set fire to buildings.

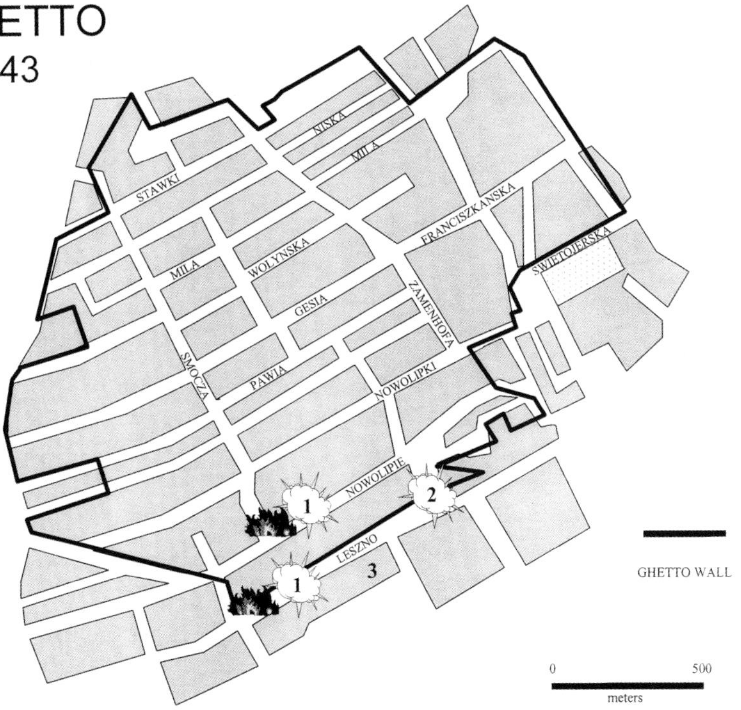

WARSAW GHETTO
24 APRIL 1943

1 1000: Germans begin attacks against Resistance defenses.

2 Germans burn Czyste-Benson-Bauman Hospital.

3 1900: Germans attack Resistance in the *Werterfassung*.

Germans intentionally set fire to buildings.

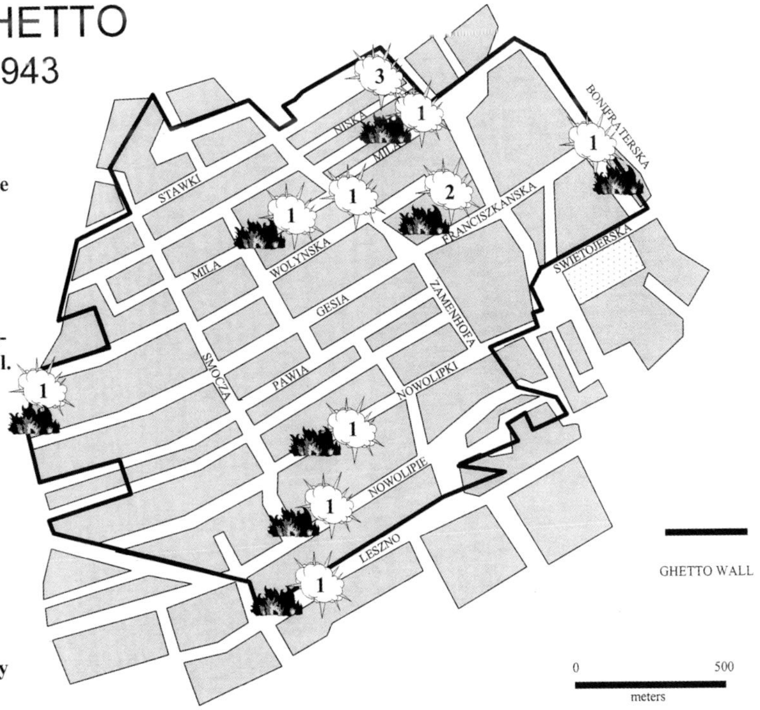

WARSAW GHETTO
25 APRIL 1943

1 1000: Germans begin executing captured Jews outside Pawiak Prison.

2 1300: Germans begin attacks against Resistance defenses.

Germans intentionally set fire to buildings.

WARSAW GHETTO
26 APRIL 1943

1 Germans attack Resistance in bunkers.

2 Germans attack Resistance in buildings.

3 1500: Germans begin executing Jewish Police outside Pawiak Prison.

4 1500: Germans set Productive Ghetto on fire at Stroop's orders.

Germans intentionally set fire to buildings.

WARSAW GHETTO
27 APRIL 1943

1 0900: Germans begin attacks against Resistance positions.

2 1200: Germans attack Muranowska Square.

3 1600: German half-tracks and infantry attack Nalewki Street.

4 1600: Special German battle group attacks Niska Street.

5 1800: Germans attack Muranowska Street.

Germans intentionally set fire to buildings.

WARSAW GHETTO
28 APRIL 1943

1 1000: Germans begin attacks against Resistance in buildings.

Germans intentionally set fire to buildings.

WARSAW GHETTO
29 APRIL 1943

Germans intentionally set fire to buildings.

WARSAW GHETTO
30 APRIL 1943

1 German patrols fight Resistance patrols.

WARSAW GHETTO
1 MAY 1943

1 0900: Germans begin attacks against Resistance in buildings and bunkers.

2 1100: German troops attacked from the rear on Nalewki Street.

3 1500: Germans begin attack on bunker at 30 Franciszkanska Street.

4 Germans begin night ambush patrols.

Germans intentionally set fire to buildings.

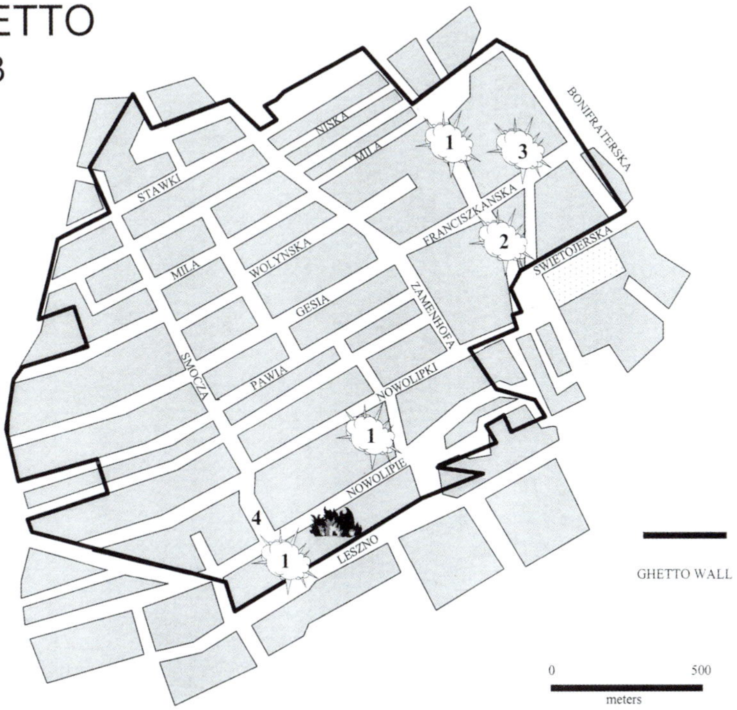

WARSAW GHETTO
2 MAY 1943

1 1000: Germans continue attack on bunker at 30 Franciszkanska Street.

2 1000: Germans burn Transavia Factory for visiting ***SS-Obergruppenführer*** **Krüger.**

3 Additional German attacks.

Germans intentionally set fire to buildings.

WARSAW GHETTO
3 MAY 1943

1 0900: Germans continue attack on bunker at 30 Franciszkanska Street.

WARSAW GHETTO
4 MAY 1943

1 1100: Germans comb out Productive Ghetto.

Germans intentionally set fire to buildings.

WARSAW GHETTO
5 MAY 1943

1 1000: Germans attack Jews near Church of the Virgin Mary.

WARSAW GHETTO
6 MAY 1943

1 0930: Germans begin attacks against Resistance positions.

WARSAW GHETTO
7 MAY 1943

1 1000: Germans begin attacks against bunkers.

Germans intentionally set fire to buildings.

WARSAW GHETTO
8 MAY 1943

1 1000: Germans attack ZOB headquarters bunker at 18 Mila Street. Resistance leader Mordechai Anielewicz probably commits suicide in bunker to avoid capture.

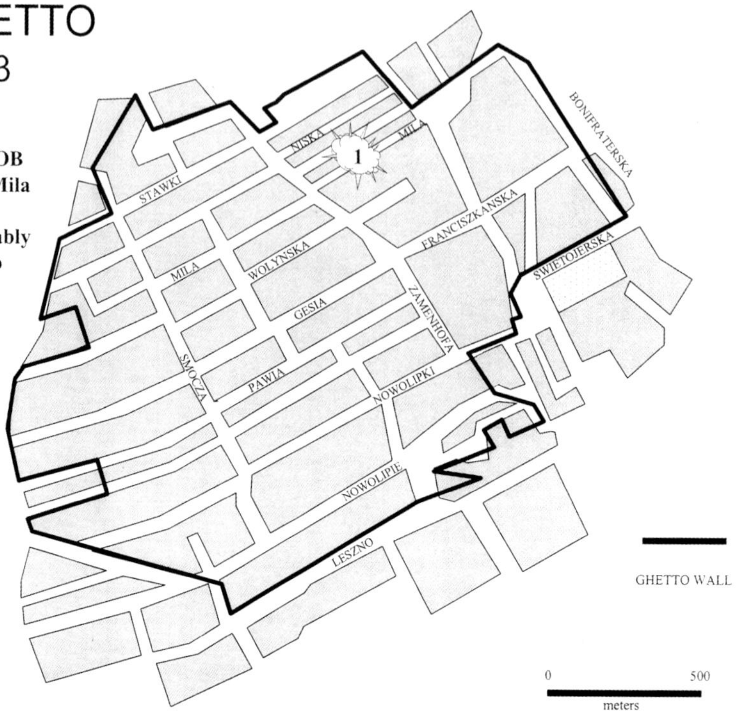

WARSAW GHETTO
10 MAY 1943

1 1000: **Germans begin attacks against Resistance positions.**

Germans intentionally set fire to buildings.

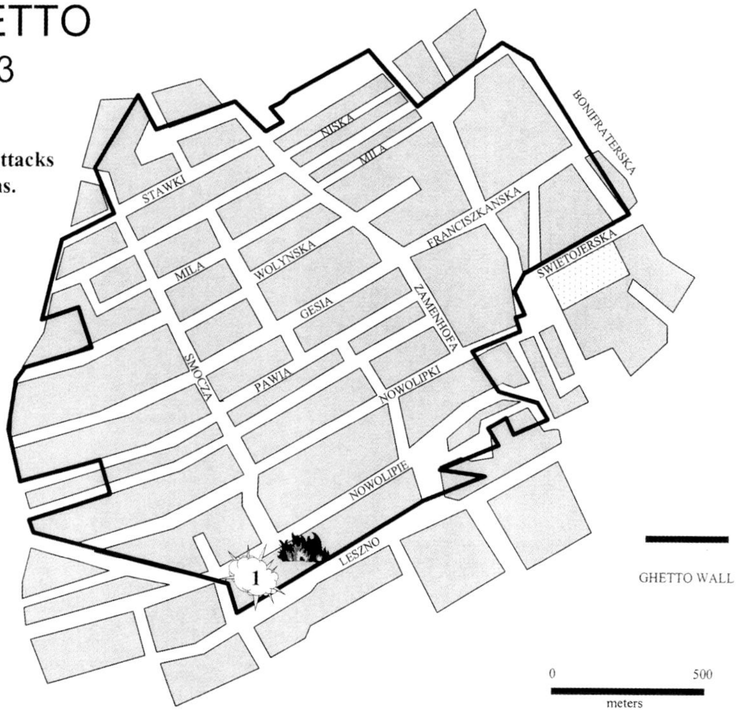

WARSAW GHETTO
11 MAY 1943

1 0930: **Germans attack Resistance in ruins on Gesia Street.**

2 **Germans attack Jewish Resistance bunker on Grzybowska Street, outside of Ghetto.**

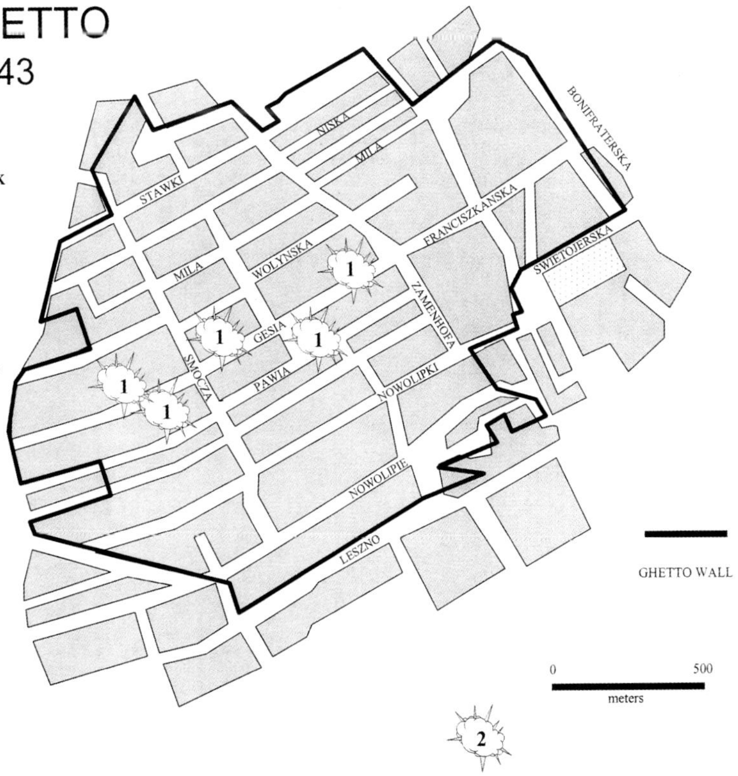

WARSAW GHETTO
12 MAY 1943

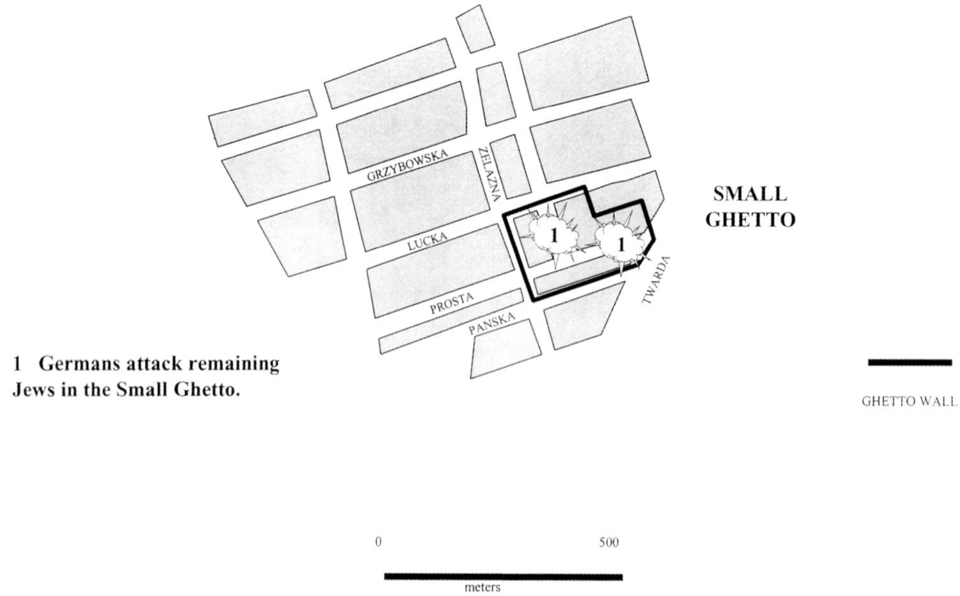

WARSAW GHETTO
13 MAY 1943

WARSAW GHETTO
14 MAY 1943

1 0130: Jewish Resistance fighters attempt to break out of Ghetto during Soviet air attack.

WARSAW GHETTO
16 MAY 1943

1 2015: Germans destroy the Great Tlomackie Synagogue marking the official end of the Ghetto operation.

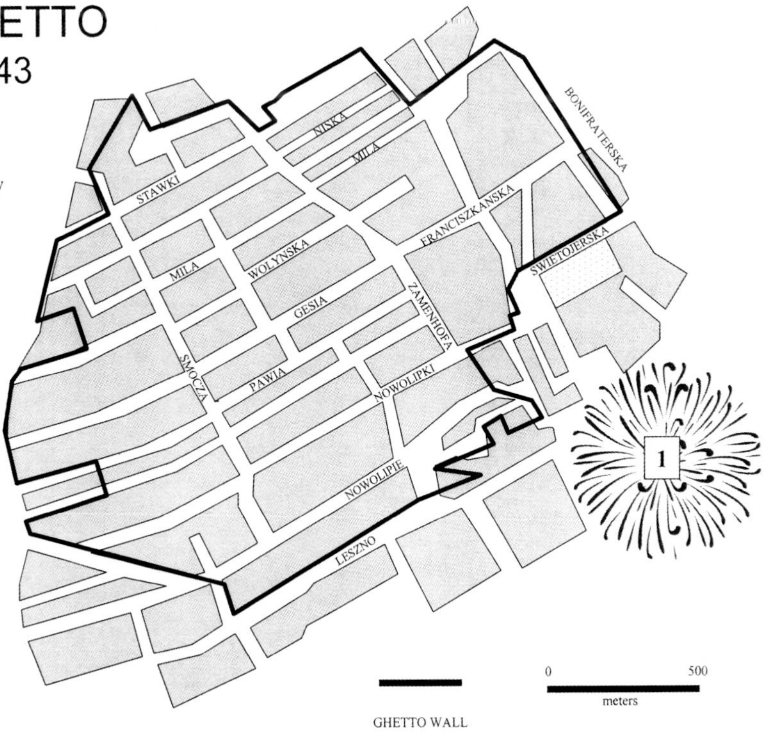

WARSAW GHETTO
MAY-JULY 1943

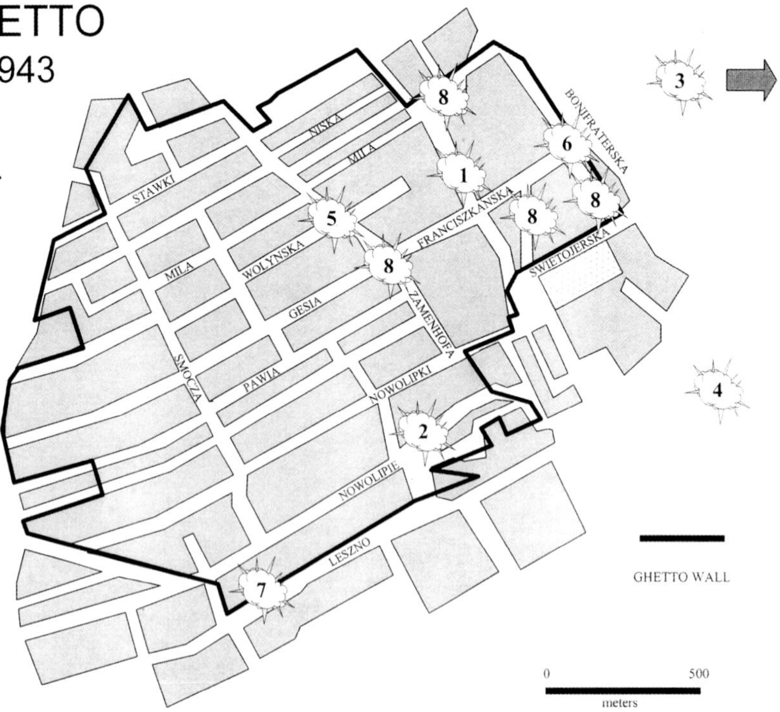

1 19 May: Skirmish at Gesia and Nalewki Streets.

2 20 May: Skirmish at Nowolipie Street.

3 25 May: Germans destroy Jewish Resistance group hiding in eastern Warsaw suburb of Praga.

4 27 May: Skirmish at Miodowa Street.

5 30 May: Jewish fighters ambush SS detachment.

6 3 June: Skirmish at Bonifraterska Street.

7 Mid-June: Skirmish at Leszno Street.

8 July: Skirmishes

CHARTS

KOMMANDEUR DER SCHUTZPOLIZEI

KdS

SS-Obersturmbannführer **Dr. Ludwig Hahn**
SS-Sturmbannführer Dr. Ernst Kah
SS-Hauptsturmführer Erich Herberholz
SS-Untersturmführer Kurt Müldner
SS-Untersturmführer Alfred Pagel
*SS-Untersturmführer*Waldemar Sterk
SS-Untersturmführer Otto Wettstädt
SS-Sturmscharführer Heinrich Theiss
SS-Hauptscharführer Fritz Bässler
SS-Oberscharführer August Lindner

I/II ADMINISTRATION & LAW — ***SS-Hauptsturmführer*** **Arthur Füssel**

III SECURITY SERVICE — ***SS-Sturmbannführer*** **Dr. Ernst Kah**

IV GESTAPO — ***SS-Sturmbannführer*** **Walter Stamm**

V CRIMINAL POLICE (*KRIPO*) — ***SS-Sturmbannführer Harry Geisler***

ADMINISTRATION & LAW

I/II

***SS-Hauptsturmführer* Arthur Füssel**
SS-Hauptsturmführer Eugen Schweizer

I A PERSONNEL

SS-Hauptscharführer Paul Hörmann
SS-Sturmscharführer Horst Jahns
SS-Sturmscharführer Willi Seitz

I B TRAINING & EDUCATION

SS-Obersturmführer Ulrich Breitenfeld

I C REGISTRATION & FILES

SS-Oberscharführer Karl Bertram

I D INTERNAL DISCIPLINE

SS-Untersturmführer Hugo Schwarze

II A POLICE ORGANIZATION & REGULATIONS

SS-Obersturmführer Ulrich Breitenfeld
SS-Untersturmführer Wilhelm Hammermeister
SS-Sturmscharführer Wilhelm Steinmetz
SS-Hauptscharführer Johann Lüthje

II B PASSPORTS & ALIENS

II C FINANCE

SS-Obersturmführer Werner Grabert
SS-Obersturmführer Richard Grudno
SS-Obersturmführer Dr. Herbert Jung
SS-Obersturmführer Gustav Steinmetz
SS-Untersturmführer Werner Weitze
SS-Sturmscharführer Otto Bindernagel
SS-Sturmscharführer Max Eibisch
SS-Sturmscharführer August Kamm
SS-Sturmscharführer Herbert Kolbe
SS-Unterscharführer Wilhelm Krömer
SS-Unterscharführer Viktor Junge
SS-Rottenführer Konrad Schweitzer

II D TECHNICAL MATTERS

SS-Hauptsturmführer Otto Oertwig
SS-Untersturmführer Willi Schmidt
SS-Hauptscharführer Gerhard Linders
SS-Hauptscharführer Hans Melzer
SS-Hauptscharführer Otto Stephan
SS-Oberscharführer Erich Brümmel
SS-Oberscharführer Fritz Dereser
SS-Oberscharführer Rudolf Fahrenberger
SS-Oberscharführer Franz Meusert
SS-Oberscharführer Helmut Merkel
SS-Rottenführer Witold Janz

SECURITY SERVICE

III

***SS-Sturmbannführer* Dr. Ernst Kah**
SS-Hauptsturmführer Arthur Potratz
SS-Sturmscharführer Alfred Schuchardt
SS-Unterscharführer Gerhard Raths

III A
ADMINISTRATION & LAW

***SS-Hauptsturmführer* Karl Müller**
SS-Hauptscharführer Karl Müller
SS-Oberscharführer Erich Kracht

III B
NATIONALITY & RACE

***SS-Untersturmführer* Hugo Hampel**

III C
CULTURE RELIGION & PROPAGANDA

SS-Obersturmführer Heinz Schnartendorff
SS-Untersturmführer Franz Avril

III D
FINANCE

***SS-Hauptsturmführer* Rudolf Albanbauer**
SS-Obersturmführer Karl Heine
SS-Untersturmführer Karl Jepsen

GESTAPO — IV

***SS-Sturmbannführer* Walter Stamm**
SS-Hauptsturmführer Gottlieb Höhmann
SS-Hauptscharführer Paul Skibbe

**IV A
HOSTILE ACTIVITIES & SABOTAGE**

***SS-Hauptsturmführer* Gottlieb Höhmann**

**IV B
RELIGIOUS BODIES, MASONS & JEWS**

***SS-Hauptsturmführer* Paul Werner**
SS-Sturmscharführer Max Köhler
SS-Rottenführer Wilhelm Renzel

**IV C
PROTECTIVE CUSTODY & FILES**

***SS-Obersturmführer* Norbert Graf Bergh-Trips**
SS-Sturmscharführer Paul Bartz
SS-Sturmscharführer Fritz Nowack
SS-Hauptscharführer Heinrich Hämmerli
SS-Rottenführer Walter Kreisel
SS-Rottenführer Karl Vorpahl
SS-Rottenführer Josef Zwerina

**IV D
EMIGRES HOSTAGES FOREIGN LABOR**

***SS-Obersturmführer* Norbert Graf Bergh-Trips**
SS-Sturmscharführer Otto Birkholz
SS-Oberscharführer Herbert Hundt
SS-Scharführer Fritz Schary

**IV E
COUNTER-INTELLIGENCE**

***SS-Obersturmführer* Willfried Jopke**

**IV N
COORDINATING INFORMATION**

***SS-Hauptsturmführer* Wolfgang Birkner**
SS-Hauptscharführer Erich Müller
SS-Hauptscharführer Willy Stoffel

HOSTILE ACTIVITIES & SABOTAGE

IV A

***SS-Hauptsturmführer* Gottlieb Höhmann**
SS-Sturmscharführer Alfred Damitz

IV A 1 COMMUNISTS POWs & RADIO

SS-Untersturmführer Gustav Grambow
SS-Sturmscharführer Siegfried Stahlhut
SS-Hauptscharführer Kurt Nicolaus
SS-Hauptscharführer Franz Reuter
SS-Hauptscharführer Walter Schween
SS-Oberscharführer Lothar Ress
SS-Scharführer Ewald Czorny

IV A 2 SABOTAGE FORGERIES AIR DROPS

***SS-Obersturmführer* Walter Witossek**
SS-Untersturmführer Wilhelm Hammermeister
SS-Sturmscharführer Walter Domröse
SS-Sturmscharführer Kurt Hörnig
SS-Sturmscharführer Wilhelm Löbig
SS-Hauptscharführer Gerhard Uebel
SS-Oberscharführer Georg Denzel
SS-Oberscharführer Wilhelm Perlbach
SS-Oberscharführer Waldemar Reichow

IV A 3 RESISTANCE ORGANIZATIONS

***SS-Hauptsturmführer* Gottlieb Höhmann**

IV A 4 PERSONAL SECURITY

***SS-Hauptsturmführer* Wolfgang Birkner**

IV A 5 CIPHERS

***SS-Hauptsturmführer* Jakob Lechner**

IV A S SPECIAL COMMANDO SPILKER

***SS-Obersturmführer* Alfred Spilker**
SS-Sturmscharführer Fritz Habel
SS-Hauptscharführer Georg Folta
SS-Hauptscharführer Herbert Schmidt

RESISTANCE ORGANIZATIONS

IV A 3

SS-Hauptsturmführer **Gottlieb Höhmann**

IV A 3 a

SS-Sturmscharführer Friedrich Kohls
SS-Sturmscharführer Otto Ebert
SS-Hauptscharführer Karl Mischke
SS-Rottenführer Lothar Roeser

IV A 3 b

SS-Oberscharführer Kurt Kelm

IV A 3 c

SS-Obersturmführer Ulrich Stern
SS-Untersturmführer Alfred Otto
SS-Sturmscharführer Max Lorenz
SS-Sturmscharführer Robert Pautz
SS-Sturmscharführer Max Vogt
SS-Hauptscharführer Arthur Henkel
SS-Hauptscharführer Wilhelm Höhmann
SS-Oberscharführer Martin Breger
SS-Oberscharführer Otto Diehm
SS-Oberscharführer Paul Drath
SS-Oberscharführer Walter Koglin
SS-Oberscharführer Hans Wiener
SS-Scharführer Edmund Langer
SS-Scharführer Paul Verch
SS-Rottenführer Josef Beresniewicz

IV A 3 d

SS-Sturmcharführer Bruno Edler
SS-Sturmscharführer Hugo Köhler
SS-Sturmscharführer Otto Möller
SS-Sturmscharführer Hermann Schimmann
SS-Hauptscharführer Heinrich Fuss
SS-Hauptscharführer Erwin Hartmann
SS-Hauptscharführer Kurt Napporra
SS-Hauptscharführer Kurt Vogel
SS-Hauptscharführer Franz Weber
SS-Rottenführer Reinhold Liedtke

RELIGIOUS BODIES, MASONIC ORGANIZATIONS & JEWISH AFFAIRS

IV B

SS-Hauptsturmführer **Paul Werner**
SS-Sturmscharführer Max Köhler
SS-Obercharführer Erich Hahn
SS-Oberscharführer Günter Weise
SS-Untercharführer Arthur Schöneborn

IV B 1
CHURCHES

IV B 2
SOLDIERS

IV B 3
FREE MASONS

IV B 4
JEWISH AFFAIRS

SS-Obersturmführer **Johannes Böhm**
SS-Obersturmführer Karl Georg Brandt
SS-Oberscharführer Gerhard Mende

COUNTER-INTELLIGENCE — IV E

***SS-Obersturmführer* Willfried Jopke**

IV E 1 GENERAL COUNTER-INTELLIGENCE

SS-Untersturmführer Erich Merten
SS-Sturmscharführer Paul Jahnke
SS-Sturmscharführer Hermann Kleist
SS-Sturmscharführer Werner Münkwitz
SS-Sturmscharführer Willi Rudolph
SS-Sturmscharführer Adolf Wild
SS-Oberscharführer Gustav Fahner
SS-Oberscharführer Werner Kressner
SS-Rottenführer Georg Rückert

IV E 2 ECONOMIC COUNTER-INTELLIGENCE

SS-Sturmscharführer Wilhelm Rietz
SS-Oberscharführer Josef Blösche
SS-Rottenführer Heinrich Schröckenstein

IV E 3 PASSPORTS ALIENS FRONTIERS

SS-Sturmscharführer Hermann Czeratzki
SS-Hauptscharführer Bruno Griesche
SS-Oberscharführer Heinz Peter
SS-Scharführer Helmut Orf

IV E S SPECIAL COMMANDO

***SS-Obersturmführer* Karl Heller**
SS-Untersturmführer Alfred Seiler
SS-Untersturmführer Emil Kirbach
SS-Sturmscharführer Reinhard Gesien
SS-Sturmscharführer Josef Kolberg
SS-Sturmscharführer Georg Müller
SS-Sturmscharführer Rudolf Richter
SS-Sturmscharführer Bruno Urbanski
SS-Sturmscharführer Gustav Willimzik
SS-Hauptscharführer Johann Tiemann
SS-Oberscharführer Alfred Böhnke
SS-Obercharführer Eduard Schlader
SS-Scharführer Eugen Walottek
SS-Unterscharführer Arthur Rättig

PAWIAK PRISON

SS-Hauptscharführer Paul Gerhard Hiersemann
SS-Oberscharführer Alfred Steinebrunner
SS-Scharführer August Albers
SS-Scharführer Franz Bürkl
SS-Unterscharführer Karl Brockmann
SS-Unterscharführer Konstantin Stegner
SS-Unterscharführer Otto Wulfes
SS-Rottenführer Fritz Arzt
SS-Rottenführer Albert Baumstark
SS-Rottenführer Eduard Hanisch
SS-Rottenführer Karl Knodelseder
SS-Rottenführer Heinrich Krooss
SS-Rottenführer Wilhelm Mechert
SS-Rottenführer Alfons Piecyk
SS-Rottenführer Waldemar Ragoss
SS-Rottenführer Fritz Rührnschopf
SS-Rottenführer Arno Schubert

N-OST

SS-Oberscharführerr Heinrich Harbusch
SS-Oberscharführer Max Krausshaar
SS-Scharführer Otto Junghart

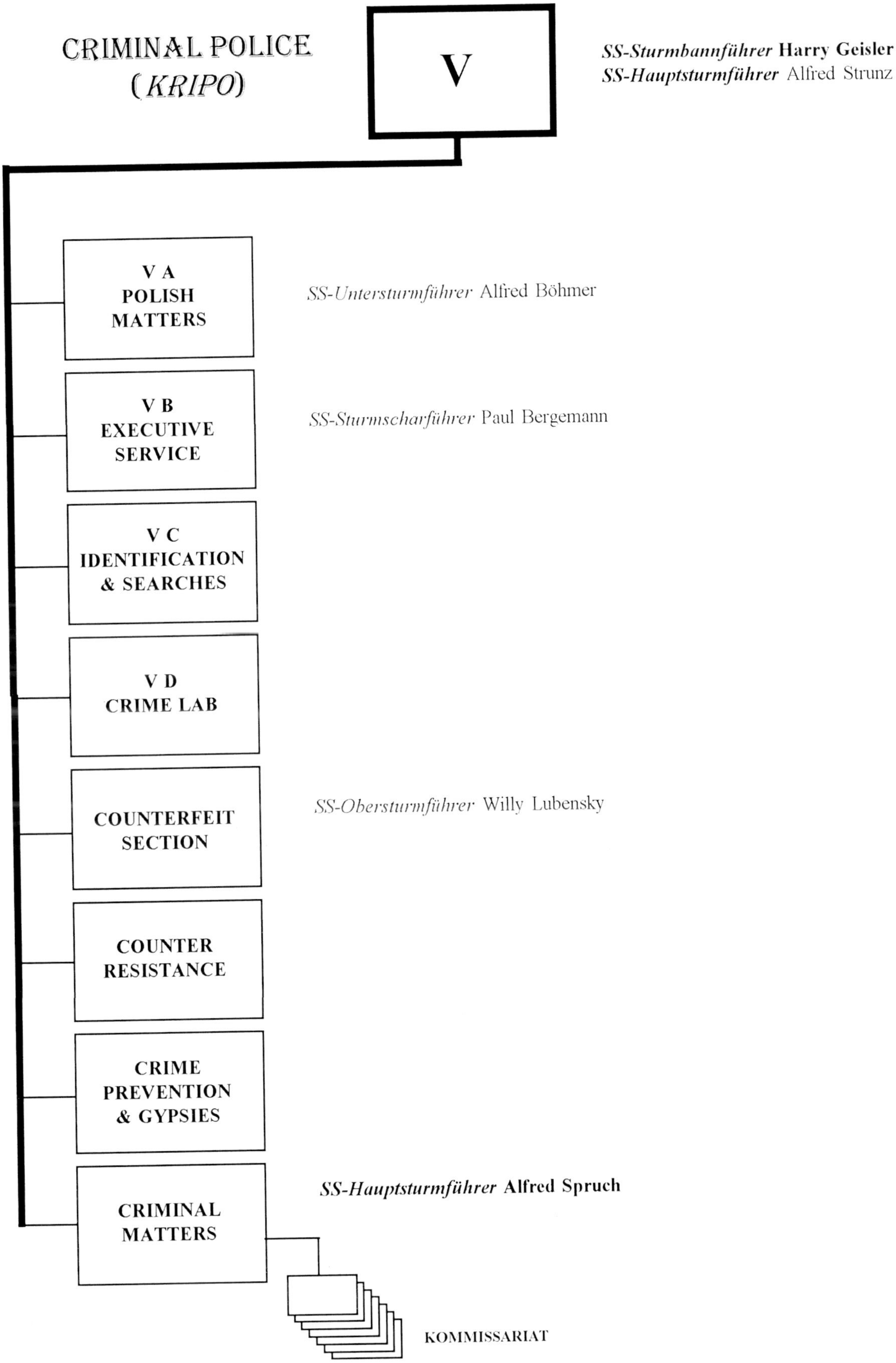
CRIMINAL POLICE
(KRIPO)
V
SS-Sturmbannführer Harry Geisler
SS-Hauptsturmführer Alfred Strunz
V A
POLISH MATTERS
SS-Untersturmführer Alfred Böhmer
V B
EXECUTIVE SERVICE
SS-Sturmscharführer Paul Bergemann
V C
IDENTIFICATION & SEARCHES
V D
CRIME LAB
COUNTERFEIT SECTION
SS-Obersturmführer Willy Lubensky
COUNTER RESISTANCE
CRIME PREVENTION & GYPSIES
CRIMINAL MATTERS
SS-Hauptsturmführer Alfred Spruch
KOMMISSARIAT

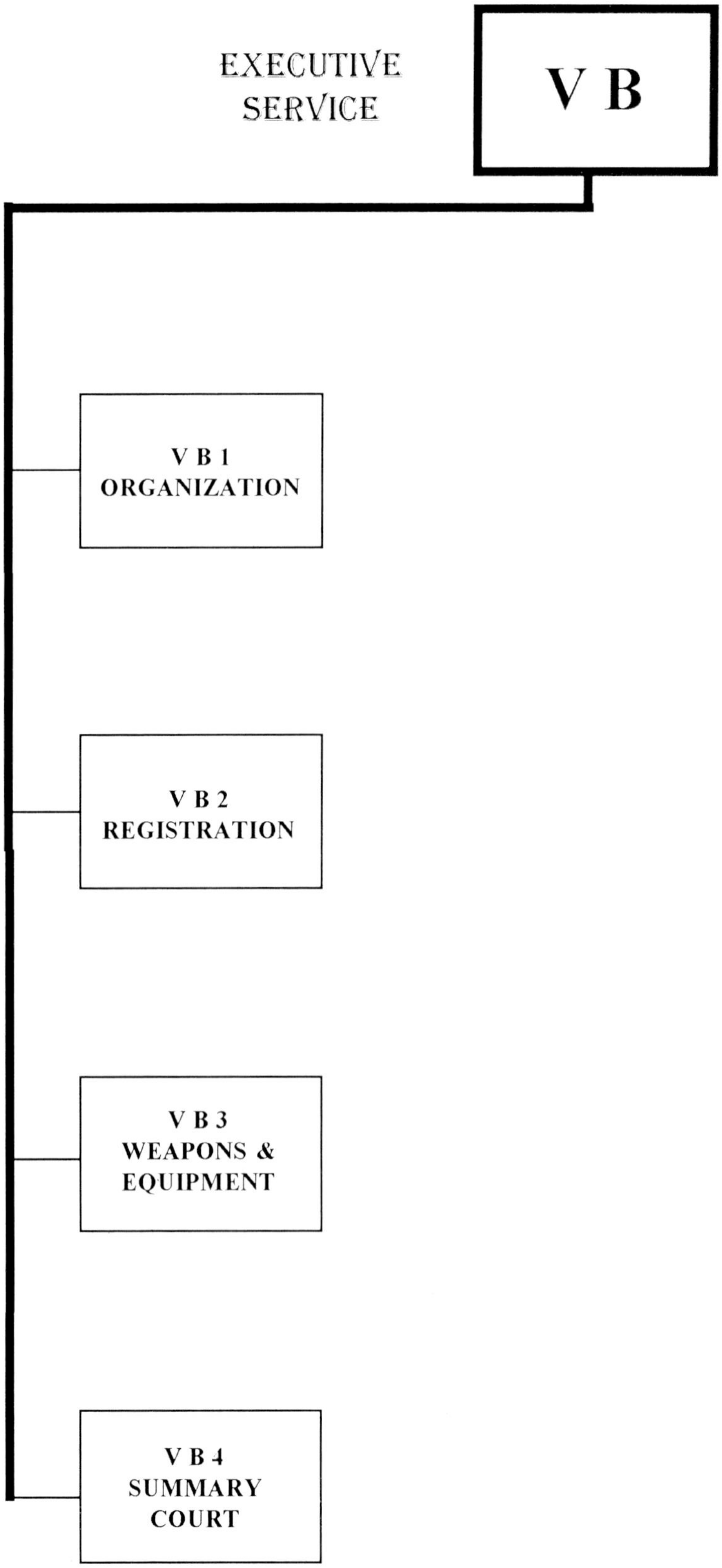
EXECUTIVE SERVICE
V B
V B 1 ORGANIZATION
V B 2 REGISTRATION
V B 3 WEAPONS & EQUIPMENT
V B 4 SUMMARY COURT

CRIMINAL POLICE (*KRIPO*)

CRIMINAL MATTERS

***SS-Sturmbannführer* Harry Geisler**
SS-Hauptsturmführer Alfred Strunz

KOMMISSARIATS

- **1ST *KOMMISSARIAT* HOMICIDE**
  - *SS-Sturmscharführer* Ernst Kaiser
  - *SS-Hauptscharführer* Otto Weber
- **2ND *KOMMISSARIAT* GRAND LARCENY**
  - *SS-Sturmscharführer* Hugo Pless
  - *SS-Hauptscharführer* Werner Ballhause
- **3RD *KOMMISSARIAT* PETTY THEFT & BLACK MARKET**
  - *SS-Sturmscharführer* Rudolf Kosmala
  - *SS-Hauptscharführer* Walter Stoll
- **4TH *KOMMISSARIAT* FRAUD**
  - *SS-Sturmscharführer* Karl Hacke
  - *SS-Sturmscharführer* Friedrich Schramm
  - *SS-Hauptscharführer* Johann Ogorrek
- **5TH *KOMMISSARIAT* VICE**
- **6TH *KOMMISSARIAT* HOTEL & TRAVEL REGISTRATION**
  - ***SS-Untersturmführer* Wilhelm Munk**
  - *SS-Sturmscharführer* Josef Baumgartner
- **7TH *KOMMISSARIAT* IDENTIFICATION PHOTOGRAPHY**
  - *SS-Sturmscharführer* Otto Nemitz

SS AND POLICE CHAIN OF COMMAND

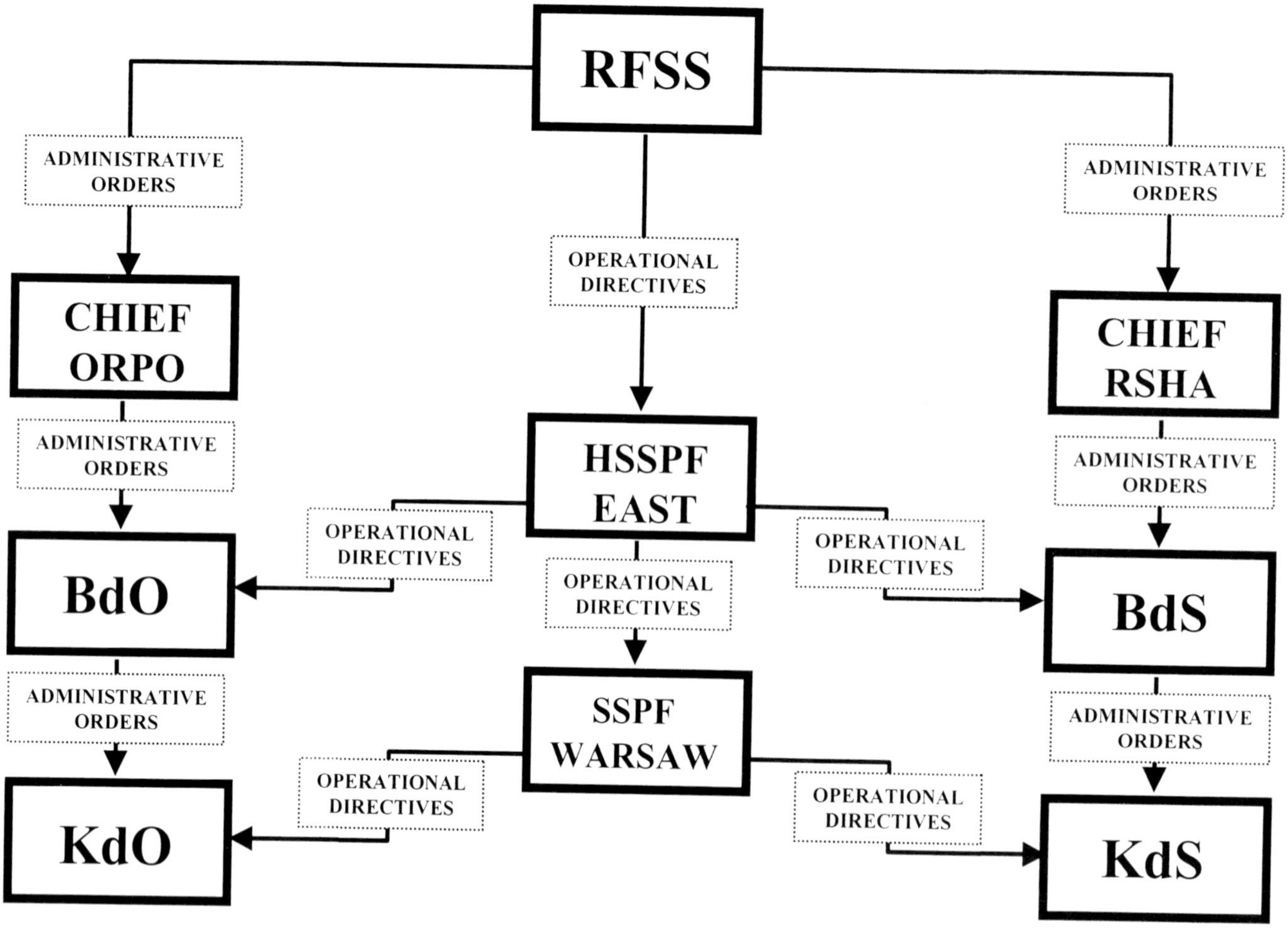